SEX, GENDER, AND KINSHIP

Sex, Gender, and Kinship: A Cross-Cultural Perspective

Burton Pasternak

Carol R. Ember

Melvin Ember

Prentice Hall, Upper Saddle River, New Jersey 07458

Library of Congress Cataloging-in-Publication Data

PASTERNAK, BURTON.
　　Sex, gender, and kinship: a cross-cultural perspective/Burton
Pasternak, Carol R. Ember, Melvin Ember.
　　　p.　cm.
　　Includes bibliographical references and index.
　　ISBN 0-13-206533-9 (pbk.)
　　1. Kinship—Cross-cultural studies.　2. Marriage—Cross-cultural
studies.　3. Sex role—Cross-cultural studies.　I. Ember, Carol R.
II. Ember, Melvin.　III. Title.
GN487.P37　1997
306.83—dc20
　　　　　　　　　　　　　　　　　　　　96-41018
　　　　　　　　　　　　　　　　　　　　CIP

Editorial/production supervision, interior design,
　and electronic page makeup: Kari Callaghan Mazzola
Editorial director: Charlyce Jones Owen
Editor-in-chief: Nancy Roberts
Editorial assistant: Pat Naturale
Cover design: Bruce Kenselaar
Electronic art creation: John P. Mazzola
Buyer: Mary Ann Gloriande

This book was set in 11/12 Goudy by Big Sky Composition
and was printed and bound by Courier Companies, Inc.
The cover was printed by Phoenix Color Corp.

© 1997 by Prentice-Hall, Inc.
Simon & Schuster/A Viacom Company
Upper Saddle River, New Jersey 07458

Printed in the United States of America
10　9　8　7　6　5　4　3　2　1

ISBN　0-13-206533-9

PRENTICE-HALL INTERNATIONAL (UK) LIMITED, *London*
PRENTICE-HALL OF AUSTRALIA PTY. LIMITED, *Sydney*
PRENTICE-HALL CANADA INC., *Toronto*
PRENTICE-HALL HISPANOAMERICANA, S.A., *Mexico*
PRENTICE-HALL OF INDIA PRIVATE LIMITED, *New Delhi*
PRENTICE-HALL OF JAPAN, INC., *Tokyo*
SIMON & SCHUSTER ASIA PTE. LTD., *Singapore*
EDITORA PRENTICE-HALL DO BRASIL, LTDA., *Rio de Janeiro*

CONTENTS

PREFACE

Americans are seriously questioning their own society and values, rethinking closely held assumptions about the nature of human nature. Many wonder whether essential institutions of family and kinship are disintegrating. As we think about such matters we wonder about what, if anything, is really necessary or natural to human society and culture. We hope this book will provide useful background and perspective, and serve as an aid to reflection in the struggle to understand the potentials and limitations of human nature. In this exploration of other cultures we can glimpse altered reflections of ourselves, facets of ourselves that are revealed only in different, even exotic, cultural mirrors.

More specifically, we will summarize what cross-cultural research has taught us about the nature and extent of variation in sex, gender, and kinship in societies around the world. The discussion is based on data drawn from the nearly two thousand human cultures that have been studied by anthropologists and other social scientists. For most of the issues we address there was little or no systematic cross-cultural research even thirty years ago—fewer than eighty relevant cross-cultural studies. Since then there have been more than one thousand studies designed to test and evaluate alternative explanations of behavior, most of which have focused on the universals and variables of human sex, gender, and kinship. We will highlight what we have learned from these studies, using illustrations from concrete ethnographic accounts to give life and humanity to our findings.

When we wrote this book we had more than one audience in mind. First, we wanted to provide an interesting window on behavioral variation for the educated lay person, for virtually anyone interested in human sexual and social behavior. Second, we wanted to produce a readable introduction to these matters that could be used in a variety of academic courses in sociology and psychology, as well as in anthropology. Indeed, we believe this text can provide an interesting and useful cross-cultural perspective for courses in human sexuality, anthropology of gender, sociology of women, sex and gender roles, marriage and the family, social organization and kinship, comparative social structures, women's studies, cross-cultural psychology, and psychological anthropology.

We hope this work will inspire in others a measure of our own wonder and curiosity about the ways humans differ yet are the same the world over. And for students soon to be on the frontiers of social science, what researchers have learned thus far and what they have failed to explain should suggest alternative explanations to be tested, new questions to be pursued, and perhaps also a different way of looking at old questions. We offer here a tempting albeit sometimes intentionally provocative challenge to students, but leave much for instructors to say. And while we do not directly address American society, this book will provide the sort of comparative perspective that can change the way we think about our own society and experience.

Burton Pasternak
Carol R. Ember
Melvin Ember

Sex, Gender, and Kinship

1

INTRODUCTION

There is such a thing called evil, and it is not the result of being a victim of society. [Westerners] have abandoned an ethical basis for society, believing that all problems are solved by a good government, which we in the East never believed possible. [The] fundamental difference between Western concepts of society and government and East Asian concepts is that Eastern societies believe that the individual exists in the context of his family. He is not pristine and separate. The family is part of the extended family, and then friends and the wider society. The ruler or the government does not try to provide for a person what the family best provides.

In the West, especially after World War II, the governments came to be seen as so successful that they could fulfill all the obligations that in less modern societies are fulfilled by the family. This approach encouraged alternative families, single mothers for instance, believing that government could provide the support to make up for the absent father. [It's] not that we don't have single mothers here. We are also caught in the same social problems of change when we educate our women and they become independent financially and no longer need to put up with unhappy marriages. But there is grave disquiet when we break away from tested norms, and the tested norm is the family unit. It is the building brick of society.[1]

This was the riposte of Lee Kuan Yew, Singapore's former Prime Minister, shortly before the highly criticized caning of Michael Fay, the Ohio teenager convicted of vandalizing cars in Singapore. It was Yew's way of telling us that we should be looking to our own house, think-

1

ing about our own problems, instead of criticizing Singaporean discipline. It is a response calculated to pinch already sensitive nerves. Explicit is the notion that educating and allowing women economic and social independence constitutes potential threat to the family unit, to the "building brick of society." We find a quite different view in the following passage from a group of women social scientists:

> The institution of marriage and the role of "wife" are intimately connected with the subordination of women in society in general. It is the constraints on women to engage freely in various social activities, whether in sexual intercourse, economic exchanges, politics, or war, that make us "dependent" on men, that oblige us to become "wives." By marrying, women enter into contracts by which we gain protection from sexual molestation by men other than our husbands (and lose our freedom to engage in sexual relationships with other men if we so choose); we gain a right to our husbands' economic support (and undertake an obligation to provide for their domestic support and comfort); and we gain a claim on their possessions and rights for our children (and accept their right to control and dispose of them as they wish). On balance, it would appear that husbands gain much more than wives. They not only gain domestic servants, sexual companions, and producers of children but also political assets, instruments for acquiring allies.[2]

Here are two very different assessments and evaluations of marriage and family, each with many adherents. Nearly everyone, however, accepts that, for better or worse, changes are occurring throughout the modern world. Families and kinship networks are shrinking, becoming more fragile, and losing control over individual lives. *The New York Times* recently summarized the findings of a study by the Population Council, an international nonprofit group in New York.[3] The study indicates that, for a variety of reasons, marriages are dissolving with increasing frequency. In many developed countries, divorce rates alone doubled between 1970 and 1990, while in less developed countries, roughly a quarter of first marriages are over by the time women reach their forties. Some observers manage to find something positive in such statistics, and in the atrophy of kinship as well, seeing these changes as indications of an overdue emancipation of women. They see growing participation in the work force and higher salaries as enabling women to assert an unprecedented independence, challenging at last the constraints of husbands and kin networks.

But the study also reveals costs. As families shrink, parents in their prime working years have heavier child care burdens, and children require more support for a longer period of time, through more years of education. Obligations to aging parents increase too, because people are living longer. And with more and more unwed motherhood around the world, the children of single-parent households are more likely to be poor.

Even where fathers are present, mothers are assuming greater economic responsibilities. Research in many countries indicates that they work longer hours than men, at home and on the job. According to the New York Times summary, women's work hours exceed men's by 30 percent in seventeen less developed countries, and data from twelve industrialized countries show that employed women work 20 percent more hours than men. Women make a substantial contribution to family economies in many countries. The Population Council study indicates that, while mothers generally earn less than fathers, they contribute a larger proportion of what they earn to household needs; husbands reserve more for themselves.

According to the Council, women contribute more of themselves to raising children as well; studies of parent-child interactions reveal no society in which fathers provide as much child care as mothers, and very few in which fathers have regular, close relationships with their young children. Liberated though they may be, divorced women are particularly hard-pressed; the Council report indicates that in countries around the world they find it difficult to collect child support. For example, three-quarters of divorced fathers in Japan, almost two-thirds in Argentina, half in Malaysia, and two-fifths in the United States do not pay child support.

For those who see the transformation of family and kinship in a negative light, the assumption is that something of value is being lost. People seem to pay a price in security and well-being for the gain in individual freedom. Indeed, some of us may be inclined to believe that particular family institutions are necessary in all healthy societies, and that they have endured and sustained our ancestors from the time humans were all hunter-gatherers. For those who see something hopeful in the transformation, however, the assumption often is that the starting point for change was a "traditional" family system in which some people, and especially women, were oppressed. But is either assumption really correct? Is there one type of traditional family that was characteristic of most of human history? Does more freedom for women inevitably go with the "breakup" of family? In later chapters, we will consider and compare families, family relationships, and the role of kin groups in societies around the world. In the course of our examination we will find a variety of marital and family possibilities, as well as societies in which women were neither oppressed nor unvalued.

At the outset, let us make clear that when we use the word *traditional*, we do not imply that such societies are stuck in time, unchanging. The truth is very much otherwise; all of them are constantly changing. We mean only that we are talking about societies described in the ethnographic literature, for the most part societies that are preindustrial (or were when first described by anthropologists and others). In important ways, then, they are as we were, although the course of their development is subject now to global economic forces. We have built our own society on foundations similar to those found in many of these societies, which continue to constrain our options and behavior in subtle, often invisible ways.

While our work will have implications for contemporary society, many sociologists, economists, and political scientists are already more directly involved in unraveling that experience. Our intention is to help in that endeavor by laying out what humans everywhere are capable of. We will explore the family and kinship structures into which they have organized themselves, not only to determine what is possible, but to highlight options that occur more or less frequently and, where possible, to see if we can account for the choices made.

Ours is a timely inquiry, given the growing concern about what many perceive to be an erosion of basic family institutions and values. Of course, this is not the first time people have agonized over that; to some extent our apprehension expresses an almost unavoidable perplexity characteristic of the relations between generations. But perhaps now there are also less transitory grounds for suspicion that something has gone wrong, that the essential "building brick" to which Lee Kuan Yew refers is crumbling, threatening the very foundations of society. Is he right that we in the West have lost our way? The issue attracts considerable media attention; candidates for office routinely accuse opponents of lacking sufficient awareness or of being too little alarmed. Some of us raised in less than "typical" American families may even wonder whether the "proper" family we never quite managed to achieve may now be forever beyond reach.

Television, movies, indeed all the media have contributed to our uncertainty. While they have the potential for deepening our engagement with the world and improving our understanding of it, the media can, as well, promote models and standards that only harden preconceptions and engender uniformity. Until recently, they exposed us daily to the typical American family, with its well-adjusted members living in what seemed the lap of luxury, the typical middle-class home in a community of families like their own. These images especially haunted the children of single parents, of immigrants, of all the underclasses, highlighting their shortcomings and reminding them of what they would have to become to escape them. Out there somewhere, where TV cameras could track it, the standard American family lived and, to some minds at least, it was far from certain that departures from that model qualified as "families." It was distressing, to say the least, not to be counted among them—to have no ball-tossing father, no psychologically sophisticated mother, no dog, no Christmas tree, linoleum instead of carpets, perhaps not even a bed, bedroom, or towel for every family member.

For better or for worse, many Americans were probably more certain a generation ago than they are today about the virtues of melting into the American pot. If some go too far today in their praise of diversity, many then saw no value at all in diversity. More than a few would have willingly and eagerly exchanged their poor imitations for the real thing, for a more traditional American family, the form of which was determined and defined by who knew whom. It took some time for us to consider the possibility of other possibilities, and to accept the idea that they, too, might have value and a proper place in nature. This book explores and attempts to account for some of those other possibilities, and to consider our own choices in their light.

Apart from whether basic institutions and their attendant values are eroding, there are questions about the building bricks themselves, and they are at the heart of our inquiry. Are there familial institutions, structures, or customs so basic and essential that their distortion or displacement anywhere can only be deleterious? Do we have a propensity, perhaps even a necessity, for certain forms of family relationship, organization, and belief, and if so, why? Are the commonalities cultural in origin, biologically driven, or perhaps a bit of both? And beyond that which we share, how much variation occurs and what is responsible for it?

As the multiple facets of an insect's eye provide a view of reality different from ours, cultures, too, are eyes, or different filters, through which we perceive, interpret, and relate to the world around us. To what extent does our social construction vary in terms of understandings provided by these different cultural lenses? Are there aspects of social life not relative, but necessary and similar regardless of differences in cultural perception? The issue of what is necessary, likely, rare, perhaps even disruptive is not simply one of academic curiosity. It underlies and guides policy at the community, national, and international levels. The position one takes can inspire confrontation between as well as conflict within individuals.

Those of us raised in a tradition of tolerance often find ourselves torn between reasonable yet contradictory points of view. Few would find no virtue in what has come to be called a *multicultural* point of view. Most people may readily accept the notion that cultures are equally valuable and worthy of respect, and are prepared to assume that "peculiar" customs and beliefs become understandable and meaningful once we consider them in relation to other things people do and think. *Cultural relativism*, an article of faith for many in and out of anthropology, does not require a suspension of moral judgment (although some might go that far), only that we understand why people do what they do in terms of their total cultural context. In educating our children, therefore, many of us want to ensure that they have some exposure to cultures and traditions other than their own, so that they may become more tolerant.

Yet, we are also attentive to voices urging caution lest we fall under the corrosive spell of *ethnocentric separatists* disguised as multiculturalists, and thus come to grief. As Arthur M. Schlesinger Jr. described it, the challenge here at home is to recognize and respect cultural differences while appreciating the important commonalities that hold us together.

The American identity will never be fixed and final; it will always be in the making. Changes in the population have always brought changes in the national ethos and will continue to do so; but not, one must hope, at the expense of national integration. The question America confronts as a pluralistic society is how to vindicate cherished cultures and traditions without breaking the bonds of cohesion—common ideals, common political institutions, common language, common culture, common fate—that hold the republic together.[4]

Few Americans would care to be considered *ethnocentric*, so culturally narrow and smug as to press our ways and values on others, yet we may set relativism aside when it comes to specific issues. People are especially likely to do so, for example, when they believe the social fabric is disintegrating, that their way of life is under siege. Then they worry about basic family institutions and basic values, assuming that there are some relationships and structures that are proper, perhaps even natural in the sense that every society needs them to work properly. Are they really under assault, subject to major and essentially negative transformation?

Perhaps we are, as Lee Kuan Yew suggests, expanding individual freedom at the expense of essential obligations traditionally defined by family and kinship. We support parity for women at home and abroad, but worry about whether its achievement may weaken basic kinship structures, the basic building blocks of society, in unforeseen ways. We may embrace the idea that women should have greater access to higher education and work opportunities outside the home, but then think about the impact of that on the stability and functioning of the family. If there are more ways for women to escape difficult marriages, does that contribute to or undermine the quality of life?

An important question, then, is whether certain institutions or values are absolute rather than relative in the sense of being necessary to the proper working of any society. It is easy to embrace a strict relativist position in theory but difficult to maintain it in practice, and we may shift between relativism and absolutism without realizing we have done so. Can we assume, for example, that all people are entitled to certain "inalienable rights,"—to life, liberty, and the pursuit of happiness—as our Constitution dictates? Are there *human rights* to which people everywhere are entitled whether they know it or not, whether they agree or not, or are these rights, too, culturally relative?

Most Americans believe they live in one of the world's most democratic and tolerant countries, and they expect their government officials to reflect that. But there are times when we, too, shift ground. At a recent international conference on human rights, for example, our Secretary of State, anticipating arguments from representatives of Third World countries interested in economic development with minimal political disruption, slipped into an absolutist mode, distancing himself and us from the relativist position:

> [The] United States warned today that it would oppose any attempt to use religious and cultural traditions to weaken the concept of universal human rights.
>
> The strong statement set the stage for a [sic] intense struggle between Western countries committed to the universality of human rights and countries that oppose what they describe as the imposition of Western values.
>
> Speaking on the opening day of the first World Conference on Human Rights in twenty-five years, Secretary of State Warren Christopher said the universality of human rights sets a single standard of acceptable behavior around the world, a standard Washington would apply to all countries. [He] noted, "We cannot let cultural relativism become the last refuge of repression."[5]

Pushed to the wall, many people will compromise tolerance. Many may insist on respect for customs and beliefs different from our own, but probably few are prepared to observe in silence culturally tolerated neglect or abuse of females. How many would refrain from supporting the struggle against female infanticide everywhere in the world? How many would not speak out against acts of genocide in Africa, Bosnia, or elsewhere, dismissing them as "their way"? Many people may endorse the rights of others to privacy or to worship in their own way, but some of them will insist that certain behaviors, such as homosexuality or abortion, are absolutely wrong and should be discouraged everywhere.

It is not our goal to solve, once and for all, the question of whether some forms of family and kinship are more natural or better than others. Before we can even consider questions of that sort, we must first find out what people do, how often, and why. That is the purpose of this book, to explore and make some sense of what people around the world do, to summarize what we know about extent and sources of variation. Let us consider, then, whether there are structural, perhaps even biological propensities (if not necessities) that determine how we organize our families and kin groups, and how we relate to one another within them. How much latitude do we have to vary what we do; are some possibilities more common than others, and if so why? In grappling with these questions we will consult ethnographic data (descriptions of societies based mainly on fieldwork and participant observation) from around the world, first to discover just how much variation there is, and then to sort out unjustified assumptions, explanations, and conclusions about the nature of family and kinship institutions. Where systematic evidence is not available, we will not shy away from educated speculation.

While we will give attention to variation within societies, the main focus will be on differences among them. The method is comparative and the units of analysis are societies, rather than individuals within societies. We describe social customs, not individual habits; customs are essential ingredients in any ethnographic or anthropological description of culture. While the comparative or cross-cultural method enables us to test the predictive value of different interpretations and explanations, we are far from having all or even most of the answers. We will undoubtedly raise more questions than we can answer, but highlighting and defining what needs to be done is the first step to understanding. At the very least, we hope that this exploration will enable us to see beyond the confines and assumptions of our own culture, and to get a feel for what is possible, what is common, and what is rare.

Individuals are ultimately the source of all culture change; what one person does one day may be the basis for what most do a decade later. But we deal here with societies and their customs, rather than individuals, for a number of reasons. First, we are interested primarily in patterns of social structure that appear to work. How can we know what works? Different theorists may judge differently what works. For example, evolutionary theorists may talk about traits that are adaptive—that appear to convey reproductive success to their carriers. Others may judge what works in terms of how long a behavior is customary. After all, if some behavior gets repeated over a considerable period of time, it probably works for the people exhibiting it. Persistence does not guarantee that something is adaptive or successful, but it is probably more likely to be so than any particular individual behavior. Suppose, for example, that one single parent arranges to share child care with another. While the arrangement may work for them, why do we find no societies in which people *customarily* rely on friendship for caretaking?

The point is that a consideration of customary behavior in many societies is more likely than individual behavior to tell us something important about what does or does not work. But we must consider what is customary, and under what conditions it is so, in *many* societies. If we look only at one or two societies, we may readily identify behaviors common enough to be thought of as customary. But such customs may be short lived. A pattern currently popular in one or two societies could well disappear in a single generation, as individuals come to realize it has not worked so well after all. Of course, if few or no societies have a certain custom, the chances are that it does not work, and we are unlikely to find deleterious behavior that is customary in many societies.[6]

Another benefit of focusing on societies is that our comparisons are more likely to reveal the causes of general patterns. In our own society, for example, we tend to live apart from kin when we marry. If we study individual variation, we might notice that people who remain with kin often have a precarious economic situation or are involved in a family business. But cross-cultural comparison would reveal something more general—that living apart from kin is generally rare in traditional societies; it is a common pattern only in more recent, commercialized societies.

In short, comparison of many societies can reveal connections not apparent from a comparison of individuals. Cross-cultural comparison may also suggest fruitful hypotheses about the sources of individual variation. If cross-cultural analysis reveals, for example, that people living in commercial societies can buy services which kin provided in the past, we might anticipate that poorer people may be more dependent on kin than are others. Still, that realization will not help us understand why only *some* wealthier people remain near kin, or why some people strike out on their own, whatever their economic circumstances. Questions of that sort ultimately require a focus on individuals, rather than on societies.

Much of human social structure is rooted in relatively stable reproductive relationships between women and men. We would not have families and kinship without sexual reproduction and relatively stable, mated relationships. We begin in Chapter 2, therefore, with a discussion of sexuality—the universals and variation that occur—in order to better understand how the possibilities and constraints of human biology shape family and kinship organization. Given that not all organisms reproduce sexually, why is human reproduction sexual, and what follows from that in terms of family organization? What insights into human sexuality can be gleaned from study of other, nonhuman primates? Where variation is possible, how does culture channel our sexuality and why? We examine the ethnographic record to see how childhood sexuality is managed in societies around the world. Do all discourage or prohibit masturbation and homosexual play, for example? And what of heterosexual relations before marriage: Do people everywhere consider premarital intercourse immoral and inappropriate? What do we know about homosexuality cross-culturally? Are there societies that find it acceptable, and are there any in which it is universal for women or men? Leaving the incidence and acceptance of various sexual practices aside, what do people *think of* sex? Do people everywhere consider it desirable and pleasurable, or are there societies in which people consider sex dangerous and frightening, and contact with the opposite sex undesirable?

In Chapter 3 we take up the matter of *gender*, and consider the factors that shape the roles women and men play in society. Are there any universals in terms of how female and male roles are assigned, and what variation do we find cross-culturally? How much of gender behavior is biologically given, how much culturally conditioned? What determines whether women or men contribute more to subsistence, and of what relevance is the division of labor to child care and family life? Are men invariably society's leaders and fighters? Is it the case that all societies favor them when it comes to privilege, power, and authority? And what is the relationship, if any, between gender and personality? Are women everywhere nurturant and gentle, and men aggressive?

Then, in Chapter 4, we turn to the basic bonds that define family, and consider the forms of marriage and other mated relationships that humans have invented for themselves around the world. Why do human females and males form stable mated relationships while most other primates do not, and what is the relationship between bonding and marriage? Do people everywhere marry, and what forms of marriage occur? Is marriage between one man and one woman most common, perhaps "natural" in that sense? We will want to discuss the conditions under which women are likely to share a common husband, or men a common wife. And, in that connection, we will consider why and with what consequences women are less likely to have multiple spouses than men.

All societies regulate sexual behavior and marriage and, in Chapter 5, we consider the most basic cultural constraint, the family incest taboo, which puts family members out of bounds when it comes to marriage, requiring us to find mates in other families. We will see if people everywhere prohibit marriage with close family members or whether incest taboos, too, are culturally relative. Just how universal are they, to what extent do they vary, and why? We continue this inquiry in Chapter 6, where we explore other ways societies regulate sexual behavior—by extending the incest taboo to other relatives, or by pressing people to find mates within or outside of certain groups.

In Chapter 7 we turn to how people get married—how mates are selected, the nature of courtship, and the sorts of exchanges that take place when people marry. In our society, individual preferences weigh heavily when it comes to marriage, but how important are choice, romance, and intimacy cross-culturally, for women as well as for men? Do most societies share our view that marriage should be based on willingness of the parties involved? Why are marriages arranged in some societies, and why are spouses captured or kidnapped in others? How important is courtship around the world? What sorts of ceremonies, celebrations, and exchanges are involved? Marriage often involves a transfer of goods and services. We will want to look at the kinds of transactions that take place (e.g., bride wealth, bride service, dowry, indirect dowry, and simple exchange of women), and consider the conditions under which they are more or less likely.

Marriage is the gateway to family life. But, as the ethnographic record (and Chapter 8) will show, the character of relations between wife and husband, too, can vary substantially. How common is it, for example, that societies insist on restricting sex to the marital relationship? Are there any that allow or even expect married people to have extramarital relationships? Is there a double standard everywhere when it comes to such matters? In this connection, does sex with multiple partners within or outside marriage necessarily evoke jealousy? Just how intimate do peoples around the world think spouses ought to be, and what determines degree of intimacy? At the other extreme, what constitutes *spouse abuse*, and how common is it cross-culturally?

Nowhere is marriage forever; at some point all marriages terminate, either by divorce or death. In Chapter 9 we examine the extent to which, and the conditions under which, societies accept the idea of divorce, for women as well as for men. We look, as well, at what becomes of widows—do they often remarry after loss of a spouse? What about the widowers? Finally, we consider cultural rules that some societies create to constrain or channel the remarriage of widows and widowers.

Chapter 10 takes up the matter of who lives where at marriage, why, and with what consequences. When are brides likely to join their grooms, or husbands their wives? What other arrangements occur and are all possibilities equally likely? As we will see, some options are more often adopted than others, and that fact has a profound impact on family life in general, and on the status of women in particular. The nature of postmarital residence is of more than academic interest. It determines the composition of families and larger kin groups, and influences the character of relations within them. It has an impact on the quality of conjugal relations, on the position of women in society, and on the opportunities available to them. For that reason it is particularly important to consider the reasons for, and the implications of, the fact that women join their husbands' relatives at marriage in most societies.

What sorts of families do we find in the ethnographic record? Before we can even consider whether there is some sort of *best* or *natural* family, we need a common understanding of what *family* means. Having that, we can at least compare societies (in Chapter 11) to see what sorts of families occur, to determine whether some are more common than others, and to consider the consequences of life in different kinds of families. What accounts for differences in family complexity within as well as between communities and societies, and what implications does complexity have for relations within families? For example, does it make any difference to a woman whether she lives in one sort of family or household rather than another, or at what stage of her life she lives in any particular family form? Does the presence of a mother-in-law, or sister-in-law, or nephews and nieces make any difference to her well-being, or to the economic and family-building strategies she and her husband will adopt?

In Chapter 12 we consider relations of kinship beyond the family. While the notion is unfamiliar to most Americans, in most of the societies anthropologists have described, people organize themselves and their society in terms of groups in which the members trace their descent from a common ancestor. Under what conditions are people likely to do that, what sorts of groups do they form, and what accounts for the variation? In that connection, why are relationships more commonly traced through men than women in societies that have descent groups? Are women invariably disadvantaged in male-oriented societies, and better off in those that trace descent through women or in those that make no distinction between relatives on the female and relatives on the male side? In short, what impact do descent groups have on the lives of individual women and men?

We conclude our inquiry by bringing together and highlighting (in Chapter 13) some of the threads that run through the book. To what general conclusions has our exploration led us? Does what we have learned suggest anything about our present condition and future? We will leave the reader with more questions unanswered than we would like, but, hopefully, also more aware of human necessities and potentialities, of what we must be and of what we can be, and better able to judge, perhaps, what we ought to be.

NOTES

1. *New York Times*, April 11, 1994.
2. Ülkü Ü. Bates, Florence L. Denmark, Virginia Held, Dorothy O. Helly, Susan H. Lees, Sarah B. Pomeroy, E. Dorsey Smith, and Sue Rosenberg Zalk, *Women's Realities, Women's Choices: An Introduction to Women's Studies* (New York: Oxford University Press, 1983), pp. 249–250.
3. *New York Times International*, May 30, 1995. The summary of the Population Council study that follows is based on the report in the *Times*.
4. Arthur M. Schlesinger, Jr., *The Disuniting of America: Reflections on a Multicultural Society* (New York: W. W. Norton & Company, 1992), p. 138.
5. *New York Times*, June 15, 1993.
6. In this book, societies and cultures are the essential units of analysis. In making our comparisons, we will frequently draw upon and refer to cultures included in the full-text database known as the Human Relations Area Files (HRAF). Complete and incomplete sets of the Human Relations Area Files (in microfiche and CD-ROM formats) are located at nearly three hundred universities and colleges in the United States and some twenty-five other countries.

2

SEXUALITY

Imagine what human relations would be like if humans reproduced asexually. We might have complex ties between us anyway, but many of the elements we see in all human societies, past and present, would be missing. Without sexual reproduction we would not, of course, have females and males. And without two sexes, we would lack a division of labor by gender, different expectations for females and males, courtship and marriage between a man and a woman, kinship terms differentiated by gender, and (as in many existing societies) kin groups organized around women only or men only. Whatever they would be, human relations and social organization would be very different in a world without sexual reproduction. What would adolescents day dream about? What would our popular music and dance be like?

As these questions make clear, the nature of human relations is responsive to characteristics of human reproductive biology. This is not to say that culture is irrelevant: The way sexuality is expressed and how females and males relate to each other do vary cross-culturally. But to understand both the universals and the variation in human sexuality, we must consider the possibilities and constraints of human biology.

WHY IS REPRODUCTION SEXUAL?

Among humans and many other complex animals, reproduction almost always involves heterosexual intercourse. That is, except for cases of artificial insemination (in vitro and in vivo fertilization), coitus brings a male's sperm to a female's egg. But reproduction does not require a combining of genetic materials from female and male organisms in all species. In some, like bacteria, organisms can reproduce asexually—by *cloning* or duplicating their own genetic material and budding off new organisms. Some organisms can even transfer or combine genetic materials (which is what biologists mean by sex) without having distinct females and males. For example, bacteria occasionally reproduce "sexually" although there are no males and females. By a process called *conjugating*, two bacteria (each a single cell) touch cell walls and a genetic copy of one bacterium's chromosome is transferred through a temporary *tube* to the other bacterium (bacteria have only one chromosome). The two chromosomes exchange genetic material by *crossing-over*, resulting in hybrid chromosomes. Then one of the hybrid chromosomes decays, leaving the receiving bacterium with just one hybrid chromosome. The sexual reproduction is completed when the hybrid organism buds off a new organism, with genetic material from two bacteria. This process, though we call it *sexual*, does not involve female and male individuals. Given that the more common cloning process takes substantially less time, biologists wonder why bacteria ever reproduce in the sexual way.[1] Why, then, should bacteria ever need to conjugate?

One theory is that sexual reproduction occurs in so many organisms, and sometimes even among unicellular ones like bacteria, because there are selective advantages to the additional intraspecies variation that results, especially in situations of environmental instability. When conditions are stable, bacterial clones survive and reproduce just fine. But when there is insufficient food, or increased predation by other organisms, or when some poison (e.g., a natural or human antibiotic) finds its way into the environment, then it may be advantageous for bacteria to reproduce sexually. This is because sexual reproduction produces more new variants, some of which may better adjust to the new conditions.[2] In short, natural selection may favor sexual reproduction because the variation so produced is adaptive in varying or changing environments.

But even if natural selection favors sexual reproduction to increase variation, why should any species require different kinds of individuals to get the job done? As a matter of fact, other animals besides bacteria, and many plant species as well, lack separate female and male organisms. For example, most flowering plants have both "female" and "male" organs.[3] But humans along with other complex animals are individually differentiated by sex—in their gametes, or reproductive cells, and in their sexual organs. Like many other sexually reproducing organisms, human females produce relatively large gametes (eggs) while males produce many small ones (sperm). Because of this difference in gamete size, biologists claim that human reproduction "costs" more for females than for males.[4]

What else do humans share with other animals that reproduce sexually? In our case, too, fertilization takes place within the female reproductive tract, usually after some kind of courtship.[5] Being mammals, human females also devote considerable time and energy to pre- and postnatal care of their offspring. Among all placental mammals, offspring grow for some period in the uterus, during which time the placenta provides nutrients and removes waste.[6] After birth, the mother continues to provide nourishment (through her milk) as well as protection and affection. Perhaps because all mammals suckle their young, females normally provide more care than males, particularly to infants. There are exceptions, of course. Nowadays, with substitutes for mother's milk, human males can successfully rear children on their own, and some fathers actually spend more time with infants and children than the mother does. But this is still relatively uncommon.

SEXUALITY IN PRIMATES

The behavior of our closest primate relatives may provide insight into the underlying nature of human sexuality. When we compare primate species, we discover considerable variability in terms of whether sex is limited to particular seasons, how much sex a species has, and whether females or males typically initiate sex. With regard to how much sex they have, the lower primates (prosimians and New World monkeys), like most mammals, have seasonal breeding with limited sexuality during the breeding seasons.[7] In common with human females, higher primates (Old World monkeys and apes) have menstrual cycles, which means that they produce eggs throughout the year and are receptive to sex at least around the times of ovulation. But how often they are sexy varies.

Comparative (cross-species) research suggests why sex may occur year round in some species, but only in particular seasons in other species. Animals that live in seasonal environments, generally those far from the equator, tend to have limited breeding seasons. Their births seem to be geared to changes in the availability of crucial resources like food and water, or to optimal climatic conditions.[8] But even if this is why some primates do not breed year-round, why do some have sex more often than others *within* each cycle? The female mountain gorilla is receptive only one to three days of each menstrual cycle, around the time she ovulates. But human females and those of a few other primate species (e.g., bonobo chimpanzees) have sex throughout their cycles.[9] Also puzzling is why some primate females advertise their sexual receptivity with conspicuous swellings in the genital area. And with regard to copulation, females are commonly the initiators among some primates, such as gorillas, while in others, such as chimpanzees, males are more likely to initiate.[10]

HUMAN SEXUALITY

Heterosexual intercourse is usually necessary for reproduction in the world of complex animals, but humans are somewhat unusual in their ability to be sexual much more often than reproduction requires. In our case, sex can and often does occur when reproduction is not possible—after menopause, during pregnancy, and at times during the menstrual cycle when conception is highly unlikely (e.g., near the actual time of menstruation). We are not unique among primates in terms of the ability to have sex at any time. As noted, bonobo chimpanzee females also have sex throughout their cycles. Compared with the other primates, humans and bonobos separate sex from reproduction to the greatest degree. Yet many other primates also have sex at clearly nonfertile times—during pregnancy, for example.[11]

Why are humans so sexy, or at least potentially so? (We say potentially so, because despite our biological capacity for sex at almost any time, societies vary considerably in how often and at what times sex is allowed, as we shall see.) Early theorists often proposed that more continuous sexuality was adaptive because it served to bind primates (early humans included) into larger social groups.[12] Interest in sex was supposedly the "glue" that kept groups together. But researchers subsequently discovered that many primates live in year-round local groups without year-round sexuality, so we no longer consider the *sex as glue* hypothesis plausible.

With regard to humans, perhaps the most often cited idea is that once we developed female-male bonding, we required more continuous sexuality to bolster the bond.[13] Of course, this assumes that bonding developed first. We will consider this explanation more fully later, when we take up marriage in Chapter 4; here we are simply concerned with whether human female-male bonding really helps account for relatively continuous sexuality.

To see if there is, in fact, a relationship between sexuality and female-male bonding, two of your authors (Melvin and Carol R. Ember) examined a sample of mammal and bird species. The reason for not using humans is that it would be impossible to determine whether female-male bonding is associated with more continuous sexuality among us, since there is little or no variation to examine (all human populations have both traits). If a trait is universal (like the ability to have sex throughout the menstrual cycle), any other universal can be invoked to explain it. To detect an association between traits, the cases must exhibit variation in the traits at issue (a trait might be present or absent in one species, or one species might have more or less of something than another). If we look at mammals and birds, then, we do find female-male bonding sometimes, and we also see variation in degree of female sexuality.

If it is true that more sexuality is necessary to keep females and males bonded, then species with bonding should have more frequent sexuality than those without female-male bonding. However, the results of the Embers' study indicate the *opposite*: Animals with female-male bonds generally have *less* sexuality throughout the year (they are more likely to have breeding seasons). If sex is not the glue for female-male bonding in other animals, why should it be so for humans?[14] Pair-bonding and more or less continuous sexuality do occur together among humans, but judging from what we have learned about other mammals and birds, it is unlikely that we became so sexy just because we bond.

But then why did humans develop the capacity for sex most of the time? Two characteristics of human social structure may be important in this regard. We are unique in having both female-male bonding and local groups containing more than a few adult males and females. This means that several potential sex partners are always nearby. Consider what might happen if females were not interested in sex throughout the year, or were only interested around their times of ovulation. The bonded males in the group might be tempted to have sex with any females who were interested at the time. The pull of those receptive females might compromise a man's bond with a particular female. Contrary to what early theorists expected, there would be less likelihood of bond disruption *even in multi-male, multi-female groups* if all or most females were interested in sex most of the time.

Why, then, did natural selection not produce more continuous female sexuality in other primate species as well? Those that, like us, live in multi-male and multi-female groups generally lack male-female bonding, so even complete promiscuity and year-round sexuality would have nothing to undermine. But what about gibbons, which *do* have pair-bonding? (In Chapter 4, we deal with why only some species have pair-bonding.) Why should they have shorter periods of female sexuality than humans? In fact, the gibbons do not challenge the explanation we propose because, unlike humans and many other primates, they live in small family units; they lack multi-male, multi-female local groups. Since bonded pairs are separated from other adults, there is little possibility of "extramarital affairs" that might threaten pair-bonds.

Still, what are we to make of bonobo chimpanzees? Are they not an exception to the Embers' theory that bonding and multi-male, multi-female groups favor more continuous sexuality? The bonobo live in multi-female, multi-male groups, as we do. Like many other primates, however, they do not form pair bonds. What reason would there be, then, for more or less continuous female sexuality? Are the bonobo an exception to the theory that pair bonding and multi-male, multi-female groups select for more continuous sexuality? We must consider the possibility of a different inducement to relatively continuous female bonobo sexuality. Perhaps it has something to do with the fact that bonobo females are more likely to get meat from males who have had sex with them. (Only males hunt and kill for meat.) Although it is not clear why this is so, perhaps continuous female sexuality developed among the bonobo because more sexy females acquired more meat and were, therefore, more likely to survive and reproduce.

Might this *sex for meat* hypothesis have implications for humans as well? Early humans also ate meat (from scavenging and/or hunting), so could it not be that the human females who could have sex more often were similarly advantaged? While that is possible, if prehistoric hunters were anything like their recent counterparts, getting a fair share of meat would not be problematic for females because (in contrast to other primate hunters) human hunters customarily share meat between as well as within families.

By now the reader may be a bit uncomfortable with our focus on pragmatic (reproductive and material) considerations, rather than interest in pleasure, as primary motives for sex. But if a desire for pleasure really was the only motive for sex, it would be difficult to explain why some species have sex less often than others. Clearly, continuous female sexuality is far from universal in the animal world. Breeding seasons (and limited sexuality) are much more common, especially in species far from the equator (a fact that seems difficult to relate to differences in desire for pleasure). Sex may be pleasurable, but how often it occurs during the year seems independent of that. Moreover, where food resources are not adequate year round and animals do not store food, or where climatic conditions are seasonally difficult, continuous sexuality and, in consequence, less seasonal births could even be disadvantageous.

When behavior is heavily dependent on learning, as it is among primates, much of sexual behavior is also learned.[15] This is especially true of humans, who use learning to control and condition sexual behavior. We create cultural rules for this purpose. Thus, while people everywhere have the capacity for frequent sex, many societies prohibit or avoid sex for a year or more after the birth of a baby, before and during certain activities such as war, or during certain seasons. Nor does our biological potential for frequent sex preclude people in some societies (as we shall see later) from believing that sex is dangerous to health. In fact, every society imposes some restrictions on sex.

CULTURE CHANNELS SEXUALITY

Although sexuality is part of human nature, no society leaves it to nature alone; all have rules and attitudes channeling proper conduct. When it comes to how much and what sorts of sexual activity societies allow or encourage before marriage, outside marriage, and even within marriage, there is considerable variation. Societies also differ in their tolerance of homosexual sexuality. We also find that restrictions of one sort or another may not apply throughout life, or to all aspects of sex. Moreover, the various cultural rules governing sexual behavior are not haphazard; within societies there seems to be some consistency among them. For example, societies that frown on sexual expression in young children are also likely to punish premarital and postmarital sex.[16]

Customs may also change over time. In our own society, attitudes were becoming more permissive until the AIDS epidemic. During the 1970s, American behavior and attitudes suggested that acceptance and frequency of premarital sex had increased markedly since Kinsey's surveys in the 1940s. Surprisingly, attitudes toward extramarital sex had not changed much from the 1940s to the 1970s; the vast majority surveyed in the 1970s still objected to it.[17] More recent surveys in the 1990s indicate a large drop in the frequency of both extramarital and premarital sex.[18]

What do we know about how sexuality and sexual relations are regulated cross-culturally? How uniform or varied are customs governing childhood sexuality, premarital sex, and sex after marriage? Do people everywhere disapprove of sexual relations among persons of the same sex? It is to these questions that we now turn. As many of our examples illustrate, acceptance of sexuality is not an all-or-nothing matter; societies differ in the sorts of heterosexual relationships they tolerate (or encourage), and with whom such relationships are proper. So in our discussion of attitudes toward sexuality, it will be useful to consider various kinds of sexuality separately.

It is important to keep in mind that the customs of a society may be reported by an ethnographer as of the time she or he was there, but often (if the culture had been severely disrupted) the ethnography pertains to an earlier time, such as before the people were confined to a reservation. So the customs of a society may have changed substantially after the ethnographic report which we refer to in our discussion.

CHILDHOOD SEXUALITY

One thing we know is that the sexual curiosity of children is not worrisome to all people; in many societies people greet it with tolerance and openness. An ethnographer working among the Aymara of Peru described a people for whom sexual relations in general were considered "normal, natural, and pleasurable." From early childhood the sexes were unsegregated and related easily and freely. Children slept near their parents and were, from early childhood, aware of adult sexuality. The Aymara viewed the sex play of young children with tolerant amusement. Masturbation was not actively disapproved and evoked neither guilt nor shame. Heterosexual activity on the part of children, too, was generally ignored, and if noted, evoked only amusement or mild ridicule. Girls and boys alike usually had considerable sexual experience by the time they reached puberty—in this society virginity had no special value.[19]

Similarly, the Cubeo Indians of the northwest Amazon considered masturbation and sex play between same sex children neither shameful nor worthy of discouragement. We are told that Cubeo boys sometimes indulged in mutual masturbation, while girls might stroke one another's nipples to produce erection. While younger people participated in this "mild form of homosexual eroticism," however, "true homosexuality" was rare.[20]

Not all societies are so permissive when it comes to sex in general or to masturbation in particular. Consider the people of East Bay, a South Pacific island, who exhibited "great concern for sexual propriety." They discouraged children from touching their genitalia in public—the boys through good-natured ridicule, the girls by scolding. By age five, children had learned to avoid all physical contact with the opposite sex and had become highly sensitive to lapses in modesty. Girls and boys were careful to maintain proper distance at all times.[21] Among the Ashanti of Ghana, a father warned his son against the evils of masturbation, of "making a pestle of his penis."[22] And among the Chinese of Taiwan, masturbation was also greeted with strong disapproval:

> If a child is discovered masturbating he is severely scolded and beaten. He is threatened with what will happen if he continues; he will be unable to urinate, or he will go crazy. Children are also expected to conceal their genitalia from the eyes of others. If a boy urinates outside, he must use his hand to conceal his genitals, while girls past the age of four are expected to use the privacy of the benjo [toilet] where no one can see them. They are reprimanded with slaps and scoldings if they expose themselves.[23]

Childhood sexuality is not just about allowing or encouraging children to be autoerotic or sexual with others of their own age. We should also consider attitudes about sexuality involving adults and children. In our society most people consider any sexual behavior involving an adult and child to be child abuse and strongly condemn it. But some societies are more tolerant of sexual behavior between adults and children. We are told that Thai mothers often tickled their sons' genitalia while feeding or playing with them, for example.[24] Among the Kogi of Colombia, mothers taught their sons how to masturbate, using this method from about age five to calm them and make them sleep.[25] What is especially interesting about the Kogi is that fathers' attitudes toward masturbation were very different from mothers'. Fathers considered masturbation a serious transgression and punished it harshly. They were especially concerned about it because of the belief that a child's masturbation endangered the father's health:

> A father condemns in general the manifestations of infantile sexuality in both sexes, but a mother does not. She, in addition to masturbating her son, shows a lively interest in the erotic pleasures which her daughter derives from her body and takes a certain pride in the fact that this instinct is developing in her children. Both parents nevertheless try to

avoid having the children observe the sexual activities of the adults, and since these are carried out almost solely at night and outside the house, the children evidently do not have any occasion to learn about them.[26]

Some societies also allowed older people special license with respect to sex with young children. Here, for example, is a description of a practice among the Truk of the South Pacific:

> Among older people no longer able for physical or social reasons to have heterosexual liaisons, two practices are reported by a number of informants. Older men not infrequently perform cunnilingus on preadolescent girls; both are said to enjoy this, the men because it is their only sexual outlet and the girls because it is so gentle…[the Trukese refer to such behavior] with tolerant amusement over the dilemma of these old people who have to resort to such devices in order to obtain sexual satisfaction.[27]

While this description might suggest that any sexuality was permitted, the Trukese were much less permissive about certain kinds of sex. When children three or four years in age were observed masturbating they were crossly told to stop, although reproofs did not go beyond "mild pats and somewhat angry sounding remarks." They believed that heterosexual activity made children sick, and that notion extended to masturbation. Yet, as the ethnographers pointed out,

> we may be fairly sure that the prohibition does not reflect disapproval of masturbation as such for this activity is permitted adults with only the restrictions of modesty which apply, for example, to urination, provided the people nearby are of the same sex.[28]

As we have seen, people are not always consistent regarding the kinds of sexual activities allowed infants and children. However, there is a general tendency for societies that allow children to express their sexuality with each other before puberty to be fairly tolerant of premarital and extramarital intercourse as well.[29] Such societies also tend not to insist on modesty in dress and do not constrain their talk about sex around children.[30] Still, no society is entirely free and open about sex. As we shall see in a later chapter, even the most permissive societies do not allow sexual intercourse between parents and children or between brothers and sisters.

HETEROSEXUALITY IN ADOLESCENCE

Do relatively permissive societies alter their attitudes toward sexuality when pregnancy becomes possible? Mostly they do not; as we have seen, tolerance of childhood sexuality generally predicts tolerance for premarital sex. Many

societies permissive of childhood sexuality get girls to marry before or shortly after puberty, so premarital pregnancy is not usually a problem. Some
make a clear distinction between sexual play and intercourse before marriage. For example, among the Kikuyu of Kenya, premarital sex was traditionally encouraged as long as intercourse was avoided. Adolescents practiced *ngweko* which involved "platonic love and fondling."[31] Girls wore an
apron over their genitals and adults taught them, and the boys, how to inter-
twine legs so as to enjoy sex without intercourse. Traditionally, they learned
to do this after initiation into an age-set, but now that the initiation and
age-set system has broken down, the practice of ngweko has diminished.
Sexual activity has not decreased, however, and premarital pregnancy is not
now unusual.

More permissive than the Kikuyu were the Trobriand Islanders who
permitted sexual intercourse before marriage. Girls were expected to have
sex with boys visiting from other villages, and could have as many lovers as
they wished. This was still the case during the 1970s and 1980s when
Annette B. Weiner did fieldwork among the Trobriand Islanders. As she
describes it,

> in the Trobriands, adultery is a crime, but premarital love affairs are
> not. For unmarried young people, each decorative element is carefully
> chosen to catch the eye of a possible lover, as each use of magic is cal-
> culated to "make someone want to sleep with you." Attraction and
> seduction are adolescent pursuits, and the presence of young people
> walking through Losuia, laughing, singing, and teasing, made Saturdays
> almost as celebratory as traditional yam harvest feasts."[32]
>
> Even while involved in the daily village routine, young people are
> preoccupied with their own plans and negotiations. Throughout the
> day, lovers send messages back and forth to arrange evening meeting
> places. Conversations between young people are filled with sexual
> metaphors that express a person's intention. Questions such as "Can I
> have a coconut to drink?" or "Can I ride your bicycle?" are Trobriand
> ways to say, "Will you sleep with me?" Dabweyowa once told me,
> "Women's eyes are different than men's. When I talk to a girl I watch
> her eyes. If she looks straight at me, I know she wants me." Young
> women are just as assertive and dominant as men in their pursuit or
> refusal of a lover.[33]

Given the frequency of premarital sex among the Trobrianders,
Malinowski was puzzled about why there was so little premarital pregnancy.
Whiting et al. suggest its rarity was perhaps due to adolescent subfecundi-
ty—Trobriand girls remained unmarried for only about three years after
puberty. Trobriand Islanders believed that pregnancy was unrelated to copulation, perhaps because the frequent sex did not often result in pregnancy.[34]

Among the Tikopia of the Pacific, masturbation was an acceptable alternative to intercourse for the young of both sexes. Their only reservation was that masturbation makes the hands unclean for food preparation. In the case of men, masturbation could involve self or mutual stimulation, and a girl might masturbate herself if she

> cannot get a man to have intercourse with her, or is too shy to ask the one she wants. It is said that only women who have already tasted sex pleasure will act thus. Such a woman "remembers the male organ," and with her finger, or a manioc root, or a peeled banana, rubs herself. She does so with increasing energy as her desire climbs up. It is because of the force used that it is customary to peel the banana; otherwise her genitals would become sore.[35]

Allowing premarital sex does not always mean that anxiety about sex is absent. For example, even though premarital sex on the Micronesian island of Truk was allowed during the late 1940s and early 1950s, courting usually involved trysts in the bush and secret visits at night to the girl's home. Discovery evoked teasing, even if there was no punishment. The Trukese believed men should initiate sex. But for young men, getting a sexual relationship started, and keeping it going, could be quite stressful. For one thing, it was not easy to find unmarried women with whom to "practice" because girls married early, usually around the time of puberty. It was easier to establish illicit relationships with married women. That was always a bit risky; if discovered, such relationships could be embarrassing, especially for the young man. Courting an unmarried (or married) woman usually required skill at writing love letters. Gladwin and Sarason noted: "It is ironic that, in terms of quantity at least, the most important use to which the art of writing has been put by the Trukese since it was taught them so painfully by missionaries and administration alike is the writing of love letters."[36] A woman could pick and choose among potential lovers, who struggled and competed to satisfy her sexual needs:

> Sexual intercourse, without which a lover's relationship has no meaning for the Trukese, by its very nature requires the expression of strong emotion not only by the man, but also by the woman. In some societies the occurrence or nonoccurrence of female orgasm is not considered of major importance; on Truk, however, it is important, particularly for more accomplished or serious lovers, and its occurrence is a function of the contribution of both partners to the relationship. For the man it determines the success or failure of his performance: If he reaches his climax before the woman he not only leaves her in some degree unsatisfied, but more importantly from his standpoint has "lost" in the contest.[37]

The woman could also exert some control over her lover by virtue of the fact that she possessed his letters, by their nature clear evidence of his intent to consummate a sexual liaison. Their purpose was unambiguous, and by answering a letter a woman essentially agreed to sex. Were she later to become displeased with her lover, she could publicize the letters to his discomfort. All-around, sexual liaisons were far more difficult and sensitive for the man (although not less exciting for that reason):

> It is the woman whose position is at every turn secure and the man who exposes himself to hazards. A man has committed himself by writing the first letter; the woman holds and can expose the incriminating document. With the entry into the house and his approach to the woman it is again the man who runs the risk: of being discovered or of being rejected. And finally during the intercourse itself it is the man who stands to "lose" if he ejaculates too soon; it must furthermore be noted that it is under these circumstances that the type of intercourse least likely to produce rapid orgasm in the woman is used.[38]

Not all peoples are as tolerant of premarital sex as those we have been describing. The Chinese certainly valued premarital chastity and wifely fidelity after marriage. They traditionally took pains to control the perambulation of women, and to limit their contact with the opposite sex. These efforts were not always successful. Constant watchfulness notwithstanding, girls did (and do) have affairs and even get pregnant before marriage, courting discovery, punishment, shame, and possibly reducing bride-wealth value. It was a heavy burden for any family to discover, after a son's marriage, that his bride was not a virgin. But, as one of Pasternak's Taiwan informants put it, "rice already cooked cannot be returned to the storage bin." Such a family usually tries to contain and hide their discovery, but the daughter-in-law can expect to pay for her indiscretion.

Watchfulness was essential among the Tepoztlan of Mexico as well, where a girl's life became "crabbed, cribbed, confined" from her first menstruation. From then on she was not to speak to or encourage boys in the least way. It was a mother's burden to guard her daughters' chastity and reputation. One mother confided to the ethnographer that she wished her fifteen-year-old daughter would marry soon because it was inconvenient to "spy" on her all the time.[39] Indeed, virginity at marriage was (and often still is) important in many cultures. In many Muslim societies, it used to be customary to display blood-stained sheets after the wedding night as proof of a bride's virginity.

With increased education, attitudes toward female/male relationships are often relaxed. In the small Moroccan town of Zawiya, adolescent girls and boys can now walk to school and study together, although dating is still taboo and marriages are still largely arranged (as of the mid-1980s). In the previous generation, just talking together was considered shameful. Even now a girl risks her reputation if people see her too often in a boy's company; they invariably suspect the worst. And a boy might well eliminate as potential mate any girl who has kissed him before.[40] Zawiya town clearly has a double standard, constraining girls more than boys. But surprisingly it is not common for societies to have a double standard regarding premarital sex.[41]

What sorts of societies are more accepting of premarital sex than others, and why? Comparative research work by Suzanne G. Frayser provides some indications.[42] To begin with, her research revealed that more societies allow premarital sex for one or both sexes than do not, and that where there are restraints, they are considerably more likely to apply to sex before marriage than to extramarital sex. Further, societies that restrict sex before marriage are likely to restrict extramarital sex as well. When the rules differ for women and men, it is always in the direction of allowing greater freedom to males. As Frayser put it, "the double standard operates only in one direction."

But why should there be more interest in restricting women's sexual relationships, or in confining them to the reproductive context (to marriage) in some societies but not in others? In this connection, Frayser draws our attention to the fact that women are more obviously linked to their offspring than men, through childbirth, nursing, and the like. For men, the linkage must be assured in other ways:

> If a man has a continuing relationship with a woman who confines her sexual relations exclusively to him, he can more easily identify any children she bears as his own. Therefore, a man indirectly affirms his physical link to his child by creating a close, social bond with the woman whose children he wishes to claim as his own. Cultural beliefs about his role in conception and the restriction of the woman's sexual relations to him further strengthen the basis for his connection with the child.[43]

Still, why are some people more concerned about paternity than others? It is clear that societies vary in the degree to which social groups have an interest in the reproductive potential of women. Consider two examples Frayser provides, one a society in which there is little interest, the other in which interest is considerable.

Among the Kimam, inhabitants of an island off New Guinea, women may have premarital sex and even take the initiative in that regard. There is considerable extramarital liberty as well, for women as well as men. It is not that having children is of no concern; everyone wants sons to work the gardens and to provide support in old age. They need daughters, too, to exchange for daughters-in-law. Interest in childbirth is so strong that a man can divorce or kill his wife for aborting her child.

Although the Kimam appreciate the biological contribution women and men make to childbearing, they base rights to children on other considerations. As Frayser puts it, "conceiving or giving birth to a child is not sufficient reason to claim the right of parenthood; people acquire this right by taking care of the child."[44] For that reason, a barren woman need not fear shame or retribution. Adoption provides an easy solution; few refuse to give a child. Establishment of paternity may not be so much an issue because adoption is acceptable. A man helps support his sister's children and has the right to adopt the sister's child.

Consider now the Kenuzi Nubians, on Egypt's Nile River, among whom strict control over women's sexuality begins early. When a girl is three or four, the custom is to remove her clitoris and practically seal her vaginal opening to guarantee virginity at marriage. And once married she can have sex only with her husband, who often spends long periods working far from home. Husbands sometimes insist that their wives' vaginas be sewn up during long absences. A husband may kill his wife at the slightest suspicion of infidelity, so conception during his absence is to be avoided at all cost.

Like the Kimam, the Kenuzi want children; women to ensure continuation of marriage (and husband's economic support), men to provide for continuity of their descent groups. In fact, reproduction is so much a group concern among the Kenuzi that a man is under pressure to remarry if his wife bears no sons. (This is a source of considerable anxiety for wives, especially given that one-third to one-half of Kenuzi children die young.) Sons, as in all patrilineal societies, belong to the kin groups of their father. For these reasons, men may feel it important to establish paternity and they attempt to do so by strictly controlling the sexuality of women. However, societies that emphasize the mother in kinship (matrilineal societies) have no comparable problem. Identification of the mother is critical for access to kin group resources but maternity is hardly problematic. Knowing the identity of the father is not vital, so controlling his sexuality is probably not as necessary in societies that have kin groups oriented around women.

Where descent is traced through women, then, establishing paternity may be less vital. There, a man's responsibility is to his sister's children; children belong to their mother's group, which is also that of the mother's brother. A man's own offspring belong to a different group—to that of his wife. Thus, a husband's contribution to reproduction can be relatively brief and limited. The link between mother and child is crucial, but motherhood requires no special confirmation.

Is the patterning of kinship crucial to the control of sexuality, then? Frayser's data do confirm that patrilineal systems are more likely to restrict women's sexual relations, and confine their reproductive potential to one man, than matrilineal systems. We find the opposite where descent is traced through women: low confinement of women's sexual and reproductive relationships to one man.

But what of societies in which descent is not traced exclusively through women or men, or in which there are no descent groups at all? Such societies, like patrilineal ones, also tend to emphasize father-child bonds. Frayser suggests this may be because most of these societies require a woman to live with or near her husband's family (patrilocally) when she marries:

> Paternity would be most important in patrilocal groups, because it is the only residence pattern whereby an individual's postmarital residence depends upon where the person's father lives. In addition, patrilocal residence means that the raw materials for community organization consist of clusters of related males.[45]

The comparative evidence confirms that patrilocality is significantly related to restrictions on women's sexual and reproductive relationships. It is even more strongly related to such restrictions than patrilineal descent is related to such restrictions. In fact, patrilineal societies may have these constraints because they are usually also patrilocal.

The nature of kinship organization clearly has an impact, but environmental factors too may play a role. The Circum-Mediterranean area is especially restrictive when it comes to female sexuality, with strong prohibitions against both premarital and extramarital sex. Divorces are difficult to obtain, and where granted the basis is usually barrenness. Remarriage after divorce or death of a husband is difficult. And, as Jane Schneider has pointed out, considerable attention is given in this region to matters of honor, shame, and virginity. There is also considerable competition for pastoral and agricultural resources, resulting in conflict within and between groups, and weak political integration. In the face of competition and social fragmentation, family and descent groups are unstable. Lacking effective political controls, codes of honor and shame provide some degree of social control.[46] In Frayser's view, there may be good reason for women to abide by these codes as well:

> In Circum-Mediterranean societies, a woman's contribution to subsistence relative to a man's is lowest in comparison with all other world areas. Therefore, if a woman's husband divorces her, her consequent economic deprivation would be of major proportions. This economic loss could over-shadow a woman's temptation to violate the regulations placed upon her sexual or reproductive relationships.[47]

Are similar sorts of societies likely, then, to be more or less permissive when it comes to premarital sex? Indeed, in societies where property and other rights are passed to children through males (patrilineal descent) and where married couples live with or near the husband's parents (patrilocal residence), premarital pregnancies tend to evoke considerable disapproval.[48]

In such societies, an unmarried woman who becomes pregnant puts her child at a severe economic as well as social disadvantage. However, if rights to property pass through the mother (matrilineal descent) and women live with or near their own kin when they marry (matrilocal residence), then illegitimate children usually enjoy access to resources.

Societies with dowry, goods and money given by the bride's family to the bride or the couple, are also likely to be restrictive of premarital sex. And, as we will see in the chapter on getting married, dowry is common in socially stratified societies, where families often use large dowries to attract high-status sons-in-law. That strategy may well fail, however, if a daughter has had sex with and become pregnant by a low-status male. So, one reason families guard daughters may be to defend against social climbers attempting to use seduction and pregnancy to force a marriage.[49]

Cross-cultural studies do indicate that complex societies—those with political hierarchies, part- or full-time craft specialists, cities and towns, and class stratification—are especially likely to restrict premarital sex.[50] Perhaps with increasing social inequality, parents become increasingly concerned about their children avoiding marriage with people "beneath them." Permissive premarital sex could complicate matters if it leads to inappropriate emotional attachments. Even worse, unsuitable liaisons resulting in pregnancy could make it difficult or impossible for a girl to marry well. Consistent with this notion, we find that societies with little premarital sex also tend to have arranged marriages.[51]

The degree to which premarital and extramarital sexuality are regulated in society are clearly not matters of chance or accident. These customs and practices are related to each other, to characteristics of kinship and political organization, and perhaps to ecological adaptations as well. Our understanding of the connections is still rudimentary, however, and much more research still needs to be done.

HOMOSEXUALITY

We discuss homosexuality separately because societal attitudes toward it are apparently unrelated to those governing heterosexuality.[52] Because many societies deny homosexuality exists and many ethnographers have ignored it, the incidence or prevalence of homosexuality cross-culturally is difficult to estimate.[53] It is easier simply to determine whether a society permits or prohibits homosexuality. We know less about female homosexuality (less often discussed in ethnographies), but we do know that if it is permitted for adolescent girls, it is almost always also permitted for adolescent boys. We are also aware that permissiveness of homosexuality in adolescence almost always predicts tolerance of it in adulthood.[54]

The consensus now is that homosexuality is not a unitary phenomenon.[55] Some researchers suggest that different types of male homosexuality should be distinguished. In some societies, for example, homosexuality is *mandatory* during a phase of the life cycle. This is the case in parts of Melanesia, where homosexuality is commonly associated with the initiation rites which all adolescent boys undergo.[56] Here, younger participants receive semen from older men in homosexual episodes. They subsequently become the inseminators of younger boys. Later still, they marry heterosexually and have children. Some examples follow.

Among the Big Nambas of Malekula, an island in eastern Melanesia, boys become lovers of older men. The custom is that, after a decision to hold circumcision rites, fathers find guardians for their sons, guardians who will possess exclusive sexual rights over the boys. The guardian becomes the boy's "husband," in a relationship that is very close and usually monogamous. (Chiefs are different; they may take many boy lovers just as they may have many wives.) The boy accompanies his guardian everywhere, and should one die, the survivor would mourn him deeply.

Homosexual liaisons elsewhere in Melanesia are not as intimate or monogamous as among the Big Nambas. Those of the Keraki, in the Trans-Fly area of Papua New Guinea, are more transitory. With respect to the Keraki, Creed tells us that

> sodomy was fully sanctioned by male society, universally practiced, and...homosexuality was actually regarded as essential to a boy's bodily growth. Boys are initiated at the bull-roarer ceremony at about the age of thirteen. On the night of the ceremony the initiate is turned over to a youth of the previous group of initiates who introduces the boy to homosexual intercourse. In all cases...the older youth was the mother's brother's son or the father's sister's son of the new initiate. After this, the boy is available to fellow villagers or visitors of the opposite moiety who wish to have homosexual relations with him. During this time the initiates live together in a seclusion hut for several months, during which they are supposed to grow rapidly with the aid of homosexual activities. At the end of the seclusion the youth becomes a "bachelor." He associates more freely with the elders and shows an increased interest in hunting, but he continues to play the passive role in homosexual relations for a year or so.[57]

Initiates then go through a ceremony during which lime is poured down their throats. People believe the burns which result ensure that the boys have not become pregnant as a result of their homosexual relationships. From that time sexual passivity is over; newly initiated youths now become the inseminators of other boys until, in time, they marry heterosexually.

The expectation that all boys will engage in homosexual relationships with older men is not limited to Melanesia. Other societies have this custom as well. For example, the Siwans of Egypt expected all unmarried males to have homosexual relations, which their fathers arranged. The custom was not entirely permissive, however, since it limited a man to one boy. Although the government eventually prohibited Siwan homosexuality, it was practiced quite openly until 1909. Almost all older men reported having had homosexual relationships as boys. Later, between sixteen and twenty years of age, they invariably married girls. As in Melanesia, then, homosexuality was a phase in every man's life.[58]

The mandatory homosexuality we have been describing usually involves relationships between older men and boys. But homosexuality finds acceptance even in societies where it is not mandatory; some researchers suggest that it commonly occurs as a form of adolescent experimentation.[59] As we noted in our earlier discussion of childhood sexuality, some societies allow casual homosexual play. Still others have special times when homosexuality can be expressed. For example, the Papago of the southwestern United States had "nights of saturnalia," during which males could have brief homosexual relationships.[60] Quite a few North American Indian societies also accommodated male transvestites, commonly referred to as *berdaches*. These men assumed the dress, occupations, and many of the behaviors of women. But whether they were homosexual as well is not clear. The evidence in the ethnographic literature suggests quite a bit of variability. In some societies, like the Papago, Crow, Mohave, and Santee, berdaches reportedly did engage in homosexual behavior. However, informants denied they were homosexual among the Flathead, Pima, Plains Cree, Chiracahua Apache, and Bella Coola.[61] Also variable was the extent to which berdaches married. Where they did, in some societies they customarily married nonberdache men and assumed a woman's role; in other cases they married women and established heterosexual relationships.[62]

In some native North American societies, females too could adopt transvestite roles, but this was much less often accepted. One survey found reports of female transvestites in 30 native North American societies, compared to 113 with male transvestites. And in societies with both female and male berdaches, the females were usually far less common than their male counterparts.[63] Female berdaches often cross-dressed and took up some male pursuits, like hunting. Homosexuality is mentioned in connection with them in some North American societies, but in others their sexual proclivities are not clearly described.

Sexuality is not necessarily either heterosexual or homosexual.[64] As we shall see in the next chapter, the notion of gender does not invariably involve just two categories—female and male. And berdache-like roles are not limited to North America. In a survey of 186 societies, Richley H. Crapo found such statuses in 41 or 22 percent of them, and about half were outside North America.[65] Only eight societies (3 percent) provided evidence of female berdaches. Just as accounts more often describe male berdaches, so do they more often report male homosexuality than lesbianism.[66] Without more research on lesbianism in societies around the world, there is no way to know whether it is reported less often than male homosexuality because it really is so, or because ethnographers have neglected to investigate the phenomenon and the members of many societies are more reluctant to discuss it.[67]

The fact that societies accepting homosexuality in childhood are generally also tolerant of it in adulthood does not imply that expectations about sexual behavior do not change in adulthood. Reproduction requires heterosexual relationships, so it is hardly surprising that, once individuals are able to reproduce, societies expect and prefer them to do so. Indeed, even in societies where most or all individuals have homosexual experiences during an early stage of their lives, most adults marry and have heterosexual intercourse. And even where people may adopt roles atypical for their sex, such individuals are rare. There are actually very few societies in which people prefer homosexuality over heterosexuality in adulthood. The Etoro of New Guinea were one such society. Although most men married and had heterosexual sex, the Etoro actually prohibited heterosexual sex for as many as 260 days a year, and never allowed it in or near the house or gardens. There were no restrictions on male homosexuality, however; the Etoro believed it made crops flourish and boys strong.[68]

While people tolerate homosexuality in most societies, in some they condemn or ridicule it, or consider it incomprehensible.[69] A few societies even eliminate persons discovered engaging in homosexual acts. For example, the Eastern Apache executed homosexuals, considering them dangerous witches. However, they did not consider cross-dressing synonymous with homosexuality; they ridiculed berdaches, but did not execute them unless they were homosexual as well.[70] Among the Azande of the Sudan, too, the reaction was severe. Lesbianism among women in princely households was punishable by death, flogging the likely response in poorer families.[71]

Several cross-cultural studies have attempted to discover why some societies are more accepting of homosexuality than others. The findings, unfortunately, have been contradictory. Part of the problem may be that most researchers have not distinguished different kinds of male homosexuality. If degree of acceptance varies according to type, then failing to make such distinctions could well obscure the results.[72] Nonetheless, an intriguing study by Dennis Werner found that societies with evidence of *population pressure* on resources, and therefore with reason to limit reproduction, are more likely to tolerate male homosexuality.

The presumption is, of course, that more homosexuality translates into less heterosexuality and, therefore, a lower reproductive rate. By way of contrast, societies that forbid abortion and infanticide for married women (most permit these practices for illegitimate births) are likely to disapprove of male homosexuality, suggesting that it may be less acceptable in societies struggling to increase their populations. These societies may discourage any behavior that inhibits population growth. Widespread homosexuality would have that effect to the extent that it decreased heterosexual relations. Another bit of evidence in support of the population pressure interpretation is that societies with famines and severe food shortages, indirect indicators of excess population, are also more likely to allow homosexuality.[73]

Policy changes in the former Soviet Union were consistent with this interpretation. In 1917, during the turmoil of revolution, the government encouraged people to have fewer children, and also revoked laws prohibiting abortion and homosexuality. Later, when a pronatalist policy emerged (1934–1936), the Soviet government rewarded mothers with many children, and once again declared abortion and homosexuality illegal.[74]

Population pressure may not be the only inducement to more relaxed attitudes toward homosexuality. We know, for example, that societies with customary rites of passage from boyhood to manhood (usually including genital operations) are also more likely to condone or encourage homosexuality, although the reasons are unclear.[75] It is important to keep in mind, as well, that while problems of population growth (too little or too much) may have something to do with *societal* attitudes toward homosexuality, such problems cannot explain why certain *individuals* become homosexual.

Let us return, now, to the matter of types. Have comparative studies thrown any light on the conditions under which different forms of homosexuality are more or less likely to occur? In one study, Richley H. Crapo compared mandatory intergenerational homosexuality (which he calls mentorship homosexuality) with voluntary same generation homosexuality, and found that they occur in different types of societies.[76] The mentorship variety appears in societies with male-centered kin groups, a good deal of segregation of the sexes in childhood, and clear role distinctions between males and females.

This is consistent with earlier suggestions that mentorship homosexuality is part of a larger syndrome reflecting strong male power and authority.[77] Where older men exercise strong control over women and younger males, institutionalizing homosexuality for younger males may increase their prospects of acquiring multiple wives. If this is so, mentorship homosexuality may have more to do with control than with some fundamental homosexual orientation or desire. Societies with voluntary same generation homosexuality (or at least a tolerance of male transvestites) may be different. Although early theorists thought that male transvestism was a way for some males to escape oppressive sex-role requirements (such as aggressive warrior roles),[78] subsequent research by Munroe, Whiting, and Hally found that male transvestism was actually more likely where sex-role distinctions are *minimal*. In societies that emphasize female-male role differences, people seem to consider transvestism less acceptable.[79]

MEN'S FEAR OF SEX WITH WOMEN

We have been talking about the degree to which societies allow or tolerate different kinds of sex, but we have not yet considered how people *think* of sex—as desirable and pleasurable, or as a duty and perhaps even frightening? Just because a society allows a certain type of sex with a certain type of person does not mean people generally desire it. On the other hand, even forbidden sex may be illicitly enjoyed by some. When it comes to attitudes toward sexuality, too, we find considerable variation, as the following examples will show.

Sex, according to the Chukchee of Siberia, was the "best thing" in the world, while for the Cayapa of Ecuador it was "a little like work."[80] And earlier in this chapter, we discussed the Aymara and Trukese, who clearly also considered sex pleasurable and desirable. Where people think of sex as pleasurable, it is not necessarily so for one sex alone. This was clearly the case on Truk, where men went to great lengths to ensure orgasm in their partners. And among the Bemba of Africa,

> puberty is eagerly looked forward to by the girls. They and their parents watch the growth of their breasts with interest and excitement and openly discuss the approach of womanhood. Girls are enthusiastic about the prospect of marriage and are taught that sex relations are pleasant and that it is their duty to give pleasure to their husbands. They do not seem to fear the first act of intercourse or to apprehend that it will be painful.[81]

Malinowski tells us that for Trobriand Islanders the most important idea about sex was that it is "purely a source of pleasure." Here is an informant's account, a description of lovemaking which clearly conveys the pleasure derived by women and men alike:

> When I sleep with Dabugera I embrace her, I hug her with my whole body, I rub noses with her. We suck each other's lower lip, so that we are stirred to passion. We suck each other's tongues, we bite each other's noses, we bite each other's chins, we bite cheeks and caress the armpit and the groin. Then she will say: "O my lover, it itches very much...push on again, my whole body melts with pleasure...do it vigorously, be quick, so that the fluids may discharge...tread on again, my body feels so pleasant.[82]

In some societies men take special pains to assure the pleasure of their sex partners. This was clearly also the case among the Toradja, a people of Central Celebes, according to the account provided by Adriani and Kruyte:

for the purpose of increasing sensual pleasure, the penis is sometimes mutilated.... One man from there even claimed that someone whose penis is not mutilated is not desired by the women. This mutilation is done by inserting under the skin of the glans of the penis little marbles of about five millimeters in diameter, which are ground from shells. The men of Kawanga had this operation done in a woods located between this place and Moengkoe-lande. The skin of the glans of the penis is pinched in a split piece of wood, so that it protrudes above. Then the skin is pierced and the little balls are pushed into the cut, after which this is rubbed with horse manure. These little marbles are called *kandoekoe* (*makandoekoe*, "uneven, bumpy"). At each operation two or three little balls are inserted, up to seven in all. (It is said that there are girls who inquire about the number of *kandoekoe* that a young man who asks to marry them has, with the words: "How many guests do you have" (*bara sangkoedja linggonamoe*). They are said to be inserted in such a way that, when the penis is limp, the little marbles are on the under side of it, and with an erection they come to lie on the upper side. The operation takes place without any ceremony. When the wound has healed, the person must not eat any peas (*tibesi*), fern greens (*bate'a*), or slimy vegetables; otherwise the little marbles will fall out.[83]

While many people consider sex pleasurable, there are also those who find it dangerous and fearful. The Mae Enga, in Highland New Guinea, are an example of a society in which men are afraid to have sex with women, even in marriage. Before and after heterosexual sex, men engage in various rituals to protect themselves against harm. Mervyn Meggitt described the situation as follows:

Each act of coitus increases a man's chances of being contaminated...copulation is in itself detrimental to male well-being. Men believe that the vital fluid residing in a man's skin makes it sound and handsome, a condition that determines and reflects his mental vigor and self-confidence. This fluid also manifests itself as his semen. Hence, every ejaculation depletes his vitality, and over-indulgence must dull his mind and leave his body permanently exhausted and withered.[84]

We do not have research yet on why some societies think of sex as a pleasure versus a duty, but we do know quite a bit about the conditions under which men will fear sex with women. Relatively few societies express fears as strong as the Mae Enga, but we find evidence of a milder fear of sex in many societies around the world. During planting, sex may spoil the harvest; dreams about sex can bring bad luck; sex before sports may result in losing the game. Carol R. Ember has conducted cross-cultural research to evaluate four explanations of men's fear of sex with women. She limited herself to men's attitudes only because women's views are not often described in ethnographies.[85]

One explanation, suggested by Meggitt on the basis of data from various places in New Guinea, is that men may fear sex with women if they usually obtain wives from their enemies, as the Mae Enga did (along with many other societies in Papua New Guinea's Western Highlands.) On the other hand, fear of sex with women is likely to be absent if marriage is not with traditional enemies (as in the Central Highlands of Papua New Guinea).

A second hypothesis Ember tested was that of Shirley Lindenbaum, who proposed that fear of sex with women may be a cultural device that serves to restrain population growth where resources are endangered.[86] If Lindenbaum is right, fear of sex with women should be found in the presence of population pressure.

Beatrice B. Whiting suggested a third possibility: If men are conflicted about their sexual identity, they are likely to exhibit exaggerated masculine behavior as well as antagonism toward, and fear of, women.[87] We might expect problems of sexual identity where there is an initial unconscious feminine identification and a subsequent (more conscious) identification with men. That sequence is likely where, early in life, boys have almost exclusive contact with mothers who exert almost complete control over them. That situation could lead to an initial feminine identification. When they later become aware that men actually control the society's important resources, boys might shift their identification to men. Accordingly, men's fear of sex with women should be particularly likely where they initially have a cross-sex identification.

The fourth proposal Ember tested was that of William N. Stephens, who suggested that some societies may produce an exaggerated *Oedipus complex*, which in turn is conducive to a fear of sex with women.[88] The idea here is that anxiety about heterosexual sex should emerge where we find an unconscious equation of *mother* with *sex partner*. If a boy's sexual interest in his mother were heightened for some reason, he would be especially frightened because of the incest taboo (fearing retaliation by the father). Under what circumstances might the Oedipus complex be exaggerated? Stephens suggests this might occur where custom frustrates a mother's sexual expression, causing her to redirect some of her sexual interest toward her son.[89] This could happen, for example, where there is a long postpartum sex taboo (a mother avoiding sex for a year or more after she gives birth).[90] But whatever the reason, the closer the relationship between mother and son, and the more contact between them, the more likely his Oedipal impulses will be enhanced, and the more likely he will fear sex with women (generalizing from his fear of sex with his mother).

When Ember tested the predictive value of these four hypotheses cross-culturally, she found support for all four. The more a society marries its enemies, the more likely men will fear sex with women. The more evidence of population pressure (food shortages or famine), the more likely men will be afraid of sex with women. Where mothers sleep closer to their infants than to their husbands *and* live with or near their husbands' families when they marry (a combination that presumably produces conflict over male sex identity), men tend to fear sex with women. As for the Oedipal interpretation, duration of the postpartum sex taboo does not by itself predict that men will fear sex with women, but Ember did find that men are likely to fear sex with women in societies where mothers customarily sleep closer physically (in the same bed or room) to their babies than to their husbands. Because all of the hypotheses tested were supported, Ember suggests the following theory to integrate them:

> "Marrying enemies" (with food shortage as a partial cause) creates emotional distance (including sleeping distance) between husbands and wives. This in turn may exaggerate a boy's unconscious sexual interest in his mother, which becomes frightening in view of the incest taboo. Given the incest taboo, this exaggerated interest may result in a general fear of sex with women.[91]

Reanalyzing Ember's data, Michio Kitahara has offered a different interpretation. He suggests that food shortages may have a more direct effect on men's fear of sex than Ember supposed; anxiety about food itself may inhibit sexual desire.[92] (The Embers now speculate that, lacking an adequate diet, people might experience dizziness and weakness during and after sex, reactions that could lead to the conclusion that sex is dangerous.) Societies in which men fear sex with women may have considerable stress of one kind or another. Food shortage is only one kind of stress; there are others. For example, if people find mates in nearby villages with which they are periodically at war, marriage with women from enemy villages might well promote sexual anxiety. We should keep in mind, however, that the risk of famine and marriage with enemies are likely to be stressful for both parties, for the women as well as the men. If Kitahara's theory is right, then, we would expect both genders to fear heterosexual sex. Unfortunately, we do not yet have comparative research that might enable us to confirm or refute this theory. One reason may be that ethnographic accounts are generally deficient about women's thoughts on sexual attitudes, probably because most of them have been written by men.

Fear of women is not only manifested in reluctance to have sex. The Mae Enga also believe that menstrual blood is dangerous, that contact with it can "sicken a man and cause persistent vomiting, turn his blood black, corrupt his vital juices so that his skin darkens and wrinkles as his flesh wastes, permanently dull his wits, and eventually lead to a slow decline and death."[93] The Onge of Little Andaman are also among those who refrain during menses, believing that swelling of the arms and legs would follow.[94] Among the Chinese, too, sex is prohibited during menstruation; women in this state are considered polluting, as they are for one month after childbirth, when sex would "endanger the health of all concerned."[95]

The notion that menstrual blood is dangerous is actually fairly common around the world, and most often the danger is to men or to the community at large. Rarely are risks to women mentioned in ethnographic accounts.[96] This raises the possibility that men's fear of sex with women, and fear of menstrual blood, may both be part of a more general pattern of husband-wife avoidance and aloofness. It should also be noted that societies in which sex is enjoyable rather than frightening, and in which marital relationships are likely to be intimate, are generally also those in which social organization does not center on men. We will return to the issue of marital intimacy and aloofness later, in our chapter on marital relationships. But first let us shift gears to pursue at greater length a matter only vaguely suggested thus far. At a number of points in this chapter, we noted that societies vary in terms of how sharply they define different roles for women and men. Just what is the relationship between sex and social roles, or between them and characteristics of personality? It is to these questions that we will turn in the next chapter.

Notes

1. "Sex" in bacteria takes about ninety minutes; cloning takes less than thirty minutes. James L. Gould and Carol Grant Gould, *Sexual Selection* (New York: Scientific American Library, 1989), pp. 18–25.
2. Ibid., p. 25; for a review of theories about why there is sex, see Chapter 3.
3. Ibid., p. 65.
4. Martin Daly and Margo Wilson, *Sex, Evolution, and Behavior*, 2nd ed. (Boston: Willard Grant Press, 1983), p. 72.
5. Suzanne G. Frayser, *Varieties of Sexual Experience: An Anthropological Perspective on Human Sexuality* (New Haven: HRAF Press, 1985), pp. 23–24.
6. Ibid., pp. 28–30.
7. Sarah Blaffer Hrdy and Patricia L. Whitten, "Patterning of Sexual Activity," in *Primate Societies*, eds. Barbara B. Smuts, Dorothy L. Cheney, Robert M. Seyfarth, Richard W. Wrangham, and Thomas T. Struhsaker (Chicago: University of Chicago Press, 1987), p. 370.
8. Melvin Ember and Carol R. Ember, "Male-Female Bonding: A Cross-Species Study of Mammals and Birds," *Behavior Science Research* 14 (1979): 42–43; Carol R. Ember and Melvin Ember, "The Evolution of Human Female Sexuality: A Cross-Species Perspective," *Journal of Anthropological Research* 40 (1984): 202–210. Length of dependency also appears to be a factor. Animals that can rear their young to matu-

rity within a season also appear to have breeding seasons; those with longer dependency periods have year-round breeding. See also Burton Pasternak, "Seasons of Birth and Marriage in Two Chinese Localities," *Human Ecology* 6 (1978): 299–323, which refers to a number of studies bearing on the effects of climate on birth seasonalities.

9. Hrdy and Whitten, "Patterning of Sexual Activity," pp. 370–384.

10. Ronald D. Nadler and Charles H. Phoenix, "Male Sexual Behavior: Monkeys, Men, and Apes," in *Understanding Behavior: What Primate Studies Tell Us about Human Behavior*, eds. James D. Loy and Calvin B. Peters (New York: Oxford University Press, 1991), p. 173.

11. Hrdy and Whitten, "Patterning of Sexual Activity," p. 371.

12. Solly Zuckerman, *The Social Life of Monkeys and Apes* (London: Routledge and Kegan Paul, 1932); Thelma E. Rowell, *Social Behavior of Monkeys* (Harmondsworth, England: Penguin Books, 1972); for specific reference to humans, see Ralph Linton, *The Study of Man: An Introduction* (New York: Appleton-Century-Crofts, 1936), p. 135; and Marshall D. Sahlins, "Origin of Society," *Scientific American* (September 1960): 76–86.

13. This view has become widely familiar through Desmond Morris, *The Naked Ape* (New York: McGraw-Hill, 1967). The role of sexuality in maintaining pair bonds has also been discussed by J. H. Crook, "Sexual Selection, Dimorphism, and Social Organization in the Primates," in *Sexual Selection and the Descent of Man, 1871–1971*, ed. B. Campbell (Chicago: Aldine, 1972), p. 254; Jane B. Lancaster, "Sex Roles in Primate Societies," in *Sex Differences: Social and Biological Perspectives*, ed. Michael S. Teitelbaum (Garden City, NY: Anchor Books, 1976), p. 51; and C. O. Lovejoy, "The Origin of Man," *Science*, January 23, 1982, p. 346.

14. Ember and Ember, "The Evolution of Human Female Sexuality."

15. Linda D. Wolfe, "Human Evolution and the Sexual Behavior of Female Primates," in *Understanding Behavior*, eds. Loy and Peters, p. 134.

16. David R. Heise, "Cultural Patterning of Sexual Socialization," *American Sociological Review* 32 (1967): 726–739.

17. Morton Hunt, *Sexual Behavior in the 1970s* (Chicago: Playboy Press, 1974), pp. 254–257.

18. Tamar Lewin, "Sex in America: Faithfulness in Marriage Is Overwhelming," *New York Times National*, October 7, 1994, pp. A1, A18. However, it is difficult to know if this is a real change or a reflection of different survey procedures. The latest surveys are likely to be accurate because they were based on random sampling procedures; earlier samples were more opportunistic—recruiting people who may have been more willing than most people to talk about sex. Since many people do not readily talk about sex, we cannot be sure that typ-

ical behavior has really changed; perhaps people who were more sexually permissive were more willing to discuss their sexuality in earlier surveys. On the other hand, it seems quite plausible that attitudes toward sexuality are less permissive now because of the fear of AIDS. For the results of recent surveys, see Robert T. Michael, John H. Gagnon, Edward O. Laumann, and Gina Kolata, *Sex in America: A Definitive Survey* (Boston: Little, Brown and Co., 1994).

19. Harry Tschopik, Jr., "The Aymara of Chucuito, Peru," *Anthropological Papers of the American Museum of Natural History* 44 (1951): 167.

20. Irving Goldman, *The Cubeo: Indians of the Northwest Amazon* (Urbana: University of Illinois Press, Illinois Studies in Anthropology, no. 2, 1963), p. 181.

21. William Davenport, "Sexual Patterns and Their Regulation in a Society of the Southwest Pacific," in *Sex and Behavior*, ed. Frank A. Beach (New York: John Wiley, 1965), pp. 164–174.

22. R. S. Rattray, *Ashanti Law and Constitution* (Oxford: The Clarendon Press, 1929), p. 13.

23. Norma Joyce Diamond, *K'un Shen: A Taiwan Village* (New York: Holt, Rinehart & Winston, 1969), p. 34.

24. Howard Keva Kaufman, *Bangkhuad: A Community Study in Thailand* (Locust Valley, NY: Association for Asian Studies, Monographs 10, 1960), p. 149.

25. Gerardo Reichel-Dolmatoff, *Los Kogi: Una Tribu de la Sierra Nevada de Santa Marta, Columbia, Toma II* [*The Kogi: A Tribe of the Sierra Nevada de Santa Marta, Columbia, vol. II*] (Bogota: Editorial Iqueima [translated from the Spanish for the Human Relations Area Files by Sydney Muirden], 1951), p. 219.

26. Ibid.

27. Thomas Gladwin and Seymour B. Sarason, *Truk: Man in Paradise* (New York: Wenner-Gren Foundation for Anthropological Research, Viking Fund Publications in Anthropology, no. 20, 1953), p. 115. The period they describe is 1947–1951.

28. Ibid., p. 252.

29. Data from Robert B. Textor, comp. *A Cross-Cultural Summary* (New Haven: HRAF Press, 1967).

30. William N. Stephens, "A Cross-Cultural Study of Modesty," *Behavior Science Research* 7 (1972): 1–28.

31. John W. M. Whiting, Victoria K. Burbank, and Mitchell S. Ratner, "The Duration of Maidenhood across Cultures," in *School Age Pregnancy and Parenthood: Biosocial Dimensions*, eds. Jane B. Lancaster and Beatrix A. Hamburg (New York: Aldine De Gruyter, 1986), pp. 281–282, refer to the traditional Kikuyu pattern as described by Jomo Kenyatta, *Facing Mount Kenya* (New York: Random House, 1979), pp. 151–152, and to the more modern situa-

tion as described by Carol Worthman, "Developmental Dysynchrony as Normative Experience: Kikuyu Adolescents," paper delivered at the Social Science Research Council meeting on School-Age Pregnancy and Parenthood, 1982.

32. Annette B. Weiner, *The Trobrianders of Papua New Guinea* (New York: Holt, Rinehart and Winston, 1988).

33. Ibid., p. 67.

34. Whiting, Burbank, and Ratner, "The Duration of Maidenhood across Cultures," p. 283.

35. Raymond Firth, *We, the Tikopia: A Sociological Study of Kinship in Primitive Polynesia* (London: George Allen and Unwin, 1936), p. 494.

36. Gladwin and Sarason, *Truk*, p. 103.

37. Ibid., p. 277.

38. Ibid., p. 113. See the HRAF file on Truk for further details.

39. Oscar Lewis, *Life in a Mexican Village: Tepoztlan Revisited* (Urbana: University of Illinois Press, 1951), p. 397.

40. Susan Schaefer Davis, "Morocco: Adolescents in a Small Town," in *Portraits of Culture: Ethnographic Originals*, eds. Melvin Ember, Carol R. Ember, and David Levinson (Englewood Cliffs, NJ: Prentice Hall/Simon & Schuster Custom Publishing, 1994).

41. Gwen J. Broude, "Cross-Cultural Patterning of Some Sexual Attitudes and Practices," *Behavior Science Research* 11 (1976): 227–262; Frayser, *Varieties of Sexual Experience*, p. 203; Alice Schlegel and Herbert Barry III, *Adolescence: An Anthropological Inquiry* (New York: Free Press, 1991), p. 121.

42. Frayser, *Varieties of Sexual Experience*, pp. 323–359.

43. Ibid., p. 327.

44. Ibid., p. 336.

45. Ibid., p. 346.

46. See Jane Schneider, "Of Vigilance and Virgins: Honor, Shame, and Access to Resources in Mediterranean Societies," *Ethnology* 10 (1971): 1–24.

47. Frayser, *Varieties of Sexual Experience*, p. 354.

48. See also Gwen J. Broude, "Variations in Sexual Attitudes, Norms, and Practices," in *Cross-Cultural Research for Social Science*, eds. Carol R. Ember and Melvin Ember (Upper Saddle River, NJ: Prentice Hall/Simon & Schuster Custom Publishing, 1996); George W. Goethals, "Factors Affecting Permissive and Nonpermissive Rules Regarding Premarital Sex," in *Sociology of Sex: A Book of Readings*, ed. James M. Henslin (New York: Appleton-Century-Crofts, 1971), pp. 9–25.

49. Alice Schlegel, "Status, Property, and the Value on Virginity," *American Ethnologist* 18 (1991): 719–734; Alice Schlegel and Rohn Eloul, "Marriage Transactions: Labor, Property, Status," *American*

Anthropologist 90 (1988): 291–309; see also discussion in Schlegel and Barry, *Adolescence*, pp. 112–116.

50. Data from Textor, *A Cross-Cultural Summary*.

51. Gwen J. Broude, "Male-Female Relationships in Cross-Cultural Perspective: A Study of Sex and Intimacy," *Behavior Science Research* 13 (1983): 154–181.

52. Broude, "Cross-Cultural Patterning of Some Sexual Attitudes and Practices," pp. 227–262.

53. See the recent discussion of problems with ethnographic data in Ralph Bolton, "Sex, Science, and Social Responsibility: Cross-Cultural Research on Same-Sex Eroticism and Sexual Intolerance," *Cross-Cultural Research* 28 (1994): 134–190; and Richley H. Crapo, "Factors in the Cross-Cultural Patterning of Male Homosexuality: A Reappraisal of the Literature," *Cross-Cultural Research* 29 (1995): 178–202.

54. Schlegel and Barry, *Adolescence*, pp. 128–129.

55. See the discussion in Crapo, "Factors in the Cross-Cultural Patterning of Male Homosexuality," pp. 183–202; and Bolton, "Sex, Science, and Social Responsibility," pp. 163–164.

56. The discussion of homosexuality in Melanesia that follows is based on an analysis and description of ethnographic reports by Gerald W. Creed, in "Sexual Subordination: Institutionalized Homosexuality and Social Control in Melanesia," *Ethnology* 23 (1984): 157–176.

57. Ibid., p. 160.

58. Mahmud M. 'Abd Allah, "Siwan Customs," *Harvard African Studies* 1 (1917): 7, 20.

59. Broude, "Variations in Sexual Attitudes, Norms, and Practices"; Schlegel and Barry, *Adolescence*, p. 127.

60. Men could also have brief heterosexual relationships during "nights of saturnalia." Women did not have quite the same freedom of expression. They participated in these feasts only with their husband's permission. As we shall see shortly, male transvestites engaged in homosexuality on a more regular basis among the Papago; there were no female transvestites, however. For a discussion of these customs among the Papago, see Ruth Murray Underhill, *Social Organization of the Papago Indians* (New York: Columbia University Press, 1939).

61. References to the relevant ethnography can be found in an extensive review by Charles Callender and Lee M. Kochems, "The North American Berdache," *Current Anthropology* 24 (1983): 443–470. See particularly pp. 449–451.

62. Ibid.

63. Ibid., pp. 445–446; Walter L. Williams, "Amazons of America: Female Gender Variance," in *Gender in Cross-Cultural Perspective*, eds. Caroline B. Brettell and Carolyn F. Sargent (Englewood Cliffs, NJ:

Prentice Hall, 1993), pp. 179–191, prefers to call females who take up some of the male role *amazons*.

64. See the discussion in Patricia C. Albers, "From Illusion to Illumination: Anthropological Studies of American Indian Women," in *Gender and Anthropology: Critical Reviews for Research and Teaching*, ed. Sandra Morgen (Washington, DC: American Anthropological Association, 1989), pp. 132–135; see also Sue Ellen Jacobs and Christine Roberts, "Sex, Sexuality, Gender, and Gender Variance," in *Gender and Anthropology*, ed. Morgen, pp. 438–439.

65. Crapo, "Factors in the Cross-Cultural Patterning of Male Homosexuality," pp. 187–190.

66. Broude, "Variations in Sexual Attitudes, Norms and Practices."

67. See Jacobs and Roberts, "Sex, Sexuality, Gender, and Gender Variance," for a fuller discussion of the work that needs to be done on lesbianism.

68. Raymond C. Kelly, "Witchcraft and Sexual Relations: An Exploration in the Social and Semantic Implications of the Structure of Belief," paper presented at the annual meeting of the American Anthropological Association, Mexico City, 1974.

69. Summarizing the results of twelve cross-cultural studies reporting attitudes toward homosexuality, Bolton, in "Sex, Science, and Social Responsibility," p. 153, says that most societies in ten of the studies ignore, permit, tolerate, encourage, or accept homosexuality as normal for some categories of persons.

70. Morris Edward Opler, *An Apache Life-Way: The Economic, Social, and Religious Institutions of the Chiricahua Indians* (Chicago: University of Chicago Press, 1941), pp. 79, 415.

71. Edward Evan Evans-Pritchard, *Witchcraft, Oracles, and Magic among the Azande* (Oxford: Clarendon Press, 1937), p. 56.

72. See Bolton, "Sex, Science, and Social Responsibility"; and Crapo, "Factors in the Cross-Cultural Patterning of Male Homosexuality."

73. Dennis W. Werner, "A Cross-Cultural Perspective on Theory and Research on Male Homosexuality," *Journal of Homosexuality* 4 (1979): 345–362, and "On the Societal Acceptance or Rejection of Male Homosexuality" (M.A. thesis, Hunter College of the City University of New York, 1975), p. 36. It is important to note, however, that political conditions, too, can lead to famine: Somalia, Ethiopia, and Bosnia provide recent vivid examples.

74. Werner, "A Cross-Cultural Perspective on Theory and Research on Male Homosexuality," p. 358.

75. Ibid.

76. Crapo, "Factors in the Cross-Cultural Patterning of Male Homosexuality."

77. See, for example, Creed, "Sexual Subordination."

78. See, for example, E. Adamson Hoebel, *Man in the Primitive World* (New York: McGraw Hill, 1949).

79. Robert L. Munroe, John W. M. Whiting, and David J. Hally, "Institutionalized Male Transvestism and Sex Distinctions," *American Anthropologist* 71 (1969): 87–91.

80. Waldemar Bogoras (Vladimir Germanovich Bogaraz-Tan), *The Chukchee: Material Culture [Part 1], Religion [Part 2], Social Organization [Part 3]* (New York: G. E. Stechert and Co., Memoirs of the American Museum of Natural History, 11, 1904 [Part 1], 1907 [Part 2], 1909 [Part 3]); and Milton Altschuler, "Cayapa Personality and Sexual Motivation," in *Human Sexual Behavior*, eds. Donald S. Marshall and Robert C. Suggs (Englewood Cliffs, NJ: Prentice Hall, 1971), pp. 38–58, as reported in Broude, "Variations in Sexual Attitudes, Norms, and Practices."

81. Audrey I. Richards, *Chisungu: A Girl's Initiation Ceremony among the Bemba of Northern Rhodesia* (London: Faber and Faber, 1956), p. 154. (Period 1930–1934.)

82. Bronislaw Malinowski, *The Sexual Life of Savages in Northwestern Melanesia*, vol. I and II (New York: Horace Liveright, 1929), p. 341.

83. N. Adriani and Albert C. Kruyt, *De Bare's Sprekende Toradjas van Vidden-Celebes (de Oost Toradjas), Tweede Deel [The Bare-Speaking Toradja of Central Celebes (the East Toradja), vol. 2]* (Tweede, geheel omgewerket druk, Koninklijke Nederlandse Akademie Van Wetenschappen, Verhandelingen, Afdeling Letterkunde, Nieuwe Reeks, vol. 55. Amsterdam: N.V. Noord-Hollandsche Uitgevers Maatschappij, 1951), p. 392.

84. M. J. Meggitt, "Male-Female Relationships in the Highlands of Australian New Guinea," *American Anthropologist* 66, no. 4 (1964): 204–224.

85. Carol R. Ember, "Men's Fear of Sex with Women: A Cross-Cultural Study," *Sex Roles* 4 (1978): 657–678.

86. Shirley Lindenbaum, "Sorcerers, Ghosts, and Polluting Women: An Analysis of Religious Belief and Population Control," *Ethnology* 11 (1972): 241–253.

87. Beatrice B. Whiting, "Sex Identity Conflict and Physical Violence: A Comparative Study," *American Anthropologist* 67 (1965): 123–140.

88. William N. Stephens, *The Oedipus Complex: Cross-Cultural Evidence* (Glencoe, IL: Free Press, 1962).

89. These proposals all focus on men's fear of sex. We have no studies that indicate what women think about sex in these societies and why.

90. While the postpartum sex taboo applies to both husband and wife, the husband can often seek satisfaction elsewhere.

91. Ember, "Men's Fear of Sex with Women," p. 677.

92. Michio Kitahara, in "Men's Heterosexual Fear Due to Reciprocal

Inhibition," *Ethos* 9 (1981): 37–50, amended Ember's model on the basis of a reanalysis of her data using path analysis. While he suggests a more direct role for food shortages, his analysis is consistent with Ember's model with respect to the effects of marrying enemies and sleeping arrangements. Note, however, that Kitahara interprets these relationships differently. See also a discussion by Lewellyn Hendrix, "Varieties of Marital Relationships," in *Cross-Cultural Research for Social Science*, eds. Ember and Ember.

93. Meggitt, "Male-Female Relationships in the Highlands of Australian New Guinea," p. 207.

94. It is interesting that the Onge explain menstruation in very young girls in terms of previous nose rubbing, their substitute for kissing. According to one account, "they ignore the unhygienic practice of kissing with the lips, and never even kiss their children. Orly nose rubbing is practiced." See Lidio Cipriani, "Hygiene and Medical Practices among the Onge (Little Andaman)," *Anthropos* 56 (1961): 492.

95. Diamond, *K'un Shen*, p. 61.

96. William N. Stephens, "A Cross-Cultural Study of Menstrual Taboos," *Genetic Psychology Monographs* 64 (1961): 397.

3

GENDER, DIVISION OF LABOR, AND SOCIAL BEHAVIOR

The females and males of a species may have different reproductive organs, but differences in such *primary sex characteristics* do not necessarily mean that the sexes will differ also in their *secondary sex characteristics* (e.g., size) or social behavior. In some species the size and coloring of females and males, and even their behavior, may be so similar that experts cannot distinguish them, except by watching who does what to whom during sex. Some primate species show striking differences between the sexes (sexual dimorphism). Gibbon females and males do not differ in size and appearance, but orangutan males weigh more than twice as much as females, and only males have large cheek pads, throat pouches, beards, and long hair. Indeed, the males in all the great ape species (orangutans, chimpanzees, gorillas) are larger. Just as gibbons manifest little physical dimorphism, they also behave much the same way, except when it comes to infant care. Neither sex dominates the other and both, as a bonded pair, defend their territory against intruders.[1]

Why some species have more physical sexual dimorphism than others is a fascinating question, but not one of concern here.[2] Our interest is in the relationship between physical sexual dimorphism and behavior in humans. Humans are sexually dimorphic, not as much as orangutans, but certainly more so than gibbons. Females and males also exhibit differences in role and personality in most societies; in none do they do exactly the same things. No society treats females and males exactly the same, or expects them to behave in the same ways. It is important for us to ask, then, whether biology or culture mainly accounts for these gender differences. Let us begin with

45

a discussion of the physical difference between women and men, and then move on to economic and political roles, personality, and status.

PHYSICAL DIFFERENCES
BETWEEN HUMAN FEMALES AND MALES

Aside from obvious differences in genitalia and secondary sex characteristics, women and men everywhere exhibit fairly marked differences in size. Females generally have wider pelvises, while males are taller and have heavier skeletons. A larger proportion of female body weight is fat, whereas males have proportionately more muscle. Males typically also have greater grip strength, proportionately larger hearts and lungs, and greater aerobic work capacity (greater maximum uptake of oxygen during exercise).[3]

What are we to make of these physical differences? Are they givens, part of the purely genetic human condition, or are they alterable? All primates descend from a common ancestral species, yet they vary enormously in degree of female/male dimorphism.

It is clear that some aspects of dimorphism changed in the course of human evolution. For example, natural selection seems to have widened the female pelvis to accommodate the trend toward bigger brain capacity (even in newborns). Those females who could not give birth to larger-brained babies (because their pelvic opening was not large enough) would have been more likely to die in childbirth, or their babies would have been more likely to be still-born. In any case, genes for a wider pelvis were favored. Similarly, natural selection seems to have favored earlier cessation of growth and smaller stature in females, perhaps to reduce the possibility that the nutritional needs of a young mother might compete with the nutritional needs of her fetus.[4] Along the same lines, there is some evidence that females tend to be less affected than males by nutritional shortages, presumably because they are generally shorter and proportionally fatter.[5] Natural selection may have favored these female traits because they made for greater reproductive success.

But while it is understandable that natural selection would favor the cessation of growth in women soon after puberty, why should it have favored the continued growth of males that is probably responsible for the average difference in height between males and females?[6] One possible explanation is that males were subject to different selective pressures because of what they did. For example, if they encountered predators more often, or fought more, smaller males might have died in greater numbers.[7] In other words, role differences could have influenced the evolution of some aspects of human dimorphism. Another possibility is that human sexual dimorphism is partly the result of *sexual selection*. Perhaps females were more likely to mate with taller, heavier males because these males could prevent smaller ones from mating, or because they were more capable hunters or fighters.[8]

But however dimorphism developed, it is clearly characteristic of all human populations today. It is likely that the common ancestor we share with apes was also dimorphic in height and weight since all existing great apes have this characteristic. Certainly the earliest known bipedal primates, the hominids we call australopithecines, were sexually dimorphic in size. But what about other differences, like those in muscle strength and aerobic capacity? Since exercise increases strength and aerobic capacity in both sexes, cultural factors could partially account for these physical differences. If society encourages boys to play physical games but discourages girls, differences in muscle strength and aerobic capacity could follow. That cultural factors like these could have this effect is indicated by the fact that, as a result of increasingly similar athletic conditioning, female/male differences in athletic performance have been narrowing recently. For example, women's marathon record performance is now closer to men's. When it comes to physique and physiology, then, the differences we observe between women and men may reflect the influence of both culture and genes.[9]

The question we now turn to is the following: To what extent are the physical differences between women and men, whatever the selective causes, accommodated and reflected in the definition of gender roles? Is the assignment of tasks to males and females completely, or not so completely, a result of their physical differences?

DIVISION OF LABOR BY GENDER

All societies assign tasks at least somewhat differently to females and males. (We will see that cultural considerations clearly influence how societies allocate responsibilities, which is why we speak of *gender* rather than *sex* roles.) What is of particular interest is not so much that all societies allocate different work to females and males, but that so many make similar allocations. Table 3-1, which summarizes the world-wide patterns in mostly nonindustrial societies (the societies traditionally studied by anthropologists), indicates 1) which activities are performed by women and men in all or almost all such societies, 2) which are usually performed by one gender only, and 3) which are commonly assigned to either or both. Does Table 3-1 provide any clues as to why males and females generally do different things?[10]

The greater strength of males and their superior capacity for quick bursts of energy have commonly been cited as the reasons for universal (or near-universal) patterns in the gender division of labor. We can call this the

TABLE 3-1 WORLDWIDE PATTERNS
IN THE DIVISION OF LABOR BY GENDER

TYPE OF ACTIVITY	MALES ALMOST ALWAYS	MALES USUALLY	EITHER GENDER OR BOTH	FEMALES USUALLY	FEMALES ALMOST ALWAYS
Primary subsistence activities	Hunt and trap animals, large and small	Fish; herd large animals; collect wild honey; clear land and prepare soil for planting	Collect shellfish; care for small animals; plant crops; tend crops; harvest crops; milk animals	Gather wild plants	
Secondary subsistence and household activities		Butcher animals	Preserve meat and fish	Care for children; cook; prepare vegetable food, drinks, and dairy products; do laundry; fetch water; collect fuel	Care for infants
Other	Collect lumber; mine and quarry; make boats, musical instruments, bone objects, horn objects, and shell objects; engage in combat	Build houses; make nets and rope; exercise political leadership	Prepare skins; make leather products, baskets, mats, clothing, and pottery	Spin yarn	

Source: Mostly adapted from George Peter Murdock and Caterina Provost, "Factors in the Division of Labor by Sex: A Cross-Cultural Analysis," *Ethnology* 12 (1973): 203–225. The information on political leadership and warfare comes from Martin K. Whyte, "Cross-Cultural Codes Dealing with the Relative Status of Women," *Ethnology* 17 (1978): 217. The information on child care comes from Thomas S. Weisner and Ronald Gallimore, "My Brother's Keeper: Child and Sibling Caretaking," *Current Anthology* 18 (1977): 169–180.

strength theory.[11] Certainly, activities that require heavy lifting (as in hunting large animals, butchering, clearing land, working with stone, metal, or lumber), throwing weapons, and running with great speed (as in hunting or fighting) may be best performed by males. None of the activities females usually perform, with the possible exception of collecting firewood, seems to require the same degree of strength or quick bursts of energy. But the strength theory cannot readily explain all the patterns we observe. For example, it is not clear that trapping small animals, collecting wild honey, or making musical instruments (nearly always male activities) require much physical strength. And are females less likely to engage in combat merely because they are generally smaller?

Another explanation for worldwide similarities in the division of labor can be called the *compatibility-with-child-care theory.*[12] Everywhere, women are primarily responsible for infant care. In most societies breast-feeding continues for about two years, so it is hardly surprising that women mostly care for infants and children. The argument here is that the division of labor has to be compatible with women's tasks, particularly infant and child care. It is not safe or easy to take infants far from home for long periods. Women's tasks should also be interruptible when infants need attention.

The compatibility theory may explain why no activities other than infant care are listed in the right-hand column of Table 3-1. Until recently, most women in every society have had to devote much of their time to nursing infants and caring for children. The compatibility theory may explain why men usually do the hunting, trapping, fishing, collecting of honey, lumbering, and mining. These are all potentially dangerous tasks, difficult to coordinate with infant care. And certainly fighting is incompatible with child care.

The compatibility theory may also explain why men take over certain crafts when societies develop full-time specialization. Making baskets, mats, and pottery are usually women's tasks in noncommercial societies but tend to be men's work in those with full-time craft specialists.[13] In our society women may be terrific cooks at home, but chefs and bakers are usually men. There is every reason to suppose that women have the physical and intellectual ability to work at such professions, and they might actually do so more often were they able to leave their young in the safe care of others.

The compatibility theory does not account for why men usually prepare soil for planting, make things out of wood, or work bone, horn, and shell. These tasks probably could be interrupted, and none of them are any more dangerous to children nearby than cooking. Why, then, do males tend to do such work? The *economy-of-effort theory* may make sense out of work assignments that, like these, are not readily accounted for by the strength or compatibility theories. For example, perhaps men make musical instruments of wood because they cut and prepare lumber and are more familiar with its properties.[14] Similarly, if women have to be near home to care for young children, it might be more economical to have them manage other chores that have to be done in or near the home.

A fourth explanation of cross-cultural regularities might be called the *expendability theory*. This one suggests that men tend to do the dangerous work because they are not as necessary for reproduction. If some lose their lives while hunting, deep-water fishing, mining, quarrying, lumbering, or fighting, reproduction need not suffer so long as there are cultural institutions (preeminently polygyny) to assure that most fertile women have regular and approved sexual access to men.[15]

Although these theories singly or in combination seem to explain much of the division of labor by gender, there are still some unresolved problems. For example, critics of the strength theory have pointed out that women do engage in very heavy labor in some societies.[16] That suggests that strength may be more a function of training than we might suppose. And while the compatibility theory suggests that women's work should be consistent with the requirements of infant and child care, there are other ways to arrange for such care. Indeed, in many societies where women spend a good deal of time working away from home, others (often an older woman in the household) tend their infants, feeding them "baby food" until the mothers are able to nurse.[17] In the mountains of Nepal, for example, women carry heavy loads up and down steep slopes and work in fields far apart most of the day, leaving infants with others for long stretches of time.[18] And although hunting is almost always, if not always, difficult to reconcile with child care, women do hunt in some societies. Among the Agta, a people of the Philippines, many women regularly hunt wild pig and deer. In fact, women bring in almost 30 percent of the large game, taking nursing babies along on the hunt.[19] It may be easy for Agta women to hunt for several reasons. Their hunting grounds are close, only about a half-hour from camp, their dogs provide protection, and the women generally hunt in groups so there is usually help available for carrying babies and carcasses while the group is away from camp.

These examples suggest that we need to know a lot more about the conditions under which work is done before we can properly evaluate the different explanations of how labor is divided by gender. How much strength is required to accomplish particular tasks, how dangerous are they, and how interruptible? We also need to know whether alternative arrangements for child care are possible. Finally, the general patterns we observe are probably not fixed in our genes. Indeed, those revealed in Table 3-1 may become blurred in many societies in the future. We know from our own experience and that of other industrialized societies that a sharp division of labor by gender begins to disappear when machines replace muscle, when women have fewer children, and when institutional structures emerge to care for and educate children.

WHY DOES ONE GENDER CONTRIBUTE MORE TO SUBSISTENCE?

According to traditional television stereotypes, the wife was manager of home and children, the husband was the breadwinner. That model is becoming more myth than reality. In addition to the women who are single parents, many married women now work away from home; in the United States, more than 50 percent of all married women now work outside the home.[20] Still, our image of family breadwinner continues to attribute special value and importance to the efforts of those who bring food (and now money) home. It is an image that minimizes the contributions of those who work primarily at home, even when what they do requires long hours and is essential to family subsistence. Is threshing, winnowing, and grinding grain, or making bread, less important to subsistence than growing or buying grain?

How then should we weigh contribution to subsistence? We really ought to consider both *primary* and *secondary subsistence activities*. In traditional societies, the primary ones include the five food-getting activities: gathering, hunting, fishing, herding, and agriculture. Secondary activities have to do with the preparation and processing of food. The problem is that, while we know a lot about how and why the primary activities of women and men vary cross-culturally, we have no systematic surveys of how the division of labor in secondary subsistence activities varies. Therefore, in assessing the overall contribution of each gender to subsistence, it is easy to exaggerate the importance of whichever gender predominates in primary subsistence activities.

Although the image of man as the breadwinner no longer fits our society very well, it does describe the situation in many societies known to anthropology. Take the Toda of India, for example, as they were described early in the twentieth century. They depended for subsistence almost entirely on the dairy products of their water buffalo, consuming them directly or selling them for grain. Only men tended buffalo and prepared their products; women largely confined themselves to household work—to preparing purchased grain for cooking, cleaning house, and decorating clothing.[21] But we know of many societies in which women contributed more than men. Among the Tchambuli of New Guinea, for example, the women went out early in the morning by canoe to their fish traps, returning when the sun was hot. The Tchambuli traded some of the catch for sago (a starch) and sugarcane, and it was the women who went on the long canoe trips to do the trading.[22]

CROSS-CULTURAL TRENDS

Given the variation in how labor in subsistence activities is divided by gender, can we discern any general trends? One cross-cultural study indicates that while both men and women typically contribute to primary food-getting activities, men usually contribute more to the diet in terms of calories.[23] Child care is almost always the responsibility of women, so it is not surprising that men usually do most of the primary food-getting work; gathering, hunting, fishing, herding large animals, and farming usually require work to be done away from home. But if we measure subsistence contribution in terms of *total work time*, and include work inside the home (preparing and cooking food) as well as outside (food-getting), we come to different conclusions about the contribution each gender makes to subsistence. In horticultural and intensive agricultural societies, for example, it appears that women typically work more total hours per day than men, even if the men do much or most of the work with crops.[24] And in hunting societies where men do most of the food collecting, women may work as many or more hours preparing and cooking food.

It is all too easy to underestimate the burden of women's work, in the fields and at home, especially if we overlook some of the less familiar but nonetheless vital contributions they make. For many traditional peoples around the world, for example, beer is more than a beverage; it is a staple food and ceremonial necessity. Indeed, there is even archaeological evidence suggesting that the earliest use of domesticated cereals may have been for beer rather than bread![25] And in most societies that make substantial use of beer, women play a major role in its preparation. The Jívaro of South America provide only one example. Michael J. Harner, ethnographer of the Jívaro, tells us that manioc beer achieved great importance in ceremony and as food in that society, and that

> the importance of wives in producing food and beer goes far beyond the subsistence requirements of the household itself. Plural wives assure a surplus production which will make possible adequate entertainment of visitors from other households. The Jívaro place a high value on drinking beer and eating (perhaps in that order), so that one's status in a neighborhood is greatly affected by one's generosity with beer and food. No one can expect to have many friends unless he is a good host; and he cannot easily meet the requirements of good hospitality without plural wives as a labor force.[26]

Jívaro women do most of the laborious garden work and are exclusively responsible for planting and harvesting the manioc they use to make beer. They plant and harvest other crops like areca species, sweet potatoes, *papa china*, red peppers, sugar cane, onions, and pineapples as well. Together with men they plant peanuts, which only the women harvest. Men plant and harvest maize; they also plant plantains and bananas, which women harvest. Women do all the weeding, using machetes. Harner tells us that this laborious work alone consumes the greatest amount of their time in the garden.[27] But a woman's reputation ultimately hangs on her beer-making abilities.

The Jívaro consider beer far superior to plain water, "which they drink only in emergencies such as when their beer canteens run dry while they are out hunting." And the role of women in the domestic manufacture of beer is crucial. Men believe the best beer is that which a pretty girl rather than an old woman has chewed. But this masticatory contribution, so important to beer making, is only part of women's beer-making labor. Here is a description of only the prefermentation phase of beer-making:

> Manioc beer is prepared by first peeling and washing the tubers in the stream near the garden. Then the water and manioc are brought to the house, where the tubers are cut up and placed in a pot to boil. When the manioc has become soft, the pot is removed from the fire and allowed to cool. The manioc is then mashed and stirred to a soft consistency with the aid of a special wooden paddle. While the woman stirs the mash, she chews handfuls and spits them back into the pot, a process which may take half an hour or longer. The mastication of the mash is considered by the Jívaro to be essential to the proper and rapid fermentation of the brew, and their view seems to be supported by Western physicians who have informally voiced the opinion that the enzymes in the saliva, as well as the bacteria in the mouth, probably hasten the fermentation process.[28]

In many societies women bear the burden of such "domestic" work. While their involvement in child care and secondary subsistence activities makes it difficult for women to contribute to primary subsistence, we nonetheless find that they do contribute as much as men to *primary subsistence* in many agricultural societies, and particularly in horticultural ones. Judging from Table 3-1, people do not define most agricultural tasks as exclusively the province of women or men in most societies. Except for clearing and preparing land for planting (usually men's work), other cultivation tasks may be done by either or both genders (see the *Either Gender or Both* column in Table 3-1). In much of Asia, Europe, and in areas around the Mediterranean, men do more, but in Africa, south of the Sahara, women generally do more than half the field work.[29] Why do women do a considerable amount of the agricultural work in some places, while men do most in others?

The type of agriculture people practice may have something to do with it. Women make a substantial contribution to primary subsistence in *horticultural societies*—those that depend on root and tree crops or shifting slash-and-burn cultivation. Intensive cultivation, particularly plow agriculture, is associated with a high level of male participation.[30] Ester Boserup has suggested that, when population increased, creating pressure to make more intensive use of land, cultivators turned to the plow and irrigation, and males then started to do more.[31]

But why should women contribute less when cultivators use plows?

One possibility is that plow agriculture requires a lot more labor time, which men have more of since they are not as involved in child care. Men usually do the clearing in horticultural systems as well, but field preparation takes even more time among intensive cultivators. Researchers estimated in one Nigerian district that one hundred days of work were needed to clear an acre of previously uncultivated land for tractor plowing, compared to only twenty days of preparation for shifting cultivation. Weeding is more easily combined with child care than clearing or plowing land, and perhaps for that reason either or both genders may do weeding. It may be significant, therefore, that plowed land requires less weeding, work commonly done by women.[32] Still, this does not explain why women do less of all agricultural tasks, not just weeding, in societies that have the plow.[33]

Another possibility is that domestic chores increase with intensive agriculture, limiting even more the time women can spend in the fields. Intensive cultivators, who mainly live in temperate climes, rely heavily on cereal grains, which take more work to make edible than root and tree crops.[34] Grains like corn, wheat, oats, and rice are usually dried before storing. They take long to cook unless treated (as by parboiling) to permit fast cooking. Consider, for example, the preparation of hominy, a staple of North America's Zuni Indians. Removing dried corn from the husk, women soak the kernels in a mixture of water and ash. After bringing it to a boil, they cook and stir the mixture for three hours, after which they rinse the corn in the river.[35] Because most people, until recently, did not have running water, or stoves using gas, kerosene, or electricity, cooking this long meant fetching a lot of wood (for fuel) and water, generally women's work.[36]

A variety of techniques can reduce cooking time (like soaking, grinding, or pounding), but the process that speeds it the most—grinding—is very time-consuming (unless done by machine). A Zapotec Indian woman spends many hours each day grinding corn, after rinsing and boiling it the night before. Only then can she make the tortillas her people eat. Even women who bring their corn to electric mills spend most of the morning there.[37] Among horticulturalists, preparation is usually less time consuming. With the exception of bitter manioc, which must be specially processed to remove toxins, most root and tree crops are cooked and rendered edible with relatively little preparation.[38] It is sufficient simply to scrape breadfruit a bit before baking, and we can eat bananas raw. Yams, potatoes, plantains, taro, and sweet manioc boil fairly quickly if cut into small pieces.

Other domestic work, too, may substantially increase with intensive agriculture. For one thing, women typically have more children to care for than in horticultural societies.[39] Given the increase in household work, it is easy to understand why women might not contribute more than, or even as much as, men to the work of intensive cultivation. Their contribution is generally substantial nonetheless; cross-cultural evidence suggests that, on average, women put in four-and-a-half hours of work outside the home each day, seven days a week, in intensive agricultural societies. Considering that these women generally work a total of about eleven hours a day, seven days a week, it is hard to imagine how they could do more in the fields or anywhere else.[40]

Assuming that horticulture usually requires less work in the fields than intensive agriculture, how can we explain why, in many horticultural societies, women do more of such work than men? Women may not have as much household work as their intensive cultivating counterparts, but neither do the men. And horticultural women still have infants and children to care for. Where are their men? Perhaps they cannot do as much because they are often involved in other activities of a sort that men in intensive agricultural societies are not pulled into. One such activity is hunting, which horticulturalists do more of than intensive agriculturalists. Another is war. Although intensive agriculturalists and horticulturalists do not differ in how often they are at war, fighting among horticulturalists often occurs precisely when some kind of cultivation work has to be done; most horticulturalists live in warmer climates, where cultivation is year-round. Unlike intensive cultivators, they rarely have standing armies; all able-bodied men fight when necessary. Thus, warfare in their case can draw men away from work in the fields at almost any time. If they are often not around to do this work, women have to assume the responsibility.[41]

EFFECTS OF THE DIVISION OF LABOR

There is substantial evidence that contribution to primary subsistence and the nature of child care are closely linked. Several cross-cultural studies suggest that when women are frequently involved in primary food-getting, they are likely to feed their infants solid foods earlier than women less involved. That enables working mothers to pass some infant care to others.[42] We also find that where women contribute heavily to subsistence, young girls are more likely to be trained for industriousness (i.e., responsible task performance), perhaps in anticipation of their later economic contribution.[43] And where women contribute more to subsistence, they seem to have more to say about some aspects of their sexuality. They are freer to engage in premarital sex and less vulnerable to rape.[44] Furthermore, people are more likely to value female babies where women contribute a lot to food-getting.[45] A positive valuation can have significant ramifications, as the following example illustrates.

During the nineteenth century, Hakka women in south Taiwan played a greater role in cultivation than other Taiwanese women, probably because men were often drawn into combat, and had to be always ready to fight their more numerous Hokkien neighbors. Training from the beginning prepared women for hard work in the fields. While other Taiwanese women had bound feet, limiting their participation in field work, the Hakka did not have this custom. Even today, Pasternak has heard their Hokkien-speaking neighbors note with no little derision that Hakka women "work like water buffalos while their men sit around doing nothing."

Because of their greater economic contribution, Hakka women were better treated, or at least less neglected, than other Taiwanese women. The difference is reflected in survival rates. Contrary to the usual Chinese pattern, Hakka women were more likely to survive to every age than Hakka men. Their prospects were also better than those of Taiwanese women in general.[46] Improved survival prospects were not accompanied by expanded political power, however. The division of subsistence labor had no direct relationship to the division of labor in politics, and, as we shall see shortly, it has no general relationship to the overall status of women.

WHICH GENDER LEADS, WHICH FIGHTS?

The lack of correspondence between economic contribution and formal political roles is not unique to the Hakka. In almost every society we know of, men generally lead in the political arena. One cross-cultural study found that only men were leaders in approximately 88 percent of societies. Where women occupied some leadership positions (in 10 percent of the societies), they were either outnumbered by, or less powerful than, male leaders.[47] Even in matrilineal societies, where descent group membership depends on blood connections through females, men occupy the important political positions. Among the matrilineal Iroquois, women controlled basic resources but men held all the important political offices. The women did have considerable indirect influence, however. Although they could not serve on the highest political agency of the Iroquois League, the Council, they could nominate, elect, and impeach male members. They could also decide between life or death for prisoners of war, forbid the men of their households to go to war, and could even intervene to bring about peace.[48]

Why have men almost universally dominated the political sphere (at least until now)? It may not be pure coincidence that they almost universally dominate warfare as well. In about 88 percent of the world's societies, women never actively participate in war.[49] Some people have suggested that it is their role in warfare that gives men the political edge, particularly because they control weapons.[50] However, there is little evidence that men usually use force to obtain their leadership positions.[51] Still, male involvement in war may be related to political power another way. Fighting occurs regularly in most societies, and decisions about warfare directly affect survival prospects. Since these decisions are so crucial in most societies, it may be advantageous to have those who know most about warfare make the decisions about it. Hence, male political power may stem, at least partially, from male predominance in warfare.

As to why males usually do the fighting, we should recall three of the explanations proposed for the worldwide patterns in the gender division of labor. Warfare, like hunting, probably requires strength and quick bursts of energy. And combat is undoubtedly one of the most dangerous and uninterruptible activities imaginable, hardly compatible with child care. Even before they have children, then, people may prefer to keep women out of combat. Their reproductive potential may be more important to a population's survival than their usefulness as warriors.[52] So the strength theory, the compatibility theory, and the expendability theory might all explain the predominance of men in warfare.

Two other factors may contribute to the leadership advantage of men. One is the sexual dimorphism in height; the second is that men more often travel far from home. While it is not clear why height should be a factor, studies in two very different kinds of societies—the United States and the Mekranoti-Kayapo of Brazil—suggest that tallness is related to leadership. The two societies are at opposite ends of the continuum in terms of economic and political development: One is an industrialized society with a central government, the other a horticultural society with politically autonomous villages. In both, leaders are likely to be taller than non-leaders.[53] It may be more than pure coincidence that, in the course of United States history, the taller candidate has almost always won the presidency.[54] The fact that females are usually shorter than males might be a disadvantage in the competition for political position.

We should also consider the possibility that men dominate politics because they get around more; the things they do in traditional societies are more likely to take them farther from home. If people choose leaders at least in part on the basis of their knowledge of the outside world, then men would usually have an advantage over women. Consistent with this expectation, Patricia Draper found that in newly sedentary !Kung bands, women no longer traveled long distances gathering food and had lost much of their influence over decision-making.[55] Heavy involvement in child care can also limit social interaction and inhibit political influence. In his study of village leadership among the Mekranoti-Kayapo of Brazil, Dennis W. Werner found that women with heavy child-care burdens were less influential than others, perhaps because they had fewer friends and missed many details of what was going on in the village.[56]

All these explanations suggest why men generally dominate politics, but why do women participate in politics more in some societies than in others? In a cross-cultural survey of ninety societies, political scientist Marc Howard Ross found considerable variability in female political participation.[57] For example, among the Mende of Sierra Leone women regularly hold high office, but among the Azande of Zaire they play no part in public life. Male-centered social structure appears to be one of the main impediments to female participation in politics. Where women have to move to their husband's place when they marry, and where kin groups are organized around males, women are much less likely to participate in political life. And the economic value of women does not necessarily confer political status. So what gives women higher or lower political status in a society?

Societies with male-oriented social structures are also more likely to exclude women from combat.[58] For reasons we will explore further in later chapters, societies with male-oriented social structures (particularly where women, upon marriage, move to another community to live with or near the husband's family) are much more likely to have internal war (i.e., within the society or language group). If they also marry only men from other communities, then wives and husbands could well find their interests and loyalties in conflict. Wives would then often come from communities with which their husbands' community and kin are periodically at war. Fighting would often pit husbands against their wives' fathers, paternal uncles, and brothers. David Adams has proposed that such conflicts of interest may encourage people to keep women from active participation in war, from meetings in which war is discussed, and from handling weapons.[59] Where there are no conflicts of interest, either because fighting occurs only with other societies (and therefore with people unrelated to both spouses), or because marriage partners always come from the same community (local endogamy), then women are more likely to participate in warfare. In other words, wives (and their male relatives) are less likely to be the enemies of husbands in societies with purely external war or local endogamy. Indeed, the two conditions—residence with husband's kin and marriage outside the community—cross-culturally predict the exclusion of women from combat.

In conclusion, what does the cross-cultural evidence suggest about the effect of biology on the assignment of roles to males and females? As we have seen, assignment to some work, like hunting, may arguably be based on some aspect of physical dimorphism (e.g., greater proportion of muscle or higher aerobic work capacity). Other task assignments may reflect a quite different biological concern—the need to survive and reproduce. That need would favor ways to allow women to avoid activities that put themselves or their infants at risk (like deep sea fishing or collecting honey from high trees). But other gender role assignments, such as who does most of the agriculture, or who participates more in politics, appear to be more influenced by social and cultural factors.

Thus far we have only been talking about factors affecting how work is assigned to women and men. But what of differences in personality and psychological characteristics? Are women and men different in these regards and, to the extent that they are, can we attribute the dissimilarities to intrinsic biological differences or to the influence of culture?

Gender and Personality

Reporting on three tribes in New Guinea, Margaret Mead claimed that "many, if not all, of the personality traits we have called masculine or feminine are as lightly linked to sex as are the clothing, the manners, and the form of head-dress that a society at a given period assigns to either sex."[60] Mead thought that there are no universal or even near-universal personality differences between the sexes; rather, societies are free to create differences or to minimize them. Mead described Arapesh women and men as essentially alike: Both sexes were gentle, cooperative, and nurturing. Mundugumor females and males, too, were similar, but in their cases both were violent and competitive. Mead reported substantial female-male differences among the Tchambuli, but of a sort opposite to what we might expect. Women, the main economic providers, were domineering, practical, and impersonal. Tchambuli men were sensitive and delicate, devoting much of their time to their appearances and to artistic pursuits.

Since Mead's work, questions have been raised about her conclusions. Were her descriptions of these three New Guinea cases accurate? We do not have independent evidence about the specific communities she studied, but we do have a reanalysis of Mead's notes on the Mundugumor by Nancy McDowell, as well as the results of McDowell's own fieldwork in a village near the one Mead wrote about. These materials reveal nothing that contradicts Mead's description.[61] But even if Mead's descriptions are accurate, we must still ask whether her broader conclusion, too, is accurate: Is personality as lightly linked to biological sex as she suggested? In part, the answer depends on what is meant by "linked." If we mean that temperament is *randomly* connected to biological sex, the answer has to be no. New methods of observation enable us to capture minute details of behavior for a substantial number of females and males. Conclusions about gender differences in aggressiveness, for example, no longer depend on subjective impressions, but emerge from counting the times particular individuals try to hurt or injure others during specific observation periods. Research based on such systematic observation does not support Mead's view that there are no consistent gender differences in temperament. To the contrary, some behavioral differences appear consistently, even in quite diverse societies. However, this is not to say that culture does not have a lot to do with how temperament is shaped. Unfortunately, as we shall see, the consistencies we observe in gender differences do not tell us anything definitive about their probable causes.

SOCIAL BEHAVIOR

What sorts of gender differences do these systematic studies indicate? The most consistent one between boys and girls is in regard to aggression: Systematic observations indicate that boys more frequently try to hurt others, physically or verbally.[62] In a comparative study of children's behavior in six cultures, this difference appeared as early as three to six years of age.[63] Other observations of the same kind are available for the Luo of Kenya, an Israeli kibbutz, and the !Kung in southwest Africa.[64] Research in the United States yields the same result: Many observational and experimental studies in this country indicate that boys are more aggressive.[65]

Still other differences have turned up with considerable consistency, although we have to be more cautious in accepting them, either because they have not been documented as well or because there are more societies that are exceptions. For example, there is some evidence that girls tend to exhibit more responsible, nurturant, helpful behavior. They are also more likely to conform to adult wishes and commands, whereas boys more often attempt to dominate others and get their own way. In play, both boys and girls display a preference for their own gender; but girls play in smaller groups and maintain less physical distance from each other than boys do.[66]

Some of these differences persist throughout the life cycle. Differences in aggressiveness decrease with age, but do not completely disappear in adulthood.[67] The studies upon which we base these conclusions all draw from observational evidence, interviews, or experiments. They do not take relatively rare homicidal events or socially approved violence such as war into account. But if we added these other arenas, males would have even higher rates of aggression. Cross-culturally, males are far more responsible for incidents of homicide. Daly and Wilson looked at same-sex homicide rates in twenty-two societies, and found that male-male homicides far outnumbered female-female ones; even in the society with the smallest difference, male-male homicides were eleven times more frequent! These numbers actually under-represent male homicides because they omit large numbers of male-female homicides.[68] And then there is rape, which Gwen Broude found occurs "commonly" in 41 percent of societies about which we have some relevant information.[69]

We must exercise some caution in interpreting these studies. Consistent sex differences are not necessarily characteristic of all societies; there are invariably cases that do not conform to the general pattern. For example, while girls are generally more nurturant than boys in many communities, a study in Nyansongo, a Kenyan community, indicated that boys actually offered help and support to others more often than girls. For reasons we shall discuss below, they may have been unexpectedly helpful in Nyansongo because, as with girls, families frequently called upon them to help care for young children.

Still, how are we to account for the general consistency with which some gender differences occur? Many writers and researchers are prepared to attribute them to biological causes, and greater male aggressiveness is most often singled out as a particularly good candidate for biological explanation because it appears so early in life.[70] But the logic is less than compelling, given that many societies socialize the genders differently from the moment of birth.[71] Even when objective observers discern no obvious personality differences between female and male newborns, parents often claim to.[72] Parents may, perhaps unconsciously, expect and want boys and girls to be different and may, therefore, encourage differences in the course of early socialization. Thus, even the earliest differences could be learned rather than genetic in origin.

Still, there is considerable evidence of biological influence, although most of it comes from experimental research on aggression in nonhuman animals. These experiments suggest that the male hormone androgen may be partly responsible for higher levels of aggression. In some experiments, females injected with androgen before or shortly after birth, when their sexual organs are developing, behave more aggressively when they are older than other females. Can this also be true of humans? Some researchers have looked at human females androgenized in the womb because of drugs given their mothers to prevent miscarriage. By and large, the results of these investigations are similar to those of the experimental studies—androgenized females are more aggressive.[73] Some investigators believe these results indicate that the male/female difference in aggression is biologically caused.[74] But others feel that these findings are not conclusive because females with more androgen may manifest disturbed metabolic systems in general, and that alone could exacerbate aggressiveness. Furthermore, androgen-injected females resemble males more than other females—for example, they may have masculinized genitalia. Perhaps they behave more like males, then, because conspecifics treat them like males.[75]

What evidence do we have that socialization, rather than genes or other biological factors, contributes to gender differences in aggression among humans? Cross-cultural studies reveal that while some societies clearly do train boys to be more aggressive than girls, apparently most do not.[76] The fact that only some train girls and boys differently in this regard can hardly account for the fact that males are more aggressive than females in most societies. But these studies are based on ethnographic accounts, and aggression or other masculine traits may be engendered in ways too subtle for anthropologists to pick up on and describe in their ethnographic reports.

Consider the possibility, for example, that girls and boys learn to behave differently because their parents ask them to do different kinds of work. In other words, they may end up behaving differently because their work assignments call for dissimilar behaviors. As a matter of fact, ethnographic evidence suggests that, in societies where children do a great deal of work, they generally display more responsible and nurturant behavior. Girls may display such behavior more than boys because they are almost always asked to do more.[77] If this reasoning is correct, we should also find that where boys are asked to do girls' work, they may learn to behave more like girls.

A study of Luo children in Kenya by Carol R. Ember supports this expectation.[78] Parents asked girls to baby-sit, cook, clean house, and fetch water and firewood. Boys did little work around the house; their traditional work was herding cattle, but most families in the community studied had few of them. For some reason, more boys than girls had been born, and many mothers without daughters had to require their sons to do girls' chores. It turned out that much of the behavior of those boys who did girls' work was intermediary between the behavior of other boys and the behavior of girls. Boys who did girls' work were less aggressive, less domineering, and more responsible than other boys, even when they were not working at girls' chores. So it is possible that task assignment has an important influence on how girls and boys learn to behave. Other subtle forms of socialization should be investigated as well. We need to look closely, for example, at whether newborn and infant boys are handled more roughly than girls, at whether they are allowed to rough-house more as youngsters (boys typically do rough-house more than girls), at the kinds of toys parents give their children (e.g., trucks versus dolls)—these differences could all provide subtle ways of differently shaping the behavior of boys and girls.[79]

Before we leave the subject of gender differences in behavior, we should note some assumptions that are probably wrong, or that at least find no support in the available evidence. We have in mind notions that females are characteristically dependent, sociable, or passive. Results of the *Six Cultures Project*, a collaborative comparative endeavor, provide reason to doubt all three assumptions.[80] If, by dependency, we mean seeking the help and emotional support of others, then girls are no more likely to be dependent than boys. However, the evidence does indicate that boys and girls have somewhat different styles of dependency; girls more often look for help in achieving goals, while boys want attention and approval. If sociability means seeking and offering friendship, then we again find no difference other than that boys generally play in larger groups. Nor does the evidence support the notion that girls are generally passive; they are no more likely than boys to flee aggression or to yield to unreasonable demands. The only difference that does find support is that older girls are less likely to respond to aggression with aggression. This does not signal greater passivity, however, but only that girls are less aggressive—which we already know.

To what extent do role dissimilarities reflect or accommodate fundamental personality differences, induced genetically or through unlike socialization? Is it not possible, for example, that most societies choose males as warriors because they recognize that they are intrinsically more aggressive? While that is certainly possible, the assignment could as well have developed for other reasons. Perhaps societies everywhere prefer men as warriors because they are more expendable than females when it comes to reproduction. Once that choice is made, parents might well be inclined to encourage their sons, directly or indirectly, to be aggressive.

Here we remain very much in the realm of speculation. The causality involved is elusive because of the difficulty of disentangling possible biological from learned effects, particularly given that girls and boys are typically reared differently. Although the task is not impossible, unraveling the effects of different causes will undoubtedly require that researchers be more attentive to natural variation. It might be useful, for example, to determine whether gender differences are greatest where assignment to different chores begins earliest. We might also want to find out if there are societies where girls do boys' work, and, if so, are girls in such societies more like boys in personality and social behavior? The answers will ultimately require more than imaginative research. Margaret Mead conducted her fieldwork among the Arapesh, Mundugumor, and Tchambuli before we developed techniques for making systematic, controlled observations of social behavior. Use of these newer methods will surely tell us more about how and to what extent unlike treatment of females and males contributes to differences in personality and behavior.

COGNITIVE, PERCEPTUAL, AND EMOTIONAL DIFFERENCES

In many respects, females and males show few cognitive and perceptual differences. However, there are a few differences which show up with considerable consistency. One is in the area of visual/spatial abilities, where males have the edge.[81] Such abilities are measured by tests involving mazes, three-dimensional pictorial representation, spatial rotation of objects and drawings, and reconstructing three-dimensional objects. A second area which may be related to the first is called *field independence/field dependence.*

These terms, referring to perceptual style, might best be explained by the tests that measure them. One test—the *rod-and-frame* test—asks subjects in a darkened room to say when a lighted rod inside a lighted frame is straight-up-and-down. Subjects are usually disoriented by being placed on a chair that is rotated and the frame and rod are moved into many different positions. Persons are classified as *field dependent* if they consistently think the rod is straight-up-and-down when it is parallel to the frame, even though the frame is actually tilted away from the vertical. Persons are classified as *field independent* if they judge the rod to be straight-up-and-down if it is close to the vertical, even though it does not line up with the frame.

In other words, a field-dependent person makes a perceptual judgment influenced by the surroundings of an object (the field); the field-independent person makes a perceptual judgment about the object independent of the surroundings. A related test, the embedded-figures test, asks subjects to find a simple figure within a more complicated drawing. Field-independent individuals seem to do this easily; field-dependent individuals, perhaps because they appear to see the complicated figure as a whole, find it difficult to separate out a part of it.

Data from the United States are fairly consistent in showing that females typically are more field dependent, while males are generally more field independent. Many communities in other cultures show the same pattern of gender difference; however, a gender difference appears to be absent in societies heavily dependent on food collection.[82] What may account for the typical gender difference in visual/spatial abilities and in field independence/dependence? Before we turn to some possible explanations, we should note that some researchers suggest that field independence/field dependence is a manifestation of visual/spatial ability.[83]

Most of the biological explanations offered to explain female-male visual/spatial differences (e.g., in terms of brain lateralization, prenatal hormones, hormones at puberty) have to deal with inconsistent evidence. For example, such explanations cannot easily accommodate the fact that gender differences have narrowed over time, or that training can considerably improve female performance. Nonetheless, there have been some intriguing findings that warn against too quick a dismissal of biological factors. One is that visual/spatial test scores vary for women in different phases of the menstrual cycle.[84] If these findings hold up, it would make it difficult to rule out the role of biological factors.

So far, relatively few studies have directly investigated socialization factors that may increase visual/spatial skill. However, there is some evidence that children who grew up playing with more "masculine" toys (e.g., blocks, cars) have better visual/spatial skills; also, the more time a child spends away from the household, the better such skills.[85] Field dependence is predicted by tight parental control and parental emphasis on conformity. Parental control creates a strong tie between the parent's actions and the child's actions; it seems that the social tie parallels the perceptual—objects are also bound to their fields.[86] These socialization explanations might predict why girls typically do not do as well on visual/spatial tests and more often score field dependent. In many societies, females are more tightly controlled and spend more time closer to home. Perhaps it is significant that food collecting societies show little gender difference in field independence/dependence. Such societies may need to have both males and females learn to negotiate their way through space to return home safely (women usually gather away from home; men hunt and fish away from home); food collectors also emphasize independence rather than obedience in child-training.[87]

Turning now from perception to emotion, some theorists suggest that women are more apt to be concerned with interpersonal relationships, and to have more empathy for the feelings of others.[88] To date, studies outside the United States, in Israel and some Asian countries, provide considerable support for this expectation.[89] Perhaps also consistent with this theory is the fact that, in a large number of studies, females showed themselves better at understanding nonverbal cues and at expressing emotions nonverbally (e.g., they have more expressive faces).[90] Even in recounting their dreams, women describe more emotion than men.[91]

Given these gender differences, it might be tempting to suggest that some of the gender division of labor results from difference in ability. After all, it is easy to speculate that men may excel at hunting and herding because they have superior visual/spatial abilities and possess a field-independent style. Women may excel at child tending because they have more empathy. Empathy suggests a connection between individuals which can be strengthened by field dependence.

However, differences in cognitive, perceptual, and emotional style may result largely from differences in training and the early performance of tasks. If boys are allowed to roam far from home because they are less constrained and/or they have less work to do, they may develop better visual/spatial skills. Ball-playing in particular could enhance such skills. If girls caretake infants and children more, they may learn to understand the needs of another. Recall that Luo boys who did more girls' work were significantly less aggressive and more responsible than boys who did less girls' work! To evaluate these possibilities we probably need longitudinal research that evaluates such abilities before and after females and males take on different roles.

ON THE STATUS OF WOMEN

Let us turn, finally, to more elusive issues: Which gender is more valued in the society? Which has access to more privileged positions? Which has more power and authority? Which has more control over their own lives? Loosely speaking, these questions all have something to do with status in society. In those terms, comparative research tells us that women have very low status in a considerable number of societies, and we know of none in which women clearly have more status than men. What might account for the disadvantaged position of women cross-culturally?

Consider the small Iraqi town of Daghara, where women and men lived very separate lives.[92] In many respects, we would have to say women there had very low status. In common with much of the traditional Islamic world, they lived their lives in seclusion, confining themselves to their houses and interior courtyards. If women had to go out, they did so only with male approval, and had to cover their faces and bodies. They always had to cover themselves in mixed company, even at home. Legally, they were subject to the authority of their fathers and husbands, and they played no part in the political activities of the larger society. Custom required they be virgins at marriage. Since women avoided even casual conversation with unfamiliar men, opportunities for premarital or extramarital relationships were very limited. There were no such restrictions on the sexuality of men.

But in other societies, as among the Mbuti Pygmies, women and men more closely approached equal status. Like many food collectors, the Mbuti had no formal political officials who made decisions or settled disputes. When arguments occurred within or among families, when decisions had to be made, women and men both expressed their ideas. Women intervened and made their positions known, and their opinions were often heeded.[93] Women usually had equal say over the disposal of resources they or the men collected, over the upbringing of children, and about whom their children would marry. One of the few inequalities is that women were somewhat more restricted than men with respect to extramarital sex.[94]

Why do some societies have relatively equal status for women and men and, therefore, little gender stratification, whereas others appear to have much more gender stratification? Many theories have been suggested, but before we can hope to evaluate them fairly we must agree on how best to assess status. It would undoubtedly be easier to find agreement on how to define and measure the contribution women and men make to primary subsistence (e.g., in terms of time spent or calories produced) than to decide how we ought to measure status. That is a concept that can have a variety of measures—material rewards, prestige, influence, power, authority, autonomy, and so on.[95] And there may be variation depending on arena or domain of life; women may have considerable authority in the family, but little in the larger kin group or community. Thus, can we really think of status as a single thing, or is it rather a concept that embraces many things? Do the various indicators of status go together? For example, can we assume that when women have equal access to economic resources, they will also have equal prestige, power, and authority?

The results of a cross-cultural study by Martin K. Whyte suggest that the various aspects or indicators we commonly use as measures of status are, in fact, not strongly associated.[96] Whyte measured fifty-two cultural characteristics that he thought might tap different aspects of status. He considered, for example, which gender inherits property, which has final authority over unmarried children, the gender of the gods, and whether parents prefer female or male children. Rather than deciding in advance which of these fifty-two cultural features would best measure status, Whyte decided to see how the measures relate to one another. In fact, he found them so *weakly* related that it makes little sense to think of higher or lower status for women (in any given society) as a unitary phenomenon. Whyte could only conclude that status is multidimensional, and that high status in one dimension is often not paralleled by high status in another.

How, then, can we hope to predict more versus less status equality between the genders? Some might argue that we cannot do so precisely because the concept is not unitary. But perhaps we can make some headway if we focus on more limited sets of status measures that do appear related to one another.[97] Indeed, Whyte identified nine clusters of related traits. He found, for example, that the following topical categories, or domains, comprised specific traits that did go together: property control; power of women in kinship contexts; domestic authority; and control over women's marital and sexual lives. Each cluster contains similar and related aspects of status. So, the one having to do with *control over women's marital and sexual lives* is actually composed of four status traits: lack of a premarital double standard; lack of an extramarital double standard; ease of remarriage; and similarity in marriage age. Together, the four traits provide a way to measure control over women's marital and sexual lives. Whyte then evaluated the predictive efficacy of different theories of why women's status differs cross-culturally, by seeing how they account for scores on each of his nine trait clusters.[98] Let us see what he found.

It is commonly assumed that if societies frequently engage in activities requiring physical strength or aggressiveness, the status of males will be much higher than that of women. To test this theory, Whyte looked to see whether men's status is substantially higher (in the nine domains) in societies with considerable warfare or heavy dependence on hunting, herding, or plow agriculture. These activities presumably require male strength and aggressiveness.[99] The results were only partly consistent with the idea that male strength has something to do with status. For while women's status (in various domains) was lower in societies with intensive (plow) agriculture and herding, as expected, women's status was closer to men's status in those societies with a good deal of hunting and warfare, which the theory would not anticipate.

Another common expectation is that status reflects contribution to primary subsistence. The presumption, then, is that women should enjoy higher status where they contribute more to primary subsistence. Whyte found no support for this theory in his data, however, nor did Peggy Sanday in a separate test.[100] Where does this leave us? Is there really no way to anticipate when women might have higher or lower status? As a matter of fact, two useful predictors do emerge from the research conducted to date. Female-centered kin groups (matrilineality) and female-centered marital residence (matrilocality), what we may call *female-centered social structure*, predicts more equal status for women. The second predictor is a low level of societal complexity.

Whyte found that female-centered social structure predicts that women will have more control over property, more authority in the home, more equal sexual restrictions, and more value attributed to their lives. The predictiveness is not perfect, because in some domains female-centered social structure does not translate into higher status. For example, women in such societies do not have more say in kin group affairs, and they are not more likely to be political leaders. Recall that Iroquois women, in a matrilocal and matrilineal society, could not hold political office. In matrilineal societies it is the men of the matrilineal kin group who are likely to be most influential in kin group decisions.[101] Even when it comes to authority in the household, women in matrilineal societies do not always have as much domestic authority as their brothers or even their husbands.[102]

What of societal complexity as a predictor of women's status? Intensive agriculture (in preindustrial societies) is one of many indicators of greater societal complexity, and Whyte found that women actually have relatively low status in such societies. They also have lower status in societies with complex political hierarchies and private property, which are other indicators of societal complexity.[103] There is one type of female influence that increases with cultural complexity—informal influence. But, as Whyte points out, greater informal influence may simply reflect the lack of real influence.[104]

It is not entirely clear why more societal complexity should be associated (in preindustrial societies) with less female authority in the home, less female control over property, and more restricted sexual lives for females. One possibility is that women have to spend more time in and around the home in societies with intensive cultivation, so their access to information about the world they live in is more limited.[105] But there are other possible explanations. More complex societies usually have more powerful centralized governments. Since men usually are the political leaders in such contexts, this may lead to other kinds of control. Western colonialism, too, has often been detrimental to women's status, partly because colonial authorities were accustomed to dealing with men. There are many examples of Europeans restructuring land ownership around men and teaching men modern farming techniques even where women were traditionally the farmers. Further, native men were usually in a better position than women to work for wages and to earn cash selling goods (such as furs) to Europeans.[106] And in societies where women and men were unequal before contact, colonial influence often further undermined the position of women.

Whatever the reasons for gender differences, they figure importantly in the way society structures human relations. As we have noted, no known society assigns women and men exactly the same jobs and responsibilities. But whether these differences are responsible for other aspects of culture and social structure is more debatable. For example, division of labor by gender does not appear to predict the overall status of women. And, as we shall see in the next chapter, the division of labor by gender may not explain why humans have marriage either, judging by the evidence about what predicts female-male bonding in other species.

NOTES

1. Barbara B. Smuts, "Gender, Aggression, and Influence," in *Primate Societies*, eds. Barbara B. Smuts, Dorothy L. Cheney, Robert M. Seyfarth, Richard W. Wrangham, and Thomas T. Struhsaker (Chicago: University of Chicago Press, 1987), p. 407.

2. For reviews of theories and research on sexual dimorphism and possible genetic and cultural determinants of variation in degree of dimorphism over time and place, see David W. Frayer and Milford H. Wolpoff, "Sexual Dimorphism," *Annual Review of Anthropology* 14 (1985): 431–432; and J. Patrick Gray, *Primate Sociobiology* (New Haven: HRAF Press, 1985), pp. 201–209, 217–225.

3. See references in Carol R. Ember, "A Cross-Cultural Perspective on Sex Differences," *Handbook of Cross-Cultural Human Development*, eds. Ruth H. Munroe, Robert L. Munroe, and Beatrice B. Whiting (New York: Garland Press, 1981), pp. 535–536; see also mean height differences in 216 societies in J. Patrick Gray and Linda D. Wolfe, "Height and Sexual Dimorphism of Stature among Human Societies," *American Journal of Physical Anthropology* 53 (1980): 441–456.

4. William A. Stini, "Evolutionary Implications of Changing Nutritional Patterns in Human Populations," *American Anthropologist* 73 (1971): 1019–1030.

5. Frayer and Wolpoff, "Sexual Dimorphism," pp. 431–432.

6. R. D. Bock, H. Wainer, A. Petersen, D. Thissen, J. Murray, and A. Roche, "A Parameterization for Individual Human Growth Curves," *Human Biology* 45 (1973): 63–80.

7. Gray, *Primate Sociobiology*, p. 201ff. Also see his book for a review of the literature and evidence regarding sexual dimorphism in primates.

8. Ibid.

9. For reviews of theories and research on human sexual dimorphism, and possible genetic and cultural determinants, see Frayer and Wolpoff, "Sexual Dimorphism"; and Gray, *Primate Sociobiology*, pp. 201–209, 217–225.

10. The following discussion largely follows Carol R. Ember and Melvin Ember, *Anthropology*, 8th ed. (Upper Saddle River, NJ: Prentice Hall, 1996), pp. 336ff.

11. See, for example, George Peter Murdock and Catarina Provost, "Factors in the Division of Labor by Sex: A Cross-Cultural Analysis," *Ethnology* 12 (1973): 203–225.

12. Judith K. Brown, "A Note on the Division of Labor by Sex," *American Anthropologist* 72 (1970): 1073–1078.

13. Murdock and Provost, "Factors in the Division of Labor by Sex," pp. 213.

14. Douglas R. White, Michael L. Burton, and Lilyan A. Brudner, "Entailment Theory and Method: A Cross-Cultural Analysis of the Sexual Division of Labor," *Behavior Science Research* 12 (1977): 1–24.

15. Carol C. Mukhopadhyay and Patricia J. Higgins, "Anthropological Studies of Women's Status Revisited: 1977–1987," *Annual Review of Anthropology* 17 (1988): 473.

16. Brown, "A Note on the Division of Labor by Sex"; and White, Burton, and Brudner, "Entailment Theory and Method."

17. Sara B. Nerlove, "Women's Workload and Infant Feeding Practices: A Relationship with Demographic Implications," *Ethnology* 13 (1974): 207–214.

18. Nancy E. Levine, "Women's Work and Infant Feeding: A Case from Rural Nepal," *Ethnology* 27 (1988): 231–251.

19. Madeleine J. Goodman, P. Bion Griffin, Agnes A. Estioko-Griffin, and John S. Grove, "The Compatibility of Hunting and Mothering among the Agta Hunter-Gatherers of the Philippines," *Sex Roles* 12 (1985): 1199–1209.

20. John J. Macionis, *Sociology*, 4th ed. (Englewood Cliffs, NJ: Prentice Hall, 1993), p. 362.

21. W. H. R. Rivers, *The Todas* (Oosterhout, N.B., The Netherlands: Anthropological Publications, 1967 [originally published 1906]), p. 567.

22. Margaret Mead, *Sex and Temperament in Three Primitive Societies* (New York: New American Library, 1950 [originally published 1935]), pp. 180–184.

23. See Table 1 in Melvin Ember and Carol R. Ember, "The Conditions Favoring Matrilocal versus Patrilocal Residence," *American Anthropologist* 73 (1971): 573. Reprinted with "Afterthoughts," in Melvin Ember and Carol R. Ember, *Marriage, Family, and Kinship: Comparative Studies of Social Organization* (New Haven: HRAF Press, 1983).

24. Carol R. Ember, "The Relative Decline in Women's Contribution to Agriculture with Intensification," *American Anthropologist* 85 (1983): 288–289.

25. See Solomon Katz, "Brewing an Ancient Beer," *Archaeology* (July/August 1991): 24–33.

26. Michael J. Harner, *The Jivaro: People of the Sacred Waterfalls* (Garden City, NY: Anchor Books, 1973), p. 81.

27. Ibid., p. 52.

28. Ibid., p. 51.

29. Ester Boserup, *Woman's Role in Economic Development* (New York: St. Martin's Press, 1970), pp. 22–25; see also Alice Schlegel and Herbert Barry III, "The Cultural Consequences of Female Contribution to Subsistence," *American Anthropologist* 88 (1986): 144–145.

30. Peggy R. Sanday, "Toward a Theory of the Status of Women," *American Anthropologist* 75 (1973): 1691.

31. Boserup, *Woman's Role in Economic Development*, pp. 22–25.

32. Ibid., pp. 31–34.

33. Ember, "The Relative Decline in Women's Contribution to Agriculture with Intensification," pp. 286–287; data from Murdock

and Provost, "Factors in the Division of Labor by Sex," p. 212; Candice Bradley, "Keeping the Soil in Good Heart: Weeding, Women, and Ecofeminism," in *Ecofeminism: Multidisciplinary Perspectives*, ed. Karen Warren (Bloomington: Indiana University Press, 1995).

34. Ember, "The Relative Decline in Women's Contribution to Agriculture with Intensification," pp. 289–290.

35. Source 4 in the Human Relations Area Files on the Zuni, Stevenson, p. 367.

36. See Murdock and Provost, "Factors in the Division of Labor by Sex," p. 210.

37. Source 24 in the Human Relations Area Files, Steininger and Velde, pp. 65–66.

38. This assertion is based on time allocation data provided by Dennis W. Werner on the Kayapo, and by Raymond Hames on the Ye'kwana (personal communications). Both confirm that processing bitter manioc is not as time-consuming as processing dried cereal grains. See also the general discussion of this issue in Ember, "The Relative Decline in Women's Contribution to Agriculture with Intensification," p. 290.

39. For data supporting this statement, see Ember, "The Relative Decline in Women's Contribution to Agriculture with Intensification." Two cross-cultural samples yield this result. One uses data from Moni Nag, *Factors Affecting Human Fertility in Nonindustrial Societies: A Cross-Cultural Study* (New Haven: Yale University Press, 1962); the second involves data from the HRAF Sixty-Culture Probability Sample Files. While the reasons for differences in fertility are not entirely clear, intensive agriculturalists do have significantly shorter postpartum sex taboos and, therefore, probably shorter birth intervals. There could conceivably also be differences in nursing patterns, given that cereals make more convenient baby food.

40. Ember, "The Relative Decline in Women's Contribution to Agriculture with Intensification," pp. 287–293.

41. See Ember and Ember, "The Conditions Favoring Matrilocal versus Patrilocal Residence," pp. 579–580.

42. Nerlove, "Women's Workload and Infant Feeding Practices."

43. Schlegel and Barry, "The Cultural Consequences of Female Contribution to Subsistence."

44. Ibid., p. 147.

45. Ibid. The evidence indicates that most societies do not show a difference in the evaluation of girls and boys, but where there is a difference, girls are apt to be more valued when women make a greater contribution to subsistence.

46. Burton Pasternak, *Guests in the Dragon: Social Demography of a Chinese District, 1895–1946* (New York: Columbia University Press, 1983).

47. Martin K. Whyte, *The Status of Women in Preindustrial Societies* (Princeton, NJ: Princeton University Press, 1978), p. 57.
48. Judith K. Brown, "Economic Organization and the Position of Women among the Iroquois," *Ethnohistory* 17 (1970): 151–167.
49. Whyte, *The Status of Women in Preindustrial Societies*, p. 58, uses the figure 89 percent; using a different sample, David B. Adams, "Why Are There So Few Women Warriors?" *Behavior Science Research* 18 (1983): 196–212, obtains the figure 87 percent.
50. See Peggy R. Sanday, "Female Status in the Public Domain," in *Woman, Culture, and Society*, eds. Michelle Z. Rosaldo and Louise Lamphere (Stanford, CA: Stanford University Press, 1974), pp. 189–206; and William T. Divale and Marvin Harris, "Population, Warfare, and the Male Supremacist Complex," *American Anthropologist* 78 (1976): 521–538.
51. Naomi Quinn, "Anthropological Studies on Women's Status," *Annual Review of Anthropology* 6 (1977): 189–190.
52. Susan Brandt Graham, "Biology and Human Social Behavior: A Response to van den Berghe and Barash," *American Anthropologist* 81 (1979): 357–360.
53. Taller Mekranoti women were also more often considered leaders. See Dennis W. Werner, "The Making of a Mekranoti Chief: The Psychological and Social Determinants of Leadership in a Native South American Society" (Ph.D. diss., City University of New York, 1980). See also Dennis W. Werner, "Chiefs and Presidents: A Comparison of Leadership Traits in the United States and among the Mekranoti-Kayapo of Central Brazil," *Ethos* 10 (1982): 136–148; and Ralph M. Stogdill, *Handbook of Leadership: A Survey of Theory and Research* (New York: Macmillan, 1974), cited in Ibid. In a study conducted in the United States of emerging dominance in newly created small groups, W. Penn Handwerker and Paul Crosbie found that men were more likely to dominate groups, but the effect of biological sex was accounted for by differences in height and weight. Taller men tend to be dominant over shorter men; taller women tend to be dominant over shorter women; and taller women tend to be dominant over shorter men. These findings are reported in W. Penn Handwerker and Paul V. Crosbie, "Sex and Dominance," *American Anthropologist* 84 (1982): 97–104.
54. Werner, "Chiefs and Presidents"; Stogdill, *Handbook of Leadership*; see also Handwerker and Crosbie, "Sex and Dominance," pp. 97–104.
55. Patricia Draper, "!Kung Women: Contrasts in Sexual Egalitarianism in Foraging and Sedentary Contexts," in *Toward an Anthropology of Women*, ed. Rayna R. Reitger (New York: Monthly Review Press, 1975), p. 103.
56. Dennis W. Werner, "Child Care and Influence among the Mekranoti of Central Brazil," *Sex Roles* 10 (1984): 395–404.

57. Marc Howard Ross, "Female Political Participation: A Cross-Cultural Explanation," *American Anthropologist* 88 (1986): 843–858.

58. Adams, "Why Are There So Few Women Warriors?"

59. Ibid.

60. Mead, *Sex and Temperament in Three Primitive Societies*, p. 206.

61. Nancy McDowell, "Mundugumor: Sex and Temperament Revisited," in *Portraits of Culture: Ethnographic Originals*, eds. Melvin Ember, Carol R. Ember, and David Levinson (Englewood Cliffs, NJ: Prentice Hall/Simon & Schuster Custom Publishing, 1994). One indication of female/male similarity in temperament, even in 1981, was McDowell's discovery of a coed basketball team.

62. Kaj Bjökqvist, "Sex Differences in Physical, Verbal, and Indirect Aggression: A Review of Recent Research," *Sex Roles* 30 (1994): 177–188, claims that the differences in aggressiveness are largely qualitative rather than quantitative. If indirect forms of aggression were studied (such as excluding someone from a group or negative gossip), the quantitative sex difference might disappear. We should note, however, that there is not sufficient research on indirect aggression to verify this possibility. For a more extensive review of the cross-cultural research on aggression, see Marshall H. Segall, Carol R. Ember, and Melvin Ember, "Aggression, Crime, and Warfare," in *Handbook of Cross-Cultural Psychology, Volume 3: Social Behavior and Applications*, 2nd ed., eds. J. W. Berry, M. H. Segall, and C. Kagitcibasi (Boston: Allyn and Bacon, in press).

63. Beatrice B. Whiting and Carolyn P. Edwards, "A Cross-Cultural Analysis of Sex Differences in the Behavior of Children Aged Three through Eleven," *Journal of Social Psychology* 91 (1973): 171–188.

64. Carol R. Ember reports differences among Luo girls and boys in "Feminine Task-Assignment and the Social Behavior of Boys," *Ethos* 1 (1973): 424–439. For differences on an Israeli kibbutz, see Melford Spiro, *Children of the Kibbutz* (Cambridge, MA: Harvard University Press, 1958). N. G. Blurton-Jones and M. Konner report such differences among the !Kung in "Sex Differences in Behavior of London and Bushman Children," in *Comparative Ecology and Behaviour of Primates*, eds. R. P. Michael and J. H. Crook (London: Academic Press, 1973), pp. 690–750.

65. Eleanor E. Maccoby and Carol N. Jacklin, *The Psychology of Sex Differences* (Stanford, CA: Stanford University Press, 1974). A more recent analysis of U.S. and Canadian aggression research by Janet Shibley Hyde, "Gender Differences in Aggression," in *The Psychology of Gender: Advances through Meta-Analysis*, eds. Janet Shibley Hyde and Marcia C. Linn (Baltimore: The Johns Hopkins University Press, 1986), pp. 51–66, also supports this claim.

66. For a more extensive discussion of behavior differences and possible

explanations for them, see Ember, "A Cross-Cultural Perspective on Sex Differences," pp. 531–580.

67. Hyde, "Gender Differences in Aggression." Consistent with the U.S. data, and on the basis of ethnographic accounts, Ronald Rohner, "Sex Differences in Aggression: Phylogenetic and Enculturation Perspectives," *Ethos* 4 (1976): 58–72, also suggests that gender differences in behavior narrow in adulthood. (We assume he does not include the domain of war or rare events such as homicide.)

68. Martin Daly and Margo Wilson, *Homicide* (New York: Aldine de Gruyter, 1988), pp. 147–148, 184–186.

69. Gwen J. Broude and Sarah J. Green, "Cross-Cultural Codes on Twenty Sexual Attitudes and Practices," *Ethnology* 15 (1976): 409–429.

70. Whiting and Edwards, "A Cross-Cultural Analysis of Sex Differences in the Behavior of Children Aged Three through Eleven."

71. See Ember, "A Cross-Cultural Perspective on Sex Differences," p. 533.

72. J. Z. Rubin, F. J. Provenzano, and R. F. Haskett, "The Eye of the Beholder: Parents' Views on the Sex of New Borns," *American Journal of Orthopsychiatry* 44 (1974): 512–519.

73. For a fuller discussion of this evidence, see Lee Ellis, "Evidence of Neuroandrogenic Etiology of Sex Roles from a Combined Analysis of Human, Nonhuman Primate, and Nonprimate Mammalian Studies," *Personality and Individual Differences* 7 (1986): 525–527. See also Ember, "A Cross-Cultural Perspective on Sex Differences," pp. 531–580.

74. For example, Ellis, in "Evidence of Neuroandrogenic Etiology of Sex Roles from a Combined Analysis of Human, Nonhuman Primate, and Nonprimate Mammalian Studies," expressed the view that evidence in support of a biological origin for aggression is "beyond reasonable dispute."

75. Ember, "A Cross-Cultural Perspective on Sex Differences."

76. Rohner, "Sex Differences in Aggression."

77. Beatrice B. Whiting and John W. M. Whiting, in collaboration with Richard Longabaugh, *Children of Six Cultures: A Psycho-Cultural Analysis* (Cambridge, MA: Harvard University Press, 1975); see also Beatrice B. Whiting and Carolyn P. Edwards, *Children of Different Worlds: The Formation of Social Behavior* (Cambridge, MA: Harvard University Press, 1988), p. 273.

78. Carol R. Ember, "Feminine Task Assignment and the Social Behavior of Boys," *Ethos* 1 (1973): 424–439.

79. For further discussion of this point and other possible social explanations, see Ember, "A Cross-Cultural Perspective on Sex Differences"; and also Segall, Ember, and Ember, "Aggression, Crime, and Warfare."

80. Whiting and Edwards, "A Cross-Cultural Analysis of Sex Differences in the Behavior of Children Aged Three through Eleven," pp.

175–179; see also Maccoby and Jacklin, *The Psychology of Sex Differences*.

81. Marcia C. Linn and A. Petersen, "A Meta-Analysis of Gender Differences in Spatial Ability: Implications for Mathematics and Science Achievement," in *The Psychology of Gender*, eds. Hyde and Linn.

82. The problem is that the differences revealed in those studies are not completely consistent by type of test or age.

83. Judith A. Hall, *Nonverbal Sex Differences: Communication Accuracy and Expressive Style* (Baltimore: Johns Hopkins University Press, 1984).

84. See, for example, Irwin Silverman and Krista Philips, "Effects of Estrogen Changes during the Menstrual Cycle on Spatial Performance," *Ethology and Sociobiology* 14 (1993): 257–269.

85. Ruth H. Munroe, Robert L. Munroe, and Anne Brasher, "Precursors of Spatial Ability: A Longitudinal Study among the Logoli of Kenya," *Journal of Social Psychology* 125 (1985): 23–33.

86. The research supporting this statement is discussed in John W. Berry, *Human Ecology and Cognitive Style* (New York: John Wiley, 1976); and Ember, "A Cross-Cultural Perspective on Sex Differences," pp. 565–566.

87. Herbert Barry III, Irvin L. Child, and Margaret K. Bacon, "Relation of Child Training to Subsistence Economy," *American Anthropologist* 61 (1959): 51–63.

88. See, for example, Carol Gilligan, *In a Different Voice: Psychological Theory and Women's Development* (Cambridge, MA: Harvard University Press, 1982).

89. See, for example, David Stimpson, Larry Jensen, and Wayne Neff, "Cross-Cultural Gender Differences in Preference for a Caring Morality," *Journal of Social Psychology* 132 (1992): 317–322.

90. Hall, *Nonverbal Sex Differences*.

91. Robert L. Munroe et al., "Sex Differences in East African Dreams," *Journal of Social Psychology* 125 (1985): 405–406.

92. This description is based on the fieldwork of Elizabeth and Robert Fearnea (1956–1958), as reported in M. Kay Martin and Barbara Voorhies, *Female of the Species* (New York: Columbia University Press, 1975), pp. 304–331.

93. Elsie B. Begler, "Sex, Status, and Authority in Egalitarian Society," *American Anthropologist* 80 (1978): 571–588.

94. Ibid. See also Martin K. Whyte, "Cross-Cultural Codes Dealing with the Relative Status of Women," *Ethnology* 17 (1978): 229–232.

95. See Alice Schlegel, "The Status of Women," in *Cross-Cultural Research for Social Science*, eds. Carol R. Ember and Melvin Ember (Upper Saddle River, NJ: Prentice Hall/Simon & Schuster Custom Publishing, 1996).

96. Whyte, The Status of Women in Preindustrial Societies, pp. 95–120. For a similar view, see Quinn, "Anthropological Studies on Women's Status."

97. The reader should note that the correlations reported within each of these clusters in Whyte, The Status of Women in Preindustrial Societies, are not that high either.

98. Some researchers advise concentrating not on clusters of traits but on specific aspects of status that seem more important. For example, Alice Schlegel, in "The Status of Women," expressed the view that traits having to do with power and authority are particularly central to status.

99. Whyte, The Status of Women in Preindustrial Societies, pp. 121–130. It is widely assumed that plowing requires considerable strength. But Ember ("The Relative Decline in Women's Contribution to Agriculture with Intensification") questions whether the difficulties women might have plowing really explain their lesser contribution to subsistence.

100. Whyte, The Status of Women in Preindustrial Societies, pp. 45, 145–146; Sanday, "Toward a Theory of the Status of Women," p. 1695.

101. David M. Schneider, "The Distinctive Features of Matrilineal Descent Groups," in Matrilineal Kinship, eds. David M. Schneider and Kathleen Gough (Berkeley: University of California Press, 1961), pp. 1–35.

102. Alice Schlegel, Male Dominance and Female Autonomy (New Haven: HRAF Press, 1972).

103. Whyte, The Status of Women in Preindustrial Societies, pp. 135–136.

104. Ibid., p. 135.

105. See Ember, "The Relative Decline in Women's Contribution to Agriculture with Intensification."

106. Quinn, "Anthropological Studies on Women's Status," p. 85; see also Women and Colonization: Anthropological Perspectives, eds. Mona Etienne and Eleanor Leacock (New York: Praeger, 1980), pp. 19–20.

4

MARRIAGE AND OTHER MATED RELATIONSHIPS

Female mammals invest a lot of energy rearing their young, from gestation in the womb until the time they are weaned—and even longer, if the young need to be taught to provide for themselves. In most mammalian species, mothers do all this without help from the fathers of their offspring. Indeed, most female mammals have hardly anything to do with the fathers after copulation. Female-male bonding—the persistence of a tie between mates—is unusual among mammals; the paternal male does not stay long with the female in most mammalian species. In the vast majority of bird species, however, there is female-male bonding for at least one breeding season, and mating for life is not uncommon. But bonding may not be limited to one female and one male (monogamy). In humans, for example, it can involve one female and two or more males (polyandry), or one male and two or more females (polygyny); the term *polygamy* includes both polyandry and polygyny.

If most female mammals do not require a male except for impregnation, why do some nonprimate mammal species, like wolves and beavers, have female-male bonding? And why do most bird species have bonding? But most important for us, why do humans generally bond with mates when most of their primate cousins do not?

In all human societies known to anthropology, most adults at any given moment are involved in a continuing, sexual, female-male relationship. Usually the parties live together at least most of the time. We commonly think of such arrangements as *marriage*, although, as we shall see later in this book, marriage in human societies often, if not always, entails more than female-male bonding. In this chapter, however, we are primarily interested in why stable mated relationships are universal or customary in all human societies, in how scholars have variably defined marriage, and with the circumstances under which marriage is likely to be monogamous, polyandrous, or polygynous. In no society known to anthropology has group marriage (multimale/multifemale) been customary.

Many scholars assume that if a custom, trait, or institution (such as marriage) is universal, it must have clear adaptive advantages. We assume this too. But what exactly are those advantages? Let us address that question first. Does research comparing humans with other animals suggest why female-male bonding would develop in some species but not in others?

THE STABLE MATED RELATIONSHIP

When we discussed why human females are capable of so much sexuality (which is also, like marriage, a universal characteristic of our species), we explained why it was impossible to test theories about sexuality if we limit consideration to humans. We cannot test theories about variation in any species that exhibits only minimal variation. We face the same problem when we consider stable mated relationships. It is not possible to evaluate the merits of different theories of marriage, a cross-cultural constant, because any other cross-cultural constant may explain it. The fact that certain characteristics are invariably found together does not necessarily indicate a causal relationship between them. If two universals necessarily implied a causal relationship, we would be forced to entertain absurd propositions such as that humans have stable mated relationships because they build shelters or laugh.

If we cannot convincingly account for one universal in terms of another, because any universal might plausibly be invoked as cause, how can we investigate why humans have stable matings? Here, too, it is useful to consider other animals, among whom mating is not a constant: Some species have female-male bonding while others do not. A comparison of such species may reveal the conditions under which some species form enduring bonds, and that might provide insights relevant to human bonding.

In a study of free-ranging mammals and birds (using data on a random sample of mammal and bird species), two of the present authors, Melvin and Carol R. Ember, evaluated the explanatory value of various proposed explanations of human bonding.[1] According to one theory, stable mated relationships are universal in human societies because they solve the problem presented by a gender division of labor. As we learned in the last chapter, women and men in all societies are likely to do different things in food-getting and other economic activities. We might suppose, then, that some mechanism is needed to enable women and men to share the products of their division of labor. (How else could males obtain some of the products females provide, and vice versa?) Female-male bonding provides one way to make this possible. But this theory cannot explain female-male bonding in other species. While few have a gender division of labor in food-getting, many bird species and some mammal species have bonding anyway.

Another supposed problem that bonding might solve is conflict arising from competition over females. (This is the *sexual competition* theory.) The reader should note that, in contrast to the idea discussed in the chapter on sexuality (that female-male bonding may have developed prior to year-round female sexuality), the sexual competition theory assumes that human females had already become sexy year-round, before bonding developed. But if females were already so sexy, would bonding minimize competition between males, as Ralph Linton assumed?[2] We think the reasoning behind this theory is questionable.

One reason we find it questionable is that it assumes that struggles among males determine who mates with whom. Yet, recent research on other animals (including primates) indicates that who mates with whom is often the female's decision, and that females do not always choose males on the basis of aggressive performance. Even where there is an established dominance hierarchy based on previous aggressive encounters in multimale groups, dominant males do not clearly have more mating opportunities.[3] Female primates have a variety of ways to indicate willingness or rejection. For example, they may avoid the advances of a male by simply sitting down, making sex difficult if not impossible.[4]

A more telling weakness of the sexual competition theory is that it begs an important question: Why should we expect males to fight over something plentiful (as would be the case if females were often interested in sex)? Just as abundant food is less likely than scarcity to evoke competition, wouldn't males be less rather than more likely to struggle for mates if females were often sexy? Bonobo chimpanzees provide a good illustration. They live in social groups with a number of females and males, have sex almost any time (and appear to enjoy it), but exhibit almost no male-male or female-female competition, notwithstanding the absence of female-male bonding![5]

Even though the logic of the sexual competition theory of marriage leaves something to be desired, we can, nonetheless, test it. Can it predict the presence or absence of female-male bonding? According to this theory, we would expect that species with more female sexuality (i.e., with more days per year of female interest in copulation) would be more likely to bond. Contrary to this expectation, however, the Embers found that species with female-male bonding did not have a significantly different number of days per year of female copulatory activity when compared to species without bonding. That is, species with bonding did not have more female sexuality.

And when amount of female sexuality was measured in terms of the absence versus presence of a breeding season, those species with more female sexuality (no breeding season) were significantly less likely to have female-male bonding than the species with less female sexuality.[6] So, for empirical as well as logical reasons, we can reject the sexual competition theory of marriage; the underlying reasoning is questionable and it does not predict female-male bonding in mammal and bird species.

Another theory is that female-male bonding is universal cross-culturally because it provides an effective way to accommodate the extremely long period of infant and child dependency characteristic of humans.[7] Human offspring especially require protection and shelter, as well as food, for many years. According to this *dependency theory* of marriage, if dependency is long, both parents need to provide care, and their participation is ensured by female-male bonding. Laura L. Betzig put it this way:

> Obviously reproduction is accomplished without marriage in the vast majority of organisms, but where, as in the human species, young benefit enough by being cared for by both parents, parents appear to have evolved to cooperate in order to provide such care.[8]

When the Embers systematically considered the behavior of other animals, however, they found that duration of dependency does not predict bonding; in fact, species with longer dependency are significantly less likely to have bonding. Primates have some of the longest dependency periods, but they generally lack female-male bonding; birds have some of the shortest dependencies, but almost all bird species bond. So duration of dependency can hardly be the cause of female-male bonding.[9]

Ethologists—scientists who study animal behavior in the wild—suggest that bonding can be expected in species where both parents participate in caring for their brood, *regardless of the period of dependency*.[10] But this suggestion borders on tautology. It leaves a basic question unanswered: Why do females and males share responsibilities for their brood in some species but not in others?

Attempting to answer that question, the Embers asked: Why can females in some species do without males? Their tentative answer: A mother might do without bonding if she can simultaneously feed herself and take care of new offspring by herself after birth or hatching. Browsing or grazing mammals, whose new offspring can travel with the mother soon after birth or hatching, should be able to manage alone, without attendant fathers. But most bird (and some mammal) mothers have a serious problem—their newborn are usually not mature enough to get their own food or fully able to move about with their mothers when the mothers search for food. If left behind in the nest or den while mothers go out to get food, predators may kill them. If their mothers remain with them, no one will eat. Thus, natural selection should favor female-male bonding if the mother's feeding requirements interfere with her baby tending.[11] When the Embers tested it on their cross-species data, this *interference* hypothesis found significant support. Indeed, interference between feeding and baby tending strongly predicts female-male bonding among birds and mammals. Almost all species with interference had bonding, and almost all without interference did not. (Recall that none of the other discussed interpretations predicted bonding in the Embers' sample of bird and mammal species.)

Of what relevance is this interference theory to human female-male bonding? Most primate females can move about to forage for plant food shortly after they give birth; their babies often travel with them, clinging to their fur. So most nonhuman primates do not require the help of another adult; the mother's feeding requirements do not interfere with her baby tending. But human mothers would have a hard time without help. For one thing, they lack the fur to which infants might cling while mothers forage. Further, humans do not exhibit a grasping reflex until a few months after birth. Thus, when humans came to depend on food-getting activities that interfere with infant care (activities like hunting or fishing that would take mothers away from babies), they probably needed help with baby tending. Bonding would have provided a solution to the interference problem: Bonded adults could either take turns watching the baby while one went out for food, or one of the adults could assume the principal responsibility for finding and bringing back food.

But why should bonding necessarily involve female and male: Couldn't females cooperate to the same end? Probably not, suggest the Embers. Two females might simultaneously have two sets of offspring. In that event, baby tending would mean watching and feeding twice the number of offspring. If one female consistently went out for food, or if they took turns, the task of watching and feeding twice the number of offspring would likely mean increased risk and less food per offspring. If a human mother would have "her hands full" tending two sets of offspring, so too would a bird mother have "her claws full" attending two broods at the same time. But a bonded male and female would have only one set of offspring to watch and feed, and among mammals and birds this probably translates into more surviving offspring than female-female bonding would provide. With female-male bonding, each guardian brings food to the same set of offspring, and there is always an adult available to provide them protection.

The disadvantage of female-female bonding would probably apply as well to male-male bonding, if both males had dependent offspring. That is, it is also unlikely that two males could feed themselves and adequately care for two sets of young. Male-male bonding would obviously also be impractical, if not impossible, in animals that suckle their young. (The males would need to keep the lactating mothers around; but of course if they did, the bonded individuals would not be a male-male pair.)

As to why a group of promiscuous females and males would not provide any better solution, the Embers note that the more uncertainty about paternity, the less a mother can count on any particular male for help. Because mothers in such groups would have to compete for help, their young would not be as assured of protection as they would be if father and mother were bonded. Even if a male bonded with two females, each would have a particular male to depend on. Some evidence that group bonding does, indeed, result in reduced reproduction comes from studies of dunnocks—a species of bird that exhibits four bonding patterns—one male/one female, one male/several females, one female/several males, as well as promiscuous group bonding. Group-bonded dunnocks (two males and two females) had the fewest surviving offspring per female.[12]

In short, the available cross-species evidence suggests that interference between a mother's feeding requirements and baby tending may explain why humans, along with some other mammals and most birds, have continuing or stable mated female-male relationships. Compared with other alternatives, the female-male bond may best assure feeding and protection of young when mothers cannot obtain food and care for young simultaneously.

THE MEANING OF MARRIAGE

In most societies, *marriage* means much more than a stable, mated relationship between woman and man. As we shall see in the chapter on "Getting Married," there may also be elaborate ceremonies, complex arrangements between the intermarrying families, and various rights and obligations. Perhaps because the details of marriage vary considerably from one society to another, scholars have tried to define marriage in a way that covers all the various forms it can take. But each definition encounters exceptions.

Consider George Peter Murdock's classic definition: Marriage "exists only when the economic and the sexual [functions] are united into one relationship."[13] In other words, marriage is an economic as well as sexual relationship; spouses share the proceeds of the division of labor by gender. Murdock also said that "residential cohabitation" was a universal feature of marriage, and he claimed that all societies have marriage, as he defined it.

However, cohabitation is not a universal feature of marriage. In some societies, there are marriages in which couples do not live together or sleep in the same house most of the time. Married men may sleep most of the time in a men's house. In other societies, work may take many or most spouses away from home for long periods of time. In our society, most people would not say a marriage has ended just because work takes a spouse away from home, even for a lengthy period of time. Finally, there are even a few societies in which most spouses customarily live apart.

There are also problems with defining marriage as an economic and sexual union. Consider the Nayar, a caste group living early in the nineteenth century on India's Malibar coast, as described by Kathleen E. Gough.[14] To be married, a Nayar woman required at least two husbands. To begin with she needed a *ritual husband*, someone who ceremonially tied an amulet around her neck signifying that she had not slept with a man of inappropriate caste. Her ritual husband might or might not have sex with her, but rarely lived with her and did not contribute to her subsistence or to the maintenance of her children. Once ritually married, a woman could enjoy several mates, or *visiting husbands*. Arriving after dinner and leaving before breakfast, they, too, contributed nothing of material significance to her or her children. A woman's only concern was that one of her visiting husbands claim parenthood of a child born to her, thus testifying that the child was not the product of a union that violated caste rules. To be married, then, a Nayar woman needed both a ritual and visiting husband (at least one). Her relationship with her visiting husbands was fragile, however; she could break a bond simply by throwing the fellow's belongings into the street.

Nayar marriages did fulfill the sexual purpose (in a polyandrous way) that Murdock points to as partly diagnostic of the marital bond, but they lacked the economic diagnostic. So can we properly speak of marriage in the Nayar case? The answer is no, if we abide by the Murdock definition. To accommodate the Nayar situation, Gough proposed a definition of marriage phrased in legal or jural rather than economic/sexual terms. She suggested that we think of marriage as

> a relationship established between a woman and one or more other persons, which provides that a child born to the woman under circumstances not prohibited by the rules of the relationship is accorded full birth-status rights common to normal members of his [or her] society or social stratum.[15]

Among the Nayar, marriage functioned almost entirely to ensure the legitimacy of children. But is it necessary to focus on legitimacy, to the exclusion of sexuality and economic functions? After all, the Nayar case is quite unusual. They were only a subgroup of their society; elsewhere in India marriage was as Murdock defined it. And even the Nayar shifted later to the usual arrangement of married couples living together, consistent with his definition. The earlier pattern was probably an adaptation to the frequent absence of Nayar men who served as hired soldiers for long periods of time in other parts of India.[16]

Gough's definition of marriage is preferable to Murdock's if we want to accommodate some unusual kinds of marriage, including female-female ones. For example, three percent of marriages among the Nandi of Kenya (as of the 1970s) were between one woman and another. If a woman married to a man did not have a son, she might "marry" a younger woman to have one. When "female husband" became "father" to the younger woman's children, she could no longer have sex with her male husband. Nor could she have sex with her "wife." The female husband had other, nonsexual rights of a husband and expected her wife to do all the domestic work.[17] Biologically speaking, these were two women marrying, but *socially* speaking they were man and woman. Thus, Nandi female-female marriage fits Gough's definition: A woman is married to someone who legitimizes her children, but in this case the children born to the new wife have a "father" who happens to be a woman.

Gough's definition that there be a woman involved does not allow us to accommodate male-male marriages, which some societies allow (for example, the Cheyenne of North America in the 1800s).[18] There are also cases of marriage with ghosts, another possibility not provided for in Gough's (or Murdock's) definition. Ghost marriages occurred in China, for example, and still occurred from-time-to-time in Taiwan and Hong Kong in the last fifty years.[19] Here is an account of one ghost marriage Pasternak witnessed while doing fieldwork in Taiwan during the 1960s.

Mr. Chang, a farmer, had a problem that showed no signs of going away. For several days, while he sought relief from the evening heat in the family ancestral hall, his peace had been shattered by an inexplicable rattling of ritual tea cups on his family ancestral altar. At night his sleep was ruined by recurrent dreams involving a wailing woman. Mr. Chang did what any sensible villager would do under the circumstances; he took his problem to the village temple where, after dinner, the community medium regularly went into trances. Whenever personal problems accumulated in the village, God provided advice and assistance through him.

And so it was that Mr. Chang's problem was resolved. Through the medium, God reminded him of a pact made long ago with his best friend. They wanted, then, to strengthen and deepen their bond by converting friendship into kinship. They belonged to different lines of descent so a more powerful consanguineal bond was out of the question, but kinship through marriage was possible. The men agreed, therefore, that should one have a son and the other a daughter, the children would marry.

Mr. Chang had a daughter and his friend a son, but the children never married because the girl died in infancy. Thus the crying of a woman in the night, and the rattling of tea cups in the ancestral hall. According to God, these were complaints and entreaties from her ghost. Aware that her intended husband was about to take a bride, she demanded her due. To placate her, the boy would have to fulfill the parental pact.

Mr. Chang appealed to his friend. Let the boy first marry his ghostly daughter and thereafter take a living bride. He would sweeten the bargain by providing a dowry without any expectation of the bride wealth usually provided by a groom's family. A ritual marriage with the ghost did take place during which the boy carried her incense burner to his home and placed it on the bridal bed. He then went to claim his living bride in full ceremony. All ghostly communication ceased and Mr. Chang and his best friend were finally relatives by marriage.

While marriage of this sort may not fit any of the definitions we have discussed so far, it reminds us that ghost marriage, like any other form of marriage, can establish potentially useful connections between families. It can also provide important services—the labor and reproductive powers of a daughter-in-law, for example. In this particular case, apart from the cost of a minimal dowry, there was little to lose. But had the son died, the ghost marriage would have imposed a bigger burden of suffering on the survivor. Custom allowed a male to take more than one wife, but a woman could not have two husbands at once. Married to a ghost, a woman would be at the mercy of her in-laws with no husband to protect her, and would remain in that unhappy state indefinitely, or at least until she could find escape from the marriage (which was unlikely). It is not difficult to understand, then, why one of the early acts of the Chinese Communist regime was to outlaw ghost marriages.

As our discussion suggests, there are a few exceptions to virtually any definition of marriage. Perhaps this is because human cultures seem to have elaborated on either the meaning of marriage or its varying functions. But that should not obscure the behavioral reality that there are commonly stable, mated relationships between females and males in every human society. (Again, the Nayar were a subcaste, not a whole society.) Stable does not mean forever, but it does mean that mated relationships generally persist for some time. To be sure, marriage means much more than that in most societies. In addition to a persistent sexual relationship, there are often ceremonies marking onset of the publicly recognized relationship, there may be continuing ties between the intermarrying families, and there usually are many specific rights and duties between a woman and a man. Even if some societies extend the concept of marriage to two females, two males, or even to a person and a ghost, female-male bonds are always most common.

FORMS OF MARRIAGE: HOW MANY DOES ONE MARRY?

However one chooses to define it, marriage takes a limited number of forms. Many societies allow multiple spouses, but no society customarily has group marriage, that is, the simultaneous marriage of two or more females and two or more males. In our own society the only legal form of marriage is monogamy—one female and one male at a time. But limiting people to a single spouse at the same time is relatively rare; the great majority of societies in the ethnographic record allow some form of polygamy, or the marriage of one individual to more than one of the opposite sex at the same time. Figure 4-1 indicates that, while most societies allow polygamous marriage, polygyny is much more commonly allowed than polyandry. (Keep in mind that a society allowing polygyny or polyandry usually has mostly monogamous marriages.) Why should so many societies allow polygyny, and why is polyandry allowed so rarely?

WHY SHARE A HUSBAND?

If a female needs a male to help rear offspring successfully, isn't it odd that hardly any human societies allow polyandry while the vast majority allow polygyny? How would polygyny serve the needs of females? One possible answer is that it does not—it may mostly serve the needs of males. Recall the earlier discussion of dunnock birds, which have a variety of forms of female-male bonding. Researchers found that, for male parents, polygyny on average produced the largest number of young that fledged (i.e., left the nest at maturity). But, for females, polygyny produced the fewest fledglings (except for group bonding, which was the least reproductive for both sexes). For females, polyandry produced the most fledglings (but only when both males fed the young).[20] This makes intuitive sense. With polyandry, there are more surviving fledglings per female because there are two or more males to help care for one set of offspring. With polygyny, females have to

FIGURE 4-1   SOCIETIES IN THE ETHNOGRAPHIC ATLAS
BY TYPE OF MARRIAGE ALLOWED

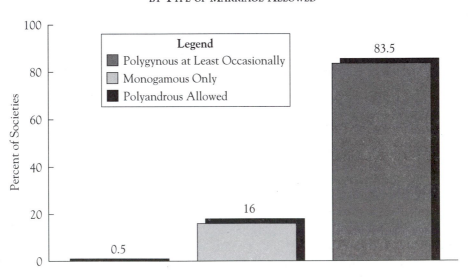

Source: Calculated from George Peter Murdock, *Ethnographic Atlas* (Pittsburgh: University of Pittsburgh Press, 1967).

share a single male to feed and protect two or more sets of offspring. But for males, having more mates means more reproduction even though each mother may have reduced reproductive success. Assuming that these conditions are true for humans as well, why should the advantage of polygyny for males outweigh the advantage of polyandry for females?

Perhaps part of the answer has to do with the traditional prevalence of male dominance. Ralph Linton suggested that polygyny derives from certain universal human biological characteristics, particularly male dominance and the general primate urge of males to collect females.[21] We question Linton's reasoning. Since we now know that primates vary considerably in their mating patterns and sexual appetites, it is not clear that there is a general primate urge on the part of males to collect females. While the males in some nonhuman primates keep harems, others show very different patterns. Gibbons are monogamous. In other species, such as the bonobo or pygmy chimpanzees, females and males both show great interest in sex without any kind of bonding at all. And what about the supposed influence of male dominance? By almost any measure, most human societies have male dominance of some sort (in leadership, sexual freedom, where couples live after marriage, inheritance), and males are generally taller and heavier than females. But how could something nearly constant (male dominance) explain something so variable (from some polygyny to consistent monogamy to some polyandry)?

William Divale and Marvin Harris also consider polygyny to be a result of male dominance, and they explain the connection as follows:[22] War promotes a *male supremacist complex* (in band and tribal societies). Males are expected to be fierce and aggressive warriors and are rewarded with sex, particularly in the form of polygyny. The male supremacist complex persists, Divale and Harris assume, because a shortage of women is created by female infanticide (males are the preferred sex) and because polygyny creates an even greater shortage (some men have more than one wife). So men engage in war to capture more women.

Note that Divale and Harris are explaining warfare in a circular way. They begin by assuming that war is frequent; they presume, therefore, that people favor males (because of the need for warriors) and hence practice female infanticide; finally, because females are in short supply, they presume that men go to war to get more women.

Divale and Harris did present a table suggesting that societies with warfare, as contrasted with those previously pacified, had sex ratios favoring males at younger ages. However, because of serious defects in their methodology, their finding about sex ratios is suspect.[23] Furthermore, subsequent research by the Embers failed to replicate their finding.[24] In fact, the Embers found a nonsignificant tendency in the opposite direction—societies with the highest proportions of males to females had the lowest frequencies of war (not the highest). It appears from their data that a shortage of women does not predict more versus less war, which casts doubt on the notion that male dominance (because of their role in war) can explain polygyny.

Variation in male dominance in some other respect could still have an effect on the forms of marriage that are practiced in a society. Generally but variably, men more than women control important economic resources. A number of studies have shown that wealthier men (if the society is not egalitarian) generally tend to have more wives than do poorer men.[25] This suggests that men might prefer to have more than one wife, if they could. But is that true? There are many ethnographic reports of problems associated with polygynous families, and we will have more to say about these problems later, in our chapter on the marital relationship. Of course, from the point of view of a male, polygyny will likely produce more progeny, as is the case with dunnock birds. But do men generally want to maximize the number of children they have?

On the other hand, polygyny might be preferred by women even if men control wealth. That is, we can adopt the woman's point of view to interpret the greater likelihood that wealthier men will be polygynous: A woman might prefer to marry a man who has access to important resources rather than one who does not, or rather than not marry at all. Needless to say, we are assuming here that women in such circumstances lack the means to live independently, which was mostly the situation in the societies known to anthropology (until the spread of commercial economies in recent times). And it is not simply wealth that might attract a woman to polygynous unions, but also the need for a male partner to help her and her offspring. But this is a need men may have as well; in noncommercial societies, where people cannot earn a living by selling their labor and/or products, men (as well as women) have to live and work with kin.[26]

Does the notion that polygyny goes with wealth explain why the form of marriage varies from one society to another? For example, are societies with substantial differences in wealth more likely to allow polygyny? The answer appears to be no. It turns out, as a matter of fact, that societies with differential wealth are slightly *less* likely than egalitarian societies to allow polygyny.[27]

The relationship between male wealth and polygyny has been interpreted another way. Perhaps men may become wealthier if they marry more than one woman, because women contribute substantially to subsistence.[28] Obtaining wealth through wives would provide an economic incentive for males to marry polygynously, in addition to the desire for more children. This theory (that polygyny increases the husband's wealth) suggests that societies with polygyny should be more likely to have females contributing a good deal to subsistence. But here too the results are equivocal. While some researchers have found evidence for a weak relationship, others have failed to find any association at all.[29]

Another explanation for polygyny links it to a long postpartum sex taboo—prohibition of sexual intercourse for a year or more after the birth of a child. John W. M. Whiting, who first directed our attention to this possibility, reasoned as follows: In societies with diets low in protein, children are subject to a disease called *kwashiorkor* which is often fatal.[30] A child's protein intake and survival chances would be greater when nursed for a long time. While frequent nursing reduces the likelihood of conception, it is not a perfect contraceptive. If the mother abstained from sex for a year or more, she could postpone conception with greater certainty and continue to nurse her last child. Thus, a long postpartum sex taboo would effectively increase the protein available to a child during the early critical stages of growth, and we would therefore expect such a taboo in societies with low protein diets.

But then a father might look to have sex with another woman, which might encourage polygyny. As a Yoruba woman said:

> When we abstain from having sexual intercourse with our husband for the two years we nurse our babies, we know he will seek some other woman. We would rather have her under our control as a co-wife so he is not spending money outside the family.[31]

Whiting collected cross-cultural data to test two hypotheses—that societies with low-protein diets (as indicated by a dependence on root and tree crops) are more likely than others to have a long postpartum sex taboo, and that such a taboo should be associated with polygyny. Both hypotheses were supported.

But polygyny is not the only possible solution to the problem of a long postpartum sex taboo. Why would a man without sexual access to his wife for a year or more have to marry another woman to satisfy his sexual needs in a socially approved fashion? He could have extramarital affairs, which are socially approved in many societies. He could masturbate during the period of the taboo. Or he could abstain completely from sexual activity. Even if he took another wife, she too might be taboo most of the time. So a long postpartum sex taboo does not have to give rise to polygyny; other responses are possible. If that is true, we have to explain why polygyny and not some other possible behavior is the response to a long postpartum sex taboo.

Is there a more compelling reason to practice polygyny? One possibility, originally suggested by Herbert Spencer in 1876, is that polygyny may be a response to an unbalanced sex ratio in favor of women.[32] This possibility was rejected for many years. For example, Ralph Linton claimed that male dominance and sexual urges would give rise to polygyny even where females outnumber males. But the possible effect of an excess of women was rejected without an empirical test.

Barring human meddling, nature provides more males than females at birth, creating a slight imbalance in favor of males that later evens out or sometimes reverses. Barring human interference, females appear to be hardier than males after birth and they normally outlive them. Complications associated with childbirth may remove some women, but this is usually more than offset by male mortality because of dangerous activities (e.g., hunting, deep-sea fishing, lumbering, quarrying, war) which are largely or completely men's activities. War is especially likely to remove males from the population. Until pacification by powerful polities (usually colonial), war was very common in the vast majority of societies known to anthropology.[33] Assuming, for reasons discussed above, that marriage in noncommercial societies is advantageous for rearing young successfully, if a population has more women than men, women may reproduce more if they marry men who are already married than if they do not marry at all. Thus, we might expect polygyny to develop if there is an excess of women because of high male mortality in war. (As noted above, polygyny would also maximize the reproductive rate for males.)

The sex-ratio explanation of polygyny warrants consideration then, purely for logical reasons. Yet no one systematically tested it until Melvin Ember did so in a 1974 paper.[34] The results of that test showed that polygynous societies do have significantly more women than men: 111 females for every 100 males on average, compared to only 94 females for every 100 males in nonpolygynous societies. It is probably no coincidence that the cross-species study of bonding discussed earlier indicated that an excess of females predicted polygyny rather than invariably monogamous bonding in other mammals and birds as well.[35] The data in Ember's polygyny study also supported the hypothesis that societies with high male mortality in warfare are likely to have an imbalanced sex ratio in favor of females.[36]

One of Ember's findings even suggests that Whiting's explanation of polygyny in terms of protein deficiency and a long postpartum sex taboo is rendered unnecessary by the sex-ratio interpretation. When he held male mortality in warfare constant (by looking only at societies with low male mortality, and by looking only at societies with high male mortality) the relationship between a long postpartum sex taboo and polygyny disappeared: There was no association between a long postpartum taboo and polygyny in either the high or low male mortality societies. When he controlled on the presence or absence of a long postpartum sex taboo, however, the strong relationship between high male mortality in warfare and polygyny persisted. He concluded, therefore, that

> in whatever way the association…between polygyny and a long postpartum sex taboo may be explained causally, the results of the present study are more consistent with the theory that polygyny may generally be a response, particularly in noncommercial societies, to an excess of females over males due to a high loss of males in warfare.[37]

But then why, he asks, couldn't excess women find support without being married? Here Ember recalls Spencer's speculation, offered more than a hundred years ago, that polygyny is favored where warfare is prevalent and male loss high because polygynous societies may be better able to replenish their numbers, and therefore may enjoy a competitive advantage over monogamous societies (other things being equal, to be sure).

So it may be that polygyny is a response to an excess of women, that an excess of females (produced by war or a high male mortality rate for other reasons) must develop first. In other words, polygyny may mostly be an effect of sex ratio. On the other hand, the causality could be just the reverse, as is suggested by the results of a recent study by John W. M. Whiting.[38] Based on data from seven Kenyan communities, Whiting suggests that polygyny itself may produce an excess of women, that more girls than boys may be born to polygynous marriages. In the communities studied, he found that the sex ratio at birth was lower (more females than males born) for polygynously married mothers than for monogamously married mothers. Whiting observes that,

> although the effect was not robust enough to permit the practice of polygyny without an adjustment of the adult sex ratio, the hypothesis that sex ratio at birth is influenced by the rate and timing of coitus and the ethnological assumption that these differences are influenced by the form of marriage were strongly supported.[39]

Bobbi S. Low has presented data consistent with another selectionist or Darwinian explanation of polygyny.[40] Her interpretation is based on the observation that environmental extremes and unpredictability increase the probability of reproductive failure.[41] In a cross-cultural study, Low focused on a particular environmental challenge, pathogen stress, which she believes might increase sexual selection and therefore favor polygyny.

Her argument is as follows: Pathogens characterized by an acute, possibly fatal initial stage of infection, and long-term chronic debilitation or recurrence of acute episodes (e.g., leishmanias, trypanosomes, malaria, schistosomes, filariae, spirochetes, and leprosy), constitute an environmental stressor that increases the probability of reproductive failure. The presence of such a stressor might favor the evolution of behavior that produces more variable offspring, because more variable offspring would on average be likelier to survive the environmental challenge. Male reproductive success might, therefore, be maximized by marriage with multiple, unrelated mates. Low's results indicated that pathogen stress and polygyny were positively associated no matter how polygyny is measured (e.g., in terms of percent of women or men polygynously married, or in terms of maximum number of wives). Further, the more pathogen stress there is, the more likely women are captured for marriage, and the more nonsororal polygyny is preferred (both would produce more variable genotypes among the offspring of polygynous men):

> These results suggest that pathogen stress may represent for humans, as well as for other species, a real stress that (1) renders fewer men acceptable as mates, resulting in greater polygyny, and (2) favors the production of more variable offspring, resulting in polygyny of specific types. The relationship appears to be of a threshold sort (at high levels of pathogen stress, monogamy, polyandry, and mild polygyny are absent), rather than a linear relationship.[42]

In other words, Low's research indicates that societies with high pathogen stress are unlikely to be monogamous or have low levels of polygyny. It would be interesting to explore the possibility that pathogen stress affects women and men differently, or at different ages, possibly producing the sort of sex-ratio imbalance (more women than men) that more generally encourages polygyny. In any case, pathogens may make some men less desirable as mates, and, therefore, the number of marriageable males may be appreciably smaller than the number of marriageable females.

Ember and Low both suggest that polygyny may have selective advantages in some circumstances. Almost certainly polygynously married men will reproduce more. But while a man can impregnate many females, a woman can have only one pregnancy at a time. So the fertility consequences for women may be less advantageous with polygyny. We might even wonder whether there is any effect at all for women.

In terms of what we know about the nature of polygynous marriages in different ethnographic contexts, we could anticipate either higher or lower fertility for polygynously married women. For example, one expectation might be that in societies where first marriages are arranged by parents, which is most commonly the case, a husband might favor a younger, second wife he has chosen for himself, and that his disproportionate interest in her might translate into more babies with her. In that case, we might expect second wives to have more offspring than monogamous women. On the other hand, plural marriages could generate so much conflict and competition among co-wives for the attention of their common husband, and over access to the estate he controls, that the frequency of coitus (and conception) is reduced for polygynously married women.

Indeed, Munson and Bumpass found that the mean number of live births in Upper Volta was less for women who had ever been polygynously married.[43] Although most studies support the view that polygynous women have fewer children, there are some contrary findings. The problem has much to do with the data used in analysis. After reviewing a number of relevant studies done on Africa and the Middle East, Moni Nag observed that all of the studies,...whether or not they took account of all variations in age or duration of marriage, had one common drawback: The cumulative fertility levels of women married polygynously or monogamously at the time of investigation were compared. Since a woman currently married to a polygynous or monogamous husband might have gone through other forms of marriage during her reproductive period, the differential effect of polygyny on fertility should not be inferred from this type of comparison.[44]

Data from the household registers of one Taiwanese site enabled Pasternak to overcome this difficulty.[45] He compared the reproductive performance of monogamously married women with that of second wives in polygynous unions, controlling on both age and years spent in each form of marriage, and found that polygynous wives had significantly lower fertility (regardless of whether the monogamous women joined their husband's families at marriage, or he joined theirs).

We cannot be certain, of course, that polygynous wives were less fertile for the reasons outlined earlier. The registers have nothing to say about the health or sperm motility of husbands. Whatever the mechanisms, however, the data are consistent with the expectation that polygynous wives have fewer children than monogamous wives. So, other things being equal, if a woman had a choice between a monogamous marriage or a polygynous one, polygyny might not be to her advantage. In fact, a woman might actually fare better under polyandry, married to more than one husband at the same time unless, of course, there were fewer marriageable males than females, or a shortage of healthy men. In that event, polyandry would mean that some women could not reproduce at all. In that situation, polygyny might be advantageous as compared with not marrying and having few or no children.

ON THE UNPOPULARITY OF SHARING HUSBANDS

George Peter Murdock's Ethnographic Atlas lists only four societies that allow marriage with more than one husband at a time (polyandry): the Tibetans, the Sherpa and Toda of India, and the Marquesans in eastern Polynesia.[46] Why is this form of marriage so uncommon? Many of the theories that we discussed regarding polygyny could be turned around to account for the uncommonness of polyandry. Although we doubted the plausibility of the male dominance explanations of polygyny on logical and empirical grounds, we have no clear examples of societies where females dominate males politically as well as in social organization. (As we will see in a later chapter, even the societies where descent passes through women mostly have male political leaders.) Could this be why there are so few polyandry cases? We think not. For none of the polyandrous cases even approach female dominance. In fact, no society we know of with inheritance in the female line has polyandry.

In light of the importance of an imbalanced sex ratio with respect to polygyny, could it be that polyandry is the result of an imbalance in favor of *men*? Toda and Marquesan ethnographies certainly do suggest an excess of males, a sex ratio imbalance that is apparently not the result of female infanticide. Another possible reason

> might be the migration of more women than men; this is a real possibility for at least one of the classical polyandrous cases, the Marquesans. It is not unlikely that in the heyday of South Pacific whaling, when Tahiti was a popular port of call for the replenishment of all kinds of provisions, more Marquesan women than men may have been drawn to the opportunities available in Tahiti.[47]

However, we should note that a large proportion of Melvin Ember's sample cases had an excess of males without polyandry, so the sex-ratio explanation of polygyny may not be generalizable to polyandry.

Some have suspected that Tibetan polyandry may reflect a sex ratio imbalance resulting from female infanticide—in turn a response to extreme poverty. But Melvyn C. Goldstein, who has studied polyandry there, reports that there has never been institutionalized female infanticide in Tibet.[48] Further, among Tibetans living in Nepal there were actually *more* marriageable-aged females than males (and many unmarried females), and still people married polyandrously. Could extreme economic deprivation alone be the reason? Perhaps life was so difficult that one man alone simply could not support a wife and children? That explanation, too, is unacceptable in light of Goldstein's data. It turns out that polyandry was not a recourse of the poor, but rather a feature of better-off families with land of their own. Worldwide, extreme poverty is common without polyandry. Goldstein suggests that while Tibetan polyandry does not stem from poverty, it may, nonetheless, reflect economic circumstances. In the Tibetan case, polyandry may have something to do with the nature of land tenure.

Traditionally, Tibet was a feudal society. In addition to powerful landed monasteries, there were aristocratic lords and several kinds of serfs. Polyandry occurred only among one class of serfs, *taxpayer serfs*, who were granted a fairly substantial portion of land that they could pass on to their children. The poorer serfs (small householders), with very small grants of nonheritable land or no land at all, did not practice much polyandry.

Why was polyandry practiced more often among serfs of more substantial means? Goldstein suggests the motivation was largely economic. Polyandry reflected the nature of feudal obligations perhaps more than differences in wealth. For the taxpayer serfs, feudal obligations (labor and taxes) were allocated by household. Among the poorer class of serfs they were allocated by person. The significance of this difference was that any family division in the wealthier group multiplied the obligations due per person. If a family divided into two families, for example, *each* was obliged to provide what had been due from both together before division, but now with fewer workers to do the work. In contrast, family division did not increase the obligations per family among the poorer serfs. There was far more incentive among the better-off serfs, then, to avoid or delay family division as long as possible. Clearly, polyandry was one way to discourage partition and keep brothers together by marrying them to the same wife. A brother that opted out of the family did so at the risk of losing his wife, and the system also prevented what Tibetans considered a major catalyst to family division—arguments among wives. In short, polyandry was an institutional way for better-off families to maintain or even increase their wealth. As Goldstein put it,

> polyandry in Tibet maximizes the potential for attaining (or sustaining or increasing) an individual's quality of life in terms of the material markers of affluence, as well as social advantage and prestige. Taxpayer serfs lose their higher ascribed status in the social hierarchies as well as economic productive potential when they split and the small household serfs…minimize their chances for attaining the good life.[49]

While the old feudal system no longer exists, many Tibetans still practice polyandry, and Goldstein suggests that the inspiration is still economic. It is difficult for Tibetans living in Limi, a two-hundred-square-mile area in the mountainous northwest corner of Nepal, to find fertile land to cultivate. To keep the land they have intact, they make special efforts to prevent family division, which by their custom would require a division of land among sons. They accomplish this by means of polyandry, since brothers share a single wife. There may be still another inducement to polyandry, one not articulated by the Tibetans themselves. This form of marriage may restrain population growth in a harsh environment with few resources. Even though there is no shortage of females, one effect of polyandry is that some women are effectively excluded from legitimate reproduction. In Limi in 1974, 31 percent of the women of child-bearing age were unmarried. Although some had children anyway, unmarried women as a group had far fewer children than married women (an average of .7 children per unmarried woman compared with 3.3 children per married woman). As further evidence in support of this interpretation, Goldstein notes that the incidence of polyandry declines when economic conditions improve:[50]

> When resources or economic opportunities requiring little or no capital were scarce, fraternal polyandry was more strictly adhered to, but when such opportunities arose defections from polyandrous unions were common. This, in turn, produced an increase in overall fertility since unmarried females previously excluded from the reproductive pool now married and were brought back into a status of high concep-

tion risk. This increased fertility and generated population pressure on the nonelastic resources finally leading to the reassertion of the conservative view of the opportunity costs of fission and stricter adherence to the fraternal polyandry alternative. The key to this process is the availability of profitable economic resources requiring little or no capital.[51]

Polyandry may serve purposes other than compensating for an imbalance in sex ratio, judging by Goldstein's comparison of the Tibetan and Pahari versions.[52] The Pahari are Indo-Aryan speakers in the Himalayas of India, Nepal, Sikkim, and Bhutan. While most are not polyandrous, some in the Indian Himalayas are and they, like the Tibetans, practice a fraternal form in which brothers share a wife. And like the Tibetans, they have other forms of marriage as well. Polyandry is not a preferred form among the Pahari, and the fact that polyandry occurs much less often than among the Tibetans suggests that it may serve a different function in their case:

> Family prestige rises with its numbers but poor families can afford only one wife shared among brothers. Elder brothers are responsible for providing wives for their younger brothers (and would themselves like to have a second wife) but can only do so when economic conditions improve.... While poor men must share a wife, prosperous men will have more than one.... This type of data suggests strongly that it is a lack of wealth (due in no small part to the traditional practice of paying bride price rather than dowry) that forces Pahari brothers to marry polyandrously and not, in sharp contradiction with Tibetans, the perceived and intended "estate conserving" advantage.... Whereas the Tibetan marriage system is oriented toward the minimization of wives, the Pahari marriage system is oriented toward the maximization of wives. Social status, esteem, and wealth are associated with maximizing the numbers of wives among the Pahari, whereas among polyandrous Tibetan populations it is associated with a corporate family's ability to minimize the number of brides per generation; i.e., to maintain fraternal polyandrous stem families.[53]

But if Tibetan polyandry found favor because it inhibited costly family division and thus preserved wealth, why are so few societies polyandrous? Surely the Tibetans are not the only people who have had to contend with limited resources and few alternative sources of income. Perhaps, then, polyandry is rare world-wide because there are other ways to accomplish the same ends. Through *primogeniture*, limiting inheritance to first sons (we will consider later why sons succeed their parents more often than daughters) or through *ultimogeniture*, limiting inheritance to youngest sons, people in Japan and parts of western Europe also minimize the number of wives per family-generation, and the number of heirs thereafter. Like polyandry, primogeniture and ultimogeniture inhibit overall fertility. With both of these inheritance systems, fewer offspring per male means a higher land-to-people ratio and higher productivity per-capita.[54]

Goldstein reminds us of the Irish experience, where the introduction of the potato increased land productivity and enabled a departure from ultimogeniture. With potatoes, less land produced more, and sons might all make a living on the land. For that reason they married sooner, which led to an increase in population. The great potato famine ended that period of growth. Many people then had to leave Ireland, and the inheritance system reverted to ultimogeniture.

The initial improvement in production per capita brought by the potato meant that the traditional mechanism for preserving wealth (ultimogeniture) could be discarded. Changes in marriage patterns followed. It is interesting that the Chinese takeover of Tibet in 1959 had similar consequences with respect to polyandry. Outside Tibet proper, Tibetans reoriented their production and trade to India. They increased their manufacture of jewelry and artifacts (admired by Westerners) for sale in India, making substantial profits with little capital investment. Tibetan nomads fleeing into Nepal sold their herds and flocks at extremely low values to other Tibetans already living there, increasing the productive potentials of the earlier residents. For them the new opportunities made family division easier, and polyandry declined. Population growth increased as more women were brought into the reproductive pool, and Goldstein suggests that this stimulated a return to polyandry as pressure once again built up on economic resources.[55]

Our discussion of polyandry does suggest, then, why it may be rare. Unless there is a serious shortage of females (which is itself rare) or a serious shortage of resources, polyandry will result in much lower reproduction for a society. An individual woman might benefit reproductively from having multiple husbands, but unless the number of marriageable women is less than that of men, the reproduction of many (unmarried) women will suffer if polyandry is common.

NOTES

1. Melvin Ember and Carol R. Ember, "Male-Female Bonding: A Cross-Species Study of Mammals and Birds," *Behavior Science Research* 14 (1979): 37–56. Reprinted with "Afterthoughts," in Melvin Ember and Carol R. Ember, *Marriage, Family, and Kinship: Comparative Studies of Social Organization* (New Haven: HRAF Press, 1983), pp. 35–64.
2. Ralph Linton, *The Study of Man* (New York: Appleton-Century, 1936), pp. 135–136.
3. Barbara B. Smuts, "Sexual Competition and Mate Choice," in *Primate Societies*, eds. Barbara B. Smuts, Dorothy L. Cheney, Robert M.

Seyfarth, Richard W. Wrangham, Thomas T. Struhsaker (Chicago: University of Chicago Press, 1987), pp. 386, 388.

4. Meredith F. Small, *Female Choices* (Ithaca, NY: Cornell University Press, 1993), pp. 110–113.

5. E. Sue Savage-Rumbaugh, "Hominid Evolution: Looking to Modern Apes for Clues," in *Hominid Culture in Primate Perspective*, eds. Duane Quiatt and Junichiro Itani (Niwot: University Press of Colorado, 1994), p. 40.

6. Ember and Ember, "Male-Female Bonding."

7. George Peter Murdock, *Social Structure* (New York: Macmillan, 1949), pp. 9–10. See also Laura L. Betzig, "Causes of Conjugal Dissolution: A Cross-Cultural Study," *Current Anthropology* 30, no. 5 (December 1989): 654–676; Richard D. Alexander and Katherine M. Noonan, "Concealment of Ovulation, Parental Care, and Human Social Evolution," in *Evolutionary Biology and Human Social Behavior: An Anthropological Perspective*, eds. Napoleon Chagnon and William Irons (North Scituate, MA: Duxbury Press, 1979); Jane B. Lancaster and Chet Lancaster, "Paternal Investment: The Hominid Adaptation," in *How Humans Adapt: A Biocultural Odyssey*, ed. D. Ortner (Washington, DC: Smithsonian Institution, 1983); and Paul W. Turke, "Effects of Ovulatory Concealment and Synchrony on Protohominid Mating Systems and Parental Roles," *Ethology and Sociobiology* 5 (1984): 33–44.

8. Betzig, "Causes of Conjugal Dissolution," p. 655.

9. Ember and Ember, "Male-Female Bonding."

10. Niko Tinbergen, *The Animal in Its World*, vol. 2 (London: Allen and Unwin, 1973), p. 207; R. L. Trivers, "Parental Investment and Sexual Selection," in *Sexual Selection and the Descent of Man 1871–1971*, ed. B. Campbell (Chicago: Aldine, 1972) pp. 136–176.

11. For a similar view, see William Etkin, "Social Behavior and the Evolution of Man's Mental Faculties," *American Naturalist* 88 (1954): 129–142.

12. N. B. Davies, *Dunnock Behaviour and Social Evolution* (Oxford, England: Oxford University Press, 1992), p. 161.

13. Murdock, *Social Structure*, p. 8.

14. Kathleen E. Gough, "The Nayars and the Definition of Marriage," in *Marriage, Family, and Residence*, eds. P. Bohannan and J. Middleton (New York: Doubleday Natural History Press, 1968 [originally published 1959]), pp. 49–71.

15. Ibid., p. 68.

16. N. Prabha Unnithan, "Nayars: Tradition and Change in Marriage and Family," in *Portraits of Culture: Ethnographic Originals*, eds. Melvin Ember, Carol R. Ember, and David Levinson (Englewood Cliffs, NJ: Prentice Hall/Simon & Schuster Custom Publishing, 1994), citing

Christopher J. Fuller, *The Nayars Today* (Cambridge, England: Cambridge University Press, 1976), p. 121.

17. Regina Smith Oboler, "Nandi: From Cattle-Keepers to Cash-Crop Farmers," in *Portraits of Culture*, eds. Ember, Ember, and Levinson.

18. E. Adamson Hoebel, *The Cheyennes: Indians of the Great Plains* (New York: Holt, Rinehart & Winston, 1960).

19. Majorie Topley, "Ghost Marriages among the Singapore Chinese," *Man* 35 (1955): 29–30, and "Ghost Marriages among the Singapore Chinese: A Further Note," *Man* 63 (1956): 71–72; Maurice Friedman, "Ritual Aspects of Chinese Kinship and Marriage," in *Family and Kinship in Chinese Society*, ed. Maurice Friedman (Stanford: Stanford University Press, 1970), pp. 165–166; Arthur Smith, *Village Life in China* (Boston: Little, Brown and Company, 1970 [originally published 1899]), p. 227.

20. Davies, *Dunnock Behaviour and Social Evolution*, p. 161.

21. Ralph Linton, "The Natural History of the Family," in *Readings in Anthropology*, vol. 2., 2nd ed., ed. Morton H. Fried (New York: Thomas Y. Crowell, 1968 [originally published 1947]), pp. 277–295.

22. William Tulio Divale and Marvin Harris, "Population, Warfare, and the Male Supremacist Complex," *American Anthropologist* 78 (1976): 521–538.

23. See Lawrence A. Hirschfeld, James Howe, and Bruce Levin, "Warfare, Infanticide, and Statistical Inference: A Comment on Divale and Harris," *American Anthropologist* 80 (1978): 110–115; Stephen M. Fjellman, "Hey, You Can't Do That: A Response to Divale and Harris's 'Population, Warfare, and the Male Supremacist Complex,'" *Behavior Science Research* 14 (1979): 189–200; and Gay E. Kang, Susan Horan, and Janet Reis, "Comments on Divale and Harris's 'Population, Warfare, and the Male Supremacist Complex,'" *Behavior Science Research* 14 (1979): 201–209. Perhaps the most serious methodological problem is the fact that sex ratios were counted for communities and some societies had many communities in the sample; others only had one. See Melvin Ember, "Alternative Predictors of Polygyny," *Behavior Science Research* 19 (1984–1985): 4.

24. Carol R. Ember and Melvin Ember, "Resource Unpredictability, Mistrust, and War: A Cross-Cultural Study," *Journal of Conflict Resolution* 36 (1992): 251–252.

25. See Barbara C. Ayres, "Intra-Societal Variation in the Incidence of Polygyny" (paper presented at the annual meeting of the Society for Cross-Cultural Research, Washington, DC, 1983). Ayres's studies suggest that wealthy men, men who were considered to be good providers (e.g., especially good hunters, herders, or farmers), political leaders, and members of hereditary elites, were all significantly likely to be polygynously married. See also Laura L. Betzig, "Roman Polygyny,"

Ethology and Sociobiology 13 (1992): 309–349, and *Despotism and Differential Reproduction: A Darwinian View of History* (New York: Aldine Publishing Company, 1986), p. 34; and Douglas R. White, "Rethinking Polygyny: Co-Wives, Codes, and Cultural Systems," *Current Anthropology* 29 (1988): 529–572, and "On the Explanation of Polygyny: Additional Source Materials," *Current Anthropology* 31 (1990): 313.

26. Melvin Ember, "The Emergence of Neolocal Residence," *Transactions of the New York Academy of Sciences* 30 (1967): 291–302. Reprinted with "Afterthoughts," in Ember and Ember, *Marriage, Family, and Kinship*, pp. 333–357.

27. See Ember, "Alternative Predictors of Polygyny."

28. See Betzig, "Causes of Conjugal Dissolution"; Jack Goody, *Production and Reproduction* (Cambridge, England: Cambridge University Press, 1976), p. 129; Dwight B. Heath, "Sexual Division of Labor and Cross-Cultural Research," *Social Forces* 37 (1958): 77–79; White, "Rethinking Polygyny"; Douglas R. White and Michael Burton, "Causes of Polygyny: Ecology, Economy, Kinship, and Warfare," *American Anthropologist* 90 (1988): 871–887; and Douglas R. White, Michael Burton, and Malcolm M. Dow, "Sexual Division of Labor in African Agriculture: A Network Autocorrelation Analysis," *American Anthropologist* 83 (1981): 824–849.

29. For the first published cross-cultural test of the relationship, see Table 3 in Heath, "Sexual Division of Labor and Cross-Cultural Research." For an analysis showing that the relationship Heath found between division of labor and polygyny is very weak, see Ember, "Alternative Predictors of Polygyny." For additional evidence showing that the relationship is weak, see White and Burton, "Causes of Polygyny," p. 880. For results suggesting that polygyny is more likely when men do more than women in subsistence, see Ember, "Alternative Predictors of Polygyny," p. 7. Finally, for results suggesting that the relationship changes direction in different types of subsistence economy, see Gary R. Lee, "Marital Structure and Economic Systems," *Journal of Marriage and the Family* 41 (1979): 701–713.

30. John W. M. Whiting, "Effects of Climate on Certain Cultural Practices," in *Explorations in Cultural Anthropology: Essays in Honor of George Peter Murdock*, ed. Ward H. Goodenough (New York: McGraw Hill, 1964), pp. 511–544.

31. Quoted in ibid., pp. 516–517.

32. Herbert Spencer, *Principles of Sociology*, vol. 1 (London: Appleton, 1876), as referred to by Robert L. Carneiro in his preface to *The Evolution of Society: Selections from Herbert Spencer's Principles of Sociology*, ed. Robert L. Carneiro (Chicago: University of Chicago Press, 1967), p. xiii.

33. Carol R. Ember and Melvin Ember, "Violence in the Ethnographic Record: Results of Cross-Cultural Research on War and Aggression," in *Troubled Times: Osteological and Archaeological Evidence of Violence*, eds. David Frayer and Debra Martin (Langhorne, PA: Gordon and Breach, in press).
34. Melvin Ember, "Warfare, Sex Ratio, and Polygyny," *Ethnology* 13 (1974): 197–206. Reprinted in Ember and Ember, *Marriage, Family, and Kinship*.
35. Ember and Ember, "Male-Female Bonding."
36. Ember, "Warfare, Sex Ratio, and Polygyny." Ember's conclusion would have been even more convincing had he been able to limit his comparison of sex ratios to people of marriageable age, since differences in age at death could also produce an excess of females. Consideration of ratio imbalances among people "at risk" of marriage produced by sex differences in age at marriage, perhaps economically (e.g., by a need to amass a large bride wealth) or politically (e.g., the demands of war), would undoubtedly have improved the finding. Unfortunately, however, age-specific measures are rarely obtainable from ethnographic accounts.
37. Ember, "Alternative Predictors of Polygyny," p. 119.
38. John W. M. Whiting, "The Effect of Polygyny on Sex Ratio at Birth," *American Anthropologist* 95 (1993): 435–442.
39. Ibid., p. 441.
40. Bobbi S. Low, "Marriage Systems and Pathogen Stress in Human Societies," *American Zoologist* 30 (1990): 325–339.
41. In this connection, Low refers to the work of R. Levins, *Evolution in Changing Environments: Some Theoretical Explorations* (Princeton, NJ: Princeton University Press, 1968); G. C. Williams, *Sex and Evolution* (Princeton, NJ: Princeton University Press, 1975); and Graham Bell, *The Masterpiece of Nature: The Evolution and Genetics of Sexuality* (Berkeley: University of California Press, 1982).
42. Low, "Marriage Systems and Pathogen Stress in Human Societies," p. 337.
43. Martha L. Munson and Larry L. Bumpass, "Determinants of Cumulative Fertility in Upper Volta, West Africa," *Working Paper* 73–76, mimeo (Madison: University of Wisconsin, 1973).
44. Moni Nag, "Marriage and Kinship in Relation to Human Fertility," in *Population and Social Organization*, ed. Moni Nag (The Hague: Mouton, 1975), pp. 11–54.
45. Burton Pasternak, *Guests in the Dragon: Social Demography of a Chinese District, 1895–1946* (New York: Columbia University Press, 1983).
46. George Peter Murdock, *Ethnographic Atlas* (Pittsburgh: University of Pittsburgh Press, 1967).
47. Ember, "Warfare, Sex Ratio, and Polygyny," p. 123.

48. Melvyn C. Goldstein, "Fraternal Polyandry and Fertility in a High Himalayan Valley in Northwest Nepal," *Human Ecology* 4 (1978): 325–337.

49. Ibid., p. 329.

50. Melvyn C. Goldstein, "Pahari and Tibetan Polyandry Revisited," *Ethnology* 17 (1978): 330, "Fraternal Polyandry and Fertility in a High Himalayan Valley in Northwest Nepal," "Culture, Population, Ecology, and Development: A View from Northwest Nepal" (Paris: Proceedings of C.N.R.S. International Conference on the Ecology of the Himalayas: The Life Sciences, 1977), and "Population, Social Structure, and Strategic Behavior: An Essay on Polyandry, Fertility, and Change in Limi Panchayat," *Contributions to Nepalese Studies* 4 (1977): 47–52.

51. Goldstein, "Pahari and Tibetan Polyandry Revisited," p. 330.

52. Goldstein, "Pahari and Tibetan Polyandry Revisited." One important source on the Pahari that Goldstein draws from is G. Berreman, "Himalayan Polyandry and the Domestic Cycle," *American Ethnologist* 2 (1975): 127–139.

53. Ibid., p. 333.

54. Ibid., pp. 330–331, 334.

55. Ibid., pp. 331–332.

5

MARRIAGE AND THE INCEST TABOO

In no society is marriage entirely a matter of individual choice. All societies have rules excluding some potential mates and favoring others. In our own society, we consider some people too "closely related" to have sex with and we eliminate them as possible marriage partners. Other people may be too old or too young to marry, or perhaps of the wrong family background. Many of us believe it is a good idea to marry people like ourselves— of the same religion, race, ethnic background, level of education—or at least people with similar attitudes, interests, and opinions. Are such restrictions and preferences characteristic of all cultures? How do they vary from culture to culture and why did these customs develop?

Two kinds of cultural rules may affect spouse selection. One kind has to do with permissible sexual behavior, the other with permissible marriage. We may put the matter this way: For a person to be marriageable, she or he must be someone with whom you may have sex; but just because no cultural rule prohibits sex with someone does not mean we may marry that person. A man of Brahmin caste could have sex with a Nayar woman, but could not marry her. While it may seem trivial, the failure to distinguish rules of sex from those of marriage can obscure aspects of marriage regulation, as we shall see when we explore why cousin marriage is permitted in some societies.

FORBIDDEN SEX: HOW UNIVERSAL IS THE INCEST TABOO?

Virtually all societies have customs restricting sex *and* marriage with people who are too closely related. We call such rules *incest taboos*. But precisely what sorts of people are "too closely related"? Would sex between a woman and her stepfather involve too close a relationship even though they are not related by blood? Further, what particular acts shall we consider incestuous? Apart from sexual intercourse, should we include acts that in themselves cannot lead to pregnancy, like fondling, genital manipulation, oral sex, perhaps even sleeping in the same bed? As a matter of fact, folk concepts display considerable variation from society to society in terms of which relatives (and other people) are too close for sex. There are striking differences as well in the specific behaviors people consider incestuous. Let us consider first whether there are any characteristics of incest regulation that are universal (or nearly so).

A pioneering attempt by George P. Murdock to systematically compare incest taboos around the world did reveal certain uniformities.[1] Most striking was the fact that sex (meaning sexual intercourse) is almost everywhere forbidden between blood relatives of opposite sex within the nuclear family (parent/child, brother/sister). Siblings did violate this proscription in a few societies, but usually only under special circumstances. Murdock noted that in precontact Inca society, as in old Hawaii and ancient Egypt, royalty could violate the taboo against sibling sex. Investigators have since discovered other exceptions. There is reason to believe that Sinhalese kings (in what is now Sri Lanka) once frequently married sisters. As a seventeenth-century account notes, "this manner of incest is allowable in kings, if it be only to beget a right royal issue, which can only be begotten that way. But in all other, 'tis held abominable, and severely punished."[2]

In at least one society, incestuous marriages were not only allowed, but fairly frequent: Commoners often practiced brother-sister marriage in Egypt during the Roman period (about 30 B.C. to A.D. 324).[3] Still, it remains true that brothers are not allowed to marry sisters in virtually any societies known to us. When royal brothers and sisters married, moreover, they were not necessarily biological siblings, children of the same parents. In old Hawaiian society, cousins were referred to as brothers and sisters (and parents' siblings were referred to as fathers and mothers). It should also be noted that while Egyptian rulers may have restricted royal succession to the children of a king or queen by his or her sibling, a king could also have offspring through unrelated polygynous wives. Relationships that we consider incestuous may be acceptable and even common elsewhere. For example, Margaret Mead tells us that it was the custom among the Arapesh of New Guinea for young girls to be raised as sisters to their future husbands:

> An Arapesh boy grows his wife. As a father's claim to his child is not that he has begotten it but rather that he has bed it, so also a man's claim to his wife's attention and devotion is not that he has paid a bride-price for her, or that she is legally his property, but that he has

actually contributed the food which has become flesh and bone of her body. A little girl is betrothed when she is seven or eight to a boy about six years her senior, and she goes to live in the home of her future husband. Here the father-in-law, the husband, and all of his brothers combine to grow the little bride.[4]

A similar arrangement was common in a region of northern Taiwan until the middle of the twentieth century. There, couples adopted daughters in infancy and raised them as sisters to their future husbands. Such marriages were common even though people considered sex among siblings a serious violation of the incest taboo.[5] And, in nineteenth-century America, Mormons had rather permissive attitudes about incest even among blood relatives, unions that were not uncommon. Indeed, in Utah there were no laws against incest until 1892.[6] That may have been because the number of possible mates was severely limited. As we shall see later in this chapter, marriage with first cousins often finds acceptance in very small societies (less than one thousand people), but is forbidden in most societies known to anthropology.

Exceptional cases aside, the reasons that virtually all societies prohibit sex and marriage within the *nuclear family* between parent and child and brother and sister, and also extend the taboo to other relatives, have been elusive. Almost all societies prohibit sex and marriage with some relatives outside the nuclear family, but there is much variation and it is difficult to predict which types of union will be forbidden in terms of biological closeness alone. Consider some examples. A number of accounts describing customs in Chinese communities during the early decades of the twentieth century report that a woman could marry her father's sister's son, and in some instances that was a preferred form of marriage. But marriage with other first cousins was not acceptable. Arab Bedouin and Kurds in the Middle East, like the Chinese, trace descent *patrilineally* (through the male line) but, according to their customs, people prefer marriage with a paternal uncle's son (father's brother's son) and no other cousin.[7] And among the *matrilineal* Akan of Africa's Gold and Ivory Coasts, a woman may marry her paternal aunt's son, but not her maternal aunt's son since he is of her clan.[8] Both, of course, are first cousins.

There is also considerable variation when it comes to marriage with relatives other than cousins. We would not look favorably on marriage with a paternal or maternal aunt or uncle but, as Murdock found, a woman can wed her brother's son among the Marquesans and Yaruro. Among the Osset and Sema, she can marry her sister's son. Although Murdock conflates rules of marriage and sex, marital preferences do have implications for sex. If a girl can marry her father's sister's son, sex with him must be allowable. And even though it is commonly the case that societies discourage sex with relatives we are not allowed to marry, it may nonetheless occur. We shall have more to say about cousin marriage and marriage with other relatives in the next chapter on "Extension of the Incest Taboo."

While there is much room for variation when it comes to extension of the incest taboo beyond primary relatives, it would be a mistake, as we shall see, to conclude that biological closeness has nothing whatever to do with the incest taboo or its extension. But first let us consider another cross-cultural generality reported by Murdock—that disapproval is stronger for incest with closer rather than with more distant relatives, even where people refer to the latter using terms for primary relatives. This suggests that people do distinguish between what we call *classificatory fathers, mothers, brothers, and sisters* in terms of degree of biological closeness.

EXPLAINING THE INCEST TABOO

Why do virtually all societies prohibit sex between primary relatives? Why do they so variably extend the taboo beyond the nuclear family? And why is the reaction to incest usually stronger than to other sexual offenses? We turn now to various attempts to answer these questions.

FORCING ALLIANCES

A common proposal has been that the incest taboo is universal because it forces adaptive connections, or *alliances*, between families. During the late nineteenth century, the British anthropologist E. B. Tylor phrased this explanation in the following much quoted way: "Again and again in the world's history, savage tribes must have had plainly before their minds the simple practical alternative between marrying-out and being killed out."[9] Much later, Leslie A. White, too, proposed that "incest is defined and prohibited in order to effect exogamous unions so that mutual aid may be fostered and, consequently, life made more secure for the members of society."[10] Albeit from a very different theoretical perspective, Claude Lévi-Strauss claimed much the same thing:

> The complete set of marriage regulations operating in human societies, and usually classified under different headings, such as incest prohibitions, preferential forms of marriage, and the like, can be interpreted as being so many different ways of insuring the circulation of women within the social group or of substituting the mechanism of a sociologically determined affinity for that of a biologically determined consanguinity.[11]

But, in fact, marriage does not invariably promote interfamilial harmony. Indeed, it is customary in some societies for people to find spouses in the villages of *their enemies*, and there is little evidence that marriage terminates or reduces hostility between villages.[12] Still, because incest taboos do require out-marriage, they may confer demographic and economic advantages, if not military ones. As Marvin Harris observed,

> the first consequence [of marrying out]…is a pooling of the reproductive and sexual potential of the constituent units. All the subgroups benefit reproductively since imbalance in the number of males and females produced by momentarily unfavorable birth and death rates can be evened out and demographic crises, which might prove fatal to isolated groups, can be overcome.[13]

PROMOTING FAMILY HARMONY

In accounting for the near universality of incest taboos, others focus less on the alliances they produce than on their contribution to harmony within families. In this view, incest taboos help avoid discord within society's basic building blocks. Embracing "without reservation" Freud's notion that incest "is a definite temptation within the family," Bronislaw Malinowski believed that were we to allow people to satisfy these incestuous desires, the result would be psychological and sociological disruption:

> Sex, with its accompaniment of courtship, jealousies, and competitions, is not compatible with the attitude of reverence and submission characteristic of child-to-parent relations. It is not compatible with the protective, sober and cooperative relations between brothers and sisters. On the social side, sex with its intrinsic rivalries and jealousies would also induce chaos. Hence the elimination of the sexual motive from the family, and from its extended counterpart, the kinship group or the clan, is a fundamental need of social structure, primitive and civilized alike.[14]

While the incest taboo may contribute to survival by linking families and reducing the risk of chaos within them, it would be a mistake to conclude that it is universal solely because it can perform these functions. For one thing, that would assume a connection between marriage and sex that may be unwarranted. Is it necessarily the case that sex within the family would preclude out-marriage or precipitate unmanageable conflict? Consider the fact that family members *do* share sexual partners in many societies. In most, as a matter of fact, women may share a common husband. In a few, brothers and even father and sons can share a spouse (so long as she is not the sons' biological mother). This was the case in traditional Tibet. Wife sharing has also been reported among the Bushmen, where extramarital sex was forbidden unless to entertain an age mate of the husband.[15] We also find sexual sharing within Yanomamö families:

> There was speculation that Kaobawa was planning to give Kaomashima to one of his younger brothers who had no wife; he occasionally allows

his younger brother to have sex with Kaomashima, but only if he asks in advance. Kaobawa gave another wife to one of his other brothers because she was *beshi* ("horny").[16]

While shared sex may arouse jealousy, not sharing could be even more disruptive where mates are hard to come by. The introduction of an outsider at marriage can also put a strain on family harmony. In any event, it has not been conclusively shown that sharing sex inevitably leads to family disruption or disintegration; if it did, 70 percent of the societies known to anthropology would not allow polygamy (almost always polygyny). Unregulated sex within the family may well be disruptive, but forbidding all sex is not the only conceivable way to regulate sexual access. It could be done in serial fashion, by stipulating in advance the time, place, and amount of access each family member has to every other member. Competition could be minimized by posting schedules and rosters, or even by assigning access according to phases of the moon. The reader might object, at this point, that none of these alternatives would require the out-marriage so many consider essential to our survival. Yet, why couldn't we require family exogamy (out-marriage) and still permit sex among family members? Why assume, as many clearly do, that people would be unwilling to release family members with whom they had sex? One anthropologist went so far as to speculate that

> the prohibition of incest...is...based on an anticipation of the loss of females. To prohibit sex, of course, does not abolish all emotional ties of parents to children and brother to sister, but certainly the consequences would be much greater if sexual relations had obtained among any of them.[17]

If sex really created such powerful emotional bonds, prostitutes would find few takers and would themselves soon marry. The rules governing sex and marriage do not correspond in so simple a fashion. As noted earlier, an Indian of highest (Brahmin) caste may have sex with a lower caste woman *he is not allowed to marry*. People may tolerate sex across racial, ethnic, or religious boundaries but criticize, even condemn, marriage across the same boundaries. Among the Rukuba of Nigeria, premarital sex involved individuals who could not marry, and married men might give their wives in marriage to others.[18] In former times, Eskimo sometimes exchanged wives when men were good friends and knew each other well. Some Eskimo men were said to be reluctant to marry because they liked the sexual liberty that went with being unmarried.[19] (But, of course, not being married does not necessarily imply a high frequency of sex.) In short, while the incest taboo may reduce the potential for conflict within the primary family, and while it requires that we find spouses in other families, both functions could be accomplished in other ways. So there must be other reasons that the incest taboo is the preferred solution in virtually all societies known to anthropology.

SHORT-CIRCUITING PSYCHOLOGICAL ATTRACTION

Another explanation, alluded to above, links the taboo to presumably universal psychological processes or needs. Most familiar is the notion that primary relatives of opposite sex have a *propensity* for sexual relations. This view has been embraced by many social scientists including, to mention only a few, Sir James Frazer, Sigmund Freud, Claude Lévi-Strauss, and Leslie A. White.[20] All argued that we find the incest taboo everywhere because it promotes social cohesion necessary for survival by thwarting sexual desire among primary relatives.

We noted this idea in an earlier citation from the work of Bronislaw Malinowski, but it is perhaps most associated with Sigmund Freud, who actually offered two versions. According to one, incest taboos emerge from a universal *Oedipus complex* (after the character in Greek legend who killed his father and married his mother). From birth, one's mother is the source of all gratification. She relieves hunger and satisfies our need for movement and physical comfort. As sensual and sexual interests emerge, we naturally address them to parents or other opposite-sex family members. Thus, a female becomes attracted to her father or brother, a son to his mother and sister.

But, so the argument goes, proximity from infancy engenders desire that might, if unchecked, generate disruptive jealousies. It could pit a young male against his father, the authority figure upon whom he depends, and a young woman against her mother. For personal safety and the good of familial and societal order, such desire must be repressed or driven into the subconscious, Freud said. Incest taboos are universal, then, because they thwart such desires, and the universal horror of incest reflects the repression of the incestuous impulse.[21] We protest "too much" (as Shakespeare said) what we refuse to ourselves.

In *Totem and Taboo*, Freud offers another, pseudo-historical version of his theory. He speculates that during the earliest stages of human existence, society consisted of very small, father-dominated groups. The father monopolized all females, driving his sons out as they approached sexual maturity. "One day," wrote Freud, "the expelled brothers joined forces, slew and ate the father, and thus put an end to the father horde. Together they dared and accomplished what would have remained impossible for them singly."[22] Having murdered and eaten their father, the brothers experienced remorse and guilt and, for that reason, agreed not to divide up their father's females. By mechanisms unstated, people passed that resolve from generation to generation and people to people; hence the universal incest taboo.

There are some problems with this formulation. Among other primates, dominant males do not invariably prevent younger, weaker ones from copulating with available females. Why should our ancestors have been different? Even if they were, why would patricidal brothers have experienced guilt after removing the source of their frustration, why would guilt have prompted renunciation of family females, and how would their original sin and renunciation have found their way into universal rules? Most important perhaps: Where are the women in all this? Were they simply passive, with no sexual desires of their own and no capability of rejecting advances?

ACCOMMODATING NATURAL AVERSIONS

Although his historical reconstruction is less than satisfactory, we cannot as easily dismiss Freud's explanation of the taboo in terms of repressed attraction. There are counterindications, however. Particularly challenging is accumulating evidence of a predisposition to *avoid* sex with close relatives. There is reason to believe that, *even without cultural rules*, primates raised together from infancy, non-human as well as human, are likely to avoid sex.[23] There is evidence, for example, of de facto incest avoidance among chimpanzees, our close primate relatives. One observer reports that "behavioral incest avoidance is well developed" among them.[24] Another confirms avoidance of sex between siblings, mother-son, and father-daughter.[25] In the course of long-term observations at Gombe National Park, Jane Goodall observed only three cases of mother-son copulation among chimps, and in two the "mother protested violently, screamed, [and] pulled away prior to ejaculation."[26] But primates are not the only animals that avoid parent-child and sibling incest. There is reason to believe most vertebrate animals do so.[27]

Edward Westermarck, an early proponent of the aversion hypothesis, suggested that long-term, early, and intimate association—the sort of familiarity associated with having been brought up and socialized in the same family—dampens sexual interest.[28] While close kin are most likely to develop such familiarity, others may as well. One may be raised with a foster brother, for example, or with a parent's companion. The key is intimate association, not necessarily kinship.[29] Westermarck was not alone in suggesting that the incest taboo reflects aversion. In *Primitive Society*, Robert H. Lowie went even further, suggesting that avoidance has an "instinctive" or "biological" basis, a daring and unpopular proposal in its time.[30] There may, indeed, be a physical underpinning to avoidance, but that is not essential to Westermarck's position. While not hostile to the idea, Westermarck stressed situational and psychological factors as leading to avoidance.[31]

Attributing incest taboos, or any other cultural rules, to instinct or biological causes has long been unpopular among anthropologists. Skeptical about facile biological, especially racial, explanations of behavior, anthropologists from early in the twentieth century rejected all *reductionist* explanations of human behavior.[32] The more accepted view was that humans differ from other animals in crucial qualitative ways, one of the most important of which was that our behavior is largely invented and learned rather than completely genetic or imprinted. Writers took pains to distance humans from other animals, noting that only humans make and use tools and communicate symbolically through spoken language. Only humans have culture; only we create, learn, and transmit behavior extra-somatically in the course of our social interactions. Here is an eloquent illustration of this position from the work of Alfred Kroeber:

> One might compare the inception of civilization to the end of the process of slowly heating water. The expansion of the liquid goes on a long time. Its alteration can be observed by the thermometer as well as in bulk, in its solvent power as well as in its internal agitation. But it remains water. Finally, however, the boiling point is attained. Steam is produced: The rate of enlargement of volume is increased a thousand fold, and in place of a glistening, percolating fluid, a volatile gas diffuses invisibly...the slow transitions that accumulated from zero to one hundred have been transcended in an instant, and a condition of substance with new properties and new possibilities of effect is in existence.[33]

In light of what we have learned since these words were written, however, the boiling water analogy seems overdrawn. We now realize that our species did not begin to move about bipedally, make tools, and communicate linguistically all at once. There was no single "missing link" between ape-like animals and ourselves; the gradual transformation to humanness as we know it required an extended period of time, perhaps millions of years, with substantial time gaps between our achievement of bipedalism, the expansion of our brains, the invention of tool kits, and the development of true language. Nor are we the only animals that adjust behavior to environmental challenges, or learn and transmit knowledge in the course of social interactions. Recent experiments with chimps and gorillas provide some reason to believe that we may not even be the only ones capable of symbolic and referential communication; chimps and gorillas can learn and use nonvocal ways (e.g., sign language) to communicate, and parrots can even vocalize symbolically.

The general rejection of simplistic racial and biological explanations of cultural behavior accounts for the hostility initially accorded Westermarck's hypothesis. Most anthropologists preferred the view that the incest taboo is a purely cultural phenomenon, perhaps the single invention that most clearly separated us from other animals, as the following passage from the work of Lévi-Strauss suggests:

> If social organization had a beginning this could only have consisted in the incest prohibition since…the incest prohibition is, in fact, a kind of remodeling of the biological conditions of mating and procreation (which know no rule, as can be seen from observing animal life) compelling them to become perpetuated only in an artificial framework of taboos and obligations. It is there, and only there, that we find a passage from nature to culture, from animal to human life.[34]

But recent fieldwork among human and other primates, and experimental research as well, has rekindled interest in Westermarck's ideas (which do not necessarily involve culture). Drawing upon data from a region of northern Taiwan, for example, Arthur P. Wolf has evaluated the explanatory power of attraction and aversion approaches to the incest taboo.[35] He describes a form of marriage (*minor marriage*), once commonplace, in which the bride entered her future husband's home as an adopted infant. Growing up as siblings, the pair experienced precisely the sort of prolonged intimate association Westermarck felt would produce sexual aversion. If Westermarck's understanding was correct, these marriages should have been less satisfactory than the more prestigious *major marriages*, which did not involve childhood association. In those, a woman joined her husband's family only after marriage. If early intimate association really engendered (rather than reduced) attraction, Wolf reasoned, the minor kind of marriage might even be preferred by those about to marry.

In fact, Wolf's data indicated strong resistance to minor marriage on the part of potential spouses, notwithstanding the fact that such marriages did not violate any Chinese incest taboo. People often expressed the view that minor marriages were "embarrassing" and "uninteresting." Wolf captures the resistance of those who had to marry in this fashion in descriptions offered by his informants:

> He had to stand outside of the door of their room with a stick to keep the newlyweds from running away; another man's adopted daughter did run away to her natal family and refused to return until her father beat her; a third informant who had arranged minor marriages for both of his sons described their reactions this way: "I had to threaten them with my cane to make them go in there, and then I had to stand there with my cane to make them stay."[36]

Minor marriages had significantly higher rates of divorce and adultery than major marriages. Perhaps a more direct indication of sexual disinterest is the fact that minor married women also had lower fertility. Their husbands were far more likely to visit "dark rooms" in town, where prostitutes offered their services. Replicating elements of Wolf's comparison in two other Taiwanese localities, one of your authors (Pasternak) also found that minor marriages more often end in divorce than do ordinary, major marriages. As expected, minor married women were also less fertile in one of his sites. In the other, where the two forms of marriage did not differ in fertility, people adopted girls for minor marriage not in infancy but only shortly before marriage. In terms of Westermarck's hypothesis, then, minor marriages should not have had lower fertility there.[37]

We find additional support for the Westermarck hypothesis in Lebanese data. There, the preferred form of marriage is with father's brother's son, with whom a girl is raised as sibling, in intimate childhood association. J. McCabe found these marriages more prone to divorce. They also produce fewer children than first-cousin marriages lacking early intimacy.[38] In addition, studies of the Israeli kibbutz indicate that children socialized in the same peer groups do not marry as adults even though they are permitted, even encouraged, to do so.[39]

Some writers have found fault with Westermarck's theory on the basis of comparisons involving different degrees of familiarity in social units larger than families (e.g., communities). In a test of Westermarck's theory, Melvin Ember predicted that, if Westermarck were right, societies with *endogamous* communities (i.e., where people find marriage partners within their community) should more likely prohibit all cousin marriage than where communities are not endogamous. In endogamous communities, all of one's cousins would likely be living in the same community and might therefore be familiar to each other. Where communities are not endogamous, however, people should be less likely to prohibit all cousin marriage since most, living elsewhere, would be "quite unfamiliar."[40] Ember further hypothesized that, if Westermarck's theory were correct, locally endogamous societies with smaller (and therefore presumably more familiar) communities should be less likely to allow first-cousin marriage than those with larger communities.

It turned out that the data from Ember's study, and from a later one by William H. Durham, failed to support these expectations derivable from Westermarck's theory.[41] But do these tests really contradict Westermarck's theory? The first author (Pasternak) thinks not. The problem with any such tests, and with concluding that the Israeli data support Westermarck as well, is that Westermarck's theory involves a narrower meaning of *familiarity* than the one used in the tests referred to. Westermarck limited the term to intimate, long-term, early, multifaceted relations—essentially to relations within the *family*, not the community. The aversion to sex with primary relatives presumably arises from having been brought up and socialized in the same domestic unit. Wolf puts the matter succinctly:

> The socialization process inevitably involves a good deal of punishment and pain, and children who are socialized together must come to asso-

ciate one another with this experience.... Because all human societies demand that children learn to control strong aggressive impulses toward other members of their family, we might expect people everywhere to exhibit an aversion to the possibility of satisfying sexual desires within the family.[42] [The reader should note that this argument assumes a link between aggressive and sexual impulses.]

A more appropriate test of Westermarck's hypothesis might be to see how cousin marriage preferences (and prohibitions) in societies with extended families (which contain cousins) compare with cousin marriage possibilities in societies of similar size that have only nuclear families (only one set of parents and children in the family). But that remains a task for the future.

Also to be considered is the possibility that long-term intimacy within the family may discourage sexual activity *even without early, common socialization*. This might explain why neither Ember's nor Durham's comparison of endogamous and exogamous communities supported Westermarck's view, while the Israeli data do. Kibbutz children are not simply raised in the same community, but in the same nursery, by the same teachers, often sleeping in the same dormitory as well. They grow up much as if they belonged to the same intimate family. Not so in endogamous Chinese communities. There, familiarity is circumscribed and limited despite the fact that couples grow up in the same community. Parker suggests a different, and somewhat broader, notion of familiarity:

A clear functional relationship exists between sexual activity and central neural mechanisms involved in processes not specific to sex. Satiation tests with mammalian species indicate that sexual activity often declines when mates are not changed over long periods and, conversely, a sharp increase in activity results from periodic mate rotation. Innate propensities of the nervous system are reinforced by cultural rules of mate selection and reduce either the probability of boredom and habituation that accompanies familiarity, or the high level of anxiety associated with the very strange. It is likely that such factors influence reinforcement contingencies in mate selection and incest avoidance in humans and other animals.[43]

A recent survey of Canadian students provides support for Westermarck's hypothesis. Bevc and Silverman compared students reporting sibling incest with a matched sample reporting no such experiences. They found that separation for more than a year during the first six years was related to *consummatory behaviors* (sexual activities culminating in anal, oral, or attempted or actual genital intercourse), but not to nonconsummatory sexual activities. On this basis they propose a modification to Westermarck's hypothesis, namely that early sustained association does not necessarily decrease sexual interest, but it does create a barrier to more mature forms of sexual activity; that is, it keeps sexual encounters between siblings at an exploratory, non-consummatory level and thus reduces procreative potential.[44]

There is substantial indication of strong inhibitions against pair formation involving parents and their young, or litter mates, in most species of vertebrates.[45] Observations and experiments involving humans and lower animals suggest that sexual excitation may be linked to aggressive or assertive reactions. If either the sexual or agonistic response is altered, the other is as well and in the same direction. There is even reason to suspect that this *sexual-agonistic linkage* may be neurologically reinforced.[46] If that is so, it would challenge the position most anthropologists have taken since the early twentieth century. In their disapproval of racist, economic, geographical, or other noncultural explanations of behavior, anthropologists have generally dismissed suggestions that cultural behavior might have even partially biological origins.

How could incest taboos reflect physical concerns when people do not always consider biological closeness when they marry? In some societies a father's sister's son is a suitable mate, but not a mother's brother's son. In others the reverse is true. How could biology matter, given that some people are reportedly even unaware of the relationship between sexual intercourse and reproduction? Malinowski reported, for example, that Trobriand Islanders believe men provide a passage for spirits to enter a woman's body, there to assume human form.[47] The Rapan, in French Polynesia, think conception requires coalescence in the uterus of blood and semen.[48] To prevent unwanted births, then, they avoid sex during and just after menstruation, reserving it for the period between menstrual periods.

That some people do not understand the mechanisms of reproduction, that even among us some may believe babies come from sitting on warm toilets, does not justify discounting a connection in peoples' minds between incest and negative outcomes. In most societies people do have a working notion of the mechanisms, and even those who may not are not without capacity to borrow ideas from others. In a recent cross-cultural study, William H. Durham found that a majority of the world's populations recognize the "deleterious phenotypic effects of inbreeding." Of those expressing awareness, about 73 percent prohibit or punish incestuous sex; 40 percent mention supernatural sanctions, most commonly disease or death; and 50 percent indicate that incest leads to "bad stock," a clear indication they are aware of deleterious physical consequences.[49] (For more discussion of the biological advantage of the incest taboo, see the next section.) Moreover, the fact that incest taboos do not everywhere apply to the same relatives outside the nuclear family does not mean that biological considerations have no weight. As Robert H. Lowie long ago observed, the taboo could originate within the nuclear family for one set of reasons and extend to other relatives variably for other (conventional) reasons.[50]

Even without reference to genetic or neurological inducements, there may be, as Westermarck and Wolf among others suggest, a *propensity for avoidance* that intimate early association triggers. Of course, this would not be inconsistent with the possibility that our bodies are also programmed for avoidance. That some people violate incest taboos in all societies, and the possibility that sociological and ecological factors may dispose against close inbreeding, is no proof that biological factors do not reinforce propensities in the same direction. Just because we may flee from threat does not mean we must, or always do so. Culture may channel responses in directions more useful to family and community; a set of individual decisions can be a collective act of heroism.

After reviewing the studies of human and other animals, Seymour Parker concluded that there is ample evidence of a relationship between the degree of complexity and novelty of stimuli, and level of arousal, exploratory behavior, and aesthetic pleasure. He summarizes it as follows:

> This model indicates that, given the nature of the nervous system and its mode of processing information, there is an optimal level of arousal and physiological activation below and above which sexual pleasure, curiosity, exploration, and aesthetic value will be progressively reduced to a point of indifference or even negative valence.... Innate propensities of the nervous system are reinforced by cultural rules of mate selection and reduce either the probability of boredom and habituation that accompanies familiarity, or the high level of anxiety associated with the very strange.[51]

It is important to reiterate that the proposition that underlying physical (biological) realities may influence our behavior does not imply concession to a reductionist position, to one that disregards the role of ecological and cultural factors. Indeed Parker emphasizes that if we are to understand mate selection or the incest taboo in humans, we must grasp the relationship between both endogenous and sociocultural factors:[52]

> It has been maintained that the familiarity or strangeness (complexity, incongruity, etc.) of stimuli influences the degree of activation and arousal in the organism. This in turn influences the experience of curiosity, efficiency in information processing, and hedonic tone [i.e., aesthetic pleasure]. The coincidence of optimal arousal, the cultural attribution of appropriateness, and social approval increases the probability of *falling in love*. Schachter, in his discussion of the determinants of emotional states, notes that "an emotional state may be considered a function of a state of physiological arousal and of a cognition appropriate to this state of arousal. The cognition, in a sense, exerts a steering function." Metaphorically speaking, the arousal level provides a

priming mechanism for sexual mate selection, while cultural rules provide the steering function. The process of natural selection has probably resulted in a strain toward a "fit" between these two sets of phenomena and optimal reproductive potential.[53]

Our neurological wiring may incline us to avoid sex without requiring that we do so, which might explain how people may sometimes violate the taboo. Westermarck suggested that we "not forget that a lack of desire, and even a positive feeling of aversion, may in certain circumstances be overcome."[54] In his view, the taboo "expresses the general feelings of the community and punishes acts that shock them, but it does not tell us whether an inclination to commit the forbidden act is felt by many or by few." Although some individuals desire what most people find obnoxious, "aversions which are generally felt readily lead to moral disapproval."[55] More recently, Patrick Bateson observed that, "fear of the unusual prompts the majority to prohibit actions to which they feel averse."[56] Rejecting the notion that a strong prohibition against behavior necessarily signals an *inclination* toward that behavior, Westermarck asked if we are to assume that the severity with which we treat parricide reflects a general desire to kill our parents.[57]

Still, if some do overcome the general distaste for incestuous sex, why should they be prevented from having such sex? Even granting a situational, possibly neurophysiological underpinning to avoidance, why should societies need rules prohibiting, and often also sanctions against, behavior that most people find uninviting or morally offensive? William H. Durham recently observed that, "incest does recur with sufficient frequency to ensure periodic reinforcement of local taboos, even in the face of aversion and moral disapproval."[58] In other words, the inclination to avoid sex with close relatives with whom one has grown up is not shared by all, so it cannot account for the near universality of incest taboos, or for variations in their extension outside the primary family, to siblings that have been raised elsewhere (perhaps as adopted children), or to people not related by blood (e.g., adopted children or stepparents). Nor can it account for the repugnance most people feel when confronted by violations of these community sensitivities. Perhaps other functions of the incest taboo will shed some light. Parker put the matter this way:

> Incest avoidance, as a behavioral propensity already existing among primates and lower mammal forms, provided for the reduction of what might have been "crippling" sexual competition in familistic units requiring cooperation. As the cultural way of life became established, additional adaptive pressures arose for this biopsychological tendency to become institutionalized as the incest taboo, because it increased the stability of the family unit, assured wider social alliances, and reduced the number of births to economically immature individuals. The incest

taboo is (by definition) a cultural phenomenon and can be explained by cultural events. But like other sociocultural aspects it is "built upon" biopsychological needs, potentials, and propensities of the organism.... Speaking teleologically, culture uses psychobiological potentials for its own purposes and can never be fully explained by the latter. Incest avoidance was certainly not a sufficient condition for explaining the incest taboo, and it may not even have been a necessary condition—it was, however, a facilitating condition. The incest taboo constitutes learned behavior, and as such is subject to principles of learning as is any other cultural item. However, insofar as it is motivated partly by biological propensities of the organism, it is easier to learn because it is subject to additional (aside from cultural) reinforcements from intraorganismic sources.[59]

BIOLOGICAL ADVANTAGE OF THE TABOO

Although anthropologists resisted the idea for years, an impressive body of data has emerged indicating that close inbreeding usually has deleterious genetic consequences, at least in recent populations.[60] There is also reason to believe that outbreeding has positive consequences in that it "increases potentially adaptive variations in the gene pool."[61] Despite the evidence in favor of the view that close inbreeding has negative consequences, some continue to insist that genetic factors can account only for the persistence and spread of incest taboos, not for their emergence. For example, Marvin Harris observed that,

> as far as a *population* is concerned, inbreeding may produce a higher death rate but it may also lead to the gradual elimination of more of the deleterious recessive genes that would be the case if completely random mating prevailed. In other words, if an inbreeding group is able to overcome the higher rate at which homozygotes initially appear, it will eventually reach a genetic equilibrium involving a lowered percentage of lethal genes. It has often been pointed out that the effects of close inbreeding in a small group are largely a matter of the original frequency of lethal and deleterious genes.[62]

In other words, while close inbreeding may have deleterious consequences in recent populations, it may not have had them in earlier ones. If the demographic characteristics of early people (e.g., short life spans, few children, high mortality and morbidity) allowed for a "weeding out" process, then early gene pools might have included few lethal recessive genes and there would have been less danger in inbreeding. The point is that if incest taboos had not been imposed initially, potentially deleterious genes might have been fewer and inbreeding would not have been so maladaptive. Even lacking incest taboos, early humans may have sought mates outside the family and local group simply because there were too few potential individuals of appropriate sex and age available locally.[63] Because contemporary populations do not permit inbreeding, lethal recessives are not as effectively weeded out and, were we suddenly to begin inbreeding, the likelihood of these genes combining would be increased.

Along the same lines, Melvin Ember suggested that humans may not have invented incest taboos until after learning to domesticate plants and animals (some ten thousand years ago).[64] Domestication opened the way for population expansion. Potentially deleterious recessives could accumulate because the chance likelihood of close inbreeding decreased as population expanded. Ember further speculated that Neolithic peoples may have deliberately adopted the familial incest taboo and purposely extended it to other relatives because they realized on the basis of experience what might happen if they did not. His algebraic modeling suggests that the difference in reproductive success between consanguineous and nonconsanguineous mating could well have been large enough to have been noticed during the initial stages of population growth, when the chance likelihood of close inbreeding was still relatively great.

But whether or not people recognize it, the likelihood of maladaptive consequences rises when recessive genes are concentrated, and the closer the inbreeding the greater the risk. Close inbreeding is problematic *even if the parties do not consider their relationship incestuous*, that is, even when their relationship does not constitute a breach of incest taboos. This was one finding in a study of Moroccan Jewish immigrants in Israel, a group who considered uncle-niece inbreeding legal and nonincestuous.[65] As the following passage indicates, some believe that concern about negative physical consequences, while probably not the only motivation for incest taboos, may be the most important reason that virtually all societies prohibit sex among primary relatives:

> We propose that the adoption of the familial incest taboo was adaptive primarily because of the genetic results of close inbreeding...and [the] familial taboo is to be considered part of the class of devices which limit familial inbreeding among intelligent, slow-maturing animals which bear few offspring at a time and which live in family units. The selection of the taboo, however, we hypothesize, occurred through efforts to solve the problem of sexual competition within the family in a cultural animal with an organized family life. Among the available mechanisms, the incest taboo solved this problem and the genetic problem. Other alternatives solved only one of these problems.... The familial taboo could be extended, by a simple evolutionary step, to a wider group of kinsmen, with great selective advantage.[66]

Although people may not know what genes are and how they work, close examination of native accounts suggests that people in many, if not all, places are aware that incest is likely to have undesired biological consequences. On the basis of a study of such accounts, Durham notes that, "even a strong aversion has less emotional impact than does sterility, death, and deformed children." Still, incest taboos are cultural rules we create, carry in our heads, and pass to our children in the course of raising them. And these rules may not reflect only biological connections. As Durham expressed it,

> incest and inbreeding must be viewed as different; there can be both nonincestuous inbreeding (as when sexual intercourse between certain categories of kin is not prohibited) and noninbred incest (as when prohibitions apply between parents and their adopted or step children).[67]

Thus, Bedouin custom permits, even prefers, that a girl marry her father's brother's son (but no other first cousin) despite the fact that he is closely related. In other instances of incest, blood ties may be tenuous, even nonexistent. One anthropologist witnessed a ceremony to expiate an act of "sibling" incest among the Mnong Gar of Vietnam. The offending "brother" and "sister" (as they were referred to by the kinship terminology) had to taste the excrement of pig and dog although their actual relationship was based upon a common ancestor fifteen generations removed![68] Ethnography provides ample examples of vagueness when it comes to the relationship between sexual behavior and genealogical closeness. Further, there may be people in every society who do not appreciate the connection between copulation and conception. But, as Roger V. Burton pointed out, it may not be necessary that everyone appreciate the connection for society to embrace and endorse the incest taboo because

> a high frequency of defective infants born to women who had sexual relations with father, brother, or son could lead to and reinforce a belief that the gods were punishing that behavior. If production of defective children was attributable to supernatural causes, it is likely that the observers of the defective offspring would see the event as some kind of punishment or immanent justice. The rarity of intrafamilial incest would make this behavior likely to be noticed as different from what people usually do and thus likely to be considered the act that displeased the supernatural. It is this belief that would account for the intense, affective horror attached to incest. Furthermore, the transmission of such beliefs could occur without every member of the society personally observing the event.[69]

People may interpret the consequences of close inbreeding as expressions of a god's wrath for inappropriate relationships, sexual or otherwise, rather than in genetic terms. But that does not say that they are unaware of a relationship between sex and its consequences. Durham may be close to the truth when he suggests that people do recognize the major costs of inbreeding and outbreeding, including inbreeding depression and/or aversion where these are significant; that they interpret these costs in locally meaningful ways, including, but not limited to, the displeasure of supernaturals; and that they evaluate them accordingly, in terms of locally evolved cultural values.[70]

Once established, the familial incest taboo is a crucial element of social structure. For family members must then seek mates and arrange marriages outside their immediate families.

NOTES

1. George Peter Murdock, *Social Structure* (New York: The Free Press, 1965 [originally published 1949]), pp. 284–313.
2. Robert Knox, *An Historical Relation of Ceylon, 1681*, cited in Nur Yalman, *Under the Bo Tree: Studies in Caste, Kinship, and Marriage in the Interior of Ceylon* (Berkeley: University of California Press, 1971), p. 332.
3. A number of studies now recommend qualifying the assertion that incest taboos are universal. See, for example, R. M. May, "When to Be Incestuous," *Nature* 279 (1979): 192–194; D. Willner, "Definition and Violation: Incest and the Incest Taboos," *Man* 9 (1983): 134–159; Russell Middleton, "Brother-Sister and Father-Daughter Marriage in Ancient Egypt," *American Sociological Review* 27 (1962): 603–611; P. L. Van den Berghe and D. Barash, "Inclusive Fitness and Human Family Structure," *American Anthropologist* 79 (1977): 809–823; P. L. Van den Berghe and G. M. Mesher, "Royal Incest and Inclusive Fitness," *American Ethnologist* 7 (1980): 300–317; and Keith Hopkins, "Brother-Sister Marriage in Roman Egypt," *Comparative Studies in Society and History* 22 (1980): 303–354.
4. Margaret Mead, *Sex and Temperament in Three Primitive Societies* (New York: Mentor Books, 1950 [originally published 1935]), p. 65.
5. For extensive treatments of this institution in northern Taiwan, see Arthur P. Wolf, "Childhood Association, Sexual Attraction, and the Incest Taboo: A Chinese Case," *American Anthropologist* 68 (1966): 883–898, "Adopt a Daughter-In-Law, Marry a Sister: A Chinese Solution to the Problem of the Incest Taboo," *American Anthropologist* 70 (1968): 864–874, "Childhood Association and Sexual Attraction: A Further Test of the Westermarck Hypothesis," *American Anthropologist* 72 (1970): 503–515, and "The Women of Hai-shan: A Demographic Portrait," in *Women in Chinese Society*, eds. Margery Wolf and Roxane Witke (Stanford, CA: Stanford University Press, 1975), pp. 89–110; see also Arthur P. Wolf and Chieh-shan Huang,

Marriage and Adoption in China, 1845–1945 (Stanford, CA: Stanford University Press, 1980); and Margery Wolf, *The House of Lim: A Study of a Chinese Farm Family* (New York: Appleton-Century-Crofts, 1968).

6. Theodore Schroeder, "Incest in Mormonism," *American Journal of Urology and Sexology* 11 (1915): 415, cited in Gregory C. Leavitt, "Sociobiological Explanations of Incest Avoidance: A Critical Review of Evidential Claims," *American Anthropologist* 92 (1990): 973.

7. For differing interpretations of this kind of cousin marriage, see Fredrik Barth, "Father's Brother's Daughter Marriage in Kurdistan," *Southwestern Journal of Anthropology* 10 (1954): 164–171; and Robert F. Murphy and Leonard Kasdan, "The Structure of Parallel Cousin Marriage," *American Anthropologist* 61 (1959): 17–29.

8. J. W. A. Amoo, "The Effect of Western Influence on Akan Marriage," *Africa* 16 (1946): 228–237.

9. E. B. Tylor, "On a Method of Investigating the Development of Institutions: Applied to Laws of Marriage and Descent," *Journal of the Royal Anthropological Institute* 18 (1888): 267.

10. Leslie A. White, *The Science of Culture* (New York: Grove Press, 1949), pp. 158–159.

11. Claude Lévi-Strauss, *Structural Anthropology* (New York: Basic Books, Inc., 1963), p. 60.

12. Gay E. Kang, "Exogamy and Peace Relations of Social Units: A Cross-Cultural Test," *Ethnology* 18 (1979): 85–99.

13. Marvin Harris, *Culture, Man, and Nature* (New York: Thomas Y. Crowell, 1971), pp. 296–297.

14. Bronislaw Malinowski, *A Scientific Theory of Culture* (New York: Oxford University Press, 1960 [originally published 1944]), pp. 208–209; see also David F. Aberle, Urie Bronfenbrenner, Eckhard H. Hess, Daniel R. Miller, David M. Schneider, and James N. Spuhler, "The Incest Taboo and the Mating Patterns of Animals," *American Anthropologist* 65 (1963): 253–265.

15. John W. M. Whiting, "The Effect of Polygyny on Sex Ratio at Birth," *American Anthropologist* 95 (1993): 440.

16. Napoleon A. Chagnon, *Yanomamö* (New York: Harcourt Brace College Publishers, 1992), pp. 27–28.

17. Elman R. Service, *Primitive Social Organization* (New York: Random House, 1962), p. 46.

18. Jean-Claude Muller, "On Preferential/Prescriptive Marriage and the Function of Kinship Systems: The Rukuba Case (Benue-Plateau Site, Nigeria)," *American Anthropologist* 75 (1973): 1563–1576.

19. Norman A. Chance, *The Eskimo of North Alaska* (New York: Holt, Rinehart & Winston, 1966), pp. 49–50.

20. For other examples of the psychoanalytic approach to the incest

taboo, see Gardner Lindzey, "Some Remarks Concerning Incest, the Incest Taboo, and Psychoanalytic Theory," *American Psychologist* 22 (1967): 1051–1059; and Melford E. Spiro, *Oedipus in the Trobriands* (Chicago: University of Chicago Press, 1982).

21. Sigmund Freud, *A General Introduction to Psychoanalysis* (Garden City, NY: Garden City Publishing, 1943 [originally published in German, 1917]).

22. Sigmund Freud, *Totem and Taboo* (New York: New Republic, 1931), p. 247.

23. This is an issue not without controversy. For a review of the primate evidence that takes exception to the notion that incest is avoided, see Leavitt, "Sociobiological Explanations of Incest Avoidance." For more positive evaluations, see Seymour Parker, "The Precultural Basis of the Incest Taboo: Toward a Biosocial Theory," *American Anthropologist* 78 (1976): 285–305; and Jim Moore, "Sociobiology and Incest Avoidance: A Critical Look at a Critical Review," *American Anthropologist* 94 (1992): 929–934.

24. Jim Moore and Rauf Ali, "Are Dispersal and Inbreeding Avoidance Related?" *Animal Behavior* 32 (1984): 94–112.

25. Anne E. Pusey, "Inbreeding Avoidance in Chimpanzees," *Animal Behavior* 28 (1980): 543–582.

26. Jane Goodall, *The Chimpanzees of Gombe: Patterns of Behavior* (Cambridge, MA: Harvard University Press, 1986), pp. 466–467, quoted in Moore, "Sociobiology and Incest Avoidance," p. 931.

27. For a review of the animal literature, see Parker, "The Precultural Basis of the Incest Taboo."

28. Edward Westermarck, *The History of Human Marriage* (London: Macmillan, 1922).

29. See Seymour Parker, "The Waning of the Incest Taboo," *Legal Studies Forum* II, no. 2 (1987): 209.

30. Robert H. Lowie, *Primitive Society* (New York: Harper, 1961 [originally published 1920]), p. 15. For another early proponent of the aversion hypothesis, see Havelock Ellis, *Sexual Selection in Man* (Philadelphia: F. A. Davis, 1906).

31. For reviews of the evidence, see Seymour Parker, "Cultural Rules, Rituals, and Behavior Regulation," *American Anthropologist* 86 (1984): 584–600, and "The Precultural Basis of the Incest Taboo."

32. For a notable example, see White, *The Science of Culture*, p. 304.

33. Alfred Kroeber, *The Nature of Culture* (Chicago: University of Chicago Press, 1952), p. 50.

34. Harry L. Shapiro, "The Family," in *Man, Culture, and Society*, ed. Harry L. Shapiro (New York: Oxford University Press, 1956), p. 278.

35. Wolf, "Childhood Association, Sexual Attraction, and the Incest Taboo," "Adopt a Daughter In-Law, Marry a Sister," "Childhood

Association and Sexual Attraction," and "The Women of Hai-shan"; Wolf and Huang, *Marriage and Adoption in China, 1845–1945*.

36. Wolf, "Childhood Association and Sexual Attraction," p. 508.

37. Burton Pasternak, *Guests in the Dragon: Social Demography of a Chinese District, 1895–1946* (New York: Columbia University Press, 1983). For data on yet another Taiwanese community indicating that minor marriages are less successful than normal, patrilocal ones, see William Kester Barnett, "An Ethnographic Description of Sanlei Ts'un, Taiwan, with Emphasis on Women's Roles: Overcoming Research Problems Caused by the Presence of a Great Tradition" (Ph.D. diss., Michigan State University, 1970, University Microfilms Dissertation no. 71–2026. Ann Arbor: University Microfilms, 1971), p. 263.

38. J. McCabe, "FBD Marriage: Further Support for the Westermarck Hypothesis of the Incest Taboo?" *American Anthropologist* 85 (1983): 50–69.

39. Joseph Shepher, "Mate Selection among Second Generation Kibbutz Adolescents and Adults: Incest Avoidance and Negative Imprinting," *Archives of Sexual Behavior* 1 (1971): 293–307, and *Incest: A Biosocial View* (New York: Academic Press, 1983); Melford E. Spiro, "Is the Family Universal? The Israeli Case," *American Anthropologist* 56 (1954): 839–846, *Children of the Kibbutz* (Cambridge, MA: Harvard University Press, 1958), and *Gender and Culture: Kibbutz Women Revisited* (Durham: Duke University Press, 1979); Yonina Talmon, "Mate Selection in Collective Settlements," *American Sociological Review* 29 (1964): 491–508.

40. Melvin Ember, "On the Origin and Extension of the Incest Taboo," *Behavior Science Research* 10 (1975): 249–281. Reprinted in Melvin Ember and Carol R. Ember, *Marriage, Family, and Kinship: Comparative Studies of Social Organization* (New Haven: HRAF Press, 1983).

41. For a similar but differently controlled test of Westermarck's thesis, see William H. Durham, *Coevolution: Genes, Culture, and Human Diversity* (Stanford: Stanford University Press, 1991).

42. Wolf, "Childhood Association, Sexual Attraction, and the Incest Taboo," pp. 892–893.

43. Parker, "Cultural Rules, Rituals, and Behavior Regulation," p. 590.

44. Irene Bevc and Irwin Silverman, "Early Proximity and Intimacy between Siblings and Incestuous Behavior: A Test of the Westermarck Theory," *Ethology and Sociobiology* 14 (1993): 180.

45. A number of relevant citations are provided in Durham, *Coevolution*, including N. Bischof, "The Biological Foundations of the Incest Taboo," *Social Science Information* 11, no. 6 (1972): 7–36, and "Comparative Ethology of Incest Avoidance," in *Biosocial Anthropology*, ed. Robin Fox (New York: Malaby Press, 1975); W. G. Holmes and P. W. Sherman, "Kin Recognition in Animals," *American*

Scientist 71 (1983): 46–55; Parker, "The Precultural Basis of the Incest Taboo"; and A. F. Read and P. H. Harvey, "Genetic Relatedness and the Evolution of Animal Mating Patterns," in *Human Mating Patterns*, eds. C. G. N. Mascie-Taylor and A. J. Boyce (Cambridge, England: Cambridge University Press, 1988).

46. See Parker, "The Precultural Basis of the Incest Taboo." Other relevant references provided in Durham, *Coevolution*, include K. Kortmulder, "An Ethological Theory of the Incest Taboo and Exogamy," *Current Anthropology* 9 (1968): 437–449; W. J. Demarest, "Incest Avoidance among Human and Nonhuman Primates," in *Primate Bio-Social Development: Biological, Social, and Ecological Determinants*, eds. Suzanne Chevalier-Skolnicoff and Frank E. Poirier (New York: Garland Publishing, 1977); and Patrick Bateson, "Optimal Outbreeding," in *Mate Choice*, ed. Patrick Bateson (Cambridge, England: Cambridge University Press, 1983), and "Rules for Changing the Rules," in *Evolution from Molecules to Men*, ed. D. S. Bendall (Cambridge, England: Cambridge University Press, 1983).

47. Bronislaw Malinowski, *The Sexual Life of Savages* (London: George Rutledge, 1929), pp. 153ff, 171.

48. Allan F. Hanson, "The Rapan Theory of Conception," *American Anthropologist* 72 (1970): 1444–1447.

49. Durham, *Coevolution*, pp. 347–349.

50. Lowie, *Primitive Society*, p. 15; see also White, *The Science of Culture*, p. 304.

51. Parker, "Cultural Rules, Rituals, and Behavior Regulation," p. 590.

52. Ibid., p. 590.

53. Ibid., p. 595.

54. Westermarck, *The History of Human Marriage*, p. 201.

55. Ibid., p. 198.

56. Bateson, "Rules for Changing the Rules," p. 501.

57. Westermarck, *The History of Human Marriage*, pp. 203–204.

58. Durham, *Coevolution*, p. 349.

59. Parker, "The Precultural Basis of the Incest Taboo," p. 299.

60. Ember, "On the Origin and Extension of the Incest Taboo." See also Aberle et al., "The Incest Taboo and the Mating Patterns of Animals," pp. 253–265. For a review of recent literature on and discussion of inbreeding and its effects, see Durham, *Coevolution*, especially pp. 286–360.

61. Parker, "The Waning of the Incest Taboo," p. 207. For a contrary evaluation, see Leavitt, "Sociobiological Explanations of Incest Avoidance," a contribution that stimulated vigorous responses from Moore, "Sociobiology and Incest Avoidance," pp. 929–932; and Allon J. Uhlmann, "A Critique of Leavitt's Review of Sociobiological Explanations of Incest Avoidance," *American Anthropologist* 94

(1992): 446–448. Leavitt provided ripostes, "Inbreeding Fitness: A Reply to Uhlmann," *American Anthropologist* 94 (1992): 448–450, and "Sociobiology and Incest Avoidance: A Critical Look at a Critical Review Critique," *American Anthropologist* 94 (1992): 932–934.

62. Harris, *Culture, Man, and Nature*, p. 286; see also Leavitt, "Sociobiological Explanations of Incest Avoidance."

63. Miriam Slater, "Ecological Factors in the Origin of Incest," *American Anthropologist* 61 (1959): 1042–1059; see also Leavitt, "Sociobiological Explanations of Incest Avoidance." Not everyone accepts that early humans had demographic characteristics that limited mating within local groups. See Ember, "On the Origin and Extension of the Incest Taboo," and his suggestion that, even with low life expectancy, there would still be plenty of opportunity for incest in early human populations. For mathematical proof of this point, see Ruth C. Busch and James Gundlach, "Excess Access and Incest: A New Look at the Demographic Explanation of the Incest Taboo," *American Anthropologist* 79 (1977): 912–914; see also Uhlmann, "A Critique of Leavitt's Review of Sociobiological Explanations of Incest Avoidance."

64. Ember, "On the Origin and Extension of the Incest Taboo."

65. K. Fried and A. M. Davies, "Some Effects on the Offspring of Uncle-Niece Marriage in the Moroccan Jewish Community in Jerusalem," *American Journal of Human Genetics* 26 (1974): 65–72, referred to and elaborated upon in Durham, *Coevolution*, pp. 307–308.

66. Aberle et al., "The Incest Taboo and the Mating Patterns of Animals," p. 264.

67. Durham, *Coevolution*, p. 289.

68. Georges Condominas, "The Primitive Life of Vietnam's Mountain People," in *Man's Many Ways*, ed. R. A. Gould (New York: Harper & Row, 1973), pp. 199–226.

69. Roger V. Burton, "Folk Theory and the Incest Taboo," *Ethos* 1 (1973): 504–516, cited in Durham, *Coevolution*, p. 326.

70. Durham, *Coevolution*, pp. 337–338.

6

EXTENSION
OF THE INCEST TABOO

In all societies, people extend the incest taboo to some persons outside the primary or nuclear family. When we take a closer look at particular societies, however, we find considerable variation both in how people react to incest and with whom sex is incestuous. In Korea (during the early 1950s), people extended their strong aversion to incest within the nuclear family to sex and marriage between people of the same surname (clan name). One ethnographer reports an incident that clearly shows this repugnance:

> When a distant and prosperous relative of the same clan name with the same place of clan origin approached a restrained, scholarly father about the possibility of marriage with his daughter, he aroused such anger and disgust that he was struck with a sickle. He nearly died from his wound but took no legal action.[1]

That this father's revulsion was not unique or limited to marital sex, but applied to any sexual relationship, is indicated by other observers. Here is a description from another study (time: 1965). It should be noted that the couple in question were sent away in disgrace and an entire clan bore a burden of collective shame as a result of their incestuous liaison:

> A monumental scandal with explosive repercussions occurred in the village when it was discovered that two third cousins of the Yi lineage, who could of course never marry because of strict exogamy rules, had been regularly having sexual relations. The incident triggered a whole series of separate, though related disputes, most of which were between

members of the Yi clan and individuals from other kinship groups. People who had economic grievances or old resentments against the former yuangban [the Yi clan] brought up the matter as an example of moral degeneracy, and bitter quarrels resulted. There was even conflict among the Yi clan members regarding who was at fault and what measures should have been taken. Women in particular were enraged over the accusations, and several hair-pulling contests took place.[2]

But aversions and sanctions may change as circumstances warrant; there is some reason to believe that Korean attitudes may be changing as far as same-name incest is concerned. Just recently, the *New York Times* reported that South Korea was ending the ban on same-name marriage to enlarge the potential pool of eligible mates by 25 percent. (Only a few dozen clan names include most of the 44 million people in South Korea; one out of five Koreans has the surname Kim, and people named Lee and Park make up another 23 percent of the population.) Lifting the ban may not make marriage easier in Korea itself, however, since that country's highest court has thus far limited its tolerance of same-name marriages to couples living abroad.

Just as the way people extend the familial incest taboo can vary over time and from society to society so, too, do the sanctions for incest vary; they range from mild ridicule to death. Among the Ashanti of West Africa, incest in any form is so offensive that it calls for death. The Ashanti term *mogyadie* ("eating up one's own blood") refers to sex with members of the same clan or descent group. Actual blood relationship need not be close. Incest is serious even where violators can trace no clear blood connection. It is enough that they have the same clan name, indicating that somewhere back in time they had a common female ancestor. An ethnographer describing the situation reports the following:

> Perhaps no other sin was regarded with greater horror among the Ashanti. Both parties to the offence were killed. Had such an act been allowed to pass unpunished, then, in the words of my informants, "hunters would have ceased to kill the animal in the forest, the crops would have refused to bear fruit, children would have ceased to be born, the *Samanfo* (spirits of dead ancestors) would have been infuriated, the gods would have been angered, *abusa* (clans) would have ceased to exist, and all would have been chaos (*basa basa*) in the world."[3]

Among the Khasi of northeastern India, the sanction for cohabitation with a member of one's clan was less severe. It was punishable not by death but by exile or fine. But the Khasi, like the Ashanti, believed that incest also triggers punishments far more severe than humans can impose—lightning may strike offenders, tigers eat them, or they might die in childbirth, for example.[4] And although people everywhere voice strong objections to incestuous unions, some nonetheless permit them under certain circumstances. The Tiv of Africa sometimes tolerated temporary (incestuous) relations within the clan so long as they did not lead to marriage. They tolerated these temporary relations when they experienced special difficulties arranging marriage exchanges outside the clan, especially for younger men.[5]

There are other examples of people looking the other way. The Ganda of Africa (in what is now Uganda) responded to incest in distinctly pragmatic fashion. Religious wars led to capture of many children, often before they were old enough to have received clan names. It often occurred that they subsequently married people of their own clan. Normally that would have been incestuous. What did the Ganda expect from such marriages and what did they think ought to be done upon discovery of their incestuous nature?

> Such a marriage was never believed to be visited by any terrible supernatural punishment. So long as the relationship of the couple was unknown, nothing happened; if it was discovered, they had to separate—but this rule, as has been mentioned, was overruled by the dignity of a mother of twins, who could even go on bearing children to her husband. The cases which were regarded as really serious were where a man turned out to have married his father's sister or maternal cross-cousin [maternal uncle's daughter]. A man who deliberately had sexual relations with either was described as *owe kive*—a phrase reserved for this context and denoting utter abomination—and put to death. But incest with a real sister—which it was admitted might occur—was atoned for in the same way as the seduction of an unmarried girl; while all that happened to a man who knowingly had intercourse with any other woman of his clan was that he was reprimanded for "disowning" her—not recognizing their relationship.[6]

The ethnographic record indicates that people may extend the notion of incest even to people with whom there is no blood relationship. Consider the matrilineal Akan, of Africa's Gold and Ivory Coasts. If, after a woman has married her paternal aunt's son, her father should die and her husband become his heir, her mother cannot become a co-wife. To put the matter simply, it would be incestuous for a man to have a woman and her daughter as co-wives even though neither are his blood relatives nor people of his clan.[7] The Masai, another African people, also classify certain unrelated people as close blood relatives with whom sex is forbidden. Once a man pays bride-price he is entitled to consider a woman's children his own. Biologically they may not be, however, since "sexual communism or something very like it prevails between all the men of one age-grade and women of the corresponding age-grade."[8] Nonetheless, sex with such children would be incestuous. They are not potential mates in any event since Masai marriage taboos prohibit members of the same clan and age group from marrying, and the penalties, while short of death, are nonetheless severe:

> If a man is knowingly guilty of incest, or has sexual intercourse with a daughter of his own sub-clan, he is punished by his relations, who flog him and slaughter some of his cattle. If he fornicates or commits adultery with a daughter of a member of his own age-grade, he is punished by the members of his age-grade. His kraal is destroyed, he is severely beaten, and a number of his oxen are slaughtered. If a warrior or boy commits adultery with a wife of a man belonging to his father's age-grade, he is solemnly cursed by the members of that age-grade. Unless he pays the elders two oxen, one for them to eat and the other to enable them to buy honey wine, and prays them to remove the curse, it is supposed he will die.... If a man unintentionally commits incest—and it is quite conceivable that a man might not know his fourth or fifth cousin, for instance, should the two live in different districts—he has to present a cow to the girl's relations in order to "kill the relationship."[9]

Some people treat incest *within* the family quite differently from incest *beyond* it. To the Mbuti Pygmies of Africa, for example, acts of familial incest are serious with potentially heavy sanctions. Colin Turnbull, who worked among them, tells us that violation of the incest taboo constitutes one of this society's "most serious offenses," and that people believe offenders should be "left to the forest," ostracized within and beyond the band. Alone in the forest they would surely die.[10] While they take a dim view of incest, the Mbuti pay little attention to genealogy and extend the taboo laterally only to first cousins. Even between them, flirtation accompanied by sexual intercourse elicits only "nominal disapproval." However, if they seem to be developing the sort of affection that would normally lead to marriage, objections become more vocal. Sex is one thing, marriage another. There is also some disapproval, "of about the same degree of seriousness, if children of the same social mother [close female relative of the true mother], but not of the same stomach, flirt with each other, but such flirtations happen."[11]

Clearly, the Mbuti are tolerant of interactions we might consider bordering on incest. And it is curious that, although they are relatively tolerant of physical intimacy between primary relatives, there is little reason to believe that such intimacy encourages incest:

> I found it impossible to discover a single admitted instance of incest closer than between first cousins, but there is some evident restraint between brothers and sisters, none between mothers and sons, little between fathers and daughters. To swear at someone by accusing them of having sex with their parent is mild; it is more serious to accuse them of having sex with their sibling of one stomach. Worst of all is to accuse someone of having sex with her or his spouse. (The degree of freedom

between sons and mothers may be seen in the fact that a mother gives strength to her children, if they are ill, by sleeping in the same bed with them. This is sometimes done between a mother and her adult son, so long as he is unmarried, without occasioning any comment.)[12]

In some societies, violations of incest taboos may even go entirely unpunished, notwithstanding expressed disapproval. Taboos of the Southern Ojibwa in North America precluded sex within family and clan. According to one early ethnographer, however, marriages did join relatives of all categories except parents and children, and siblings. And even among such primary relatives there was occasional incest.[13] Ojibwa shamans, or curers, sometimes had incestuous relations with close family members with little serious retribution:

> His adolescent stepdaughter was ill, and he treated her with his special curing method. After a time he commenced giving the girl "some medicine to make her sleep. Then he would play over her, until at last the girl knew she was going to have a baby, only she did not know who its father was." After the baby was born, the man married his stepdaughter, making her a co-wife to her own mother. The mother accepted this status horrified and shamed, but anxious to care for her duped daughter [sic]. Shortly thereafter the girl became violent, "crazy from shame and worry," and died. The stepfather conducted the girl's funeral services. "After everything was over, they went home, and his wife took the axe to cut his head off. But some men grabbed her before she hit him. She was so mad. She said, 'You killed my daughter!' Then she got ready and returned to her (family's) home, taking the boy with her."[14]

The Ojibwa considered sex between a woman and her stepfather incestuous despite the fact that they are not consanguineal or blood relatives. Sex among them occurred nonetheless and was hardly the exclusive prerogative of shamans. In fact, people felt there was a considerable risk of incest whenever a mature stepdaughter returned to her parental lodge following divorce or death of her spouse or even simply on a visit. The hope was that she would be sophisticated enough to fend off an incestuous approach, but it wasn't always easy:

> Kota was a woman who had left several husbands and had returned to her mother's home. After she had lived there a year, "her stepfather commenced going after her at night. He used to go out (of the lodge) and pretend to come in again. Later he would sneak in and lie down by her, but she thought it was someone else. Then she began to hit him and send him away. She could tell by his actions in the daytime that he was trying to get her. One time she got a stick that was burned because she wanted to find out who it was that came and bothered her in the night. So that night she lay down with the burned stick. Again that

night he came along, went out and pretended to come in, and a little
while after he came and lay down beside her. So she took the stick and
hit him across the back. The next morning she knew it was her stepfather that was bothering her because his shirt was marked with the
charred coal of the stick. So she told her mother, and then she went
away and stayed with another old woman."[15]

The ethnographer from whose work we have drawn these excerpts
assures us that not all Ojibwa stepfathers pursue their stepdaughters. Indeed,
some have only "a tender and disinterested love that withstands all temptation." Still, "this is so uncommon that they are suspected nevertheless."[16]
Incidents of incest between fathers and daughters, or grandfathers and
granddaughters, though considerably less common, occurred as well. They
were not violations of the same order, but Ojibwa punishments were not
nearly as severe as the Ashanti (for whom, as we have noted, death would
have been unavoidable). Consider the following account from Ojibwa
ethnography:

> One widower, Nahwi, lived alone with an adolescent daughter and
> eventually violated her. When she announced the fact to the village,
> the man was greeted with the most insulting scorn, his relatives repu-
> diated him as a "dog", and until the end of his life he was ostracized by
> the Indians.... Grandfathers are also likely to err, as was the case with
> Tibish. He and his wife lived with their widowed daughter and her
> young daughter. The girl dutifully accompanied her grandfather on his
> hunting trips. "At last he camped out and wouldn't come home at
> night. He used to have some excuse...it was too windy, or it was too
> late for him to come home. And he kept on like that until at last the
> girl was to become a mother. Her mother knew that she was to have a
> baby, and she got angry and kept on asking who the father was, but the
> girl wouldn't even speak to her mother (because she was ashamed). So
> when the baby was born the old woman said she would kill the baby if
> the girl refused to tell who the father was. And while she was talking
> and just about to kill the baby, the old man came in and grabbed the
> baby. Then they all knew that it was his baby. So the girl took the old
> man away from her own grandmother, and she had five children with
> the old man. This girl's own grandmother became her co-wife, and her
> own mother became her niece." The grandfather was not scorned, as a
> father would have been in his place. Apparently this was not consid-
> ered to be a primary incest, such as incest with the father or father-in-
> law; and the origin in rape was overshadowed by the succeeding mar-
> riage.[17]

The Ojibwa were also more tolerant of clan incest than the Ashanti.
Unions among clansmen constituted ordinary, albeit "harmlessly scan-
dalous," marriages. The couples lived together openly as husband and wife.

Their children were fully legitimate, but bore a "certain malicious stigma." But public disdain faded after some years. Even violators of the taboo against sex within the immediate family did not face execution or incarceration, although their offenses did not go unnoticed or unpunished. The reputations of fathers, grandfathers, and (more commonly) stepfathers who violated daughters or granddaughters were tarnished. Curiously, incest placed a greater burden on women, even when they were victims of rape. Among the Ojibwa, such women usually had to leave home and perhaps community as well. We hope future researchers will determine how general such gender asymmetry is cross-culturally, and also whether sanctions are commonly heavier for women than for men.

COUSIN MARRIAGE AND THE INCEST TABOO

Scholars averse to reductionist explanations often consider cross-cultural inconsistencies in extension of the incest taboo to relatives beyond the primary family as evidence of the taboo's cultural rather than biological origin. Recall that the rules we create to regulate marriage do not always coincide perfectly with those that govern sex. Still, marriage normally involves sexual rights. For that reason alone, marriage rules, while not identical to those regulating sex, can tell us something about how and why incest taboos may be extended. Consider, first, cousin marriage customs in societies around the world.

In most, including our own, there is little tolerance for marriage with a first cousin. According to Murdock, 57 percent of societies disapprove of such marriage.[18] At first blush, that fact suggests that we may prohibit incest to stave off the deleterious consequences of close inbreeding. But why, then, do a substantial minority of societies allow first-cousin marriage (43 percent)? Nine percent of Murdock's sample not only allowed, but preferred such marriage, and with any first cousin. Another 18 percent exhibited more limited preference, either for *FaSiSo* (father's sister's son) or *MoBrSo* (mother's brother's son); 10 percent preferred only the FaSiSo, and 3 percent only the MoBrSo. Anthropologists use the term *cross-cousins* for all cousins related through siblings of opposite sex (father's sister's children or mother's brother's children). Preference for marriage with *parallel* cousins (related through siblings of the same sex (father's brother or mother's sister) is less common, occurring in only 3 percent of Murdock's sample.[19] In a few societies, even nephews and nieces are acceptable spouses, even though they are twice as closely related genetically, compared with first cousins.

Many have argued that the irregular extension of the incest taboo to cousins undercuts the relevance of biological considerations. They prefer explanations in terms of psychological processes, or alliance theory. As a result of his fieldwork among the Trobriand Islanders, for example, Bronislaw Malinowski suggested why people who trace descent through women might prefer marriage with a MoBrSo. He proposed that men have a special problem in such (matrilineal) societies. Custom requires that they pass property to their sisters' sons, but fathers would really prefer to give it to their own sons. Marriage of a girl with her MoBrSo resolves the conflict because, assuming a woman married her biological MoBrSo, a father ends up passing his estate to his son's son (through his sister's daughter).[20]

A structural model showing exactly how this happens is hardly necessary here since, as E. R. Leach has already pointed out, the people Trobrianders refer to as MoBrSo are not invariably biological cousins.[21] They may simply be people classified as such, in which case the problem Malinowski describes persists in spite of the preference for MoBrSo marriage. Furthermore, the supposed problem itself should not be taken for granted. Do men in matrilineal societies really want to pass property to their own offspring? If they do, why does MoBrSo marriage not occur in all matrilineal societies? How could Malinowski's interpretation anticipate which of them would have the preference? With all of these questions left unanswered, Malinowski's attention to psychological issues, and the connection he suggested between descent and one kind of cousin marriage, were not lost on others.

According to one formulation, psychological processes may still partially account for the fact that we sometimes find a preference for MoBrSo marriage in matrilineal societies.[22] Psychological processes may also partially explain why FaSiSo preference occurs where descent is traced through males.

In the preceding discussion, preferences have been stated from a woman's point of view, or, as anthropologists used to say, woman-speaking. Let us shift, now, and examine the logic of the argument from a man's point of view.

In patrilineal societies family authority is vested in the father; the mother is a more indulgent figure. As children grow up, they generalize the different sentiments they develop with respect to each parent to uncles and aunts and then to cousins. Thus, a boy extends relaxed attitudes he has toward his mother to her brother. He, too, becomes a friendly, indulgent figure. Marriage with that uncle's daughter (MoBrDa) is easy under the circumstances since it only requires a further extension of warm feelings to a potential sex partner. Where descent is traced through women, however, the mother's brother, not the father, is the authority figure. He is concerned about the discipline and well-being of his sister's children, his heirs. His relationship with his own children can be one of relative indulgence. Thus, warm feelings a boy develops toward his father are extended to his father's sister, already a gentle figure by virtue of her sex, and through her to the FaSiDa, a potential sex partner.

But there are problems with this reasoning.[23] One is that it assumes a questionable and unproven psychological extension of sentiments. More troublesome is the fact that it is suspiciously male-oriented. Are we to suppose that females do not extend sentiments the way males do? Should we not assume that a girl, too, would extend warm sentiments from father to FaSiSo where descent is matrilineal, and from mother to MoBrSo in patrilineal contexts? But in fact she ends up marrying boys she should *not* be drawn to. Nor does the formulation anticipate when sentiments will or will not be extended, or the conditions under which generalization of sentiments will or will not be associated with cross-cousin marriage. While a specific matrilateral cross-cousin preference is significantly more likely in patrilineal societies than the opposite cross-cousin preference (more often found in matrilineal societies), most patrilineal and matrilineal societies actually do not allow any kind of cousin marriage, as Murdock pointed out.[24]

Then there are *alliance* theorists who also dismiss biological considerations in the matter of cousin marriage. Rather, they emphasize the role such marriage can play in cementing ties among groups. In short, they propose that some forms of cousin marriage produce more enduring social integration than others. The most renowned proponent of this view has been Claude Lévi-Strauss. Along the lines of his theoretical predecessor, Émile Durkheim, he argues that a basic function of trade and exchange is to promote social solidarity through interdependence. In the creation and perpetuation of alliances, exchange of women assumes special importance, and the mode of their exchange determines the quality of social integration. Albeit from a very different theoretical perspective, Leslie A. White took a similar position:

> Life is made more secure, for the group as well as individual, by cooperation. Articulate speech makes cooperation possible, extensive, and varied in human society. Incest was defined and exogamous rules were formulated in order to make cooperation compulsory and extensive, to the end that life be made more secure. These institutions were created by *social* systems, not by *neuro-sensory-muscular-glandular systems*.[25]

There is the proposal that cross-cousin marriage, especially with FaSiSo, is more common because, *if consistently practiced*, it promotes the most enduring interdependency.[26] This formulation, too, is problematic. For one thing, it confounds rules governing sex with those of marriage. Even if various forms of cousin marriage do promote different degrees of social integration, why would we need to rule any cousins out as sex partners? Why couldn't we allow sex with cousins but require marriage with others? Moreover, if cousin marriage creates or reinforces alliances, and if some forms engender more enduring ties than others, why did Murdock find that 57 percent of his sample societies prohibited all kinds of first-cousin marriage? And why should some of those that allow it prefer forms less effective in terms of social integration? Why, for example, should marriage with any first cousin be most common (as compared with systems allowing marriage only with some first cousins), given that such a general preference produces the weakest integration, according to alliance theorists?

What else could account for some societies allowing or even preferring cousin marriage? In testing various explanations, Melvin Ember suggests that we consider anew the possibility that biological considerations may underlie both the origin and the extension of the incest taboo, and may explain as well why a substantial minority of societies allow first-cousin marriage.[27] He found that extension of the taboo to first cousins is most likely in small genetic isolates—low density societies in which the chance probability of close inbreeding would be highest in the absence of a taboo. Conversely, extension of the taboo to cousins is least likely in large genetic isolates, where the chance probability of cousin marriage is lowest.

Some of the societies in Ember's sample did not fit these conclusions; that is, some with middle range populations (one thousand to twenty-five thousand people) allowed first-cousin marriage when they should not have, according to the biological theory. It turned out that depopulation may explain those exceptional cases; depopulation (because of introduced diseases) may have induced a relaxation of taboos against first-cousin marriage, perhaps to enlarge the set of eligible mates. Similarly, societies that are very small (less than one thousand people) may permit marriage with first cousins to provide enough mating possibilities, even if depopulation has not occurred. (In a breeding population of three hundred—and there are some in the ethnographic record—there may be only a handful of potential spouses, unmarried adults, even including first cousins.) In such cases, the difficulty of finding a mate may outweigh the cost of inbreeding if the situation is long-standing enough so that harmful recessive genes have already been removed from the gene pool.[28]

In fact, Ember's interpretation of cousin marriage accommodates the ethnographic evidence better than alliance theory because the latter would lead us to expect that cooperation would be most needed, and cousin marriage most likely, in small societies with simple political structures. But, as Ember notes, "it is the societies at the highest levels of political complexity which are the most likely to permit cousin marriage."[29]

A more recent cross-cultural study by William Durham builds upon Ember's earlier attempt to explain the existence and variable extension of incest taboos. Consistent with an earlier (1967) cross-cultural observation by the psychologist Gardner Lindzey (noted, as well, by Ember), Durham found that people everywhere take a "more than casual interest in harmful phenotypic consequences of inbreeding."[30] Further, repeated manifestations of such consequences call forth local interpretations. The negative results of such unions may be attributed to spirits of the dead, for example, and for that reason may not require human sanctions at all. Fear of divine or spirit retribution, and sensitivity to the consequences of offense, may be sufficient to ensure general compliance with incest taboos. As for variation in extension of incest taboos beyond primary relatives, Durham proposes an explanation in terms of *rational choices* people make to ensure reproduction. His approach joins natural and cultural selection in an evolutionary process that favors and reproduces adaptive ideas as well as the carriers of those ideas. Reinforcing and modifying Ember's argument (and consistent with the algebraic model originally offered by him), Durham suggests that people everywhere behave in such a way as to optimize reproduction. He concludes that people have generally been

> guided by a recognition of inbreeding effects together with a folk theory of their causation by supernatural agents or inferred natural laws. People have commonly "figured out" that inbreeding is deleterious, and have reacted accordingly.[31]

People often verbalize the choices they make in this regard. Incestuous relationships were sometimes tolerated among the Tiv, for example, because of a shortage of women, exacerbated by the fact that older men were in a better position than younger ones to accumulate bride wealth and acquire multiple wives. According to one account, the shortage of women led to both *irregular* or *transitory unions* and incestuous unions involving members of the same clan:

> Shortage of women is one of the commonest causes of incest, and these appear to have been incestuous connections, tolerated, but not encouraged, by society to mitigate the hardship of remaining single, which arose from the difficulty of finding wives for the young men, and husbands for the girls, when these had to be procured from outside the group. Apart from the question of finding sufficient [bride wealth], it must have been very difficult to arrange exchange marriages with other clans, when the tribe grew and covered a large area of country, especially in the unsettled times before the British occupation. There were constant journeyings backwards and forwards with presents for the bride's relations; there were long delays while the elders of each group met together to discuss the proposed alliance, and sent word to, or visited, the other party. Finally, when the agreement had been reached, and the bridegroom went to fetch away the girl, there was always a chance of her being seized while passing through the territory of another clan on the way home.[32]

Yet, Durham's formulation explains no better than Ember's why, when restrictions against cousin marriage are relaxed, some forms occur more often than others. Neither can distinguish societies likely to allow marriage with any cousin from societies that allow marriage with only parallel-cousins or cross-cousins. In the end, after providing more evidence that incest taboos and their extension "tend to enhance human survival and reproduction," Durham leaves us hanging with the vague suggestion that "additional functions have sometimes been added (as when incest taboos grade into lineage exogamy), and the taboos are clearly part of larger systems of kinship rules and regulations."[33]

At this stage we have no convincing answers to these more specific questions of extension. Answering them may also require a joining of biological and sociological approaches. It may turn out, for example, that distinctions among first cousins are usually less necessary in large genetic isolates because the chance probability of marrying a cousin is small. In small societies distinctions may more often be made, but for sociological reasons, a speculation not incompatible with a biological interpretation of why they are obliged to allow some first-cousin marriage. Where people organize on the basis of common descent, often the case in smaller and politically simpler societies, the way people reckon descent may influence notions of closeness. It could lead people to expand and elaborate the notion of biological closeness developed within the family to relationships beyond, but for other reasons. We know that societies in which people trace descent through men (and allow just one type of cross-cousin marriage) are more likely to favor FaSiSo than MoBrSo marriage.[34] If early familiarity breeds sexual disinterest, then the rule of marital residence together with the rule of descent may influence attitudes toward marriage with certain cousins. Cross-culturally, descent groups tend to be exogamous—members most often must find spouses in other descent groups. For that reason, parallel cousins (MoSiSo and FaBrSo) would often be people with whom, or near whom, one would have been raised. Cross-cousins would usually live elsewhere.

Comparison of societies around the world indicates that, in most of those with descent groups, people refer to at least some uncles and aunts using terms appropriate to parents; MoSi is also "mother," and FaBr is "father." We do not classify relatives that way, but neither do we organize groups on the basis of common descent. Where people do, however, the grouping of parents and their siblings does not indicate a misreading of nature; some individuals may not know who their fathers are, but most know their mothers. Classifying father with his brother and mother with her sister may simply signal that relatives grouped under the same kin term share sociologically important characteristics. Any "father" is a male of my father's generation and a member of his descent group. In the same fashion any "mother" is a woman of my mother's generation and in her descent group.

As noted above, custom usually requires that people find mates in other descent groups. Therefore, "mother" is someone that a person I call "father" could marry. The children of aunts and uncles I classify as parents are, of course, "brothers" and "sisters." For that reason they are too closely related to marry. These particular cousins either are, or might be, members of my descent group. Thus, the fact that most societies form exogamous descent groups may account for the rarity of parallel-cousin marriage (i.e., cousins related through relatives of the same sex).

But why should cross-cousin marriage be allowed? A father's sister cannot be thought of as mother—she is not of mother's descent group. Using a different term, like *aunt*, may simply indicate that she is a "woman of my father's generation and descent group." Similarly, mother's brother cannot be father because he belongs to a different descent group—to that of mother. We may signal that by calling him "uncle" rather than "father." The children of these uncles and aunts are not siblings but cousins, by definition not members of my descent group. If common descent implies closeness, then cross-cousins are not as close as siblings. Thus, marriage with cross-cousins may be more common than marriage with parallel-cousins for that reason alone.

Why, then, do any societies allow marriage with a parallel cousin? Some anthropologists propose, on the basis of ethnography on Arab Bedouin, that this form of cousin marriage keeps wealth, in the form of bride-price and/or dowry, within the descent group, since FaBrSo is also a member of a woman's (or man's) descent group.[35] It is not clear, however, why so few societies do this. Another suggestion, arising from work among the Kurds, is that parallel-cousin marriage unifies closely related segments of a descent group in the face of struggles with more distant patrilineal relatives.[36] Yet others, again on the basis of Bedouin ethnography, propose that the custom contributes to an *extreme fission process*, adaptive because it enables families to split and consolidate as circumstances require.[37] Without considering these proposals in depth, we simply note that none explains why only a few societies overcome concerns about closeness, or why descent should be traced through males in all of them.[38] Once again we must consider the possibility that, in highly mobile and dispersed societies, the difficulty of finding a mate may be more burdensome than the risks of marrying a cousin living nearby who, in these cases, would be a parallel cousin.

Before leaving the matter of incest taboos and their extension, we might note (but leave hanging for lack of a certain response) a provocative question about the meaning and relevance of incest taboos in contemporary society. Seymour Parker recently confronted the issue head-on when he proposed that "sex relations among closely related consenting adults are best left to personal choice."[39] Why did he feel that this should be the case? For one thing,

> the statistical probability of genetic ill-effects of randomly occurring low levels of incest would be insignificant. It is assumed that ideas of

romantic love, relative courtship freedom of the young, choice among large numbers of potentially available mates, and the biosocial propensities toward inbreeding avoidance would make incestuous matings relatively unusual. In addition, the development of birth control technology adds to the benignity of the entire issue.[40]

Similarly, kinship ties among families are no longer as important in our bureaucratized industrial societies as they once were, and families have become more unstable and heterogenous in composition. As society assumes their functions, extended families and kin groups become structurally and functionally less important. As Parker puts it, "Kinship is no longer the kingpin of the organizational integrity of modern industrial society. With regard to its social alliance functions, the incest taboo is no longer very relevant."[41] There is no longer reason to believe that the family is the exclusive agent of socialization. Children enter group settings outside the home at progressively earlier ages. The mothers of school-age children typically have jobs outside the home, and fewer children now live in traditional two-parent families:

> What is important to note…is that the socialization of the child is now being carried out increasingly by individuals who are not part of the kinship network, and in settings over which the immediate kin group has little direct control. In such bureaucratized (non-kin) environments the *incest taboo* has little relevance for protecting the child against sexual abuse. It is no longer an effective cultural mechanism.[42]

Further, as divorce and remarriage rates rise, children increasingly end up in reconstituted families, sometimes with people who are relatives neither by blood nor marriage. In such circumstances the coincidence of incest violation and sexual abuse of children may collapse or vanish. There is evidence that stepfathers are far more likely to abuse children sexually than are fathers, and the severity of that abuse is often far more serious.[43] Given the circumstances of contemporary life, then, Parker's view is that we should focus on preventing child abuse rather than incest. To Parker's observation we might add one of our own: that if the aversion hypothesis is correct, then perhaps we should reformulate interactions within the immediate family. Stepfathers may be more likely to pursue sexual relations with youngsters because they normally appear on the scene too late to have developed the long-term, early familiarity fathers usually have with daughters. If a society encouraged closer rather than more aloof parent-child and sibling bonds, it might short-circuit rather than stimulate incestuous desires. In that light, the Mbuti custom of having a mother join her unmarried, adult son in bed when he is ill may not be all that problematic.

Other Marital Shoulds and Shouldn'ts

Custom may dictate whom one may or may not marry, and also whom one should or even must marry. We already have some examples—societies where marriage with certain types of cousins is prohibited, allowed, or preferred. Custom may also require or encourage people to marry *endogamously* (to find a spouse within a certain group) or *exogamously* (outside some group). Both terms are always used with respect to a clearly specified group such as a village, system of villages, marketing area, language group, caste, religious group, or descent group. It is also important to be clear as to whether we intend them to refer to preferences or to the way people actually arrange marriages. There is no expressed preference for kibbutz exogamy (marriage outside the collective community) in Israel, but studies indicate that people actually tend to marry exogamously. Many Americans believe that spouses ought to have the same religion, class, race, or ethnic origin, but even people who spurn such restrictions usually end up marrying people like themselves. While many old boundaries are eroding, in some instances new ones have been erected to replace them. Consider now some Chinese ethnographic materials that point to the causes and different consequences of exogamy and endogamy.

In most of China, people are of the view that one should find a spouse outside one's own community. They provide various explanations for the preference. Some point out that if a girl were to marry a boy within the community, she would find it too easy to run home to her parents with complaints about him or, more likely, about her mother-in-law. And, how could a mother-in-law effectively train and discipline her daughter-in-law if her parents were so near? Proximity might even put a strain on relations between the families if a girl's parents could easily "see the redness of her eyes" after her in-laws or husband had abused her.

While village exogamy is preferred virtually everywhere in China, there is considerable variation in practice. Given a strong preference for descent group exogamy, villages containing only one such group must be exogamous. But where several descent groups live together, marriage within the community is possible; in any case the ethnographic record indicates that in some communities people do depart from the principle of village exogamy. Even where villages are exogamous, however, the local system of communities tends to be an endogamous one, in which marriage is only one of many unifying strands. The communities that make up these larger systems commonly intermarry and participate in ritual exchanges. They may share economic, political, ritual, and perhaps military interests as well. Often they engage in similar family sidelines, raise the same kinds of crops, and exchange labor.[44]

Chinese villages may depart from the exogamic ideal where relations of descent are less important than those of marriage and common interest, for economic and/or political-military reasons. Consider the case of Tatieh, a farming village in south Taiwan settled some three hundred years ago by Hakka-speaking migrants from southeastern China. Their movement into this region followed a familiar pattern: small groups of individuals related patrilineally first settled unobtrusively, renting land from absentee Hokkien-speaking landlords, or opening new land and leading water to it from nearby rivers and mountain streams. As their number grew, so did their thirst for irrigation water. The Hokkien villages, which were settled earlier nearer the coast and further from the mountain water sources, soon became aware of the relationship between growing Hakka numbers and water shortages. The "Guest People" were now less an asset to their landlords than a menace. Like guests anywhere who remain, multiply, and invite relatives, they eventually outstayed their welcome.

From the beginning, the Hakka were prepared to defend themselves, first against head hunters in the nearby mountains, and later against the more numerous and better organized Hokkien. Small groups of families representing different descent groups unified and organized, submerging differences for the sake of common defense. They used various devices to forge ever-larger alliances throughout the plain—the region of common peril. The most extraordinary manifestation of Hakka confederation in south Taiwan was their Six Unit military organization which drew men from Hakka communities throughout the plain. Within communities, too, emphasis was on affiliations that would minimize internal struggles and contribute to more effective common defense.

Descent groups, generally important in southeastern China, were given a special twist. The most significant here were not those within communities, but those that linked communities. While descent groups had neither the structural complexity nor the functional importance they enjoyed elsewhere in southeastern China, cross-kin associations were unusually common, varied, and functional. Anticipation of violence was also responsible for the emphasis Hakka in this region place on marital alliances, within as well as between villages.

This brings us back, then, to the matter of variation in community endogamy and its implications. For the sake of common defense against a more numerous enemy, the Hakka in south Taiwan were prepared to compromise any preference for community exogamy. While village endogamous marriage accounted for less than 25 percent of marriages in other Taiwanese villages for which we have data, nearly half those in Tatieh were endogamous.[45] To appreciate the implications of this statistic for family dynamics, we need to appreciate certain salient characteristics of the Chinese family.

Since, by custom, property passes to sons on the basis of equivalent shares, women have access to the benefits of productive resources only through men—first their husbands, later their sons. This creates conditions for conflict among women. Concerned about her own well-being and that of her offspring, now and in the future, after the passing of her husband, a woman endeavors to exert her influence over her husband and over the son(s) upon whom she will depend in old age. This pits her against her mother-in-law, who has a similar interest in controlling her son and her grandsons. Given family rather than individual ownership of property, the daughter-in-law is in competition as well with sisters-in-law, who are determined to protect the interests of their nuclear units (wife, husband, and children).

It is, perhaps, understandable under the circumstances that men would attribute family division to arguments among women. Because there are good reasons for women to argue, customs evolved to mitigate or at least delay conflict. Virtually all rituals (for births, marriages, deaths, ancestor worship, village festivals, and the like) are occasions for elevating the parent-child bond. Indeed, all custom conspired to strengthen the parent-child bond at the expense of the conjugal one.

Thus, marriage was not primarily arranged in response to the needs, desires, or appetites of individuals, but for the good of the family and for its perpetuation. People expected a daughter-in-law to serve her in-laws, to care for them in their old age and feed their ghosts after they were dead, and to continue their line by bearing sons. Under these circumstances, it was useful to arrange marriage in such a way that bride and groom did not know each other. The longer it took for affection and intimacy to develop between them the better, since the flourishing of such emotions would be a threat to the parent-child bond, and to the larger family itself.

Consider, in this light, the implications of a higher incidence of village endogamous marriage. In this case the bride is likely to know her groom and his parents. Marriage does not tear her from familiar surroundings and drop her into a family of unknown entities, into a new women's network with which she is unfamiliar.[46] She knows the community and the man, even if only superficially. Her parents and siblings are near enough to provide support and assurance. This provides an advantage in her struggle with other women, with her mother-in-law and sisters-in-law. It is far more difficult to control such a woman.

One might even anticipate that the lower level of stress associated with village endogamous marriage might affect reproduction and, in fact, there is some evidence of that. When Pasternak compared the total fertility of endogamously and exogamously married women in a nearby Hakka community, he found a clear difference in favor of the former.[47] Once again we observe a connection we noted earlier in our discussion of Westermarck's familiarity hypothesis and in the context of cousin marriage, between how people marry and demographic outcome.

In the chapter on marriage and the incest taboo, and again in this chapter, we have been discussing customs that govern whom people can and cannot marry, or should marry. It is time now to turn to customs related to how people get married.

NOTES

1. Eugene I. Knez, "Sam Jong Dong: A South Korean Village" (Ph.D. diss., Syracuse University, 1959, University Microfilms Publication no. 59-6308. Ann Arbor: University Microfilms, 1960), p. 53.
2. Vincent S. R. Brandt, *A Korean Village between Farm and Sea* (Cambridge, MA: Harvard University Press, 1971), p. 209.
3. R. S. Rattray, *Ashanti Law and Constitution* (Oxford: The Clarendon Press, 1929), p. 304; see also K. A. Busia, *The Position of the Chief in the Modern Political System of Ashanti: A Study of the Influence of Contemporary Social Changes on Ashanti Political Institutions* (London: The Oxford University Press for the International African Institute, 1951), p. 71.
4. Philip R. T. Gurdon, *The Khasis* (London: David Nutt, 1907), p. 94.
5. Rupert East, trans. and ed., *Akiga's Story: The Tiv Tribe as Seen by One of Its Members* (London: The International Institute of African Languages and Cultures, Oxford University Press, 1939), p. 123.
6. Lucy P. Mair, *An African People in the Twentieth Century* (London: George Routledge and Sons, 1934), p. 79.
7. J. W. A. Amoo, "The Effect of Western Influence on Akan Marriage," *Africa* 16 (1946): 228–237.
8. A. C. Hollis, "A Note on the Masai System of Relationship," *Journal of the Royal Anthropological Institute of Great Britain and Ireland* 40 (1910): 480.
9. Ibid.
10. Colin M. Turnbull, *Wayward Servants: The Two Worlds of the African Pygmies* (Garden City, NY: The Natural History Press, 1965), p. 190.
11. Ibid., p. 112.
12. Ibid.
13. Ruth Landes, *The Ojibwa Woman* (New York: Columbia University Press, 1938), p. 62; for a similar report, see R. W. Dunning, *Social and Economic Change among the Northern Ojibwa* (Toronto: University of Toronto Press, 1959), p. 111.
14. Ibid., p. 32.
15. Ibid.
16. Ibid.
17. Ibid., p. 34.
18. Percent of societies in the World Ethnographic Sample for which there were relevant data. See George Peter Murdock, "World Ethnographic Sample," *American Anthropologist* 59 (1957): 687. In a sample Melvin Ember looked at, an even higher proportion (63 percent) of societies prohibited all kinds of first-cousin marriage. See Melvin Ember, "On the Origin and Extension of the Incest Taboo," in Melvin Ember and Carol R. Ember, *Marriage, Family, and Kinship:*

Comparative Studies of Social Organization (New Haven: HRAF Press, 1983 [originally published 1975]), p. 83.

19. In an earlier study, Murdock presented data on a smaller sample of societies in terms not of preferences but simply of whether marriage was "conditionally or freely permitted." Those data indicate acceptance of marriage with FaSiSo in 39 percent of the societies, MoBrSo in 32 percent, FaBrSo in 5 percent, and MoSiSo in 6 percent of the societies. See George Peter Murdock, *Social Structure* (New York: Macmillan, 1949), p. 286. Whether one considers preference or simply acceptance, it is clear that some form of cousin marriage is tolerated in many societies, and that cross-cousin marriage is more often allowed or preferred than parallel-cousin marriage.

20. Bronislaw Malinowski, *The Sexual Life of Savages* (London: George Routledge, 1929), p. 81.

21. Edmund R. Leach, "The Structural Implications of Matrilateral Cross-Cousin Marriage," in *Rethinking Anthropology*, ed. Edmund R. Leach (London: The Athlone Press, 1961), pp. 54–104.

22. G. Homans and D. M. Schneider, *Marriage, Authority, and Final Causes* (New York: Free Press, 1955).

23. For an extensive critique of this reasoning, see R. Needham, *Structure and Sentiment* (Chicago: University of Chicago Press, 1962).

24. Murdock, "World Ethnographic Sample," pp. 664–687.

25. Leslie A. White, *The Science of Culture* (New York: Grove Press, 1949), p. 329.

26. Claude Lévi-Strauss, *The Elementary Structures of Kinship* (Boston: Beacon Press, 1949). For a fuller elaboration, see Burton Pasternak, *Introduction to Kinship and Social Organization* (Englewood Cliffs, NJ: Prentice-Hall, 1976), pp. 69–74.

27. Ember, "On the Origin and Extension of the Incest Taboo."

28. See also William H. Durham, *Coevolution: Genes, Culture, and Human Diversity* (Stanford: Stanford University Press, 1991), p. 356.

29. Ember, "On the Origin and Extension of the Incest Taboo," p. 82.

30. Durham, *Coevolution*, p. 349. See also Gardner Lindzey, "Some Remarks Concerning Incest, the Incest Taboo, and Psychoanalytic Theory," *American Psychologist* 22 (1967): 1051–1059; and Ember, "On the Origin and Extension of the Incest Taboo."

31. Durham, *Coevolution*, pp. 357–358.

32. East, *Akiga's Story*, p. 123.

33. Durham, *Coevolution*, p. 359.

34. Murdock, "World Ethnographic Sample," p. 687.

35. Henry Rosenfeld, "An Analysis of Marriage Statistics for a Moslem and Christian Arab Village," *International Archives of Ethnography* 48 (1957): 32–62; Hilma Granqvist, "Marriage Conditions in a Palestinian Village," *Helsingfors, Commenationes Humanarum, Societas*

Scientarium Fennica 3 (1931). Howard Kaufman offers much the same explanation of incidents in which first cousins married in a Thai community, noting that they involved well-to-do families, and "served to keep wealth intact." See Howard Keva Kaufman, *Bangkhuad: A Community Study in Thailand* (Locust Valley, NY: Association for Asian Studies, Monographs 10, 1960).

36. Fredrik Barth, "Father's Brother's Daughter Marriage in Kurdistan," *Southwestern Journal of Anthropology* 10 (1954): 164–171.

37. Robert F. Murphy and Leonard Kasdan, "The Structure of Parallel Cousin Marriage," *American Anthropologist* 61 (1959): 17–29.

38. Murdock, "World Ethnographic Sample," p. 687.

39. Seymour Parker, "The Waning of the Incest Taboo," *Legal Studies Forum* 11, no. 2 (1987): 206.

40. Ibid., p. 211.

41. Ibid., p. 212.

42. Ibid., p. 213.

43. Ibid., p. 214. See also D. Finkelhor, *Sexually Victimized Children* (New York: Free Press, 1979); D. E. H. Russell, *Sexual Exploitation* (Beverly Hills: Sage Publications, 1984); and Hilda Parker and Seymour Parker, "Father-Daughter Sexual Abuse: An Emerging Perspective," *American Journal of Orthopsychiatry* 56 (1986): 531–549, cited in Parker, "The Waning of the Incest Taboo."

44. For a more detailed discussion and illustration, see Burton Pasternak, *Kinship and Community in Two Chinese Villages* (Stanford: Stanford University Press, 1972), and *Guests in the Dragon: Social Demography of a Chinese District, 1895–1946* (New York: Columbia University Press, 1983). On local systems in China generally, see G. William Skinner, "Marketing and Social Structure in Rural China," *Journal of Asian Studies* 24 (1964–1965): 3–43, 195–228, 363–399. For an introduction to local systems and regional analysis, see Carol A. Smith, ed., *Regional Analysis* (New York: Academic Press, 1976).

45. Pasternak, *Guests in the Dragon*, pp. 94–99.

46. On the importance and influence of women's networks in Chinese villages, see Margery Wolf, *Women and the Family in Rural Taiwan* (Stanford: Stanford University Press, 1972).

47. Pasternak, *Guests in the Dragon*, p. 98.

7

GETTING MARRIED

I was sitting in Rengsanggri one afternoon when three shy looking youths from another village wandered in and inquired where they might find Unon. Everybody chuckled, and somebody replied that he might be out in the fields, and suggested that the boys go out there to look for him. The boys walked out in the direction of the fields, until they came over the crest of a hill from which Unon could be seen cultivating in the company of half a dozen other people. Here the boys split up, so as to close in on him from all sides. Unon did not realize his peril until one boy was almost next to him. He started to flee but was caught, and after a brief struggle he recognized the uneven odds, surrendered, and let himself be led calmly to Waramgri, where a girl was waiting, hoping to become his bride. During Unon's brief battle, his fellow villagers ostentatiously continued their cultivating and ignored Unon's plight. Only when the struggle was nearly over did a few of them look up, but even then no one interfered, and as the captors led Unon away they continued their work. This was by no means a lack of interest, but only a studied noninterference; for when I returned to the village after watching from a nearby hilltop, everybody eagerly asked me what had happened—"Did they catch him? Did they take him away?"—with no effort to hide their intense interest and even glee. I had just witnessed one of the most exciting events in the life of every Garo man, the bridegroom capture, which is considered the only decent way to invite a man to become a husband. The boy should know nothing about it beforehand, though his family must be consulted if he is being asked to marry an heiress.[1]

Having described the forms of marriage, and having treated gender and sexuality, we turn now to how people get married—the way mates are selected, the nature of courtship, and the sorts of exchanges that take place when people marry. We begin with the way marriage is arranged. Does the couple decide by themselves to marry, or is the union arranged by others? Why do some societies allow freedom of choice and romantic love?

COURTSHIP AND MATE SELECTION

In traditional Chinese contexts, as we have seen, marriage reflected family more than individual concerns, so that couples frequently had little or no contact before the wedding. Ghost marriage was simply an extreme expression of this pattern of arranged marriage. It should be apparent from the description of Garo groom capture as well that mate selection is not everywhere responsive to the tastes and preferences of those who marry, nor does it invariably even require mutual consent. Among the Garo, who trace descent through women and, by custom, have the husband join his wife's family at marriage, women's preferences are fundamental. "Boys never seem to tire of chasing through the jungle in pursuit of a bridegroom," in fulfillment of some girl's desires. Captured, a prospective groom typically struggles to escape and may have to be recaptured several times before consenting to settle down. That may take several years and, until he stops trying, no one can be sure the marriage exists. The boy has only limited control over the situation; if he really does not want to marry and persists in attempts to flee, his captors will eventually release him.[2]

Marriage by capture occurs in a number of societies, and most commonly it is women rather than the men who are kidnapped. For example, bride capture was an acceptable mode of marriage among the Santal of India.[3] As the following description indicates, however, it was not without risks:

> [A] method open to an impatient bridegroom is to waylay the girl of his choice and forcibly place the vermilion on her head. This is usually accomplished with the aid of his friends and often with the secret connivance of the girl concerned. Marriage by this means has to be recognized, but the fellow villagers of the outraged girl's parents do not accept the situation without protest. They march to the young man's village and if on their arrival they receive a friendly welcome and are asked to be reasonable they sit down and talk and make arrangements, which include an enhanced bride-price by way of compensation to the girl's parents. If, on the other hand, they are received sullenly and the young man hides from them they become angry and do all the damage they can to his home, from pulling down the roof to killing any animals that may belong to his family.[4]

As this passage suggests, we should not simply assume that kidnapped brides are invariably without voice or initiative. Their consent before or after the event is frequently implicit or explicit, and in some cases they may even take the initiative. Indeed, a Santal girl may take matters entirely into her own hands, forcing her way into the home of a young man she wants to marry. People assume such behavior is a ruse, that she would not try this were she not certain of welcome.[5]

Serbian art and folklore actually commend bride capture. In a study of three hundred Yugoslav villages, Vera St. Erlich notes that the custom of bride capture was widespread, especially in Bosnia, and that the government was unable to stamp it out. Abductors were rarely punished because kidnapped females usually refused to testify. Brought before a magistrate, they invariably claimed they had followed by their own free will. During the period of Turkish domination, the standard assertion in court was that the woman had been willing to follow the man "into the mountains and into the water."[6]

Why were females so acquiescent? Erlich suggests several reasons. For one thing, an abducted woman would thereafter find it difficult to attract a man. Further, her kidnapper's aggressiveness fit a model of manliness enshrined in local lore, so his act might well impress her. And in many instances the girl was not unknowing or unwilling to begin with. As Erlich put it, "The transition between brute force used by the young man and semi-initiative on the part of the girl is so gradual that it is almost impossible to establish limits."[7]

But implicit or explicit complicity is not invariable either. Where women are captured during fighting, or are simply kidnapped, their feelings may carry little or no weight. This is the case among the Yanomamö, as the following description makes clear:

> Marriages are arranged by older kin, usually men, who are brothers, uncles, and the father. It is a political process, for girls are promised in marriage while they are young, and the men who do this attempt to create alliances with other men via marriage exchanges. There is a shortage of women due in part to a sex-ratio imbalance in the younger age categories [more males than females], but also complicated by the fact that some men have multiple wives. Most fighting within the village stems from sexual affairs or failure to deliver a promised woman—or out-and-out seizure of a married woman by some other man. This can lead to internal fighting and conflict of such intensity that villages split up and fission, each group then becoming a new village and, often, enemies to each other.[8]

The possibility of capture during raids is so great that women usually take their children, especially the younger ones, when they go out to work. That way they will not be separated should an enemy seize them. One might suppose that Yanomamö interest in wife capture signals that women are valued and well treated. That this is not so is indicated by the fact that female infanticide is not uncommon, and by the abuse women invite if they react too slowly to their husbands' demands:

> Most physical reprimands meted out take the form of blows with the hand or with a piece of firewood, but a good many husbands are more severe. Some of them chop their wives with the sharp edge of a machete or ax or shoot them with a barbed arrow in some nonvital area, such as the buttocks or leg. Some men are given to punishing their wives by holding the glowing end of a piece of firewood against them, producing painful and serious burns.... Women who are not too severely treated might even measure their husband's concern in terms of the frequency of minor physical reprimands they sustain. I overheard two young women discussing each other's scalp scars. One of them commented that the other's husband must really care for her since he has beaten her on the head so frequently![9]

An appreciable number of societies in the ethnographic record allowed (or preferred) bride capture or bride theft.[10] Judging from the sample Barbara C. Ayres examined, as many as 25 percent of societies may have had the custom of bride theft. What were they like? They did not usually have social classes, nor were they characterized by differential access to occupations and property. You might expect that bride theft would be associated with little choice in marriage, yet Ayres found that in societies with bride theft, parents exercised only moderate control (as opposed to absolute or no control) over their daughters' marriages.

Cross-culturally, control over marital choice is hardly ever left to the daughter. That is, the importance we attach to premarital familiarity and romance is quite unusual. In most societies, people consider marriage too important to leave to the whims of prospective couples. According to one study, males select and/or court partners *autonomously* (parental approval not required) in only 31 percent of the world's societies; females select or court autonomously in only 8 percent.[11] Clearly, parental consent is important in most societies, especially for women. Where couples join the family of one spouse at marriage (which is usually the situation in the ethnographic record), kin normally have some say about who marries whom. However, this does not mean that parents (or others) arrange marriages without any consultation. In fact, parents feel no need to consult sons in only 13 percent of societies, and daughters in 21 percent. In most cases, then, women as well as men can express their views in some fashion.

The degree of choice allowed has an impact on other customs regulating marriage. For example, Rosenblatt and Cozby hypothesized that couples with some free choice (control over some portion of the decision process) are likely to marry people with whom they are familiar and with whom they have frequent contact.[12] In other words, left to their own devices, women and men are likely to marry people they know. If so, Rosenblatt and Cozby reasoned, then we might expect to find that marriage is more often community endogamous in societies allowing considerable choice. Where there is less choice, familiarity and personal attachments might complicate arrangements that others have in mind.[13] In that case it might be better if prospective spouses came from different communities and had few opportunities to meet. In fact, the cross-cultural evidence does indicate that local endogamy often occurs with freedom of choice.[14]

Rosenblatt and Cozby reasoned that if marital choice and premarital familiarity go together, then societies allowing more choice should also provide opportunities for young people to meet, for example at public dances.[15] As they put it,

> dances allow contact without an enormous amount of verbal interaction. This can help one to get to know another without risking self-esteem…. [The dance] may heighten interpersonal attraction through the combination of rhythm, expectation of romance, special adornment and the like.[16]

As it turns out, the evidence does indicate a relationship between public dances and freedom of choice.[17] Dances, of course, provide only one context in which young people can meet. A measure of familiarity may also develop at work, in the market, at ceremonies, or while traveling, and Rosenblatt and Cozby also report positive associations between opportunities of these sorts and freedom of marriage choice.[18] Their data reveal still other associations of interest. For example, the greater the choice allowed, the more people tend to focus upon and exaggerate the personal qualities of potential mates. They are likely to judge prospects less on pragmatic, objective grounds—social rank, food-getting skills, potential in terms of alliance building, strength, or health, for example—than on romantic grounds. The more choice, the more important are sexual attractiveness, affection, and "courtly love." Thus, these researchers propose that where people experience little pressure from others and do not rely on objective criteria in choosing a spouse, they may "need to justify their choices, by more overt expressions of affection, exaggeration of qualities, and so on."[19]

In the course of our discussion of the incest taboo, we noted a possible relationship between sexual and agonistic (aggressive) responses. Consider that possibility in the present context. If marriage freely chosen is based on romance and physical attraction, might that heighten agonistic courting? Rosenblatt and Cozby approach this question as follows:

> One might suppose from the work of Kanin (1967) that violence, conflict, and antagonism might be relatively common in courtship where

there is freedom of choice. This stems partly from the mere fact of frequent interaction but also from the relative lack of definition of the situation where young men and women are more or less on their own and from the possibility of frustrated expectations in such a situation. Emotions associated with male-female antagonism may also produce physiological arousal that promotes the belief that one is experiencing feelings of attraction.[20]

As a matter of fact, Rosenblatt and Cozby found a positive relationship between courtship *antagonism* (measured in terms of insults, teasing, verbal argument, physical battles, wrestling, stone throwing, and playing pranks) and freedom of choice.[21] They provide some clear instances of agonistic courtship. Here, for example, is their description of courtship among the Aymara:

> Ordinarily, people of nubile age are supposed to be shy of one another, and while tending herds pass one another by many times without apparently seeing each other. Around Camata, if a boy in such a situation wishes to take notice of a girl, he picks up a handful of fine earth or dust and throws it at her. This is a first step of courtship in the Jesus de Machaca region. The next time they meet, the boy picks up some fine gravel, and the girl may do likewise. If they continue to be interested this goes on until finally they throw rocks at each other. Informants told me that there were two cases of deaths in Camata during the last four years from such a cause.[22]

It is possible that romantic courtship, characteristic of societies affording more choice, has implications for the quality of married life as well. If so, it would be useful to discover why some societies leave more room for romance and free choice than others, and to explore more closely the effects, if any, on marital stability. A study by Coppinger and Rosenblatt provides a start by addressing the conditions under which romantic love is likely to be important. They begin with the following hypothesis:

> In the absence of subsistence dependence, marital relations may be relatively unstable unless some alternative bond develops. It is the hypothesis of this study that romantic love is such an alternative bond, that where subsistence dependence between spouses is strong, romantic love is unimportant as a basis of marriage, while where subsistence dependence between spouses is weak, romantic love is important as a basis of marriage.[23]

It is commonly assumed that romance does not produce stable marriages unless there are compelling reasons to overcome differences and tensions between spouses. Where romance is important, nonrational and nonpragmatic criteria may produce fragile relationships that are potentially disruptive of other important social bonds. For that reason, romance should be important only in societies that lack less costly ways to hold couples together. *Subsistence dependence* (in which husband and wife make relatively balanced contributions) constitutes a more common, less delicate alternative to romance.[24] One result in Coppinger and Rosenblatt's study is consistent with the notion that romance is more fragile than subsistence dependence: There is an *inverse* relationship between degree of female-male subsistence dependence and importance of romantic love.[25]

Research by Gary R. Lee and Lorene H. Stone may help explain why romantic love is an important basis for marriage in only some societies.[26] Romantic love may be nearly universal, but it is far from being a universally important basis for marriage.[27] Rather, romantic love and *autonomous mate selection* (relative freedom of choice) are more common in societies with nuclear (rather than extended) family systems. The theory Lee and Stone suggest to explain the relevant findings is as follows:

> Arranged marriages based on nonromantic criteria should be most prevalent in extended family systems, because in these cases the new spouse is incorporated into an ongoing family, and must function as a junior member of that family as well as a spouse and prospective parent. Under these circumstances, we expect senior family members to have a substantial voice in, if not complete control over, the selection process.

According to this theory, then, romantic love is an important basis for marriage wherever, as in the United States, most people grow up and spend their adult lives in nuclear families. Under these circumstances, romance can be the major consideration in finding a mate because marriages are not arranged by elders.

TRANSACTING MARRIAGE

In most societies, marriage involves a transfer of goods and/or services, as well as of people, between families and larger kin groups. According to one survey, only 23 percent of preindustrial societies lack such transactions.[28] What forms do they take, and under what circumstances do various options occur? Schlegel and Eloul identify several major types.[29] Bride wealth (prevailing in 29 percent of all societies) consists of substantial property (e.g., animals, money) which the groom or his relatives give to the bride's kin. Token bride wealth (in 4 percent of societies) is similar except that the prestation (or obligatory gift) is symbolic or of little value. Bride service (15 percent of all societies) involves a transfer of labor (rather than goods) to the bride's family. Where parties exchange items of similar value, we have gift exchange (8 percent). The balance is not perfect, of course, since one side loses a daughter; it is more so where families or groups exchange sisters (5 percent of sample societies). In the case of indirect dowry (10 percent of the sample), kin of the groom provide gifts to the bride, or to her father who in turn passes some to her in the form of dowry. Where ordinary dowry prevails (6 percent of all societies), the bride's family gives gifts to her when she marries.[30] In Schlegel and Eloul's terms, this last practice *concentrates* rather than *circulates* family property since it remains with a family member when she moves away to live with her husband.

The work of Schlegel and Eloul confirms that marital transactions reflect, at least in part, the kind of property that exists in the society.[31] If there is little or no property, marriage transactions tend to be absent. If there is communal property, then marital transactions tend to circulate wealth. For example, bride wealth is likely where land is communally owned, and among subsistence pastoralists with small herds and communally owned pastures and water. But where people recognize private property in the form of land, money, or marketable herds, we find dowry or indirect dowry, customs that concentrate rather than circulate property.

Some researchers consider bride wealth, bride service, and woman exchange to be compensation for loss of the daughter's labor and reproductive powers.[32] Indeed, the cross-cultural evidence supports that idea; all those circulating transactions are more likely in societies that customarily have the bride go to live with or near her husband's kin.[33] But the puzzle is this: If these transactions really are compensation for the loss of a daughter, why do the wife's kin *not* provide such gifts in societies where grooms rather than brides leave home (matrilocal societies)? Further, Schlegel and Eloul's finding that 80 percent of societies *with dowry* are *patrilocal* makes little sense in terms of compensation theory, unless we are prepared to believe that families pay to have daughters removed! Perhaps bride wealth, bride service, and woman exchange do compensate for labor loss nonetheless, but *only where women contribute heavily to production*.[34] There is some indirect evidence of this; we find bride wealth mainly in horticultural societies, where women are likely to contribute considerably to subsistence, as for example in tropical regions of Africa. But since there are also quite a few societies that have bride wealth where women's contribution is low, it appears that subsistence contribution is not the only important factor.

There is another characteristic of African horticulture, which Schlegel and Eloul point to, that might also encourage bride wealth. Perhaps the reproductive potential of women assumes special importance in underpopulated regions (like much of Africa until recent years), where labor shortages can impose a more serious constraint on family economy than lack of land. Thus, bride wealth may be especially likely in food producing societies where women make an important economic contribution either through their labor or indirectly through their reproduction of sons.

In such contexts, the bride wealth received for a daughter may underwrite the acquisition of her replacement.[35]

It is clear that dowry is characteristic of agricultural societies with property owning classes and considerable social differentiation.[36] As noted earlier, dowry concentrates property. Although women's labor is usually less important than in societies with bride wealth, the property they bring at marriage balances (pays for) claims they make on their new families. And while families have to give up wealth as well as daughters, there are compensations:

> Families can use a daughter's dowry in two ways to enhance their well-being: They can exchange it for a high-status son-in-law, a common practice in India, or they can use it to attract a poorer but presentable son-in-law whose loyalty will be assured through his wife's wealth—in other words, to gain a client son-in-law…. This form would be particularly appropriate for the maintenance of family businesses, where a loyal and clever son-in-law can make up for the lack of a clever son. The mercantile families of preindustrial Latin America, for example, often married in promising sons-in-law, using either the daughter's dowry or her anticipated inheritance as an economic inducement. Men can acquire client sons-in-law in bridewealth societies, such as the Nuer, but they do so by foregoing bridewealth for their daughters, thus reducing their chances of bringing in wives for their sons.[37]

Indirect dowry, too, occurs where there are differences in status and wealth, but especially in regions that have considerable potential for instability,

> where fortunes can change rapidly due to drought (in the Middle East), epidemics of animal disease, and military success or failure. At the same time, status positions are unstable, being based on achievement as much as, or more than, heredity, and upon luck. The stakes are high but the outcome is unpredictable. Status is negotiable rather than a given, and it is in a constant state of renegotiation. Under such conditions, status competition becomes fierce, and neither the groom's side nor the bride's side can afford to lose face by receiving more than they give. Indirect dowry solves that problem. The groom's household gives goods to acquire a bride, so it is not in the bride's household's debt. However, the bride's household cannot keep the goods, for this would end the transaction and close off further status negotiation. It cannot be returned to the groom's household in the form of gifts (i.e., gift exchange), for that would put that household further into debt; by giving it to the bride, the honor of both households is satisfied, and the bride's household has laid claim to a continuing interest in their daughter and her children.[38]

While their interpretation of marriage transactions focuses on economic and political objectives, Schlegel and Eloul suggest another purpose as well. These arrangements also provide some assurance that children will be well-treated after marriage:

> They reassure the parents of daughters that the men marrying them are capable of supporting them and their children. With bridewealth, the groom either comes up himself with property or demonstrates a kin network that is willing to contribute to his well-being. With bride service, the groom establishes his productive capacity directly. When families give dowry, they not only ensure by their own efforts a daughter's economic security, but they can also use it to "buy" the best possible husband for her as well as son-in-law for themselves. Indirect dowry combines the security features of both bridewealth and dowry. Transfers of property can thus be seen as one means for ensuring the security of daughters and their children.[39]

But this argument assumes that only some societies are interested in ensuring the security of daughters and their children. We cannot simply take it for granted that this is the case and, even if it is, we would need to understand why.

Another explanation of dowry appears to fit the cross-cultural data even better than the notion that dowry guarantees future support of a woman and her children. This other theory suggests that dowry provides a way to attract the best bridegrooms in monogamous societies with a high degree of social inequality.[40] The dowry strategy presumably increases the likelihood that the daughter and her children will do well reproductively. But even if dowry reflects competition among females for mates, there is still an unanswered question: Why is it that many stratified societies (including our own), in which women and men have only one spouse at a time, do not practice dowry? Do we not also have competition among females for mates? Part of the answer may be that competition among women for mates is softened and offset in many complex commercial societies by alternative life styles—in our own society, for example, women can make their own living , and even reproduce, without marrying.

CELEBRATING MARRIAGE

> Marriage celebrations are the most positive means that a group has of offering its stamp of approval for the relationships that it wants to encourage. Thus, the degree of social elaboration present at the celebration may be a preview of the amount of social concern that will be associated with later phases of the marital relationship.[41]

In our society, we usually expect marriage to be celebrated, set off from routine events. Even when they elope, couples may visit a justice of the peace, possibly with friends or witnesses, and they are likely to go off on a honeymoon. In some societies, however, there is little or no public attention to how couples get to be considered married. This was the case in 28 percent of the societies Suzanne G. Frayser compared.[42] By way of example, she cites the Tupinamba, who had no public rites at all; a man simply brought his sister or daughter to her betrothed. Frayser also mentions the Havasupai, among whom there was simply an agreement to marry, then a gift to the bride's parents (sometimes preceded by nocturnal visits to the girl's home), and finally coresidence in her home—all without any particular ceremony.[43]

The wedding night is special in our society—a time of seclusion and privacy, worthy of "do not disturb" signs. Friends may tease before and after, with innuendo or indirect reference, but few would have bad enough taste to refer directly to the couple's behavior in bed. Our notion that wedding nights are special and private is shared in some but certainly not all societies. As a matter of fact, 67 percent of societies do not share this view, according to a cross-cultural survey.[44]

Where people consider the wedding night special, custom usually allows newlyweds some measure of privacy, as we do.[45] At least they will modify normal schedules in some fashion. The bride and groom may go off on their own for some time (11 percent of societies), or spend special time together at work or visiting others (13 percent). It is not always the case that bride and groom spend this special time together, however. They may independently observe altered work schedules. The bride may abstain from housework or spend time in seclusion, or the bride and groom may receive visitors separately (38 percent). In fact, there are quite a few societies that make no special arrangements at all for newlyweds (23 percent of the sample societies), and some that even expect them to avoid each other for a time (15 percent). Why people have different customs in this regard is not yet clear.

Although we have much to learn about why people celebrate marriage one way rather than another, there is reason to believe that various marital customs are related. For example, the research by Broude and Greene indicates a set of relationships between how marriage partners are chosen and other marriage customs.[46] They find that where couples choose their own partners, living arrangements usually allow some degree of privacy. Where a woman's spouse is chosen by a third party, this is not as likely. Further, where restrictive premarital sex norms for females are likely, female virginity is usually a matter of considerable concern, and consummation of marriage is treated as a special occasion in these societies. Broude and Greene suggest that these connections tell us something important:

> The association between customs for choice of marriage partner and newlywed living arrangements suggest that societies may exhibit some

consistency in their attitudes toward marriage as a private affair between the partners themselves *or as an arrangement in which the larger kin network has a voice and a place* [emphasis ours]. Where the couple moves in with the family of one spouse after marriage, it is not surprising that kin also expect to have a say as to whom their children will marry. The correlation between arranged marriages for women and the elaboration of the wedding night may reflect a tendency for societies to be concerned with the virginity of females when marriages are arranged.[47]

Still, why should kin groups be more concerned with these matters in some societies than in others? This is a more basic question to which we will return shortly. For the moment, let us continue to focus on the possibilities, returning to the nature of marriage ceremonies. As noted above, we find considerable variation in this regard, from very simple to very complex. The Trobriand Islanders of Melanesia had very rudimentary marriage ceremonies, like the Tupinamba and Havasuapi mentioned above, and like them, in a context where women enjoyed considerable liberty. Bronislaw Malinowski tells us that Trobrianders expected girls to be sexually active before marriage, and there were even ceremonial occasions during which such activity was called for. For example, there were occasions when village girls went as a group to another village, there to "publicly range themselves for inspection." Then they were chosen by local boys with whom they spent the night.

When visiting parties arrived from different districts it was customary for unmarried girls to bring food, and also to have sex with the visitors. When people went to funerals in other villages, unmarried girls among the visitors were expected to "comfort the boys of the bereaved village, in a manner which gives much anguish to their official lovers." And during communal garden weeding, an unfamiliar man entering the district did so at his own risk: in Malinowski's words, "The women will run after him, seize him, tear off his pubic leaf, and ill-treat him orgiastically in the most ignominious manner."[48] These liberties are additional to the affairs that go on, especially during festive seasons when work is slack.

In this matrilineal society descent is traced through women, and children belong to the descent group of their mothers. They inherit, not from their fathers, but from their mother's brothers. Although political authority resided with men, women enjoyed considerable influence and control. They did the important garden work, a privilege as well as a duty. They played special roles in ceremonials, and had a monopoly over certain magic. Women of rank expected respectful treatment from men beneath them. And marriage occurred with little public or private ceremony and did not subject women to their husbands' unquestioned authority. As Malinowski described it,

the woman simply joins her husband in his house, and later on, there is a series of exchanges of gifts, which in no way can be interpreted as purchase money for the wife. As a matter of fact, the most important feature of the Trobriand marriage is the fact that the wife's family have to contribute, and that in a very substantial manner, to the economics of her household, and also they have to perform all sorts of services for the husband. In her married life, the woman is supposed to remain faithful to her husband, but this rule is neither very strictly kept nor enforced. In all other ways, she retains a great measure of independence, and her husband has to treat her well and with consideration. If he does not, the woman simply leaves him and returns to her family, and as the husband is as a rule economically the loser by her action, he has to exert himself to get her back—which he does by means of presents and persuasions. If she chooses, she can leave him for good, and she can always find someone else to marry.[49]

Not all peoples are as casual as the Trobrianders about either premarital sex or marriage ceremony. Among the Kurds, children belong to the descent group of their fathers. This patrilineal people have far more complicated procedures marking the transition to married life, and much less tolerance of female premarital sex. A daughter's chastity must be guarded at all cost. Proof of her virtue is essential and of great significance, as the following description will show:

> The virginity of a maiden must be attested, and from the white undergarments and bedding, the maid who makes up the room in the morning is able to report on her "virtue," for the only test is the blood of the hymen. Occasionally the youth will smear a handkerchief with this blood and present it to his mother. In either case, the mother kisses the girl on the forehead and praises her for her chastity. The stained handkerchief, accompanied by an expensive gift, may be sent to the mother of the girl. If no blood is in evidence, a suspicious husband can return the girl to her father's house, and her relatives are more or less obligated to kill her. If, however, the youth's father is "pious," he requests his son to pardon the girl and to say nothing. [50]

Getting married the Kurdish way requires preparation and complex procedures. Once a potential wife has been selected (by the boy's mother), a formal visit is made at which the girl serves tea or coffee but remains silent unless addressed. If the boy likes what he sees, formal negotiations begin over the sorts of clothing and gold jewelry his family will need to provide:

> The cost to the groom's family is substantial. The amount varies depending on the social and financial status of the families involved. Between poor families, the groom's family will be expected to buy a complete set of clothes, including shoes, and perhaps a dresser. They must also provide at least one each of the following items of gold: a bracelet or watch, a ring, a neckchain, a pair of earrings, and a gold coin to be hung from the chain. The proceeds from selling animals and hides

are used to buy the gold (at least five to ten sheep are required to pay for the gold listed above). If the families are wealthy, more gold is required. The number of rings, earrings and bracelets, lengths of chain and number of coins are all stipulated and may cost several thousand dollars. The gold signifies the groom's family's respect for the bride and her family, and acts as insurance for the bride in the event that the marriage fails or she runs short of funds to pay doctors, to feed her children, etc. The bride's family provides her with a cow or a couple of sheep, and the bride brings her woven *minder* [cushions] and bolsters, and embroidered linen to use in her new home.[51]

Once the prospective couple's fathers have settled upon these arrangements and drawn up a contract, they set a time for the wedding. The girl has little or nothing to say about any of this. She remains with her parents until old enough to marry, during which time the groom's family sends gifts of clothing, cloth, or gold jewelry. The gifts they provide before and after marriage are important; they are matters of status and honor, and also serve to discourage any girl from contemplating divorce.[52]

On the eve of her wedding, the bride's family provides a *henna party* for her female friends and relatives, and the groom's female relatives. There is dancing and singing, and various ceremonies, like the rubbing of palms with henna to bring good luck. Guests from the groom's family may remain overnight, in which case they must be generously fed. On the wedding day there is a party in the groom's home for friends, relatives, and neighbors, with food and music. The bride's young brothers arrange themselves along the route the groom's entourage will take to claim their bride, and demand coins for right of passage. She is supposed to go sadly, and as a modest young woman she should display no affection for her groom. Before she crosses his threshold, family members break a ceramic water pitcher and the bride throws an egg to the ground, to ensure that the marriage will prosper. Among the Kurds, marriage is a family matter more than an individual matter:

> Even after the wedding, the bride and groom are expected not to display affection when others are present. In fact, their daily lives do not overlap much. The groom works with his father and brothers. The bride begins her new life helping the unmarried daughters and her sisters-in-law who married into the family, under the guidance of her mother-in-law. The groom's family will refer to her as "our bride," for she is now a member of their family.[53]

Earlier, in the chapter on sexuality, we addressed the issue of why people like the Kurds may be so concerned about the chastity of daughters that they guard them from any contact with men outside the family, while other societies consider the matter of little interest. We discussed, as well, whether a restrictive attitude toward premarital sex signals constraints on extramarital sex. We will have more to say about these issues in the next chapter, on the marital relationship. For the moment, let us simply consider whether people unconcerned about premarital chastity tend to be more casual about marriage ceremonies as well.

Recall, from our chapter on sexuality, Frayser's observation that women are more obviously linked to their offspring than men, through childbirth, nursing, and the like, and her suggestion that men assert their contribution in other ways.[54] This may help us make some sense of variation in marriage celebrations. Marriage is the means by which men establish reproductive claims, and Frayser suggests that elaborate celebrations, like sexual restrictions, indicate the interest social groups have in reproductive bonds. They confirm marriage and affirm group claims on the offspring it provides. Indeed, Frayser found that societies which restrict women's sexual relationships to the childbearing context (i.e., marriage) are also likely to have elaborate marriage celebrations. Those with few sexual restrictions usually have small or no celebrations. They are almost always small, or even nonexistent, when marriage is established simply by birth of a child or cohabitation, practices we find where the social group has little need to affirm its claim on offspring, as among the Trobrianders, who assign group membership through women rather than through men.

Not surprisingly, societies with elaborate marriage celebrations are also likely to restrict women to a single husband, reducing ambiguity over claims to her children. And Frayser finds moderate or elaborate marriage celebrations in societies with bride wealth, which also confirms marriage and a husband's claim over children. In addition to these affirmative expressions of group involvement, there are also negative ones. Frayser's data reveal that, where illicit sex and reproductive problems commonly provide grounds for divorce, we are also likely to find elaborate marriage celebrations:

> As social interest in marriage increases, confirmation of the union centers on factors that a group of people can share and control. The birth of a child or cohabitation of spouses may depend on fortuitous, individual circumstances, such as a couple's fecundity or compatibility. Ritual and the transference of bride-price are subject to social management. The group has the flexibility to encourage a reproductive union by participating in an elaborate marriage celebration and by investing its economic resources in the couple.[55]

We see, then, that the way marriage is arranged and the nature of marital transactions and celebrations are not matters of whim or accident. Although our understanding of the connections is still rudimentary, it is already clear that these customs, along with rules governing premarital and extramarital sexuality, are related to each other and to other aspects of social structure.

NOTES

1. Robbins Burling, *Rengsanggri: Family and Kinship in a Garo Village* (Philadelphia: University of Pennsylvania Press, 1963), p. 83.
2. If he has had sexual intercourse with the girl in the interim, however, his release may be contingent on payment of a fine.
3. Charulal Mukherjea, *The Santals* (Calcutta: A. Mukherjee and Co., 1962).
4. W. J. Culshaw, *Tribal Heritage: A Study of the Santals* (London: Lutterworth Press, 1949), p. 145.
5. Ibid.
6. Vera St. Erlich, *Family in Transition: A Study of 300 Yugoslav Villages* (Princeton, NJ: Princeton University Press, 1966), p. 200.
7. Ibid.
8. Napoleon A. Chagnon, *Yanomamö* (New York: Harcourt Brace College Publishers, 1992), p. 7.
9. Ibid., pp. 124–125.
10. Barbara C. Ayres, "Bride Theft and Raiding for Wives in Cross-Cultural Perspective," *Anthropological Quarterly* 47 (1974): 238–252.
11. Gwen J. Broude and Sarah J. Greene, "Cross-Cultural Codes on Husband-Wife Relationships," *Ethnology* 22 (1983): 263–280.
12. Paul C. Rosenblatt and Paul C. Cozby, "Courtship Patterns Associated with Freedom of Choice of Spouse," *Journal of Marriage and the Family* 34 (1972): 689–695.
13. W. J. Goode, "The Theoretical Importance of Romantic Love," *American Sociological Review* 24 (1959): 38–47.
14. Rosenblatt and Cozby, "Courtship Patterns Associated with Freedom of Choice of Spouse," p. 691.
15. Ibid., p. 692. Rosenblatt and Cozby used measures of the frequency of dance participation by unmarried but marriageable people, and of the importance of dances in courtship, defined as "male-female interaction with a reasonable chance of leading to marriage as opposed to interaction only for sexual or recreational purposes." Women and men did not have to dance with each other, only to be present at the same dances.
16. Ibid., p. 691.
17. Ibid., p. 692. But Rosenblatt and Cozby suggest some caution in interpreting this finding: Whether the association represents special characteristics of dances or merely the obvious effect of restriction of all contact in societies with minimal freedom requires data on the psychological effects of dances not to be found in most ethnographies. The rhythm and excitement of the dance may have another important effect not previously mentioned: The emotion that is aroused may stimulate the individuals to believe they are experiencing strong feelings of attraction.

18. Ibid., p. 692.
19. Ibid., p. 693.
20. Ibid., pp. 693–694. See also E. J. Kanin, "An Examination of Sexual Aggression as a Response to Sexual Frustration," *Journal of Marriage and the Family* 29 (1967): 428–433.
21. Ibid., p. 694.
22. Ibid., p. 694. Citation from W. LaBarre, "The Aymara Indians of the Lake Titicaca Plateau, Bolivia," *Memoirs of the American Anthropological Association* 68 (1948): 1–250.
23. Robert M. Coppinger and Paul C. Rosenblatt, "Romantic Love and Subsistence Dependence of Spouses," *Southwestern Journal of Anthropology* 24 (1968): 310–319.
24. Coppinger and Rosenblatt find that the mean female subsistence contribution in their sixty-nine-society sample was 40 percent. They suggest that men generally make a greater contribution because women "must bear and nurse children." This echoes earlier research by Melvin and Carol R. Ember, which suggested that women generally contribute less to primary subsistence than men because they devote a lot of time to child-tending; see their article on "The Conditions Favoring Matrilocal versus Patrilocal Residence," *American Anthropologist* 73 (1971): 578. Reprinted with "Afterthoughts," in Melvin Ember and Carol R. Ember, *Marriage, Family, and Kinship: Comparative Studies of Social Organization* (New Haven: HRAF Press, 1983). However, we are talking only about *primary* subsistence activities here, like hunting, gathering, fishing, herding, and agriculture. When it comes to *secondary* subsistence activities such as preparing and cooking food, women may generally do more than men, judging from societies with simple or complex agriculture, which comprise the majority in the ethnographic record. On this point, see Carol R. Ember and Melvin Ember, *Anthropology,* 8th ed. (Upper Saddle River, NJ: Prentice-Hall, 1996), pp. 341–343.
25. There were exceptions, however. Of particular interest were those in which there was an imbalance in the contribution of women and men together with low scores on romantic love. In each such case, the researchers found functional substitutes for romantic love that mitigated at least some of the potentially negative consequences of imbalance in subsistence contribution and resultant marital instability — by obliging support from other kin or larger kin groups, for example, or by facilitating remarriage.
26. Gary R. Lee and Lorene Hemphill Stone, "Mate-Selection Systems and Criteria: Variation According to Family Structure," *Journal of Marriage and the Family* 42 (1980): 319–326.
27. On the occurrence of romance, see William R. Jankowiak and Edward F. Fischer, "A Cross-Cultural Perspective on Romantic Love,"

Ethnology 31 (1992): 149–155; and William Jankowiak, *Romantic Passion: a Universal Experience?* ed. William Jankowiak (New York: Columbia University Press, 1995).

28. Alice Schlegel and Rohn Eloul, "Marriage Transactions: Labor, Property, Status," *American Anthropologist* 90 (1988): 291–309.

29. Ibid.; see also George Peter Murdock, *Ethnographic Atlas* (Pittsburgh: University of Pittsburgh Press, 1967).

30. See Jack Goody, "Bridewealth and Dowry in Africa and Eurasia," in *Bridewealth and Dowry,* eds. Jack Goody and S. J. Tambiah (Cambridge, England: Cambridge University Press, 1973), pp. 1–58.

31. Jack Goody earlier observed that bridewealth and dowry are not "mirror images," in "Bridewealth and Dowry in Africa and Eurasia," pp. 1–58. Schlegel and Eloul also give credit to Goody and Tambiah (*Bridewealth and Dowry*), and to Steven Harrel and Sara A. Dickey, "Dowry Systems in Complex Societies," *Ethnology* 24 (1985): 105–120, for highlighting the connection between dowry and social stratification.

32. See, for example, George Peter Murdock, *Social Structure* (New York: The Free Press, 1965 [originally published 1949]), p. 207; and Melvin Ember, "Taxonomy in Comparative Studies," in *A Handbook of Method in Cultural Anthropology*, eds. Raoul Naroll and Ronald Cohen (New York: Columbia University Press, 1973), pp. 697–706.

33. Ember, "Taxonomy in Comparative Studies," p. 704.

34. See Murdock, *Social Structure*; and Alice Schlegel and Herbert Barry III, "The Cultural Consequences of Female Contribution to Subsistence," *American Anthropologist* 88 (1986): 142–150. Table 8 in Schlegel and Eloul, "Marriage Transactions," confirms that most bride wealth societies, and those with women exchange, have high female contribution to subsistence, in contrast to those societies with other types of transactions; however, bride service societies mostly have low female contribution.

35. This may also explain why women exchange is common in regions that also commonly have bride wealth (Africa and Oceania); women exchange replaces daughters with daughters-in-law.

36. We find it, for example, in the old elite castes and classes of the Middle and Far East and in the Mediterranean, as well as among the elites, artisans, and land-owning peasants of preindustrial Europe.

37. Schlegel and Eloul, "Marriage Transactions," p. 301.

38. Ibid., p. 303.

39. Ibid., pp. 305–306.

40. See Steven J. C. Gaulin and James S. Boster, "Dowry as Female Competition," *American Anthropologist* 92 (1990): 994–1005.

41. Suzanne G. Frayser, *Varieties of Sexual Experience: An Anthropological*

Perspective on Human Sexuality (New Haven: HRAF Press, 1985), p. 274.

42. Ibid.
43. Ibid., pp. 274–275.
44. See Broude and Greene, "Cross-Cultural Codes on Husband-Wife Relationships," p. 277. While the wedding night is special in most societies, however, there are quite a few (47 percent) in which it is not considered a special occasion.
45. Ibid., p. 277. In only 11 percent of the societies in Broude and Greene's sample was the wedding night special but not private.
46. Broude and Green, "Cross-Cultural Codes on Husband-Wife Relationships."
47. Ibid., p. 269.
48. Bronislaw Malinowski, *Argonauts of the Western Pacific: An Account of Native Enterprise and Adventure in the Archipelagoes of Melanesian New Guinea* (London: George Routledge and Sons, Ltd., 1922), p. 54.
49. Ibid.
50. William M. Masters, "Rowanduz: A Kurdish Administrative and Mercantile Center" (Ph.D. diss., University of Michigan, 1953), p. 272.
51. Annette Busby, "Kurds: A Culture Straddling National Borders," in *Portraits of Culture: Ethnographic Originals*, eds. Melvin Ember, Carol R. Ember, and David Levinson (Englewood Cliffs, NJ: Prentice Hall/Simon & Schuster Custom Publishing, 1994), pp. 10–11.
52. Ibid., p. 11.
53. Ibid., p. 13.
54. Frayser, *Varieties of Sexual Experience*, pp. 323–359.
55. Ibid., pp. 329–330.

8

THE MARITAL RELATIONSHIP

In all societies known to anthropology, most people get married at least once in their lives. But this does not mean that the marital bond is the same in all societies. In fact, there is great variety in the kinds of relationships wives and husbands have. One expectation people in all societies have is that married couples will have sex, at least to have offspring. But sex may be frequent and fun in some societies, infrequent and perfunctory in others, and feared in still other societies, as we learned in the chapter on sexuality. Sex aside, we might wonder whether there is generally also an expectation that spouses will love each other and be companions. Or do some people anticipate that they will seek love and affection elsewhere? These are questions we will address in this chapter. We will also discuss the conditions under which jealousy and anger are associated with marriage. If there are co-wives or co-husbands, for example, does that provoke jealousy? Are wives or husbands more likely to exhibit jealousy? Under what circumstances are jealousy and anger likely to lead to marital violence, and which spouse most commonly initiates it?

SEX WITHIN MARRIAGE

Sexual intercourse is always considered proper for married couples, but how much is proper? Here, societies run the gamut from frowning on any sort of abstinence to frowning on frequent sex. The extremes are in the minority—in most societies marital sex is frequent except at certain times, such as during menstruation, pregnancy, or for months or even years after the birth of a child (which we call a *postpartum sex taboo*).[1]

Some people rule sex out entirely during menstruation, some for only part of that time, others have no strong feeling about the matter one way or the other, and still others consider sex during menses desirable. Consider some examples. The Onge of Little Andaman are among those who refrain from sex during the menses, believing that swelling of the arms or legs would follow otherwise. (It is interesting, in passing, that the Onge explain menstruation in very young girls in terms of previous sexual contacts stimulated by nose rubbing, their substitute for kissing.)[2]

The Chinese, too, avoid sex during menses and consider menstruating women polluting, as they are for one month after childbirth, during which time sex can "endanger the health of all concerned."[3] Although other people share the Chinese view, avoidance of sex during menstruation does not everywhere imply notions of pollution. Mischa Titiev tells us, for example, that while the Hopi refrain from sex during menses they "show an exceptional disregard for 'contagion' and have no fear of menstrual blood. No tabus [sic] are imposed on menstruating women, who may even participate at will in the dances of women's societies."[4]

Then there are the Trukese, who do not favor intercourse during menses but allow it.[5] And beyond them, the Mbuti Pygmies of Africa who do have sex during menstruation, and through most of pregnancy as well, restricting it only in the final months before and for several months after childbirth. Some Mbuti reportedly enjoy sex during menses, others find it less enjoyable, but the Mbuti generally believe that sex at that time is the best way to ensure conception.[6]

The Mbuti notion that couples should avoid sex during the final months of pregnancy is not widely shared. In Bang Chan (Thailand), according to one account, people felt that "it was necessary that the father with his semen during intercourse 'strengthen' the baby." The ethnographer tells us that, "there was less, if any, intercourse in the last weeks of pregnancy, though no prohibition against it."[7] The Kanuri of Africa, too, continue sex throughout pregnancy, believing that it "makes for an easier labor at birth by keeping the passage open and providing fluids for the child and the mother."[8] While intercourse is "freely permitted" during pregnancy among the Kurds as well, women are "impure" for forty days after birth and cannot have intercourse with their husbands during that time.[9]

What accounts for these cross-cultural differences in how people think about marital sex and in sexual behavior itself? The attitudes people have toward marital sex are undoubtedly related to their views about sex in general. In societies where people consider sex wonderful, marital sex is also likely to be enjoyable and frequent. Where people think of sex as dangerous to one's health, marital sex is likely to occur minimally, perhaps only when reproduction demands it. Lack of privacy in living arrangements, too, may influence the frequency of marital sex.

In most societies people do prefer some measure of privacy for their sexual activities.[10] In many, married couples sleep in the same room with children and other adults and prefer to wait until others are asleep. Or they may seek a place away from home that affords some privacy. The Siriono of Bolivia had as many as fifty hammocks for sleeping in their unpartitioned huts, and couples there usually chose a place in the bush for their sexual activity.[11]

But perhaps we should not take living arrangements as given as a reason for infrequent sex. It is possible that in some instances living arrangements are intentionally arranged to avoid considerable sexuality. Recall the Mae Enga men of Highland New Guinea, who feared sex with women and spent little time with their wives. They preferred the company of other men in separate men's houses, where they lived and slept apart from their wives and children. Mervyn Meggitt observes that even though men buy spells to protect themselves during marital intercourse, they are likely to experience "disquiet rather than pleasure" in their sexual relations. The Mae Enga husband has intercourse with his wife only as necessary to have children, and regards foreplay as abhorrent.[12] Unfortunately, the ethnographer does not tell us what married women think about sex with their husbands, but given that they marry men from enemy villages, who fear sex with them, it is hard to imagine that they find marital sex very pleasurable.

The way marriage is arranged has its own effect on sexual relationships. One cross-cultural study confirms, not surprisingly, that sex is more likely to be enjoyed and thought of positively, as indicated by time spent in foreplay, where people choose their own spouses. Where marriages are arranged, sex is more likely to be perfunctory.[13]

EXTRAMARITAL SEX

Since married couples typically live in communities, it should not be surprising that extramarital liaisons sometimes occur. As a matter of fact, research indicates that such relationships are not uncommon, for women as well as for men, in a majority of societies.[14] However, the occurrence of extramarital sex does not necessarily imply societal acceptance or a high frequency of it. Many more societies disapprove than approve of extramarital sex, although there is a lot of variation in the degree to which it is prohibited and punished.

Some societies are actually rather relaxed about extramarital relationships. It was reported about the Trukese of Micronesia, for example, that extramarital liaisons were more common than premarital ones. Such relationships evoked no real concern or penalty, although the Trukese did think them less appropriate during the later years of marriage than earlier on. But in general these people considered extramarital relationships far more satis-

fying and exciting than marital ones, which were more functional, obligatory, and reserved:[15]

> The early stages of any marriage are looked on as an experiment. If it
> doesn't work out, there is little hesitancy in getting a divorce. Young
> people, even though married, engage in numerous extramarital affairs,
> so that in a sense courtship activities continue even after marriage.
> Even when a husband and wife feel themselves well matched, it is
> assumed that if they must be separated for a while, they will satisfy their
> sexual urges with other partners until they can be reunited. Husbands
> are jealous of their wives in this connection, however, and a wife may
> be compelled to live with her husband's mother while he is away. This
> is especially likely if gossip gets started about her.[16]

There are other societies in which sex is also permitted outside marriage, and for both sexes, but under more circumscribed conditions. In the
case of the Dogon of West Africa, for example, women and men could have
extramarital liaisons openly until the birth of their first child, after which
they were strictly prohibited on penalty of death. Denise Paulme indicates
something else of interest: In Dogon society it was clearly the woman who
took the initiative. She proposed and pursued the relationship, going periodically to her lover's home with the consent, even encouragement, of her
mother:

> The young woman most frequently is the legitimate wife, *ya biru* of
> another man; she sleeps in the house of the girls and young women of
> her natal quarter or of her village, goes now and then to spend the
> night at the house of her husband, takes her meals and spends all her
> days in the paternal house. She will have met, in the village or at the
> market, a young man to whose compliments she does not show herself
> indifferent; by her smiles, even by her silence, she has encouraged the
> boy, who becomes more urgent; after two or three brief encounters, the
> young woman, yielding to the entreaties of the young man, agrees to
> join him one evening, actively encouraged by her mother, who sees in
> the presence of a *sile* [lover] a source of appreciable gain. The night
> agreed upon, at the hour "when the sorceresses go into the bush," the
> young woman will go to find the boy in his village, in order to spend
> the night at his side: *Sile*, she says to him as she approaches, "let the two
> of us be friends;" the young man will keep this name, he will be the *sile*
> of her whom he henceforth calls his *ya dimu* (literally, woman who fol-
> lows). At the hour "when the sorceresses return to the village," the *ya
> dimu* leaves her friend, and he does not give her anything. At their sec-
> ond meeting, he hands her a certain number of cowries [shells], from
> five hundred to one thousand, it is said; the young woman hides the
> cowries, which she will share with her mother, in a covering that she
> carries rolled on her head. At the third visit of the young woman, the
> *sile* is not supposed to give her any gift; on the fourth, if his means per-

mit it, he will again offer her cowries, etc.... He never gives her jewelry; only the legitimate husband, the *iga biru*, has the right to offer his
wife a bracelet or a necklace. The husband, for his part, will be careful
never to give his wife a sum of money, for the act, on his part, would be
a rudeness: Cowries are the gift of a *sile*, jewelry the gift of the husband.[17]

Among the Masai of East Africa, women could have extramarital relations even after the birth of children, but there were some complicated limitations. L. S. B. Leakey tells us that Masai husbands did not mind if their
wives had sex with other men so long as they didn't do so when the husbands themselves were in need. Even then there was no punishment for a
wife's infidelity, and no claim against her lover so long as he was not a member of the woman's subclan (which would have made their relationship
incestuous). Other limitations on extramarital (and other) sex were that
women could not have intercourse (even with their husbands) while pregnant or menstruating, women and men alike could not have sex with uninitiated youths, warriors were not to have sex with married women, and sex
was prohibited between a woman and any member of her own subclan, or
with the son of any member of her husband's age-group.[18]

Among the Tlingit in North America, custom allowed extramarital
sex as well, but only within the clan. Parties to an extramarital relationship
outside the clan, woman and man alike, faced execution. But if a man
caught his own wife in an adulterous relationship with a clansman he would
likely ignore the matter. If someone else uncovered it, the woman might
well endure the social stigma and continue it or, as was common in families
of higher rank, she might even take the man as a second husband. In that
event, there was little her first husband could do. There was no marriage
ceremony, but the woman henceforth exerted considerable control over her
lover. She could prevent him from marrying another as long as she wished
to keep him.[19]

Thus far, we have been considering societies in which parties to an
extramarital relationship, limited perhaps in their choices, nonetheless
made their own arrangements privately. But in some societies extramarital
sharing is generally expected, and even organized by a spouse. Trukese men
developed sexual skills by practicing as boys, either with married women or
under the tutelage of their brother's wives. Brotherly sharing might involve
married as well as unmarried men, as the following description makes clear:

> Variety may enter into the sexual experience of a married woman with-
> out social repercussions through the visits of her husband's "brothers."
> This...is not infrequent if the husband is away and has given a partic-
> ular "brother" permission. Usually in such cases the preference of the
> wife should be consulted; during our stay on Romonum, however, a
> major fracas was occasioned by a man who beat his wife when she

refused to continue sleeping with his [classificatory] "brother" who was a widower. While a man's wife's [classificatory] "sisters" are supposed to be sexually available to him, in practice this is far less often realized than relations with a "brother's" wife. These relationships, through which variety may be realized without the anticipation of social disapproval or difficulties if they are discovered, partake largely of the character of married intercourse, being confined among other things to the house at night.[20]

Later in this chapter we will discuss at more length whether sharing sexual favors promotes jealousy. Let us simply note, here, that among the Trukese at least, there is little evidence that sharing of female favors, if approved by the brother, provoked jealousy. Indeed, a man might well invite a "brother" to enjoy his wife, as the following incident indicates:

Andy's first sexual experience was with the wife of a somewhat older artificial "brother," who said he felt sorry for Andy because he had no one with whom to sleep and invited him to his house. Andy did not find this an entirely satisfying experience for his "brother" remained in the house, obviously wide awake, throughout his embarrassing first attempts, thus robbing him of what little assurance he had been able to muster for the occasion.[21]

Sex with a brother's wife not approved by her husband could, however, evoke jealousy and even lead to divorce. The ethnographers tell us that, after overcoming his initial embarrassment, Andy began an intensive affair with this "brother's" wife which did elicit outrage and considerable jealousy and ultimately led to divorce.

Interest in creating or reinforcing useful alliances appears to be an important motive in some cultures where, by custom, people offer a spouse (most commonly the wife) to another. Such wife trading was fairly common in the polar regions where families lived at a considerable distance from each other. For example, during the late nineteenth and early twentieth centuries, the Chukchee of Siberia, who often had to travel long distances, allowed a married man to have sex with his host's wife on the understanding that he would offer the same hospitality when the host visited him. Further, cousins and other relatives also entered into regular wife-exchange arrangements. An early account described the visiting arrangement as follows:

The men belonging to such a marriage union are called "companions in wives." Each "companion" has a right to all the wives of his "companion," but takes advantage of his right comparatively seldom, namely, only when he visits for some reason the camp of one of the "companions." Then the host cedes him his place in the sleeping-room. If possible, he leaves the house for the night; goes to his herd, for instance. After such a call, the companion visited generally looks for an occasion to return the visit, in order, in his turn, to exercise his rights.[22]

Diamond Jenness has reported similar practices among the Eskimo during the first decades of the twentieth century. He observed that in a society like theirs, in which strangers were potential enemies, the custom of exchanging wives enabled people to travel in safety. Through the custom of exchanging wives, a visitor ceased to be a stranger and became, instead, a kind of relative even to the point that the children of men exchanging wives became "brothers" and "sisters" and were, therefore, precluded from marrying:

> A Kanghiryuak family, for example, arranged such an exchange with a visiting Puivlik family in the summer of 1915. Often, however, the same bond is found uniting two families that live more or less permanently in the same district. An exchange is then most likely to occur when they come together again after being separated for a few months.... [In one case] the exchange took place in the most casual and informal manner, without the slightest attempt at concealment. It was repeated a week later, although on the second occasion, instead of the women temporarily changing huts, it was the men who moved over. Similar instances occurred frequently later; in fact they were so usual that they passed almost unnoticed in the communities.[23]

There could also be very immediate, concrete, and practical advantages to such arrangements. Jenness described a case in which a woman openly traded husbands for a few days in order to visit her relatives, living where the borrowed husband was traveling. Ethnographic accounts are often silent on what women think about these exchanges, but note that this account, at least, implies that Eskimo women were not necessarily passive or unwilling participants. The economic importance of women in Eskimo society gave them considerable say in domestic affairs and they could be quite aggressive when it came to matters of sex as well.[24]

Ernest S. Burch, Jr., suggests that what is commonly referred to as *wife trading* in this context is actually a misreading of the situation. It was more than that. After a man and woman had sexual intercourse during one of these occasions, they were thereafter considered married for the rest of their lives. The two men effectively became co-spouses (as in polyandry), as did their wives (in polygyny). The children of all four became siblings.[25] Of course, if the arrangement really constituted an example of group marriage, as Burch proposes, then we probably should think of sex here as marital rather than extramarital sex.

A less symmetrical and more clearly extramarital arrangement is found among the Yanomamö in South America. Describing their customs during the mid-1960s, Napoleon A. Chagnon tells us that another form of permitted affair is called *hoimou*—"to befriend" or "act like a friend" to a woman. This type of relationship might occur, for example, when the members of a village have to take refuge with an ally. The allies invariably enter in *nohimou* relationships with the women of the refugees. The refugees are reluctant to give their women as wives to the men of the host village, but they are obliged to permit them to have sexual access to the women. These kinds of affairs also develop within a village between a man and the wife of a friend, or, with single girls. Again, when men go on visits to other villages and bring trade goods, they frequently are permitted to have affairs with the hosts' women, particularly if the men have brought goods that are highly prized by the hosts.[26]

It should be clear, then, that not all peoples share our view that spouses should limit their sexuality to the marital relationship. There are societies in which custom actually makes that unlikely. While there certainly are such societies, however, it is also the case that most societies in the ethnographic record disapprove of extra- marital sex. The Azande in Africa are especially hostile to adulterers, male as well as female, and impose severe penalties when they discover them. Describing the Azande during the late 1920s, the Seligmans wrote that

> although to-day adultery is far more common than formerly, it has probably always been the most frequent class of case brought before the courts, for owing to the Zande system of marriage young men were forced to choose between adultery or continence. Formerly a man up to the age of thirty to thirty-five was in the main deprived of access to women, as they were monopolized by older men, who would marry girls young enough to be their grand-daughters. If a man was caught committing adultery he could be and often was ferociously mutilated, his genitals, ears, upper lip, or both hands being cut off, while if he escaped this penalty he would have to pay an indemnity of a woman and twenty spears, or failing a woman thirty spears, to the husband. Nor did the woman go free; on the slightest suspicion a woman would be flogged, cut with knives, bound and tortured to make her confess the name of her lover.[27]

Severe human sanctions were not the only deterrent: The Azande believed adultery brought misfortune in other ways. A man might lose his life in battle because of his wife's infidelities which was why, before going off to war or on major hunting expeditions, men sometimes asked their wives to reveal any lovers they might have.[28]

It is interesting that the Azande aversion for adultery did not extend to sex with unmarried persons. The fact that people are restrictive in one area of sexuality does not invariably mean they will be so in others. Certainly, the Azande were not at all offended by sex between a married man and an unmarried woman, or between unmarried boys and girls:

Only the sexual relation of any man and a married woman, that is to say, one regularly paid for by her husband, is considered to be adultery. This act is reputedly so serious that formerly the husband could with impunity kill the intruder whom he surprised in this flagrant offense. But the relation of a husband with any free woman does not carry the notion of adultery. This act is not even considered reprehensible in conscience. It can lead to annoyances, arouse the jealousy of his legitimate wives, cause momentarily a little trouble in the household. The husband will encounter no remorse if he succeeds in hiding his occasional relations from his legitimate wives. Simple fornication by an unmarried man with an unmarried woman presents no serious problem in the eyes of the Azande. Only the father of the girl will intervene occasionally, notifying his daughter that he does not approve of these premature relations, not because he sees any wrong in it, but he fears that his daughter will continue this misconduct after marriage and thus bring about a great palaver. This brings us to state that the sexual act is not blameworthy in the eyes of the Azande except in the sole case where it harms justice, that is to say when one abuses the wife of another.[29]

This case clearly reveals a double standard in which the extramarital sex of wives is viewed as much more serious. In sharp contrast to Azande premarital sex prohibitions, which are usually somewhat equal for females and males, their extramarital sex prohibitions are much more restrictive for wives than for husbands.

The Double Standard   In most societies there is such a double standard, and usually sexual restrictions are considerably greater for women than for men. For example, one cross-cultural sample revealed that a slight majority of societies (54 percent) permit extramarital sex for men, while very few (only 11 percent) allow it for women.[30] Why should this be the case? Gwen J. Broude has evaluated various attempts to explain why men might be much more sensitive to spousal infidelity than women.[31]

One possibility, arising from psychoanalytic theory, is that men with exaggerated Oedipal complexes are particularly fearful that their wives may abandon them after having sex with other men. While psychoanalytic theory assumes the Oedipus complex to be universal, it may take exaggerated form in some societies. This could occur, for example, where the mother-son bond was unusually strong, and that might in turn be likely where custom prohibits a husband from having sex with his wife for a year or more after she has given birth. What does a long postpartum sex taboo have to do with a strong mother-son bond? In such societies boys often sleep with their mothers, often in the same bed, while their fathers sleep elsewhere. In terms of psychoanalytic theory, when the father eventually returns to his wife's bed, the son feels abandoned by the mother. The double standard, then, is the presumed effect of this experience. And consistent with this theory, Broude found that societies with long postpartum sex taboos are indeed more likely to impose greater restrictions on women's than on men's sexuality.

A second theory Broude evaluated, and one possibly related to the theory just discussed, suggests that men are especially boastful of their sexual prowess when they unconsciously fear sexual inadequacy. The double standard, according to this view, may reflect such a fear. To the extent that inadequately regulated female sexuality can threaten manly self-respect, it must be restricted, and that may be particularly so with regard to extramarital sex. Broude found some empirical support for this interpretation as well; her results do confirm a relationship between male boasting and the double standard.

But we are still far from really understanding how double standards come to be. We are aware of still other cultural characteristics associated with them, and we need further research to tell us which of the various predictive conditions have independent effects and which are the most important.[32]

TO BE OR NOT TO BE CLOSE

What is marriage like once the dust has settled and the honeymoon, if any, is over? How close a relationship is it, physically and emotionally? As for physical living arrangements, in our society we expect that couples will usually sleep and eat together when both are home. We do not all do so, of course, but people are likely to be suspicious if young marrieds regularly sleep or eat separately, and we are not alone in that regard. While there are people, like the Mae Enga, who insist that husband and wife sleep and eat apart, it turns out that in most societies *monogamously* married husbands and wives normally sleep together. In only 6 percent of the societies analyzed by Broude and Greene did monogamously married couples sleep in different rooms or in different houses.[33]

The situation in *polygynous* societies is quite different, however. John and Beatrice B. Whiting, in a cross-cultural study, found a strong association between polygyny and rooming apart. Commonly, co-wives each have their own bedroom and husbands rotate, sleep in their own bedroom, or share sleeping quarters with other males.[34] As we noted earlier in this chapter, sleeping in the same room is no guarantee of marital privacy. Indeed, Broude and Greene found that husband and wife sleep together alone or just with infants in only 6 percent of societies in which couples sleep in the same room. In the vast majority of societies, unmarried children or other adults sleep with the couple (81 percent of the sample).

As for eating, we find that there are quite a few societies (26 percent) in which spouses take their meals entirely apart. In a few, there is a partial togetherness at meal time; the wife customarily serves and perhaps converses with her husband while he eats (9 percent). On the other hand, research indicates that our own preference in this regard is actually most common; spouses do eat together in most societies (65 percent).

But while spouses sleep and eat together in most societies, other aspects of togetherness are less widespread. For example, companionship during leisure time is much less common than eating and sleeping together. Indeed, Broude and Greene report that in 53 percent of societies husband and wife spend most of their leisure time apart or in the company of others. In only 5 percent of societies did spouses usually spend their leisure time at home, alone or with family members.[35] Still, where couples sleep near each other, they are also likely to eat and spend leisure time together.[36]

The Trobriand Islanders provide a good example of a society with intimate marriages. The intimacy developed gradually. After living together for some time, couples who wanted to remain together in marriage "advertise this fact by sleeping together regularly, by showing themselves together in public, and by remaining with each other for long periods of time."[37] The transition to married state arrived with little fanfare; the woman simply joined her husband. Once married, the companionship matured further. As Malinowski described it:

> Husband and wife in the Trobriands lead their common life in close companionship, working side by side, sharing certain of the household duties, and spending a good deal of their leisure with each other, for the most part in excellent harmony and with mutual appreciation.[38]

A married woman is supposed to remain faithful to her husband although "this rule is neither very strictly kept nor enforced." Indeed, the Trobriand wife enjoys a remarkable measure of independence and considerable leverage over her husband, who "has to treat her well and with consideration," because otherwise she can simply return to her family and, if she chooses, find someone else to marry.[39]

In the opposite direction in terms of marital intimacy, with distinctly aloof marriages, are the Mae Enga of the Western Highlands of Papua New Guinea. Each local kin group has a special house where men meet and sleep (as do boys older than about six).[40] Women may not enter these *men's houses*. Wives live in dispersed homesteads in the vicinity, sharing their houses with unmarried daughters and infant sons. A man's visit to his wife's house is brief and, while there, he never enters the sleeping room because it is used for seclusion during menstruation.[41] Sexual intercourse almost never occurs in the house but rather takes place on cropland lying fallow.

Aloofness characterizes public as well as private relations between the spouses. On public occasions women and men keep to different sides of the living room or courtyard. A man's avoidance of his wife applies to her newborn child as well. Since the placenta is associated with menstrual blood, men consider a baby polluted for two or three months, during which time the father will not see it.

It is not clear whether Mae Enga women share these beliefs. Do they, too, consider themselves unclean and dangerous? Do they have reciprocal beliefs about men? Are men unclean? It is not really surprising that the ethnographer, Mervyn Meggitt, did not explore women's beliefs and attitudes. In such a strictly segregated society, it would have been very difficult for a male ethnographer to interview women about these matters.

Why do we find opposite patterns of conjugal intimacy among the Trobrianders and Mae Enga? One possibility is that warfare (which was frequent among the Mae Enga, but not among the Trobrianders, as of the times described) is conducive to spousal aloofness. Indeed, the Whitings suggest that in societies in which all able-bodied men are involved in war, this condition can lead to male bravado and aloof marriages.[42] Why do they think so? They propose that if a boy perceives during the first years of his life that his mother controls important resources, he will unconsciously wish to emulate her. (This may be especially likely where spouses live mostly apart, as do husbands among the Mae Enga; when they are in the village, they spend most of their time and sleep most of the time in the men's house.) In later years, when the boy discovers that men actually control the important resources (which is particularly the case in patrilocal, patrilineal societies, like the Mae Enga), the boy will develop a masculine identification. Contradictory identifications generate a conflict which, the Whitings propose, is typically resolved by exaggerating masculine behavior—acting super tough and brave. In addition, boys avoid the company of women because it arouses anxiety. It is a syndrome that perpetuates itself: Aloof marriages lead to hypermasculine behavior in sons, which in turn leads to avoiding the company of females and to aloof marriages.[43]

The Whitings suggest that spousal separation and aloofness may be advantageous in certain midrange (precommercial, prestate) societies that need all able-bodied men to be warriors.[44] Exaggerated masculine behavior could result in especially brave and tough warriors. However, we wonder whether we should take on faith just how well super-masculine males do as warriors? Indeed, overly aggressive men, difficult to control, can be problematic, either in a police force or in an armed force. Perhaps we need further research on this matter.

There is another way that spousal aloofness may be adaptive. Recall that in the sexuality chapter we found reason to believe that spousal aloofness may also serve to restrain population growth in a society subject to frequent food shortages and famine. In light of such findings, we must entertain the possibility that Mae Enga fear of sex with women may actually be adaptive. Indeed, Mervyn Meggitt estimates that within a fifty-year period from 1900 to 1950, there were two hundred intergroup wars among the Mae Enga themselves, mostly over limited resources such as land.[45]

Although the Whitings point to an association between war and spousal aloofness, it is not likely that the mere presence of warfare can completely account for such a pattern. For war is virtually universal in the ethnographic record (in the absence of forced pacification by dominant world powers), but marital aloofness is not nearly as common.[46] This suggests that particular aspects of war, such as a high incidence of polygynous marriage (associated, as we discussed in a previous chapter, with high loss of men in battle) or frequent marriage with women from enemy villages, may particularly engender aloof marriages. Recall that the Mae Enga marry their enemies. As they put it, "we marry the people we fight."[47] And we already know that marrying enemies is associated with fear of sex with women.[48]

Clearly, we still have much to learn about the conditions that give rise to intimate or aloof marriages. As Lewellyn Hendrix noted in a review of the subject, "Marital aloofness research has answered many questions and raised a few in the process."[49]

JEALOUSY

Jealousy is probably normal in any human relationship, at least some of the time. But consider two contexts for jealousy that frequently receive mention in ethnographic reports. Both express concern over the attention one's spouse gives others. Jealousy often accompanies the relations of co-wives in the ethnographic literature. And then there is jealousy over extramarital sexual partners. There are some commonalities; jealousy of either sort is usually rooted in concern about the disposition of resources (economic as well as sexual), the only difference being that co-wives are entitled to resources, whereas extramarital partners may not be. But some societies have to deal with much more jealousy than others and, apart from the commonalities, the different forms of jealousy reflect dissimilar circumstances.

Jealousy between Co-Spouses   Polyandry is so rare that it is difficult to generalize about rivalry between co-spouses. In a review of four polyandrous cases—the Toda of India, the Marquesans of the South Pacific, the Tibetans, and the Nayar of India, William N. Stephens indicates that there is actually little ethnographic evidence of jealousy among co-husbands in these cases. Perhaps this is so in two of them (Tibet and Toda) because in those societies the husbands were brothers. As we shall see later, when we discuss sororal polygyny, there is reason to believe that jealousy is less of a problem in polygamous marriages if co-spouses (female or male) are siblings. Stephens also points out that polyandrous societies all appear to have relatively open attitudes toward sex in general (allowing it in childhood, adolescence, and outside of marriage). The inconspicuousness of jealousy in polyandrous societies, then, may simply reflect more casual attitudes toward sex generally.[50]

But jealousy amongst co-wives is often mentioned in descriptions of polygynous societies, particularly where the women are not sisters. Among the Lozi of Africa, for example, "jealousy among co-wives of one man for his sexual and other favours is pronounced and is accepted as normal; the Lozi fear that if it is too great it may lead to sorcery." If a man is partial to one wife, the Lozi suspect she has "corrupted him with medicines or that he is a bit crazy and a fool."[51] And among the Wolof of Gambia, jealousy over a husband's sexual favors is also a problem:

> On the night that a wife cooks supper, she goes to her husband's house after everyone else has gone to bed. In some families the wife sleeps with her husband whether they have intercourse or not; in others the wife returns to her own house after the act is completed. Acute jealousy results when a wife who is to sleep with her husband finds another wife in her place. Of course, the husband is a co-creator of this kind of friction and can avoid it by strict adherence to the schedule of rotation. However, jealousy may occur even when the schedule is rigidly maintained, for a wife may have a belief, often imaginary in fact, that she is receiving a lesser share of her husband's attention on her visits to him than her co-wives.[52]

Competition for a husband's sexual favors is not the only reason for conflict among co-wives; there are also economic concerns. Among the Wolof, considerable jealousy results if a husband favors one wife by giving her money, jewelry, or cloth. He must take pains to properly and fairly maintain all his wives.[53] Economic concerns have also been a major source of conflict among co-wives in China. In the course of fieldwork in Taiwan during the 1960s, several polygynously married men complained to Pasternak about the constant uproar among their wives. They analyzed the problem in distinctly economic terms: The women were fighting to ensure a proper patrimony for their children, and one that would ensure their own security in old age as well. Villagers fully expected co-wives to argue about such things, which is why many families tried to discourage fathers or sons from taking second wives.

Jealousy may lead to attempts to hurt or injure others. A cross-cultural survey of female aggression in 317 societies by Victoria K. Burbank reveals that while males typically exhibit much more aggression than females, females also exhibit aggression, but much less often. And female aggression is usually verbal or gestural; physical aggression is relatively uncommon. The targets of female aggression are usually female too, with co-wives being the most frequent. When co-wives aggress against each other, the stated reasons are usually jealousy, the husband's distribution of favors, services, or goods, or the appearance of a new wife. Burbank found that while women sometimes assault men, they do not do so as often as they assault women. And when they aggress against men, it is usually against husbands for reasons having to do with inequities in the distribution of family resources.[54]

There are fewer reports of jealousy where polygny is *sororal*, where a man marries sisters. Why should that be so? Perhaps, as Murdock some time ago suggested, sisters, having grown up together, have already worked out their adjustment. If they become co-wives, then, they may carry that adjustment with them.[55] Indeed, sororal polygyny is quite common in the ethnographic record. Murdock's survey indicated that it occurs in 23 percent of societies in which polygyny is permitted but infrequent, and in 42 percent of those in which polygyny is general. In 14 percent of societies with general polygyny, such unions are exclusively sororal.[56] While sororal polygyny may ameliorate some of the strains to which polygynous marriages are subject, however, we must be aware that it is not a perfect solution; less jealousy is not the same as no jealousy. The jealousy of co-wives often leads to aggression. Even in societies with customary sororal polygyny, there are reports of aggression by females against co-wives (who are mostly sisters).[57] So sororal polygyny probably does not inhibit co-wife aggression entirely.

Given that jealousy is common among co-wives, especially when they are not sisters, we would expect that people would invent customs to deal with or at least to minimize the problem, especially in societies with nonsororal polygyny. And, indeed, we do find a number of customs and practices that have that effect.[58]

Whereas co-wives who are sisters almost always live together, those who are not sisters tend to have separate living quarters. Indeed, Murdock found that co-wives live in separate dwellings in 51 percent of societies with nonsororal polygyny, compared to only 14 percent in those with exclusive sororal polygyny.[59] For example, among the Plateau Tonga in Africa, who practiced nonsororal polygyny, the husband shared his personal goods and sexual favors according to principles of strict equality, among wives who lived in separate dwellings. But the Crow Indians practiced sororal polygyny, and co-wives in that society usually shared the same tepee.

Fairness is not characteristic of the Tonga alone; by custom co-wives usually have clearly defined and equivalent rights in matters of sex, economics, and personal possessions. The Tanala of Madagascar require the husband to spend a day with each co-wife in succession. Failure to do so constitutes adultery and entitles the slighted wife to sue for divorce and an alimony of up to one-third of the husband's property. Furthermore, land is shared equally among all the women, who expect their husband to help cultivate it when he visits.

Even where custom calls for fairness, however, husbands do not always find it possible to satisfy that admonition. Usually secondary wives are younger than first wives, and sometimes he, rather than his parents or kinsmen, has chosen them. Later wives are likely to be more attractive to him. For that reason, we usually find compensatory customs that bring things back into some sort of balance. Thus, greater prestige is usually accorded the senior wife. In the case of the Tonga of Polynesia, for example, she is *chief wife*. Her house is located in a favored spot to the right of her husband's, and is called *the house of the father*. The other wives are *small wives*, and their houses are to the left of their husband's. The chief wife enjoys other privileges as well. She has the right to be consulted first, and her husband is expected to sleep under her roof before and after a journey. Although such distinctions might seem grounds for jealousy, they usually amount to little more than compensation for the disadvantages of age.

Do these rules actually minimize jealousy among co-wives? Maybe they do, but we don't know for sure. In any case, there may still be jealousy, even with rotation rules, if unrelated co-wives have to share the same living space. For example, a recent news story describes the situation of some African women living polygynously in France. Mrs. Keita from Senegal tells us what happened when her husband came back to France with a new wife who was to share their cramped apartment: "You hear everything, your husband and the other wives... You hear how he behaves with his favorite, usually the new one. The women end up hating the man. Everyone feels bad inside." Madine Diallo from Mali says: "In Africa there is space. Even if co-wives live around the same courtyard, at least each wife has her own room or her house. The man visits her there, in her own bed. Here two, three families are packed into two rooms."[60]

But jealousy, even in nonsororal polygyny, is not completely inevitable, judging by the Arapesh of New Guinea. Margaret Mead tells us that married life there "is so even and contented that there is nothing to relate of it at all."[61] We should be aware that the circumstances surrounding Arapesh polygyny were somewhat unusual. First, polygyny was not thought of as the ideal form of marriage, monogamy was. Second, in most polygynous marriages a younger brother inherited his elder brother's wife (we will discuss this custom, called the *levirate*, in the next chapter). This means that men were not *choosing* to marry a second wife; custom obliged them to do so. Moreover, being widows of an older brother, leviratic wives were not likely sexual threats to a younger woman. Finally, the first and leviratic wives usually knew each other, having spent time in the same community as married women. The situation is thus quite different from that in most other polygynous societies, where secondary wives are usually younger and often come from different communities.

Sexual Jealousy   It is not really possible to compare the jealousy co-husbands experience with that of co-wives because there are so few polyandrous societies. On the basis of the cases we have, however, there is reason to believe that co-husbands are less likely to be jealous then co-wives. On the other hand, when it comes to jealousy about sexual relationships outside marriage, men are far more likely than women to be jealous. Moreover, jealousy is much more likely to provoke violence in men. Indeed, male sexual jealousy often escalates to violence. This is an idea certainly not unfamiliar to us; reporting figures on the United States and Africa, Daly et al. indicate that a considerable number of homicides have sexual jealousy as a motive.

Anthropologists and others with a Darwinian orientation have suggested why men are so inclined to react with jealousy to marital infidelities. They point out that fathers, unlike mothers, always have some measure of uncertainty as to which children are theirs. Men, therefore, have reason to guard against rivals, especially where custom obliges them to help care for a baby that might not be theirs.[62] Could it not be, then, that through jealousy and the threat of violence, men increase their control over wives? While mention of male sexual jealousy is quite common in the ethnographic record, its expression and importance varies considerably from society to society. The Darwinian interpretation just outlined cannot easily account for such variation.

Consider, then, some other explanatory possibilities. We noted earlier that, cross-culturally, custom far more often prohibits women from having extramarital sex than men. And in connection with that double standard, we discussed some psychological theories that purport to explain why men in some societies might suffer unusual insecurity and, for that reason, be inclined to impose greater restrictions on their wives. Those same theories could also account for the fact that men exhibit more jealousy in some societies than in others.

There are other possibilities. For example, a cross-cultural study by Hupka and Ryan indicates that variation in male sexual jealousy is related to the importance society places on marriage as the gateway to adulthood and its privileges, and to the degree to which society limits sex to the marital relationship. In short, the more a society stresses the importance of marriage, and the more it limits sex to marriage, the more likely men are to respond to apparent infidelities with violence.[63] In such societies, wifely infidelity threatens a crucial relationship, one that defines adulthood and one's place in society. Hupka and Ryan also found that male sexual jealousy is more likely where private property is important.[64] And that might well be because infidelity is a threat to that property.

What is puzzling, however, is that women's sexual jealousy is apparently not related to these same factors. Hupka and Ryan suggest that the response options available to women when it comes to their husbands' infidelity are so few and limited that there is not much variability to explain.[65] Clearly more research needs to be done if we are to better understand why infidelity provokes more jealousy in men than in women cross-culturally, and why its expression varies. In attacking the problem, we may need to follow a more eclectic research strategy. Along these lines, Lewellyn Hendrix has suggested that a combination of Darwinian and social interpretations may be useful: The former may explain men's ferocity in jealousy situations, while cultural factors may account for jealousy being differentially restrained or encouraged.[66]

VIOLENCE AGAINST SPOUSES

While most Americans consider violence against spouses and children abusive now, the meaning of abuse, and what goes into it, has actually changed over time. For example, is it abusive to administer physical punishment to a child? Not so long ago, teachers in the United States routinely disciplined children by hitting them with rulers or paddles, and many parents used switches or belts at home. Today, many of us consider such practices abusive, but were they also abusive when they were still generally accepted as appropriate forms of discipline? Some would hold that abuse is violence that goes beyond what a culture considers appropriate. But by this reasoning, we would have to consider wife-beating in some societies not "abuse" since those cultures find it acceptable. For example, the Serbs (as in many other societies) believed that a husband had the right to beat his wife for any reason.[67] Most current researchers prefer to focus on the violent acts themselves, ignoring what the culture deems appropriate or excessive. For example, one can study whether wives or husbands are physically assaulted (and how often) without labeling that behavior *abuse*.[68]

Spousal assault is quite common in the United States. In 1985 alone, one out of six couples experienced some sort of violent episode. And the figures indicate that there is a greater likelihood of being assaulted by a family member than by a stranger; for women the risk is more than two hundred times greater.[69] Somewhat surprisingly, surveys in the United States find that wives and husbands are equally likely to assault one another. Nonetheless, we consider wife battering a more serious social problem because they are much more likely than husbands to be seriously injured.[70]

Are wives and husbands equally likely to assault each other in most cultures? The answer appears to be no. In an extensive cross-cultural study of family violence focusing on physical assault, David Levinson found that, cross-culturally, wife-beating is the most common form of family violence; it occurs at least occasionally in about 85 percent of the world's societies. And in about half the sample, it is sometimes serious enough to cause permanent injury or death. Husband-beating occurs much less often (in 27 percent of the societies surveyed), and never occurs in the absence of wife-beating. And in societies where both forms of violence are present, husband-beating usually occurs less often than wife-beating.[71] Clearly, there is a double standard when it comes to violence against spouses—women are the more likely victims. And in more than half the wife-beating societies, violence against women may result in death or permanent injury.

What accounts for differences in the incidence of wife-beating from one society to another? Cross-cultural evidence indicates that wife-beating is related to broader patterns of adult violence. Societies that have violent methods of conflict resolution within communities, physical punishment of criminals, higher frequencies of warfare, and cruelty toward enemies generally also have more wife-beating.[72] It is often assumed that wife-beating is also more likely in societies where males control economic and political resources. In a cross-cultural test of this assumption, Levinson found that while not all indicators of male dominance predict wife-beating, many do. Specifically, wife-beating is more common where men control the products of family labor, have the final say in domestic decision making, where divorce is more difficult for women to obtain, where widow remarriage is controlled by the husband's kin, and where society lacks female work groups.[73] These particular indicators of male dominance do predict a greater likelihood of wife-beating. Evidence from the United States specifically indicates that the more one spouse dominates decisions, the more likely domestic violence will occur. Wife-beating is even more likely where husbands control the household but are out of work.[74]

Societies vary widely in the quality of marital relationships. Some societies clearly have warm and intimate relationships; in others, marriage is characterized by aloofness and even hostility. But even though marital relationships are sometimes less rewarding, no societies have chosen to do without them. And whether personally rewarding or painful and abusive, marital relationships inevitably come to an end, either by death or divorce. In the next chapter we consider those possibilities, along with the options that present themselves thereafter. Just how accessible is divorce, cross-culturally, for women as well as men? Under what conditions is it possible for women and men to end painful marriages this way, and do we find here, too, a double standard? What determines the likelihood of remarriage after divorce, for women and men? And what of widows and widowers—what is the likelihood they will try again? These are some of the questions to which we turn in the next chapter.

NOTES

1. Gwen J. Broude, "Variations in Sexual Attitudes, Norms, and Practices," in *Cross-Cultural Research for Social Science*, eds. Carol R. Ember and Melvin Ember (Upper Saddle River, NJ: Prentice Hall/Simon & Schuster Custom Publishing, 1996).

2. Lidio Cipriani, "Hygiene and Medical Practices among the Onge (Little Andaman)," *Anthropos* 56 (1961): 492.

3. Norma Joyce Diamond, *K'un Shen: A Taiwan Village* (New York: Holt, Rinehart & Winston, 1969), p. 61.

4. Mischa Titiev, *Old Oraibi: A Study of the Hopi Indians of Third Mesa*, Harvard University, Peabody Museum of American Archaeology and Ethnology, Papers 22, no. 1 (New York: Kraus Reprint Co., 1971), p. 16.

5. Thomas Gladwin and Seymour B. Sarason, *Truk: Man in Paradise*

(New York: Wenner-Gren Foundation for Anthropological Research, Viking Fund Publications in Anthropology no. 20, 1953), p. 115.

6. Colin M. Turnbull, "The Mbuti Pygmies: An Ethnographic Survey," *Anthropological Papers of the American Museum of Natural History* 50 (1965): 181, 122.

7. Jane Richardson Hanks, *Maternity and Its Rituals in Bang Chan* (Ithaca: Cornell University, Department of Asian Studies, Southeast Asia Program, Data Paper no. 51, 1964), p. 31. See also Howard Keva Kaufman, *Bangkhuad: A Community Study in Thailand* (New York: Association for Asian Studies Monographs 10, 1960), p. 219. The view there, according to Kaufman, is that frequent sexual activity during the first three months of pregnancy gives strength to the fetus.

8. Ronald Cohen, *The Kanuri of Bornu* (New York: Holt, Rinehart & Winston, 1967), p. 54.

9. William M. Masters, "Rowanduz: A Kurdish Administrative and Mercantile Center" (Ph.D. diss., University of Michigan, 1953), p. 254.

10. Broude, "Variations in Sexual Attitudes, Norms, and Practices."

11. Clellan S. Ford and Frank A. Beach, *Patterns of Sexual Behavior* (New York: Harper, 1951), p. 69.

12. M. J. Meggitt, "Male-Female Relationships in the Highlands of Australian New Guinea," *American Anthropologist* 66, no. 4 (1964): 210.

13. Broude, "Variations in Sexual Attitudes, Norms, and Practices." It is not clear from this study, however, that sexual relations continue to be perfunctory *throughout marriage* in the case of arranged marriages.

14. Gwen J. Broude and Sarah J. Greene, in "Cross-Cultural Codes on Twenty Sexual Attitudes and Practices," *Ethnology* 15 (1976): 416, report that in 69 percent of the sample societies surveyed, extramarital sex was not uncommon or was even universal for men; the figure for women was 57 percent.

15. Gladwin and Sarason, *Truk*, p. 101.

16. Ward H. Goodenough, *Property, Kin, and Community on Truk* (New Haven: Yale University Press, Yale University Publications in Anthropology no. 46, 1951), p. 121.

17. Denise Paulme, *Organisation Sociale Des Dogon (Soudan Français)* [*Social Organization of the Dogon (French Sudan)*] (Paris: Editions Domat-Montchrestien, F. Loviton et Cie., 1940), p. 377.

18. L. S. B. Leakey, "Some Notes on the Masai of Kenya Colony," *Journal of the Royal Anthropological Institute of Great Britain and Ireland* 60 (1930): 202.

19. Kalvero Oberg, "Crime and Punishment in Tlingit Society," *American Anthropologist* 36 (1934): 145–155.

20. Gladwin and Sarason, *Truk*, p. 112.

21. Ibid., p. 102.
22. Vladimir Germanovich Bogoraz Tan, *The Chukchee: Material Culture [Part 1], Religion [Part 2], Social Organization [Part 3]* (New York: G. E. Stechert and Co., Memoirs of the American Museum of Natural History 11, 1904 [Part 1], 1907 [Part 2], 1909 [Part 3]), p. 602.
23. Diamond Jenness, *The Life of Copper Eskimos*, Report of the Canadian Arctic Expedition, 1913–1918, 12, part A (Ottawa: F. A. Acland, 1992), p. 86.
24. Ibid., p. 272.
25. Ernest S. Burch, Jr., "North Alaskan Eskimos: A Changing Way of Life," in *Portraits of Culture: Ethnographic Originals*, eds. Melvin Ember, Carol R. Ember, and David Levinson (Englewood Cliffs, NJ: Prentice Hall/Simon & Schuster Custom Publishing, 1994).
26. Napoleon A. Chagnon, "Yanomamö Warfare, Social Organization, and Marriage Alliances" (Ph.D. diss. submitted to the University of Michigan, University Microfilms Publications no. 67–8226. Ann Arbor: University Microfilms, 1967), p. 64.
27. Charles Gabriel Seligman and Brenda Z. Seligman, *Pagan Tribes of the Nilotic Sudan* (London: George Routledge and Sons, Ltd., 1932), p. 516.
28. Edward Evan Evans-Pritchard, *Witchcraft, Oracles, and Magic among the Azande* (Oxford: Clarendon Press, 1937), p. 77.
29. C. R. Lagae, *Les Azande ou Niam-Niam: L'organisation Zande, Croyances Religieuses et Magiques, Coutomes Familiales* [*The Azande or Niam-Niam: Zande Organization, Religious and Magical Beliefs, Family Customs*], Bibliotheque-Congo, XVIII (Bruxelles: Vromant and Company, 1926), p. 77.
30. Broude and Greene, "Cross-Cultural Codes on Twenty Sexual Attitudes and Practices."
31. Gwen J. Broude, "Extramarital Sex Norms in Cross-Cultural Perspective," *Behavior Science Research* 15 (1980): 181–218.
32. Ibid.
33. In 41 percent of societies the couple sleep in the same bed, under the same blanket, touching, or in adjacent sleeping places. In 13 percent they sleep in the same room but in different beds, hammocks, or in different sections of the room. These data come from Gwen J. Broude and Sarah J. Greene, "Cross-Cultural Codes on Husband-Wife Relationships," *Ethnology* 22 (1983): 277. Since in most polygynous societies the husband and the co-wives do not share the same quarters (each wife usually has a separate room or hut), the rating was made for the monogamous marriages alone.
34. John W. M. Whiting and Beatrice B. Whiting, "Aloofness and Intimacy of Husbands and Wives: A Cross-Cultural Study," *Ethos* 3 (1975): 186–187.

35. In 25 percent of the societies, same-sex leisure activities predominate, and in 50 percent the couple may spend time together, but group or sex-segregated activities are salient. In yet another 21 percent they sometimes spend leisure time together at home, and sometimes together in groups (with visitors or visiting). Same-sex activities may be present but are not salient.

36. Whiting and Whiting, "Aloofness and Intimacy of Husbands and Wives," p. 189. This pattern of associations is supported by the subsequent research of Gwen J. Broude, "Male-Female Relationships in Cross-Cultural Perspective: A Study of Sex and Intimacy," *Behavior Science Research* 18 (1983): 166–167.

37. Bronislaw Malinowski, *The Sexual Life of Savages in Northwestern Melanesia* (New York: Halycon House, 1932), p. 77.

38. Ibid., p. 109.

39. Bronislaw Malinowski, *Argonauts of the Western Pacific: An Account of Native Enterprise and Adventure in the Archipelagoes of Melanesian New Guinea* (London: George Routledge and Sons, Ltd., 1922), p. 54.

40. The description of the Mae Enga here is based on Meggitt, "Male-Female Relationships in the Highlands of Australian New Guinea."

41. Contact with menstrual blood is thought of as dangerous and as possibly leading to a man's death.

42. Whiting and Whiting, "Aloofness and Intimacy of Husbands and Wives," p. 192.

43. Girls in such a society might also wish to be male at that point, but a gender identity conflict is not as likely for them as for boys because girls end up where they started, identifying mostly with their mothers.

44. Whiting and Whiting, "Aloofness and Intimacy of Husbands and Wives," p. 198. These researchers do not suggest that people will be consciously aware that aloof marriages will produce superior warriors, but that a gender identity conflict will be adaptive if the society needs males to be warriors. Patricia Draper and Henry Harpending, "Father Absence and Reproductive Strategy: An Evolutionary Perspective," *Journal of Anthropological Research* 38 (1982): 255–273, also argue that father absence may be adaptive in certain circumstances but they offer different reasons. Consistent with the Whitings' suggestion, J. Patrick Gray and Rob Brubaker, "Aloof Marriage, Subsistence, and the Socialization of Boys: A Multivariate Analysis," *World Cultures* 7 (1993): 7–23, found that aloof marriages are more common in preindustrial mid-range societies (agricultural and herding societies). Aloof marriages are also likely with two other indicators of mid-range cultural complexity, permanent villages and important kin groups—see Gwen J. Broude, "The Relationship of Marital Intimacy and Aloofness to Social Environment: A Hologeistic Study," *Behavior Science Research* 21 (1987): 61.

45. M. J. Meggitt, *Blood Is Their Argument: Warfare among the Mae Enga Tribesmen of the New Guinea Highlands* (Palo Alto, CA: Mayfield Publishing Company, 1977), pp. 11–15.

46. Carol R. Ember and Melvin Ember, "Resource Unpredictability, Mistrust, and War: A Cross-Cultural Study," *Journal of Conflict Resolution* 36 (1992): 242. See also Carol R. Ember and Melvin Ember, "Violence in the Ethnographic Record: Results of Cross-Cultural Research on War and Aggression," in *Troubled Times: Osteological and Archaeological Evidence of Violence*, eds. David Frayer and Debra Martin (Langhorne, PA: Gordon and Breach, in press).

47. Meggitt, "Male-Female Relationships in the Highlands of Australian New Guinea," p. 218.

48. Carol R. Ember, "Men's Fear of Sex with Women: A Cross-Cultural Study," *Sex Roles* 4 (1978): 657–678.

49. Lewellyn Hendrix, "Varieties of Marital Relationships," in *Cross-Cultural Research for Social Science*, eds. Ember and Ember.

50. William N. Stephens, *The Family in Cross-Cultural Perspective* (New York: Holt, Rinehart & Winston, 1963), p. 46.

51. Max Gluckman, "The Lozi of Barotseland in North-Western Rhodesia," in *Seven Tribes of British Central Africa*, eds. Elizabeth Colson and Max Gluckman (Manchester: Manchester University Press, 1959), p. 79.

52. David W. Ames, "Plural Marriage among the Wolof in the Gambia: With a Consideration of Problems of Marital Adjustment and Patterned Ways of Resolving Tensions" (Unpublished Ph.D. diss. Evanston, IL: Northwestern University, 1953), p. 109.

53. Ibid., p. 108.

54. Victoria K. Burbank, "Female Aggression in Cross-Cultural Perspective," *Behavior Science Research* 21 (1987): 88–92.

55. See George Peter Murdock, *Social Structure* (New York: The Free Press, 1965 [originally published 1949]), pp. 30–31. See also George Peter Murdock and John W. M. Whiting, "Cultural Determination of Parental Attitudes: The Relationship between Social Structure, Particularly Family Structure, and Parental Behavior," in *Problems of Infancy and Childhood*, ed. Milton J. E. Senn (New York: Josiah Macy Jr. Foundation, 1951), as referred to in Stephens, *The Family in Cross-Cultural Perspective*.

56. Murdock, *Social Structure*, pp. 29–30.

57. Burbank, "Female Aggression in Cross-Cultural Perspective," p. 87.

58. The notion that these practices constitute cultural adjustments to the potentiality for jealousy was taken from Stephens, *The Family in Cross-Cultural Perspective*, p. 63. Elaboration of the idea, and the examples described in the three following paragraphs, come from Carol R.

Ember and Melvin Ember, *Anthropology*, 8th ed. (Upper Saddle River, NJ: Prentice Hall, 1996), p. 375.

59. Murdock, *Social Structure*, p. 31.

60. Marlise Simons, "African Women in France Battling Polygamy," *The New York Times International*, January 26, 1996, pp. A1, A6.

61. Margaret Mead, *Sex and Temperament in Three Primitive Societies* (New York: New American Library, 1950 [originally published 1935]), p. 101.

62. Martin Daly, Margo Wilson, and Suzanne J. Weghorst, "Male Sexual Jealousy," *Ethology and Sociobiology* 3 (1982): 11–27. Daly et al. acknowledge that there is considerable variation in power relations between the sexes cross-culturally, and suggest that the degree of economic autonomy women enjoy is an important determinant of whether they are likely to succumb to male domination. But in all societies, they maintain, there is an inclination for men to control the sexual behavior of their mates.

63. Ralph B. Hupka and James M. Ryan, "The Cultural Contribution to Jealousy: Cross-Cultural Aggression in Sexual Jealousy Situations," *Behavior Science Research* 24 (1990): 51–71.

64. Ibid. Hupka and Ryan suggest that this finding is consistent with K. Davis's idea, in "Jealousy and Sexual Property," *Social Forces* 14 (1936): 395–405, that people determined to protect their property interests are likely to extend that idea to mates.

65. Hupka and Ryan, "The Cultural Contribution to Jealousy," pp. 61–62.

66. Hendrix, "Varieties of Marital Relationships."

67. David Levinson, *Family Violence in Cross-Cultural Perspective* (Newbury Park, CA: Sage Publications), p. 34, citing Vera St. Erlich, *Family in Transition: A Study of 300 Yugoslav Villages* (Princeton, NJ: Princeton University Press, 1966), p. 270.

68. See Jill E. Korbin, "Introduction," in *Child Abuse and Neglect: Cross-Cultural Perspectives*, ed. Jill E. Korbin (Berkeley: University of California Press, 1981), p. 4. To complicate matters, many would now argue that *abuse* should not be restricted to physical violence. Are not verbal aggression and neglect just as harmful (if not more so) and as painful as physical aggression? Few would disagree that inflicting injuries serious enough to kill or maim constitutes abuse, but there would likely be less agreement when it comes to other, less extreme behaviors.

69. Murray A. Straus, "Physical Violence in American Families: Incidence Rates, Causes, and Trends," in *Abused and Battered: Social and Legal Responses to Family Violence*, eds. Dean D. Knudsen and JoAnn L. Miller (New York: Aldine de Gruyter, 1991), pp. 17–34.

70. Straus, "Physical Violence in American Families," p. 17.

71. Levinson, *Family Violence in Cross-Cultural Perspective*, p. 31.
72. Gerald M. Erchak, "Family Violence," in *Research Frontiers in Anthropology*, eds. Carol R. Ember and Melvin Ember (Englewood Cliffs, NJ: Prentice Hall/Simon & Schuster Custom Publishing, 1995), pp. 44–45.
73. Ibid., p. 71. Gerald M. Erchak and Richard Rosenfeld, in "Societal Isolation, Violent Norms, and Gender Relations: A Reexamination and Extension of Levinson's Model of Wife Beating," *Cross-Cultural Research* 28 (1994): 111–133, suggest that the relationship between wife-beating and women's status is somewhat curvilinear, with higher levels of beating occurring in societies in the middle range of female power. They propose that power may cause more trouble in the middle range because it is more ambiguous there.
74. Richard J. Gelles and Murray A. Straus, *Intimate Violence* (New York: Simon and Schuster, 1988), pp. 78–88.

9

DIVORCE
AND REMARRIAGE

In all societies, most adults at any given moment are married. We might suppose, then, that divorce should be rare or nonexistent in most societies. But that is not true. Divorce or other termination of marriage is common or frequent in many societies, not just in modern societies like our own. Divorce occurs at varying rates in the societies known to anthropology, including many that anthropologists (and others) have deemed highly deserving of emulation. Many people in our society consider our high divorce rate to be a sign of societal decay. But is it? It is doubtful that most of our problems would be cured if we simply reduced the rate of divorce. Would the AIDS epidemic subside? Would affordable housing become more available, or homelessness disappear, if we divorced less often?

While divorce is not the source of all our problems, it is nonetheless more frequent than we would like. In many societies known to anthropology, the gender division of labor is quite strict and the absence of commercial exchange makes it difficult, if not impossible, for a person to live independently, without the aid of spouse or kin. (If you could not sell your labor or products so that you could buy what you need to live, how could you live independently?) We may assume, therefore, that our high divorce rate is at least partly caused by the fact that women and men in our highly commercial society can manage on their own, individually.[1] But such an assumption could be misleading because, if capacity for independent living really caused divorce, then wouldn't most divorced adults remain unmarried? As in many other societies, the vast majority of people who get divorced in our society usually remarry soon afterward. A high divorce rate clearly does not mean that many individuals will choose to live independently just because they can.

Divorce is not exclusively a characteristic of advanced industrial-commercial societies; it occurs in less complex societies as well. To be sure, the rate varies. Cross-cultural research indicates that societies vary widely in their tolerance (as well as rate) of divorce. They also vary as to the grounds for divorce that are acceptable, in the degree to which women and men have equal rights to divorce and remarriage, and in the extent to which remarriage (after divorce or the death of a spouse) is obligatory. (In many societies known to anthropology, a widow or widower was obliged to marry the dead spouse's sibling, real or classificatory.) Let us first explore how divorce and remarriage vary cross-culturally, and how divorce could occur even in nonindustrial, noncommercial societies, where we might least expect people to divorce or to find it feasible. Cross-cultural comparison may reveal sources of divorce that are important but less apparent in complex societies like our own.

DIVORCE

The fact is that divorce is not unthinkable in most societies. A study by Broude and Greene found divorce strongly disapproved and stigmatizing in only 16 percent of the societies considered. But that only has to do with values—with attitudes toward divorce. Divorce itself turned out to be a rare occurrence in only 30 percent of their sample societies.[2] It is clearly not a phenomenon unique to modern societies. This does not mean, of course, that other societies encourage or welcome divorce, or that they make it easy.

A variety of constraints almost unavoidably discourage divorce in most societies. Who will get the children and who will get the property? Usually divorce means that at least one spouse must endure substantial loss (emotional if not economic); children rarely remain with both parents after divorce, and even if property is divided equally, each party ends up with less than before. Given the special bond between mother and children that we have described, we might suppose that most societies would naturally favor her when it came to the disposition of children following divorce. But, in fact, not all people are convinced that children should remain with the mother after divorce, nor do they invariably prefer some form of joint custody. A survey of societies conducted by Suzanne G. Frayser revealed that 42 percent of societies have a clear preference for keeping children with only one parent, and of these, about half (22 percent of all sample societies) prefer that they remain with the father.[3]

In any event, concerns about child custody clearly serve to discourage one or both parties from seeking divorce in most societies. The threat of property loss, too, is a brake on divorce. In many societies, property distribution depends on which party was at fault (in 41 percent of all sample societies), presumably inhibiting some behavior that might lead to divorce. Only 21 percent of societies favor an equitable distribution of resources at divorce, regardless of fault. More often, where fault is not determining, one spouse (or the kin of one spouse) is likely to suffer a greater loss. And of the societies for which this is true, the wife or her kin are somewhat more likely to be the losers (in 23 percent of all societies, compared to 15 percent for husbands or their kin).

REASONS FOR DIVORCE

In most societies, divorce is not something couples simply decide on their own because they are no longer in love. Socially acceptable grounds must usually be cited, and these vary considerably among societies as well as between women and men. In Laura L. Betzig's cross-cultural study, adultery constitutes the most common ground for divorce (55 percent of the sample societies).[4] In that connection, Betzig notes a "double standard," in that "almost every one of the causes of conjugal dissolution that might be related to infidelity is ascribed significantly more often to one sex than to the other."[5] Where adultery is the principal ground for divorce, for example, people most often view it as solely the fault of women (67 percent of societies in which adultery is an important ground for divorce). Divorce is attributed to infidelity on the part of either spouse in fewer societies (31 percent of the cases), and men are exclusively responsible for adultery in only 2 percent of the societies in which adultery constitutes an important ground for divorce.[6]

But why should adultery be the most common reason for divorce? One possibility is that "the neglected spouse risks losing everything she or he had hoped to gain by marrying, including social, economic, and reproductive resources."[7] Then why the double standard? Here, Betzig offers a Darwinian explanation:

> Though there is no reason that adultery on the part of a wife should compromise her social or economic contribution to a marriage any more than adultery on the part of the husband should compromise his, the reproductive consequences of even a single extramarital sexual encounter are likely to be vastly more important for a woman. If pregnancy is the result, she may spend nine months gestating, several years lactating, and many more years caring for her child. The man responsible for the pregnancy has the option of providing equal or even greater investment in the child, but he also has the option of providing nothing but sperm. Clearly, the injured wife has lost little, reproductively, if her husband exercises the latter option, while the injured husband is likely to lose much more.[8]

We find some support for this interpretation in the fact that sterility is the second most commonly reported cause of divorce (47 percent of the sample societies).[9] Related but less often cited grounds include death of children, absence of male children, production of too few children, sexual neglect, refusal to have sex, and old age (which clearly also impacts fertility). In Betzig's view, sterility and these other conditions are frequent grounds for divorce because, like adultery, they threaten reproduction.

Betzig identifies still other grounds for divorce that she believes are all, in one way or another, similarly related to infidelity. For example, cruelty or mistreatment, often "prompted by a wife's adultery or by the perceived risk of it," is the third most commonly reported reason for divorce (in 34 percent of the sample societies).[10] Disobedience or disrespect (which most often means that a wife has gone out without her husband's permission) is a source of divorce in 9 percent of societies. Co-spouse conflict associated with polygyny (which Betzig considers institutionalized adultery), another common cause of divorce (17 percent of cases), is usually blamed on the husband since it was he who brought these women together. But elopement with a lover (24 percent of the societies) is more often attributed to the woman. When men want another lover they can take a second wife in most societies, but women must leave one husband to take another in most. (Polyandry is extremely rare cross-culturally.) Lack of virginity is grounds for divorce in 4 percent of societies, and is always a defect of women.

Negative personality attributes, too, can be grounds for divorce. Indeed, simple "displeasingness" is the fourth most common ground for divorce (32 percent of societies), followed closely by divorce by mutual consent (26 percent). As Betzig points out, all of these grounds can also result in infidelity and infertility.

There may be economic grounds for divorce as well (e.g., laziness; inadequate provision of support, housing, food, clothing; unsatisfactory food preparation or other wifely service). However, these grounds are reported less often than adultery, sterility, displeasingness, and cruelty.[11] Betzig proposes that economic grounds, too, ultimately relate to reproduction, observing that

> if economics were all that mattered, nonsupport by a husband should be no more often cited as a cause for divorce than failure to provide by a wife. If, on the other hand, reproduction were paramount, then a wife's unparalleled contributions to child care in gestation and lactation, education, etc., could be compensated only by contributions her husband made in other ways. Wives may contribute subsistence and labor to a marriage; in fact, they may provide more than their mates do of both. But a woman may be a reproductive asset to her husband even if she offers neither, while a husband is less likely to be a reproductive asset to his wife if he is an economic failure.[12]

Rarely are political considerations grounds for divorce. In terms of Betzig's Darwinian approach, this is not surprising. Political assets provide a social, economic, and reproductive edge, so it is reasonable to assume that marriages will be made or unmade with political objectives in mind in many societies. But that is likely to be so only so long as the marriages people arrange with these goals in mind also serve reproductive purposes. Ritual grounds for divorce are mentioned only slightly more often than political ones. In many cases, accounts make it clear that ritual issues (e.g., witchcraft, broken taboos, and bad omens or dreams) are themselves intimately linked to infertility.

In short, the most common reasons given for divorce are usually related in one way or another to failure to have children. It is not simply that people want and need children for economic and/or social reasons. Children are not economic and social assets in all societies. However, even where the costs of raising them are substantial, and their contribution to the domestic economy comes late, children are always *reproductive assets* and, as Betzig argues, this fact is consistent with the idea that infertility is a major cause of divorce, and with a Darwinian interpretation that sees marriages as made and broken mainly for the sake of reproduction.

Although most of the societies in Betzig's cross-cultural sample are preindustrial, she finds some support for her interpretation in studies of industrial societies as well. One study of thirty modern societies confirms that the likelihood of divorce is lower when couples have more children. In the United States, for example, even when length of time married is controlled, couples with no children are more likely to divorce than those with two, who are in turn more likely to divorce than those with three or more children. Betzig is led to the conclusion, therefore, that

> the association between infertility and divorce, in modern as in traditional societies, is consistent with most theories of marriage. Again, social and economic theories can be consistent if they allow that marriage ties are strengthened by children; and the correlation between divorce and infertility follows directly from reproductive theories of marriage. The idea that people marry to produce economically valuable children fails more often in modern societies, where children are generally regarded as costly. The theory that people marry to produce children as reproductive assets works irrespective of their net economic benefit or cost—although no theory could question that where children are "cheap" they will be easier to produce.[13]

Betzig has identified the most frequent reasons for divorce, but are they the same for women and men? Suzanne G. Frayser looked at the principal grounds women and men use to justify divorce in societies around the world (see Table 9-1).

TABLE 9-1   COMPARISON OF PRIMARY GROUNDS
FOR DIVORCE USED BY MEN AND WOMEN

GROUNDS	MEN (PERCENT OF CASES)	WOMEN (PERCENT OF CASES)
No Divorce Allowed (Regardless of Grounds)	7.1	10.4
Reproductive Problems	28.6	6.3
Illicit Sex	16.1	10.4
Physical Violence	0.0	14.6
Incompatibility	21.4	22.9
Desertion or Neglect	5.4	2.1
Incompatibility with Affines	1.8	4.2
Failure in Economic or Domestic Duties	14.3	18.8
Trivial Reason or No Reason	5.4	10.4
Number of Societies	56.0	48.0

Source: Suzanne G. Frayser, *Varieties of Sexual Experience: An Anthropological Perspective on Human Sexuality* (New Haven: HRAF Press, 1985), p. 258.

She found that women most often seek divorce on grounds of incompatibility, a husband's failure to fulfill his economic duties, or his physical violence. Men are also likely to claim incompatibility, but they also voice complaints that are quite different from those of women, citing in particular reproductive problems or a wife's infidelity. Women are much less likely to complain about reproductive failure. In fact, failure to have children, the most common ground men use to justify divorce, is rarely cited by women. Given the concern men have in societies around the world for reproduction, Frayser expresses some surprise that illicit sex ranks only third in importance as a ground for divorce for men, and suggests a possible reason:

> It is possible that many of the marriages that would be terminated by divorce on the grounds of illicit sex never reach a stage of litigation; they cease with the death of the wife.... Violent retaliation for extramarital liaisons seems to be mainly a male prerogative. Although I have read many descriptions of cases where the husband kills his wife for an extramarital affair, I have not found one that says it is a socially accepted alternative for the wife.[14]

But if men respond to wifely infidelity with violence in many societies because infidelity menaces the men's reproductive goals, why should they be less likely to kill wives for failure to beget children? Frayser suggests this may be because when a woman commits adultery she not only violates a social rule, she also assaults her husband's "basic sense of control." She risks pregnancy with another man, and "this assaults a man's investment of resources; he is likely to commit them to his own children but not to those of another man."[15] The frequency of husbands beating wives may reflect the husband's need for control.

Even so, most societies discourage divorce and make it difficult for one or both spouses to get one, and women more commonly have obstacles in their paths than men. Most societies also allow divorced people to remarry (78 percent of Frayser's sample), but when it is difficult to do so, it is usually more so for the woman than for the man. The cross-cultural evidence also indicates that if divorce is difficult to obtain, then remarriage too is likely to be difficult to manage. Where it is relatively easy to get a divorce, remarriage is also easy. One might speculate that where the prospects of remarriage are few, divorce is probably more likely to be avoided, especially by men. However, Frayser found that in societies that put obstacles in the way of divorce, but are less restrictive when it comes to remarriage, it is most often the men that benefit from the lack of symmetry. They are the ones most likely to remarry.

Under what conditions are we likely to find that societies impose restrictions on divorce for women? The results of a study by Hendrix and Pearson show that women are unlikely to have broad grounds for divorce in agricultural economies in which there is considerable spousal interdependence—that is, where women and men both do important but different work. Women's grounds for divorce are also likely to be limited in male-focused societies—where people trace descent through males, inherit real property (land) patrilineally, and where women live with or near their husbands' kin when they marry.[16]

So gender inequality and interdependence both limit the grounds upon which women can seek divorce. Women also have more restricted grounds for divorce in male-focused than in female-focused societies. On the other hand, Hendrix and Pearson found that where real property passes through the male line, men tend to have limited grounds for divorce as well. The grounds then seem to be limited for both genders. But where women have greater economic and/or political influence (i.e., more equality), men's grounds for divorce tend to be broader. It appears that husbands' rights increase with wives' rights.

We have been talking about the effect of gender focus and interdependence on *grounds* for divorce. Contrary to what we might suppose, however, these factors do not have a clear effect on the *actual frequency* of divorce. It is all too easy to mistakenly leap from data on divorce grounds to conclusions about the rate of divorce. The former have to do with norms and attitudes toward marriage. Divorce rate has to do with actual behavior. Let us turn now to what cross-cultural studies tell us about behavior.

WHAT EXPLAINS HIGHER DIVORCE RATES?

Implicitly or explicitly many researchers have suggested a relationship between the incidence of divorce and *female status* or, more properly, between divorce and various presumed indicators of female status. In short, the hypothesis is that rates of divorce rise as women's status improves. Although most such claims have been based on studies of particular societies or regions, there have been a few important cross-cultural studies addressing this issue. In one by Trent and South, the matter is put this way:

> Those who argue that divorce varies directly with the status of women see economic gains by women lessening their dependence on husband's income. Increases in economic opportunities for women provide the requisite independence for dissolving unhappy marriages.[17]

As Pearson and Hendrix point out, this hypothesis directs attention to features of the family itself, such as the nature of family authority, or to forces outside having to do with the character of economic opportunities available to women.[18] These factors all presumably have an impact on female status. One might suppose that preindustrial American families may have been more stable than now because there were fewer opportunities for women to work outside the home, and because families then were more male dominated (*patriarchal*).[19]

A number of scholars have suggested still other cultural characteristics impacting women's status that may influence the incidence of divorce. For example, Max Gluckman believed that divorce is less likely where descent is traced through males, a feature that presumably minimizes female status.[20] Another possibility is that differences in the degree to which a bride becomes incorporated into her husband's kin group, or notions about marriage as a relationship of groups rather than individuals, may be important. And then there is the possibility that bride wealth and dowry may inhibit divorce if their return is required when couples split up.

In their cross-cultural study of traditional (nonindustrial) societies, Pearson and Hendrix attempted to systematically evaluate the effect of female status on divorce frequency.[21] They measured status in terms of a number of indicators, such as whether women inherit real property and moveable property, whether polyandry is allowed, adultery by husband or wife, and a number of other variables related to women's roles in religious and political activity. They chose these indicators because most ethnographic accounts address them and because they "seem to relate to the extent to which women have behavioral alternatives open to them."

Pearson and Hendrix found that societies with higher female status as measured in these ways do show higher divorce rates. They then considered a few of the other commonly suggested correlates of divorce—whether or not goods are exchanged at marriage, whether women share their husband's social network at marriage (community endogamy), whether women go to live with or near their husband's kin at marriage (nature of marital residence), and whether descent is traced through males or not.[22]

It turned out, however, that none of these factors affected divorce rate; and when they controlled on each to see if the effect of female status would decrease, they found it did not. They concluded that divorce is more directly related to female status than to any of the other suggested causes. However, while female status seemed to have an important impact on divorce, the number of exceptions found suggested that there were other factors still to be discovered.

A subsequent cross-cultural study by Seccombe and Lee suggested that the *degree of independence* women enjoy is an even more powerful predictor of divorce than female status.[23] In light of that finding, Hendrix and Pearson took another cross-cultural look at the relationship between divorce and gender inequality, considering degree of female independence as well. (Female independence is low when men and women perform different tasks, when there is *high spousal interdependence* and the spouses need each other's production; female independence is high when both genders perform the same tasks, when there is *low spousal interdependence*.) Hendrix and Pearson's hypothesis was that there might be an interaction at work here, that divorce rates might be "heightened by the combination of high gender equality and high independence [of females]."[24]

It appears that the connections between female independence, female influence (gender equality), and divorce are not simple. On the basis of their statistical analyses, Hendrix and Pearson draw two main conclusions. The first is that greater female influence (i.e., less gender inequality) does push divorce up, but only where there is low female independence as indicated by a sharp division of labor by gender (*task segregation*). A second conclusion is that a strict division of labor alone is no guarantee of stable marriages. Under some conditions, it may even be disruptive. It turns out, for example, that task segregation is associated with more divorce where women enjoy greater economic and political influence (hold power resources). Nor does responsibility sharing, on its own, necessarily increase the likelihood of divorce. Hendrix and Pearson discovered, for example, that where fathers are much involved in raising infants, we actually find lower rates of divorce. This finding hardly supports the simple notion that a strict division of labor in itself makes for marital stability. As Hendrix and Pearson put it,

> functional interdependence is apparently only one of several possible effects coming from the division of labor. A rigid division of labor

requires increased coordination and control of task performance. If the resources for power of the spouses are different, but to a degree counterbalancing, there may be limited ways of ensuring that necessary work is done, should either spouse be recalcitrant. The system may lack an effective mechanism for coordination and dispute settlement needed for its stability. The spouses' functional interdependence can even be used as a weapon by either partner, should conflict escalate. One only has to do one's work poorly to punish the partner. Under these circumstances, marriages might be full of ambivalence, conflict, and especially divorce prone. Restricting access to divorce for women, as some societies do, would not reduce the amount of divorce, since dissatisfied women may do poor work to force their husbands to divorce them.

Also, when men's work in production and reproduction is segregated from that of women, relationships between the sexes are affected. A rigid separation in labor may lead to a more general segregation of the sexes and differing interests between spouses, enhancing the ambivalence and conflict in marriage. When women and men work in different locations on different tasks, their concerns and values may be shaped in divergent ways by their experiences and relations at work. With differing values for women and men, there might be more frequent marital conflict. This conflict could result in marital instability unless there were a strong authority system to hold the conflict in check. In this explanation, work segregation makes for marital ambivalence. Task segregation makes spouses depend on each other for satisfying basic needs, but at the same time may provide reasons for wanting to end marriages. Female power in this situation becomes important in that it consists of resources which may enable wives to leave husbands, thus activating the causal link between marital conflict and divorce.[25]

Keeping in mind that the relationship is not a simple one, Hendrix and Pearson believe the results of their research are more supportive of the notion that an increase in gender equality often increases divorce. They find less support for the idea that a decline in spousal interdependence alone (more female independence) does that as well. More significant, in their view, is the joint effect on divorce of gender inequality and the division of labor. This interactive relationship may provide some insight into rising divorce rates in the United States:

> The controversy on the divorce proneness of gainfully employed wives in America can be viewed in light of the interaction effect found here. If our findings may be applied to the American scene, the implication is that researchers need to look more closely at the division of labor in marriage as it works with other factors to affect divorce. Much attention has been given to the employment pattern of spouses, which is but one aspect of the marital division of labor. Yet it is one that affects many aspects of marriage: the balance of power, the division of labor in

housework and in child care, and depending on other factors, the level of marital satisfaction....

A common idea has been that divorce rose in many western nations following industrialization because of the decline of patriarchal authority. Our research suggests that this is only a part of the story. Some recent works note that the marital division of labor may have become more segregated with industrialization also. Specifically, the role of housewife is argued to have developed after industrialization as men's work was defined as paid labor outside the home. The findings of this study suggest that a sharpening both in the division of labor and in the balance of power in marriage is needed to account for the historical rise in divorce in America and other western nations.[26]

The rise in divorce rates is a worldwide phenomenon. According to Population Council research, divorce rates doubled in many developed countries between 1970 and 1990. Even in less developed countries, about a quarter of first marriages end by the time women are in their forties.[27] Given the worldwide nature of this trend, it is reasonable to suppose it has something to do with modernization. But which specific features of this general process are responsible for increasing the rate of divorce, and why?

Many observers have suggested some sort of connection between modernization and changes in both family complexity and stability. The general idea is that with urbanization and industrialization, families become smaller and more independent of larger kin groups. They lose many traditional functions (like defense, education, and care of the sick and elderly) to other agencies. As a result, marriages become less stable.[28] Some have also suggested that ideational and value changes associated with development also play a part. The fact that romantic love assumes greater importance, for example, may also render marriage less stable.[29] The stigma of divorce presumably decreases as modernization brings greater anonymity and impersonalization.

Another common proposal is that the status and independence of women increase as they enter the labor market and pursue educational and career goals, rendering divorce more possible and likely.[30] Then there is the possibility that societies with a relative under-supply of women (high sex ratio) value women more than those with an oversupply.[31] In such a situation, men may be less inclined to divorce their wives. The age at which women marry may also have an impact on divorce rates. Indeed, there is some evidence that divorce rates are higher where people marry younger, perhaps because they are less mature.[32] Or perhaps religious beliefs can restrain or facilitate divorce.[33] We know, for example, that Roman Catholicism bans divorce while Islam has traditionally been relatively permissive.

Looking at a sample of sixty-six developed and developing nations, Trent and South found support for some of these suggestions. They found lower divorce rates where there is an undersupply of women among people of reproductive age (fifteen to forty-nine), or a late average marriage age for women. They also generally found higher divorce rates with more participation by females in the labor force, but the relationship is not linear.[34] Rather, it is curvilinear. Where few women are in the labor force, small increments in participation actually *reduce* divorce rates. Once there are larger proportions, however, small added increments do *increase* divorce rates. It is not entirely clear why divorce should decline during the earliest stages of modernization, but it is clear that economic development and work outside the home probably make marriages less stable later on in development. The research on traditional societies is difficult to compare with that on complex nations because the two kinds of research do not use precisely the same measures. Nonetheless, both bodies of research, in their own ways, suggest that when women acquire more access to and control over economic resources (whether through matrilineal descent or trade and wages), divorce is likely to be higher.

Thus far we have been discussing the termination of marriage by divorce or separation of spouses. We have little cross-cultural data on what happens to people afterward—on their prospects for remarriage, or on the factors that affect those prospects. Those are matters awaiting further research. So we leave the matter of divorce here and turn to the second and certainly more common way that marriage comes to an end.

WIDOWS AND WIDOWERS

Unless nature is tampered with, slightly more males are born than females. Once born, however, females are hardier and, barring cultural interference, they are more likely than men to reach every age level, and to outlive them. We have already seen that this imbalance, combined with interdependence of the genders, encourages a tolerance of polygyny in most societies. When their husbands die, widows may remarry for much the same reasons. Rarely do societies prevent them from remarrying. A survey by Broude and Greene found remarriage absent, uncommon, or strongly disapproved in only 7 percent of societies.[35]

In a substantial number of societies in Frayser's sample (37 percent), widows could theoretically remarry anyone they chose. In most societies, however, they often refrained from remarrying (33 percent), perhaps to remain with their children, or to avoid the pain of having to join new families and communities. In Frayser's sample, too, only a few societies (5 percent) strongly discouraged or prohibited widow remarriage. If a high caste girl in Uttar Pradesh married before puberty, for example, she could not hope to remarry even if her husband died before she attained puberty. According to some accounts, when a Fijian husband died, it was customary to strangle his wife and bury her with him. But all cross-cultural research indicates that such opposition to remarriage is uncommon.

Where remarriage is possible, the customs governing widow remarriage are often quite different from those that determine the selection of first spouses. In many societies families may be more concerned about the reproductive and labor potentials of young brides than of widows, and may therefore be more concerned about their selection. Broude and Greene found that, while societies rarely allow women to choose their own first husbands on their own (only 8 percent of the societies in their sample), widows can more often do that (in 30 percent of the cases). In another 34 percent of societies the only restraint on widows was the preference or requirement that they choose from among their husband's kinsmen. In only 30 percent of societies do her husband's kin make the choice for her.

In most societies, then, remarriage is most often possible under conditions that suggest a residual interest in the widow and her issue on the part of her husband's kin, an interest less evident following divorce. Frayser, too, found that societies commonly expect widows to give preference to their husband's kin when they remarry.[36] One consequence of channeling a widow to her husband's kin is that it provides them continued control over her reproductive potential and labor. This makes sense in terms of the argument that marriage customs serve to assure the reproductive claims of a man and his kin, and to guarantee the investment they make in the children of a woman.

A disturbing but possibly revealing finding of the Broude and Greene study was that there is a relationship between wife-beating, common in human societies (in 80 percent of them), and the way widows acquire replacements for their husbands. Widows were not free to choose their own next husbands in societies where wife-beating was common. It is not clear why this should be the case, but Broude and Greene speculate that

> there may be a reflection here of an overall attitude toward women within a given culture. Thus, where wife-beating is absent and widows choose their own new husbands, societies may be seen as viewing women as deserving of a high degree of autonomy and respect. This is in contrast to cultures where wife-beating is present and where the choice of a new husband for a widow is dictated by her previous husband's kin.[37]

The notion that customs governing second marriages may differ from those affecting first marriages should be familiar. We have already learned that some societies with a tolerance for polygamous marriage may exhibit a preference for certain kinds of second spouses—for brothers in the case of polyandry (*fraternal polyandry*), and for sisters in the case of polygyny (*sororal polygyny*). It should come as no surprise, then, that where people take spouses successively, after the death of a husband or wife, custom may also recommend that they be the brother of one's dead husband (*levirate*) or the sister of one's dead wife (*sororate*). Certain other customs may even set the stage for such marriage. It is probably no coincidence that all societies allowing patterned sexual license with a spouse's sibling, and most of those that allow joking or kidding around between them, also have a strong preference for levirate or sororate.[38]

Indeed, Murdock found levirate and sororate very common in his sample of 250 societies around the world. Fifty-one percent preferred the levirate. In only 23 percent was levirate absent or only occasional.[39] A strong preference for sororate was evident in 40 percent of the societies; it was absent or only occasional in only 24 percent of the sample societies. Murdock's data also indicated that custom frequently restricted these marriages to the younger siblings of spouses (called the junior levirate and sororate). Robert H. Lowie suggested a reason for that some years ago:

> In probably an overwhelming number of instances only a younger brother inherits the widow. This is reasonable since the seniors are almost certain to be already married. Correspondingly, since girls married at puberty, the sororate…applied to a younger sister.[40]

Common as they are, we do not yet really understand the conditions under which we are more or less likely to find these customs. Most explanations, in one fashion or another, point to the fact that such marriages repeat, and presumably therefore stabilize and reinforce, bonds between families and perhaps larger kin groups as well. Since alliances are thought to be selectively advantageous, such customs should be common. And Murdock suggested that, apart from the fact that siblings represent the same families and kin groups, their "likenesses provide the requisite conditions for the generalization of behavior patterns, including sex responses.…"[41] Then there is the possibility that institutions like levirate and sororate are advantageous in the sense suggested by Frayser—they provide some continued control over a woman's reproduction. Still, if levirate and sororate reinforce existing alliances, if a dead spouse's sibling is a likely mate, and if obligatory remarriage perpetuates others' control over a woman's reproduction, why aren't the levirate and sororate universal?

While restrictions on widow remarriage in general, and customs like levirate and sororate in particular, may serve a number of purposes, including that of reserving a woman's reproductive capacity for a larger kin group, individual ethnographic accounts suggest that the matter may be even more complicated. Patrilineal descent groups were strong and highly functional in traditional southeastern China, but ethnographic accounts indicate that the levirate and sororate were rare. In fact, the levirate was strictly proscribed in imperial legal codes:

> The punishment in T'ang, Sung, Ming and Ch'ing times was one hundred strokes for marrying the widow of a kinsman beyond the mourn-

ing system; for marrying a widow of a kinsman in the fourth degree, one year's imprisonment. Marrying the widow of a kinsman in the third, second, or first degree was considered adultery. Marrying the widow of a nephew or a great uncle, or a father's paternal first cousin was punished by strangling; marrying the widow of a father's brother's son, or a grandfather's brother's grandson, or a brother's son, or a brother's grandson was punished by three years' imprisonment. In Ming and Ch'ing times the punishment for marrying a paternal uncle's widow was beheading, for marrying a brother's widow, strangling.[42]

Clearly then, the imperial codes strongly discouraged widow remarriage. Indeed, considerable official praise was lavished on "virtuous widows," who remained faithful to their husbands. In some cases, memorial arches were erected by elite families in their honor.

But this aversion to the levirate, as Wolf and Huang have suggested, exacerbated the difficulties widowers and divorced men had in finding replacements for their wives. And widows were generally unwilling to remarry in rural China. Why? On the basis of fieldwork in Hai-shan, northern Taiwan, Wolf and Huang propose that a kin group's interest in preserving a widow's reproductive potential may have been less important than the fact that widows were unwilling to leave the homes and communities of their husbands:

> There were very practical reasons for remaining unmarried and a member of her deceased husband's family. For one thing, she retained her rights as the mother of her children, her best hope for support in her old age. For another, she gained (through her children) effective control of her husband's share of the family estate, an opportunity for economic independence of a kind ordinarily denied to women.[43]

In the Chinese case, widowhood did not necessarily mean that a woman's sex life was over. The Hai-shan data indicate that nearly 40 percent of all young widows bore at least one illegitimate child. Those data also indicate that the older a widow was, the more likely she was to have grown children upon whom to depend and the less likely she was to remarry. Unless she had sons old enough to support her, however, a widow needed the help of some adult male. This did not require remarriage, however, and, as Wolf and Huang point out,

> there are at least two ways to explain the fact that many widows did not remarry but continued to bear children. The former husband's parents (or the woman's own parents in the case of an uxorilocal [matrilocal] marriage) may have needed their daughter-in-law to raise their grandchildren and therefore insisted on an uxorilocal marriage or none at all. Since it was always difficult to find a man willing to marry into his wife's family, the more so when the wife was older and a widow, many

widows could not remarry and instead entered into a series of casual sexual relationships. Alternatively, it could be argued that women who had borne children and established what Margery Wolf calls a "uterine family" were reluctant to remarry. Their children gave them the rights to a share of their husband's father's estate, and this in turn allowed them an independence normally denied to women. Had they married out of their husband's family, they would have lost both their children and their claim to family property. They therefore preferred informal to formal relationships and resisted marrying a second time.[44]

In Chungshe, a Taiwanese village studied by Pasternak, widows and widowers alike were more inclined to remarry. But a widow with young children had special reason to replace her husband there. As we shall learn in the next chapter, dependence on rainfall rather than canals put a premium on male labor. A widow might well have preferred to avoid having to deal with a new mother-in-law, family, and community, but there was little choice. And because widows were likely to remarry, widowers too enjoyed better than usual prospects of finding another mate. After all, even an old man could work a plow.

It should be clear from our discussion in this chapter that we have raised far more questions than we can answer, even tentatively. In terms of a comparative understanding, researchers have merely scratched the surface on many important issues. We hope, however, that our discussion stimulates further investigation. Certainly, if a high rate of divorce has unfortunate consequences, we need to understand more about why it occurs and how it could be avoided.

NOTES

1. According to a graph in a recent Population Council study (reported in Tamar Lewis, "Family Decay Global, Study Says: Troubled Households Are Not Just a U.S. Phenomenon," *New York Times International*, May 30, 1995, pp. A4–A5), there were about fifty divorces for every one hundred marriages in the United States in 1985 (the last year for which many countries could be compared).
2. Gwen J. Broude and Sarah J. Greene, "Cross-Cultural Codes on Husband-Wife Relationships," *Ethnology* 22 (1983): 275.
3. Suzanne G. Frayser, *Varieties of Sexual Experience: An Anthropological Perspective on Human Sexuality* (New Haven, CT: HRAF Press, 1985), p. 262.
4. Laura L. Betzig, "Causes of Conjugal Dissolution: A Cross-Cultural Study," *Current Anthropology* 30 (1989): 654–677.
5. Ibid., p. 658.
6. The total number of cases in which adultery constitutes a ground for

divorce does not include societies in the sample that could not be coded on this variable. Other studies also indicate that adultery in general, and female adultery in particular, constitute major grounds for divorce. See, for example, Mark V. Flinn, "Uterine versus Agnatic Kinship Variability and Associated Cousin Marriage Preferences: An Evolutionary Biological Analysis," in *Natural Selection and Human Social Behavior*, eds. Richard Alexander and Donald Tinkle (New York: Chiron, 1981), pp. 439–475; Martin Daly, Margo Wilson, and Suzanne Weghost, "Male Sexual Jealousy," *Ethnology and Sociobiology* 3 (1982): 11–27; Steven J. C. Gaulin and Alice Schlegel, "Paternal Confidence and Parental Investment: A Cross-Cultural Test of a Sociobiological Hypothesis," *Ethology and Sociobiology* 1 (1980): 301–309; and John Hartung, "Matrilineal Inheritance: New Theory and Analysis," *The Behavioral and Brain Sciences* 8 (1985): 661–688, cited in Betzig, "Causes of Conjugal Dissolution."

7. Betzig, "Causes of Conjugal Dissolution," p. 661.
8. Ibid.
9. Here again, Betzig points to a gender asymmetry. Sterility is attributed to the wife alone in 40 percent of the cases, to the husband alone in 16 percent.
10. In this case, too, we observe a gender imbalance. Cruelty by the husband only is mentioned in 85 percent of societies in which cruelty is a cause of divorce; the wife is never the only offender mentioned. Only 9 percent indicate that cruelty on the part of either may be grounds for divorce.
11. Laziness is a ground for divorce in 20 percent of the societies, and is more often attributed to women. Inadequate support (13 percent of the societies), however, is invariably blamed on husbands.
12. Betzig, "Causes of Conjugal Dissolution," pp. 665–666.
13. Ibid., pp. 667–668.
14. Frayser, *Varieties of Sexual Experience*, p. 259.
15. Ibid.
16. Lewellyn Hendrix and Willie Pearson, Jr., "Spousal Interdependence, Female Power, and Divorce: A Cross-Cultural Examination," *Journal of Comparative Family Studies* 26 (1995): 217–232.
17. Katherine Trent and Scott J. South, "Structural Determinants of the Divorce Rate: A Cross-Societal Analysis," *Journal of Marriage and the Family* 51 (1989): 393.
18. Willie Pearson, Jr. and Lewellyn Hendrix, "Divorce and the Status of Women," *Journal of Marriage and the Family* 41 (1979): 375–385.
19. See, for example, John Scanzoni, "A Reinquiry into Marital Disorganization," *Journal of Marriage and the Family* 27 (1965): 483–491; and Pearson and Hendrix, "Divorce and the Status of Women."

20. Max Gluckman, "Kinship and Marriage among the Lozi of Northern Rhodesia and the Zulu of Natal," in *African Systems of Kinship and Marriage*, eds. A. R. Radcliffe-Brown and D. Forde (Oxford: Oxford University Press, 1950) pp. 166–203. But many have since questioned Gluckman's hypothesis, noting that patrilineal groups vary in their divorce rates. See Lloyd A. Fallers, "Some Determinants of Marriage Stability in Bugosa," *Africa* 27 (1957): 106–121; and Edmund R. Leach, "Aspects of Bridewealth and Marriage Stability among Kachin and Lakher," *Man* 57 (1957): 50–55, both cited in Pearson and Hendrix, "Divorce and the Status of Women."

21. Pearson and Hendrix, "Divorce and the Status of Women."

22. The notion that social networks affect divorce rates has been explored by others. In one cross-cultural study, Charles Ackerman proposed that divorce may be more likely where husbands and wives have separate social networks (*disjunctive affiliations*). Indeed, his data indicate that divorce is less likely where custom encourages cousin marriage, marriage within the community (community endogamy), and the levirate (a widow marrying the brother of her deceased husband). All of these customs keep marriage within a group that is familiar to both spouses. See Charles Ackerman, "Affiliations: Structural Determinants of Differential Divorce Rates," *American Journal of Sociology* 69 (1963): 13–20, cited in Pearson and Hendrix, "Divorce and the Status of Women."

23. Karen Seccombe and Gary R. Lee, "Female Status, Wives' Autonomy, and Divorce: A Cross-Cultural Study," *Family Perspectives* 20 (1987): 241–249. In that study, father proximity to infants, father proximity to children, joint leisure activities of spouses, and inheritance of widows were indicators of greater dependence. Indicators of less dependence for wives were the relative closeness of husband and wife to their families of orientation, and women's control of property.

24. Hendrix and Pearson, "Spousal Interdependence, Female Power, and Divorce."

25. Ibid.

26. Ibid.

27. See Lewis, "Family Decay Global, Study Says."

28. See, for example, Tamara K. Hareven, "Modernization and Family History: Perspectives on Social Change," *Signs* 2 (1976): 190–206; Gary R. Lee, *Family Structure and Interaction: A Comparative Analysis*, 2nd ed. (Minneapolis: University of Minnesota Press, 1982); Meyer F. Nimkoff, ed. *Comparative Family Systems* (Boston: Houghton Mifflin, 1965); and William F. Ogburn and Meyer F. Nimkoff, *Technology and the Changing Family* (Boston: Houghton Mifflin, 1955).

29. For examples, see William J. Goode, *World Revolution and Family Patterns* (New York: Free Press, 1963); Alan C. Kerckoff, "The

Structure of Conjugal Relationships in Industrial Societies," in *Cross-National Family Research*, eds. Marvin B. Sussman and Betty E. Cogswell (Leiden, The Netherlands: E. J. Brill, 1972), pp. 53–69; and Lee, *Family Structure and Interaction*.

30. Many have suggested this. See, for example, Akbar Aghajanian, "Some Notes on Divorce in Iran," *Journal of Marriage and the Family* 48 (1986): 749–755; Gary S. Becker, Elisabeth M. Landes, and Robert T. Michael, "An Economic Analysis of Marital Instability," *Journal of Political Economy* 85 (1977): 1141–1187; Andrew J. Cherlin, "The Effect of Children on Marital Dissolution," *Demography* 14 (1977): 265–272, "Work Life and Marital Dissolution," in *Divorce and Separation*, eds. G. Levinger and O. C. Moles (New York: Basic Books, 1979), pp. 151–166, and *Marriage, Divorce, Remarriage* (Cambridge, MA: Harvard University Press, 1981); William J. Goode, *World Revolution and Family Patterns*, and "Family Disorganization," in *Contemporary Social Problems*, eds. Robert K. Merton and Robert Nisbet, 3rd. ed. (New York: Harcourt Brace Jovanovich, 1971); Joan Huber and Glenna Spitze, "Considering Divorce: An Expansion of Becker's Theory of Marital Instability," *American Journal of Sociology* 86 (1980): 75–89; Kenneth Land and Marcus Felson, "A Dynamic Macro Social Indicator Model of Changes in Marriage, Family, and Population in the U.S.: 1947–1974," *Social Science Research* 6 (1977): 328–362; Heather L. Ross and Isabel V. Sawhill, *Time of Transition: The Growth of Families Headed by Women* (Washington, DC: Urban Institute, 1975); John Scanzoni, *Sexual Bargaining: Power Politics in the American Marriage* (Englewood Cliffs, NJ: Prentice-Hall, 1972), and "A Historical Perspective on Husband-Wife Bargaining Power and Marital Dissolution," in *Divorce and Separation*, eds. Levinger and Moles, pp. 20–36; and Scott J. South, "Economic Conditions and the Divorce Rate: A Time-Series Analysis of the Post-War United States," *Journal of Marriage and the Family* 47 (1985): 31–41.

31. See Marcia Guttentag and Paul F. Secord, *Too Many Women? The Sex Ratio Question* (Beverly Hills, CA: Sage, 1983); Goode, *World Revolution and Family Patterns*; and David M. Heer and Amyra Grossbard-Shechtman, "The Impact of the Female Marriage Squeeze and the Contraceptive Revolution on Sex Roles and the Women's Liberation Movement in the United States, 1960–1975," *Journal of Marriage and the Family* 43 (1981): 49–65.

32. See Alan Booth and John N. Edwards, "Age at Marriage and Marital Instability," *Journal of Marriage and the Family* 47 (1985): 67–75; Phillip S. Morgan and Ronald R. Rindfuss, "Marital Disruption: Structural and Temporal Dimensions," *American Journal of Sociology* 90 (1985): 1055–1077; and Scott J. South and Glenna Spitze,

"Determinants of Divorce over the Marital Life Course," *American Sociological Review* 51 (1986): 583–590.

33. For example, see Norval Glen and Michael Supancic, "Sociological and Demographic Correlates of Divorce and Separation in the United States: An Update and Reconsideration," *Journal of Marriage and the Family* 46 (1984): 563–576; and Goode, "Family Disorganization."

34. Trent and South, "Structural Determinants of the Divorce Rate." Most studies in the United States point to a connection between women's working outside the home and divorce. See Hendrix and Pearson, "Spousal Interdependence, Female Power, and Divorce," for citations to this finding.

35. Broude and Greene, "Cross-Cultural Codes on Husband-Wife Relationships."

36. Not only are there usually some restrictions on whom a widow can remarry, but societies usually also require a period of restraint and mourning. In most cases (77 percent) the period does not exceed two years, but there is some variation in this respect (Frayser, *Varieties of Sexual Experience*, p. 266).

37. Ibid., p. 272.

38. George Peter Murdock, *Social Structure* (New York: The Free Press, 1965 [originally published 1949]), p. 281.

39. There were insufficient data to make a judgment one way or the other for 26 percent of the cases.

40. Robert H. Lowie, *Social Organization* (New York: Rinehart & Company, 1956), p. 103.

41. Murdock, *Social Structure*, pp. 269–270.

42. T'ung-Tsu Chu, *Law and Society in Traditional China* (Paris: Mouton & Co., 1961), p. 97.

43. Arthur P. Wolf and Chieh-Shan Huang, *Marriage and Adoption in China, 1845–1945* (Stanford, CA: Stanford University Press, 1980), p. 227.

44. Arthur P. Wolf, "The Women of Hai-Shan," in *Women in Chinese Society*, eds. Margery Wolf and Roxane Witke (Stanford, CA: Stanford University Press, 1975), p. 108.

10

MARITAL RESIDENCE: WHO GOES WHERE, WHY, AND WHAT ARE THE CONSEQUENCES?

In our society, couples about to marry usually decide for themselves where they will live after marriage. It is a decision of no little consequence, and couples may discover that they disagree on this issue. For one of the partners, the most important consideration may be convenience in terms of work. For the other, proximity to friends may be of overriding importance. Sometimes one or both want to live close to relatives. Whatever their individual preferences in these regards, neither is likely to want to live at home, with either set of parents, except as a last resort. In our society, marriage means one has arrived at full maturity. It is time, then, to leave the nest for good, and go off on one's own. Anthropologists refer to this pattern of postmarital residence with the term *neolocality* (new place).

Assuming that newlyweds have the necessary income, we usually expect them to live independently when they marry, "on their own," as we say. This means living in their own apartment or other domicile. This pattern of residence is so common among us, in fact, that we might be tempted to think of it as only natural. Cross-culturally, however, this way of doing things is actually relatively uncommon. In the vast majority of cultures known to anthropology, couples live with or near parents and other relatives. Usually, society does not leave the matter up to the individual couple's choice—everyone lives with or near kin. Living in this way seems to be necessary for survival. Our own preference, neolocality, is not only rare in the ethnographic record, it is also a relatively recent phenomenon in the world, probably nowhere more than a few thousand years old and usually a pattern that has emerged only in the last few hundred years.

But if most people live with kin when they marry, which kin are they likely to live with, the husband's or the wife's? It turns out that this, too, is usually not a matter of individual decision. And while we might imagine all sorts of arrangements, living with various sorts or categories of kin, some possibilities are actually more common than others, and some theoretical ones do not occur at all. In this chapter, we will describe the options that actually occur, as well as their relative frequency, and see what we know about why some are more common than others. As we shall see, moreover, the rule of postmarital residence we adopt is of more than casual interest; it affects many things we do—the kinds of families we have, the sorts of larger kin groups we form, and the way we relate to one another, all of which connections we will discuss in this chapter.

Because of the familial incest taboo, people everywhere must find mates outside the immediate family. Since wives and husbands usually live together, one (or less commonly both) of them must leave her or his parents. It is the wife who moves away in most societies, and we will want to think about why that is. One thing is clear from the ethnographic record: Where people depend more on kin than on employers or the government for making a living, defending themselves, and for support in old age, newlyweds usually live with or near close relatives. And in most societies (see Figure 10-1) those relatives are the husband's; couples most often live with or near his immediate family (patrilocality). But there are also some soci-

FIGURE 10-1   PERCENT OF SOCIETIES IN THE ETHNOGRAPHIC RECORD
WITH VARIOUS MARITAL RESIDENCE PATTERNS

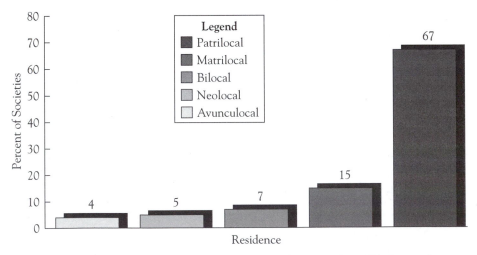

Source: Calculated from Allan D. Coult and Robert Habenstein, *Cross Tabulations of Murdock's World Ethnographic Sample* (Columbia: University of Missouri Press, 1965).

eties in which men customarily live with or near the immediate families of their wives (matrilocality). Less often, couples may live with or near either set of parents (bilocality). Our own preference for independence (neolocality) is quite rare; very few of the societies described in the ethnographic record have this custom. A practice even rarer is *avunculocal* residence, in which the couple lives with or near the husband's mother's brother. There are even a few societies in which *duolocality* is the norm: Husband and wife live apart after marriage.

We could, of course, imagine other possibilities (like living with the wife's father's sister), but none actually occurs as the prevailing or most common pattern in any known society. Why we do not find other alternatives is an interesting question to which we will return later. Let us consider, first, some examples of residence patterns unlike our own. What are they like, which are more common, and why?

RESIDENCE, FAMILY, AND KIN GROUPS

Why should we even care about why people have different customs when it comes to marital residence? What difference does it make? For one thing, where we live after marriage determines a lot about how we live, and particularly whom we cooperate with and rely on. That is because the pattern of marital residence shapes our families, determining who the insiders and outsiders are; and the kinds of families we form have an impact on the sorts of larger kin groups we belong to (as we shall see, people do belong to larger kin groups in most societies).

We noted above that in most societies it is the woman who moves at marriage. For her, it is rarely a matter of little consequence. Consider what patrilocal marriage meant to a woman in rural China. Margery Wolf conveys some sense of her condition in the following passage:

> In the recent past, a bride entered the home that was to be hers for the rest of her days as a stranger. She may previously have met her mother-in-law, but rarely her husband, and probably none of the other family members. A farm family goes to considerable trouble and great expense to acquire a daughter-in-law, and the members of the household expect more from their bargain than any naive, ignorant young country girl can provide. The go-between exaggerates the girl's domestic competence (drudgery from which her mother spared her) in order to bring the future mother-in-law to a decision; her new sisters-in-law are resentful of her before she appears for the tightened budget her marriage has required of the family; her father-in-law is irritated at the stiff bargaining her family put him through; and her husband, who probably was in no hurry to marry anyway, solaced himself with fantasies of a delicately beautiful young woman, the type his mother who wanted a

daughter-in-law capable of bearing numerous sons and of coping with heavy farmhouse work told the go-between not even to consider.[1]

It is a situation bound to create disappointment all around. Almost unavoidably, it creates in the bride a "sense of isolation, of emotional aloneness," for which there is no easy remedy. As Wolf points out, even her husband offers little solace. Initially, at least, he is "well on the path to being her arch-enemy," since she sees him alone only in the bedroom, "where he forces unpleasant attentions on her after a trying day." Nor could her parents provide relief. It is "bad form" to visit them, and they would not likely encourage frequent visits. She can expect little direct help or protection from them in the likely event that her in-laws or husband abuse her.[2]

Eventually other women in her husband's community will, with their gossip, provide a measure of restraint upon her husband's family in this regard, but initially they, too, view her with suspicion and contribute to her feelings of isolation.[3] While we do not have comparable information about how men react when custom requires that they live matrilocally, there is reason to suppose that their situation may not generally be as stressful since, as we shall see in the next chapter, matrilocal societies rarely have villages with only one kin group. Consequently, men often move to their wife's place in another part of the same village, so they remain in familiar surroundings, close to their own families.

But the rule of postmarital residence has structural as well as psychological consequences. When local families in precommercial and politically simple societies organize families into more inclusive groups (which they usually do), they normally do so by elaborating familiar notions of kinship. Most often they create groups on the basis of descent from a common ancestor. How they trace descent, through women and/or men, seems mostly to depend on the rule of marital residence. If men stay put at marriage, over time the local group comes to include a core of men related through their fathers. That being the case, patrilocal people are likely to conceive of themselves as a descent group going back through males to a common male ancestor. Their wives are outsiders from different places and blood lines. But if the men instead live with or near the parents and kin of their wives, descent will more likely be traced through women because then it will be the men who will have married in from different blood lines.

Bilocality and neolocality both create local groups in which some people are related through females, and others through males. These customs, therefore, are not conducive to tracing descent exclusively through one gender. In bilocal societies people may trace descent through either parent, or may provide some other basis for supra-family organization apart from common descent. Neolocal residence, by its nature, emphasizes independence of the married couple, and societies with that preference rarely have descent groups of any sort.

Even kinship terms are affected by marital residence. As we learned earlier in regard to incest and cousin marriage, the terms used to refer to relatives signal important relationships. Thus, while we refer to the siblings of our parents as uncles and aunts, without distinguishing those on our father's and mother's sides, in many more societies people use the terms *father* and *mother* for father's brothers and mother's sisters, respectively. Their children, therefore, are not *cousins* but *brothers* and *sisters*. Again, these usages indicate the presence (or past presence) of kin groups larger than the nuclear family. Where there are such descent groups, a "father" may simply be a male in the father's generation and descent group, and a "mother" can be any woman of mother's generation and descent group (and someone eligible to marry one of my "fathers").

It is because kinship terms reflect kinship organization that anthropologists have been so attentive to them. In some situations these terms may even provide a window on the past. If the rule of marital residence has changed, for example, it may have produced adjustments in family composition and descent that are not yet reflected in kinship terms. Unexpected or special terms may signal forms of organization that used to be present. For example, in societies that have kin groups tracing descent through females, members are likely to reserve special terms, different from those used to refer to father's brothers, for the senior males of their descent group (i.e., for their mother's brothers). They might continue to distinguish between the two kinds of uncles even after their traditional descent groups have vanished.

Let us take a closer look, now, at a few societies that have adopted different patterns of postmarital residence, to see how these customs affect people's lives. Consider, first, the patrilocal Luo of western Kenya in East Africa.[4] Most lived in the rural countryside, in communities of scattered homesteads. At first glance, there was little that indicated where one community began and another left off. Homesteads of one to four thatched houses dotted the rolling hills. Each homestead, surrounded by a high circular hedge, was separated from the next by only a few hundred feet of cropland and pasture. Which homesteads belonged to the local community was more socially than geographically defined, and while it was possible to distinguish each homestead from its neighbors, the larger social groupings to which they belonged were not so apparent.

According to custom, a son built his own house in his father's homestead when he became a young man or just before he married. When he married, his wife joined him, and they lived there until their own children reached marriageable age, or until the son, now husband, took a second wife. When either (or both) of these events occurred, the son took his family out of his father's homestead to begin one of his own in the same community.

Each homestead farmed land close by, the wife or wives doing most of the work. There could be more than one wife if the family was extended, or if marriage was polygynous. All male homestead heads (and their children) in the area traced descent from a common male ancestor. Male-focused (patrilineal) descent groups were large, embracing all descendants of an ancestor fourteen generations removed. Female descendants married out, often to places quite far since custom prohibited taking wives from within the local descent group. And because most male members of the kin group lived contiguously, it usually occupied a substantial territory. In the area where Carol R. Ember did fieldwork, the largest descent group covered an area fourteen miles across. But what defined the community? If we think of a community as a group of people who live near each other, who have frequent face-to-face interaction, and who feel a sense of unity, then the community studied by Ember consisted of those homesteads whose male heads had a common ancestor three to five generations back.

Before British colonial authorities imposed peace, the Luo had engaged frequently in warfare. Over the past few hundred years, they had fought their way into Kenya from Uganda, seizing land as they went. They not only fought with other peoples, they fought among themselves as well, kin group against kin group. Those at the center pushed outward against other Luo groups, and descent groups on the frontier pushed against non-Luo. And because custom prohibited marriage within the descent group, wives often came from enemy groups (Luo and sometimes non-Luo). Indeed, the Luo claimed it was their custom to "marry the enemy," and traditional wedding ceremonies involved mock battles between kin of the bride and groom, as well as the ostentatious display of strength and wealth (cattle).

Patrilocality is the basis of Luo social structure, from families to homesteads to communities to districts. It is the reason that, in organizing their groups, the Luo trace descent through men rather than through women. But patrilocality is not the only rule of postmarital residence in which women move out at marriage while men remain near each other. This is true of avunculocality as well. Where avunculocality prevails, women also move away to join their husbands; but, in contrast to patrilocality, the men who remain together in avunculocal societies are related not through males, but rather through females. Men bring their wives to live with or near their own mother's brothers. Thus, brothers join mothers' brothers.

It should come as no surprise, then, that if avunculocal societies have descent groups (and most do), they almost invariably trace descent through females (matrilineally). In this case, then, children belong to the group of their mother. The famous Trobriand islanders of the South Pacific, studied by Bronislaw Malinowski in the early years of the twentieth century, were prevailingly avunculocal. At adolescence, a boy moved from the home of his parents into a bachelor house. When he later married, he established his household on land belonging to his female-centered kin group, where his mother's brothers were also living. His mother did not reside there, however, because she had left to live with her husband (and his brothers and mother's brothers).[5]

Avunculocality is very rare in the ethnographic record. It is unusual to localize related males when important kin groups trace descent through females; most matrilineal societies have matrilocal residence. The Iroquois of northeastern North America are one of the classic matrilocal societies. In the seventeenth century, Iroquois villages usually contained more than fifty multifamily long houses, and one thousand or more people. The village's long houses formed a compact cluster, surrounded by cleared fields of maize, beans and squash. Each village included people belonging to a number of female-centered (matrilineal) kin groups. A group of women, with a common female ancestor, lived out their lives in the same or neighboring long houses. By custom, a man at marriage left the long house he grew up in and moved to his wife's long house. Even so, the man continued to play a role in his own kin group. Here is a clear and important difference between patrilocal and matrilocal custom. In patrilocal societies, the out-marrying spouse (the bride) has no residual interest in her own descent group, and no role to play as far as it is concerned; in matrilocal societies, however, the man continues to play an authoritative role in his descent group (and usually lives close by).

Marriage was fragile, and divorce quite commonplace, in Iroquois society. And in this matrilocal, matrilineal society children not only belonged to the descent group of their mother, but they also remained behind with her if she sent her husband (their father) back to his own people. As we noted earlier, even though women were quite important in Iroquois society, the important political offices were all held by men. Still, women were not without indirect political influence; female kin group elders helped select the men who filled important political positions, and they retained the right to remove incompetent leaders when they deemed it necessary.[6]

MARITAL RESIDENCE AND THE PLACE OF WOMEN

Apart from the impact postmarital residence rules have on family, descent, and kinship terms, there is another reason we must be attentive to them, and especially to the circumstances that account for the cross-cultural predominance of patrilocality. So long as women leave their families (and often their communities as well) when they marry, they are losses. Their labor and reproductive contributions ultimately belong to others. Patrilocal residence thus has profound implications for the status and well-being of women. As we have noted earlier, there is some cross-cultural evidence suggesting that women in matrilocal, matrilineal preindustrial societies enjoy somewhat higher status in terms of some indicators. Summarizing his findings in this regard, Martin K. Whyte observed that the clearest pattern is for women in matrilineal and matrilocal cultures to have more control over property than women in other cultures, but the weaker patterns show women in such societies with somewhat more domestic authority, more ritualized female solidarity, more equal sexual restrictions, and perhaps more value placed on their lives…. The best general summation…is that, in keeping with the writings…[of] Murdock, Gough, and Schlegel, matrilineal descent and matrilocal residence are associated with certain benefits for women. However, with the exception of control over property, these benefits are not very powerful.[7]

The dynamics and economics of family life in preindustrial patrilocal societies invariably operate to women's disadvantage. In most, people rely on offspring for care in old age. Rarely can they count on welfare, pensions, or public institutions like old age homes, nursing facilities, or hospices. If marriages transfer daughters to others, parents have little motivation for investing heavily in them. Parents are more likely to favor sons when it comes to food, attention, and education and, if resources are in short supply, females may even be at higher risk of early death. There is hardly a level playing ground for the two genders. As Murdock (and Margery Wolf) pointed out, where women marry into different communities as well as different families, which is most commonly the case in patrilocal societies, there may also be other, more subtle disadvantages:

> Where marriages are exogamous with respect to the community…spouses of one sex find themselves living among comparative strangers, to whom they must make new personal adjustments and upon whom they must depend for the support, protection, and social satisfactions which they have previously received from relatives and old friends. They thus find themselves at a considerable psychological and social disadvantage in comparison with the sex which remains at home (Murdock 1949: 18).[8]

In her study of the effects of the Communist takeover in China, Norma Joyce Diamond (1975) powerfully illustrated the problems this combination of patrilocality and community exogamy can bring to women.[9] From the outset, the Communists had promised to liberate women and remove constraints which the traditional patriarchal family and descent group had imposed on modernization. But they fell far short of their goals and attributed that failure to wrong thinking—to the persistence in China of *feudal patriarchal ideology*. Their hope had been that enlightened reeducation would correct the situation. Yet, despite many campaigns designed to alter traditional notions, preference for sons endured and people still commonly asserted that "boys are precious, girls worthless." It is not that they did not want daughters (they did), but sons still constituted "large happinesses," daughters only small ones.

Diamond argued that, in reality, the problem had less to do with ideology than with economic reality. Despite all the transformations—land reform, collectivization, drawing women into the labor force, and so forth—the rule of postmarital residence had remained unchanged. Ironically, when land was collectivized—transferred from families to collectives and later to teams, brigades, and communes—the persistence of patrilocality meant that land was still vested in groups of men related through the male line. Despite a concerted effort to undermine descent groups and to politically emasculate their wealthy leadership, the Communist transformation actually recreated and incorporated de facto patrilineal descent groups. Even with the recent privatization of the economy that began in the early 1980s, women have continued to be "losses." If postmarital residence continues to be patrilocal, this situation is unlikely to change in China, or wherever else marriage requires the bride to move.

Not unexpectedly, women in China who are matrilocally married may fare better, depending on why they married that way. Matrilocality can serve different purposes; the particular functions intended can influence how these marriages are arranged and what their consequences will be. In the following section, we consider the example of Chungshe, a village in central Taiwan where Burton Pasternak did fieldwork.[10] There, matrilocality benefited women not simply because it enabled them to avoid the stresses associated with being wrenched from familiar surroundings; matrilocality also had positive demographic consequences as well.

"CALLING A SON-IN-LAW" IN A CHINESE VILLAGE

The inhabitants of Chungshe, poor farmers much like those in other Taiwanese villages, had a special problem. Whereas farmers in other regions of the island could grow two crops of rice, and often other crops as well, those in Chungshe could grow only one, and that was usually poor and unreliable. The problem was water; the entire region lacked irrigation canals and groundwater resources. Farmers watered their fields not from canals, but from the sky. But the rainy season was short, and rainfall irregular. Farmers were all busy during the short periods when rain was sufficient to soften the earth for plowing and transplanting. Because they could not be certain when it might rain again, they maintained higher than usual ridges around their plots to hold rainwater and were reluctant to release water to aerate their fields. These practices hardened the heavy clay soils, rendering them even harder to prepare without water, and reducing yields.

The fact that farmers were all busy preparing and transplanting their fields during the same short rainy period meant that periods of labor demand were unusually short and intense. Since the number of days between transplanting and harvest was fixed, the period of harvest in the region was also short and labor needs intense then, too.

While water scarcity intensified periods of labor demand throughout the region, one cultural restraint hampered effective response. Until about 1900, when the practice was terminated under pressure from Japanese colonial occupiers, women had bound feet. That severely limited their participation in weeding, harvesting, and processing grain. But the most pressing shortage of labor was during field preparation because plowing was exclusively men's work. Cooperation among families was difficult since no one knew when it might rain again.

We have already learned that patrilocality is the preferred and most common mode of marital residence in China. While that was true in Chungshe as well, families without sons frequently responded to the heightened need for males by "calling in a son-in-law." Under other circumstances this mode of marriage was rare and frowned upon in China. For the most part, matrilocality was a device used by parents who lacked a son, or were too poor to attract one by way of adoption. The parents of boys who married matrilocally were commonly blessed with too many sons but little land.

While matrilocal marriage solves a problem on both sides, people consider it morally questionable and potentially unstable. A matrilocal groom's own preference would have been not to marry this way; by allowing his sons to take their mother's name and carry her family line, he turns his back on his own ancestors, inexcusable in the Chinese context. To make matters worse, for access to his wife's family property, he must leave his family and community and join hers, as a woman normally does. Under these circumstances it is the male who confronts uncertainty, stress, and even more—humiliation. The fact that his wife is at home, with her own mother rather than under the thumb of a mother-in-law, gives her an edge over her husband as well as a greater measure of security. It is no wonder, then, that Chinese believe such marriages are more prone to divorce.

Anticipating the instability of matrilocal marriages, parents try to arrange them in such a way as to increase the chance that, should the son-in-law eventually leave, he will not take their daughter and grandchildren along. As in the case of patrilocal marriage, when the parents want their son to marry a girl he does not know, from a distant place, the parents in a matrilocal marriage prefer their daughter to marry a boy unknown to her, because doing so weakens the conjugal bond for the sake of the parent-child bond.

Comparison with other Taiwanese villages indicates that matrilocal marriages were unusually frequent in Chungshe. As we have seen, however, their purpose there was not to ensure family continuity but to solve a labor problem. For that reason, arrangements were designed to reduce the likelihood that a matrilocal son-in-law would run away. Accordingly, matrilocal unions were more likely to be community endogamous than the more common patrilocal marriages (matrilocal marriages elsewhere were also not so likely to be community endogamous). The bride and groom usually knew each other before they married. The groom, almost invariably a long-term worker in the community, knew her parents and remained in familiar surroundings. For the sake of his labor, his bride's parents were prepared to compromise the parent-child bond to promote a more intimate and enduring conjugal one.

There are indications that the special twist to matrilocal marriage in Chungshe accomplished what was intended. That parents were unusually tolerant of premarital familiarity is suggested by the fact that, compared to patrilocal marriages, the rate of premarital conception was significantly higher for matrilocal unions. Also, while the rate of divorce was higher for matrilocal than patrilocal unions in other localities, this was not the case in Chungshe. Furthermore, the total fertility of matrilocally married women was higher than for patrilocally married women in Chungshe, and also higher than that of matrilocally married women elsewhere. Widows, widowers, and divorcees were all more likely to remarry in Chungshe than elsewhere, probably because young widows and divorcees without grown sons still needed the labor of men.

In addition to the usual advantages that come from being able to remain at home after marriage, matrilocality conferred other advantages for women in this still essentially patrilocal village. Apart from those already mentioned, we find that girls were less likely to be given away in adoption in Chungshe than elsewhere. Female adoption, in infancy or childhood, has always been common in China. Girls were adopted as servants, for prostitution, and sometimes because parents either had too many of them or simply wanted to have one. In Chungshe, however, parents were inclined to hold their daughters longer—at least until they were certain they had sons who would survive to adulthood. Until then it was important to keep at least one daughter as a potential lure for a son-in-law.

The fact that daughters were adopted later and less often in Chungshe is not a trivial one because there is reason to believe the delay reduced the risk of early death. In the course of studying *minor marriages* (in which people adopted infant daughters and later married them to sons) in north Taiwan, Arthur P. Wolf discovered that girls adopted in infancy were significantly more likely to die by age fifteen than other daughters.[11] The explanation he proposed was that inadequate nursing under conditions of poor sanitation may have increased their risk of early death. Replicating his analysis elsewhere, Burton Pasternak also found evidence of greater risk for adopted daughters, *but not in Chungshe*. The reason for Chungshe's departure from expectation became clear on closer inspection—there, girls were older, close to puberty, when families adopted them.[12]

Given the importance of marital residence in structuring relations within and among families, and considering what we have just learned about the disadvantages of patrilocal residence for women, and the possible advantages of matrilocal residence, we can see that the popularity of patrilocality in human societies is a matter of considerable consequence, and we can appreciate why it is important to explain why it is so popular.

DETERMINANTS OF POSTMARITAL RESIDENCE

What does cross-cultural research tell us about the circumstances that lead societies to adopt one residence practice rather than another, and why is patrilocality preferred in so many? Are we to suppose that it reflects a basic and inevitable human condition—male dominance? Were that the case, wouldn't all societies be patrilocal? After all, males are politically dominant even in matrilocal and avunculocal societies.

Some theorists have thought that the human propensity for patrilocality has something to do with economics and particularly with the division of labor by gender, and with the fact that in most societies men do most of the primary subsistence work (getting food). For example, Murdock expressed the following view:

> [W]hile male dominance in consequence of physical superiority may be partially responsible for the vastly greater frequency with which women move to a new community in marriage, the author is inclined, with Linton, to seek the explanation mainly in economic factors, particularly those which derive from the division of labor by sex.[13]

Indeed, Murdock believed that differences in the division of labor by sex (gender) may account for residential variation in general. But in accounting for the reason so many societies prefer to keep men at home after marriage, Murdock suggested that this particular pattern would be

> promoted by any change in culture or the conditions of life which significantly enhances the status, importance, and influence of men in relation to the opposite sex. Particularly influential is any modification in the basic economy whereby masculine activities in the sex division of labor come to yield the principal means of subsistence.[14]

A similar suggestion is that the popularity of patrilocality may have something to do with the fact that the activities of men more often require cooperation than those of women, especially where there is a potential for violence. In the writings of Elman R. Service we find an explicit example of the position that cooperation in general, and for defense in particular, may encourage a pattern in which women join their husbands at marriage (*virilocality*, in his terms):

> Virilocality is expectable in exogamous band society because of the importance of the solidarity of the males in hunting, sharing game, and

particularly in offense-defense. This necessity could be expected to continue from early to late times, until the epoch of modern acculturation when hunting diminished in importance, or individualized fur-trapping took its place, and especially when the aborigines became enclaved within a powerful modern society which enforced peace.[15]

However plausible that expectation, cross-cultural research indicates that neither the division of labor by gender nor male cooperation in hunting or war really help us predict whether people are likely to be patrilocal or matrilocal. We find no relationship between contribution to subsistence and residence, or between frequency of fighting and likelihood of patrilocality over matrilocality.[16]

How then can we anticipate whether a society will be patrilocal or matrilocal? In a cross-cultural study focusing on this problem, Melvin and Carol R. Ember suggest that earlier explanations may have predictive value when we combine elements of them—if we simultaneously consider the nature of warfare and the division of labor in primary subsistence activities. Indeed, it turns out that where fighting occurs only between groups of people with different cultures and languages (purely external warfare), the division of labor in primary subsistence by itself predicts quite well whether patrilocality or matrilocality will prevail. If men contribute most to primary subsistence, the society will be patrilocal; where women contribute equally or more, it will be matrilocal. But if people fight among themselves (if the warfare is at least sometimes internal to the society or language group), residence will likely be patrilocal *regardless of the gender division of labor*.[17] (See Figure 10-2 for a summary of the main predictors of variation in patterns of residence.)

Why should the division of labor be relevant when warfare is purely external, but not relevant if fighting is sometimes internal? The answer may be that men normally do the fighting, and therefore it may be advantageous to localize them (keep them where they grew up), *regardless of the division of labor*, if there is a possibility of sudden attack from nearby (which is likely with internal warfare). But where the enemy provides earlier warning (more commonly the case with purely external warfare), keeping sons and brothers together may be less crucial, and the gender division of labor might then be more important in determining where a couple lives after they marry.

The reader should note that the theory we have been discussing (why matrilocality versus patrilocality) is not the only possible one we might entertain. So far we have been suggesting that matrilocality versus patrilocality is a consequence mostly of the prevailing type of warfare (purely external versus sometimes internal) interacting in the case of matrilocality with the gender division of labor in primary subsistence. (That is, matrilocality is the consequence of purely external war and high contribution by women to primary subsistence.)

FIGURE 10-2   THE MAIN PREDICTORS
OF MARITAL RESIDENCE PATTERNS

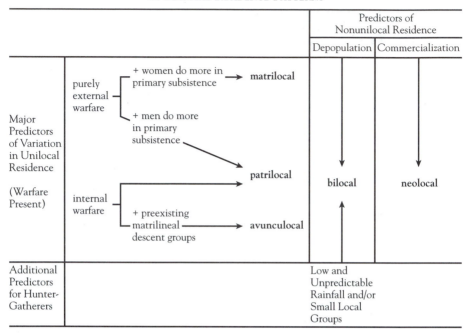

Source: Adapted from Melvin Ember and Carol R. Ember, *Marriage, Family, and Kinship: Comparative Studies of Social Organization* (New Haven: HRAF Press, 1983).

William T. Divale suggests a very different explanation for matrilocal societies having purely external warfare while patrilocal societies have internal warfare.[18] First, Divale assumes that residence will normally be patrilocal because males are usually dominant. We do not think that is a satisfactory explanation of patrilocality because males are usually dominant in all societies, yet not all societies are patrilocal. Divale further believes that matrilocal residence emerges under the special circumstances of migration. According to him, when a society (we would say a prestate society) or a large segment of a society begins to move into an already inhabited area, warfare between the intruders and the intruded upon is likely to be intense. In such a situation, Divale thinks, cessation of internal fighting amongst the intruders would be adaptive. The adoption of matrilocal residence presumably would make for the cessation of internal war because it would scatter related males and thereby foster harmony within the society (related males living in different places would be reluctant to fight each other). Hence, warfare if present would be purely external, that is, only with members of other societies. Consistent with Divale's theory is the significant relationship already discussed between external war and matrilocality, and a significant relationship between matrilocality and migration within five hundred years.

The major problem with this theory is that only half of the migrating societies in Divale's sample are matrilocal. At best, therefore, migration could only be a partial cause of matrilocality. In addition, how would a migrating society come to adopt matrilocality? Is Divale correct that people might anticipate the peace-keeping qualities of matrilocality, and deliberately adopt it for that reason in order to direct their hostilities solely toward members of other societies? We are skeptical about that reasoning. Many societies have both internal and external warfare (and usually patrilocal rather than matrilocal residence). Why did most of them not decide to adopt matrilocality to discourage fighting internally?[19]

Perhaps because childbearing and menstruation periodically remove women from labor outside the home, men normally have principal responsibility for crucial tasks that must be completed at specific times. But if fighting periodically requires them to be away when those tasks need doing, women may assume a greater role and people may then prefer to localize them. This would explain why matrilocality is so rare—we should expect it only in those relatively rare situations where we find purely external warfare of a sort that imposes heavier obligations on women. That is, matrilocality will occur only when the timing of purely external warfare requires women to do at least as much as men in primary subsistence.[20]

Internal warfare discourages matrilocality regardless of the division of labor, and there may even be a structural incompatibility between matrilocal residence and internal warfare. Consider some salient characteristics of matrilocal societies. When they form multifamily kin groups they are likely to trace descent through women. While succession and property pass through females, however, authority is still vested in men (their brothers). Because they play an important authoritative role in matrilocal, matrilineal societies, and because their sister's children are their heirs, brothers rarely move far when they marry. Often they just move "across the street."

Murdock found that fully 71 percent of the matrilocal societies in his sample were community endogamous, or exhibited a tendency to be so, compared to only 7 percent of the patrilocals.[21] Even when the men do leave their communities in matrilocal societies, they do not go far. Most commonly they marry women in nearby communities. The situation is quite different in patrilocal societies, where women are neither channels for descent nor sources of authority. Daughters are dispensable; there is no need for them to remain close after marriage.

Consider, then, what might happen were neighboring matrilocal communities to begin fighting among themselves. The danger of surprise raids would increase, as would the desirability of keeping brothers together. And since a man exercises authority in his sister's home and village even after he has married and moved away to live with his wife, he might have to defend his sister's group against a raid by his wife's local group (which is now also his local group)! We might well expect people in such a situation to change to a postmarital residence option that localizes males rather than females; this would be the result of a switch to avunculocality after a matrilocal society starts to have internal warfare.[22]

There are, in fact, only two ways males could be localized. A matrilocal people without important matrilineal descent groups could simply shift to patrilocality. That might be highly destabilizing if there were functional matrilineal descent groups, however. In that event, they would be better off finding a way to localize males *without disturbing their matrilineal descent groups*. Only avunculocality, by localizing men related through the female line, would do that.

We can better appreciate, now, why patrilocality is so much more common than matrilocality. It is not often that a society fights only externally (that is, never among themselves), and only in some societies with purely external warfare do women contribute a lot to primary subsistence. We can also see why avunculocality is even less common. To produce it you would have to confront a matrilocal society with conditions that favor keeping brothers together (like the development of internal warfare), and there would also have to be important matrilineal descent groups. This is an uncommon combination. Matrilocality is not that common to begin with, not all matrilocal societies have matrilineal descent, and even fewer of those societies will develop internal war.

Hence, avunculocal societies should be very uncommon (as of course they are). And we can also see now why avunculocality is the only residence pattern where a couple moves to some relative *other than a parent*. The mother's brother occupies a special position in a society with female-centered kin groups because of the separation of authority and descent, and warfare considerations prompt a need to localize related men (in this case matrilineally related men). There is no analogous reason for couples to move to some other relative, such as the father's sister.

Thus far we have only been discussing factors that might predispose societies to unilocal residence (patrilocal or matrilocal or avunculocal residence). But why do many societies have two or more prevalent patterns of residence (usually called *bilocal* residence when about half the couples live with or near either set of parents)? We prefer the more general term *multilocal* residence because it accommodates combinations of unilocal residence other than patrilocal and matrilocal, and includes the situation where one pattern is prevalent and two or more are frequent alternatives. While it may seem that couples in such a situation have a choice of where to live, most research suggests otherwise—that bilocal residence and more generally multilocal residence may be necessary.

There is one predictor of bilocality and multilocality which appears to reflect choice. George Peter Murdock suggested that bilocality reflects sexual equality, that "where women own and inherit property on a parity with men, it is common for a newly married couple to adopt the domicile of the spouse with the greater wealth or higher social status."[23] Indeed, research by Carol and Melvin Ember provides cross-cultural support for this idea.[24] However, sexual equality is a very weak predictor of bilocality and multilocality since most of the societies with alternative residence patterns do not have equal inheritance.

Building on the work of Gertrude Dole and Robert B. Lane, Elman Service suggested a more powerful reason for bilocality—depopulation.[25] Over the last four hundred years, contact with Europeans in many parts of the world has resulted in severe population losses where indigenous peoples lacked resistance to the Europeans' diseases. The Chukchee, Ila, Jivaro, Tiv, and Trobriand Islanders are just some examples.[26] The Embers found that depopulation predicted most cases of bilocality and multilocality. If couples need to live with some set of kin to make a living in noncommercial societies, it seems likely that couples in depopulated, noncommercial societies might have to live with whichever spouse's parents (and other relatives) are still alive. Consider the Trobriand Islanders. While they were often avunculocal, there were also many marriages that were patrilocal.[27] The Samoans also experienced severe depopulation and, in their case, some couples lived patrilocally and others matrilocally.[28]

In hunter-gatherer societies, a few other circumstances may also favor bilocal or multilocal residence. Bilocality tends to occur among those that have very small bands, or who have to deal with unpredictable and low rainfall. Residential choice in such societies may reflect an attempt to adjust marital residence in such a way that couples will have the best chance of surviving, or of finding close relatives with whom to live and work.[29]

The connection between bilocality and depopulation has evolutionary implications. Most cases of bilocality and multilocality are probably relatively recent. The vast majority of societies in the recent past have been food producers, not hunter-gatherers living under difficult conditions. And not all hunter-gatherers had to cope with unpredictable and low rainfall either (particularly in the distant past, when all humans were hunter-gatherers and lived in many nonmarginal environments). If bilocality is, in fact, most often a product of depopulation associated with Western contact, which is itself a relatively recent phenomenon, then some form of unilocality (patrilocality, matrilocality, avunculocality) was more likely to have been the norm in most traditional societies.

Neolocality may also be a recent phenomenon. This is a residential pattern particularly common in relatively recent and complex, industrial-commercial societies (like our own), where conditions encourage independent nuclear families consisting only of husband, wife, and immature children.[30] In such societies, education and ability are usually more important than kinship when it comes to finding work. When employment requires movement, people take their spouses and children along but rarely their brothers and sisters. Many burdens of the extended family in simpler societies—education, defense, welfare, and care of the elderly—pass to public institutions, which is another reason that kinship (and extended kin groups) tend to become less important. Cross-cultural evidence does suggest that commercial exchange (money), not necessarily involving an industrial economy, is a major predictor of neolocality (either as the major pattern of residence or as a common alternative).[31] For example, on the Six Nation Reserve in Canada, the Iroquois, who still rely on agriculture, now mostly live neolocally rather than matrilocally.[32] Whereas female-focused kin groups formerly owned the land, individuals now own it, and land is divided among male as well as female children. As a result, couples now tend to live wherever one of them finds or inherits land or, if both have land, they live wherever the situation is better. If neither has land, the couple may settle off the reservation, usually in a place the husband has chosen.[33]

We have now seen how and why different patterns of postmarital residence shape family composition. We have explored, as well, how residence preferences influence the nature of multifamily kin groups, find their way into kinship terms, and even structure the relations within families. We have explored their effects in terms of gender status, and have even considered some demographic consequences. We have learned that, by aggregating relatives of a particular gender, residence rules provide the basis for extended families. In the next chapter, we turn directly to how family and household vary, and particularly to the question of why most societies known to anthropology have extended families.

NOTES

1. Margery Wolf, "Women and Suicide in China," in *Women in Chinese Society*, eds. Margery Wolf and Roxane Witke (Stanford, CA: Stanford University Press, 1975), p. 123.
2. Ibid., p. 124.
3. Ibid.
4. The information on the Luo was collected by Carol R. Ember in the course of 1967–1968 fieldwork.
5. See Edmund R. Leach, "Concerning Trobriand Clans and the Kinship Category Tabu," in *The Development Cycle in Domestic Groups*, ed. Jack Goody (Cambridge, England: Cambridge University Press, 1971), pp. 120–145; Marguerite S. Robinson, "Complementary Filiation and Marriage in the Trobriand Islands," in *Marriage in Tribal Societies*, ed. Meyer Fortes (Cambridge, England: Cambridge University Press, 1972), pp. 121–157.
6. Thomas S. Abler, "Iroquois: The Tree of Peace and the War Kettle,"

in *Portraits of Culture: Ethnographic Originals*, eds. Melvin Ember, Carol R. Ember, and David Levinson (Englewood Cliffs, NJ: Prentice Hall/Simon & Schuster Custom Publishing, 1994).

7. Martin K. Whyte, *The Status of Women in Preindustrial Societies* (Princeton, NJ: Princeton University Press, 1978), pp. 132–134.

8. George Peter Murdock, *Social Structure* (New York: Macmillan, 1949), p. 18; see also Wolf, "Women and Suicide in China."

9. Norma Joyce Diamond, "Collectivization, Kinship, and the Status of Women in Rural China," in *Toward an Anthropology of Women*, ed. Rayna R. Reiter (New York: Monthly Review Press, 1975), pp. 372–395.

10. For a more lengthy discussion of Chungshe, see Burton Pasternak, *Kinship and Community in Two Chinese Villages* (Stanford: Stanford University Press, 1972), and *Guests in the Dragon: Social Demography of a Chinese District, 1895–1946* (New York: Columbia University Press, 1983).

11. See Arthur P. Wolf, "Childhood Association, Sexual Attraction, and the Incest Taboo: A Chinese Case," *American Anthropologist* 68 (1966): 883–898, "Adopt a Daughter In-Law, Marry a Sister: A Chinese Solution to the Problem of the Incest Taboo," *American Anthropologist* 70 (1968): 864–874, "Childhood Association and Sexual Attraction: A Further Test of the Westermarck Hypothesis," *American Anthropologist* 72 (1970): 503–515, and "The Women of Hai-shan: A Demographic Portrait," in *Women in Chinese Society*, eds. Wolf and Witke, pp. 89–110; and Arthur P. Wolf and Chieh-shan Huang, *Marriage and Adoption in China, 1845–1945* (Stanford, CA: Stanford University Press, 1980).

12. Pasternak, *Guests in the Dragon*. It is interesting that Pasternak's data indicate that sons adopted in infancy are also more likely to die by age fifteen than other sons. Since people do not give sons away easily in China, couples that succeed in adopting one are not likely to neglect or mistreat him the way they might an adopted daughter. This supports Wolf's notion that inadequate nursing rather than neglect was responsible for the greater mortality risk of adopted daughters.

13. Murdock, *Social Structure*, pp. 18–19.

14. Ibid., p. 206.

15. Elman R. Service, *Primitive Social Organization* (New York: Random House, 1971 [originally published 1962]), pp. 54–55.

16. See Melvin Ember and Carol R. Ember, "The Conditions Favoring Matrilocal versus Patrilocal Residence," *American Anthropologist* 73 (1971): 571–594. Reprinted with "Afterthoughts," in Melvin Ember and Carol R. Ember, *Marriage, Family, and Kinship: Comparative Studies of Social Organization* (New Haven: HRAF Press, 1983), pp. 151–198; and William T. Divale, "Migration, External Warfare, and

Matrilocal Residence," *Behavior Science Research* 9 (1974): 75–133. However, a study of only hunting-gathering societies does indicate a relationship between division of labor and marital residence. Where men contribute most to subsistence in such societies, residence is more often patrilocal; where women predominate, the rule is more likely to be matrilocal—see Carol R. Ember, "Residential Variation among Hunter-Gatherers," *Behavior Science Research* 10 (1975): 199–227. Reprinted in Ember and Ember, *Marriage, Family, and Kinship*, pp. 275–312.

17. Ember and Ember, "The Conditions Favoring Matrilocal versus Patrilocal Residence."

18. Divale, "Migration, External Warfare, and Matrilocal Residence."

19. Carol R. Ember, "An Evaluation of Alternative Theories of Matrilocal versus Patrilocal Residence," *Behavior Science Research* 9 (1974): 135–149. Reprinted in Ember and Ember, *Marriage, Family, and Kinship*, pp. 199–218).

20. Ibid. For theory and cross-cultural research suggesting that matrilocal residence precedes, rather than follows, the development of purely external warfare, see Divale, "Migration, External Warfare, and Matrilocal Residence." And for theory and research that suggests a way to resolve the disagreement between the Divale and Ember interpretations, see Ember, "An Evaluation of Alternative Theories of Matrilocal versus Patrilocal Residence."

21. Murdock, *Social Structure*, p. 19.

22. Melvin Ember, "The Conditions That May Favor Avunculocal Residence," *Behavior Science Research* 9 (1974): 203–209. Reprinted with "Afterthoughts," in Ember and Ember, *Marriage, Family, and Kinship*, pp. 249–260.

23. Murdock, *Social Structure*, p. 204.

24. Carol R. Ember and Melvin Ember, "The Conditions Favoring Multilocal Residence," *Southwestern Journal of Anthropology* 28 (1972): 382–400. Reprinted in Ember and Ember, *Marriage, Family, and Kinship*, pp. 219–248. Their research looked at *multilocality* (rather than bilocality), which they defined as "two or more fairly frequent patterns of consanguineal residence—some combination of matrilocal, patrilocal, and avunculocal...." (A few societies have all three patterns of unilocal residence, hence the term *multilocal*.)

25. Service, *Primitive Social Organization*, p. 137.

26. Ember and Ember, "The Conditions Favoring Multilocal Residence," p. 228.

27. Robinson, "Complementary Filiation and Marriage in the Trobriand Islands," reporting data from Powell.

28. This observation is based on data from Melvin Ember's fieldwork (1955–1956) in three villages of American Samoa.

29. Ember, "Residential Variation among Hunter-Gatherers," pp. 135–149.
30. See William J. Goode, *World Revolution and Family Patterns* (New York: Free Press of Glencoe, 1963); and Melvin Ember, "The Emergence of Neolocal Residence," *Transactions of the New York Academy of Sciences* 30 (1967): 291–302.
31. Ember, "The Emergence of Neolocal Residence."
32. Annemarie Anrod Shimony, *Conservatism among the Iroquois at the Six Nations Reserve* (New Haven, CT: Yale University Publications in Anthropology, Yale University, 1961).
33. Ibid.

11

FAMILY AND HOUSEHOLD

The idea that the family is a stable and cohesive unit in which father serves as economic provider and mother serves as emotional care giver is a myth. The reality is that trends like unwed motherhood, rising divorce rates, smaller households and the feminization of poverty are not unique to America, but are occurring world-wide.[1]

Around the globe, people are concerned that the building blocks of society—of any society—may be crumbling as families lose their traditional form and functions. The number of single-parent families has dramatically increased in Western countries recently, and in most cases (about 90 percent) these are female-headed families. During the 1960s, 9 percent of families in the United States were of this sort; by the mid-1980s the figure had jumped to 24 percent. Sweden once led in single-parent families (13 percent during the 1970s), but the United States now has the record. Many suspect that these *unnatural* families are the products of deep-rooted social problems and moral disintegration, and only exacerbate those problems.

A common assumption behind such concerns is that there is a time-tested "natural" family that works better than alternative forms. If so, we should expect to have to pay a considerable social price for deviations from that model. But is it really the case that there is one optimal family type, and if so what is its nature? Are *alternative families* truly dysfunctional or aberrant? Before we even consider such questions, it would be well for us to determine what sorts of families people "naturally" form in societies around the world, how much variation there is, and to see if we can account for the differences. That is our purpose in this chapter. And if we are to compare families in societies around the world, we must first agree on a definition of family. How will we know when we find a satisfactory one? At first blush the question might seem ludicrous. After all, don't we all know what families are? Perhaps not. As one long-term student of families around the world put it,

> we know too much about the family to be able to study it both objectively and easily. Our emotions are aroused quickly by the behavior of families, and we are likely to feel that family patterns other than our own are queer or improper. We are too prone to argue about what is *right*, rather than coolly to demonstrate what *is*. In addition, we have had an opportunity to observe many people engaged in family behavior, so that when we consider almost any generalization (such as "the lower social strata have a higher divorce rate than the upper") we can often find specific experience that seems to refute the generalization. Thus our personal experience is really a narrow sample of the wide range of family behavior, but it is so vivid to us, that we are likely to see no reason to look for broader data with which to test it.[2]

Once we look beyond ourselves, assumptions about what is natural, based on what we ourselves do, begin to crumble and the difficulties of comparison become acute. Just as there are ethnographic instances that seem to defy a universal definition of marriage, there are also situations that frustrate attempts to formulate an all-embracing definition of family. Consider a definition proposed some years ago by George Peter Murdock. Certainly not the only one possible, it illustrates the difficulties inherent in any attempt to arrive at a formulation that will satisfy everyone:

> The family is a social group characterized by common residence, economic cooperation, and reproduction. It includes adults of both sexes, at least two of whom maintain a socially approved sexual relationship, and one or more children, own or adopted, of the sexually cohabiting adults.[3]

After comparing families in societies around the world, Murdock identified three distinct forms—nuclear (married couple and offspring), polygamous (two or more nuclear units affiliated by plural marriage), and extended (two or more nuclear units affiliated through extension of the parent-child or sibling relationship rather than by plural marriage). His study persuaded him that the nuclear family exists as a "distinct and strongly functional group in every society" and that it is universal because it everywhere performs four functions essential to human life—sexual, reproductive, economic, and educational or socializing. One shortcoming of Murdock's definition was an additional stipulation of common residence, which would exclude cases in which husband and wife live separately or children live apart from parents. To require that family members live together is, in effect, to confuse qualitatively different social units—family and household. We will have more to say about this shortly.

There are other problems. Although the nuclear family does provide an institutionalized context for satisfying sexual needs and appetites, we have already learned that there are societies in which pre- or postmarital sexual license is allowed, even encouraged. Sex can be a reward of family life without being its cause. There are also instances of economic cooperation without sex, and of sexual unions without economic cooperation. Even some nonhuman species form family-like units in the absence of an economic division of labor between the sexes.[4]

Yet, in Murdock's view, marriage exists only when sexual and economic functions are combined. He follows this with the dubious assertion that only when marriage exists do we have families.[5] But why should marriage be universal and the family inevitable if sexual and economic functions may be otherwise performed? Murdock's response is to call upon reproductive and socializing functions for additional support. What then of the Nayar, among whom the legal, productive, distributive, residential, socializing, and consuming family unit was not a married couple or nuclear family, and where those involved in reproduction were not even members of the same family? And what are we to make of the single-parent families that occur and are even increasingly common in some societies, including our own?

Others echo Murdock's insistence that "the burden of education and socialization everywhere falls primarily upon the nuclear family," some even proposing that this function especially requires some sort of family in all societies. Only socialization, the argument goes, requires small units, and only kin-organized groups are capable of effectively doing the job.[6] But it is clear from ethnographic accounts and from experience in this and other complex societies that aspects or phases of the socialization process may be handled by different groups, particularly schools. Unrelated people bear the major burden of education in societies with schools or communes. Nor is the minimal family necessarily nuclear. Where marriages are polygamous or families extended, it is not nuclear. In addition, unmarried siblings, surviving parents, or other relatives, may all play some part in socializing the young. It was for such reasons that Levy and Fallers proposed defining the family as "any small, kinship-structured unit which carries out aspects of the relevant functions."[7]

The definitional problem has by no means been resolved.[8] As we suggested in connection with marriage, however, lack of scholarly consensus and differences in folk definitions from society to society should not deter us from formulating a working definition for the purpose of relating family, however defined, to other phenomena. It is useful to begin with some definition, recognizing its limitations, and go on to explore family variants and the conditions under which they occur. Most definitions minimally require parents and children. Since single parent families are not uncommon, in our society or in others, we prefer a definition of family that requires the presence of at least one socially and economically responsible parent (biological or other) and at least one child. While this definition enables us to compare families in societies around the world, we must keep in mind that folk notions of family may be quite different. Whenever appreciation of such notions may further our understanding of family dynamics, we will draw attention to them.

FAMILY EXTENSION AND SOCIETAL COMPLEXITY

While our definition of family requires the presence of only two people, the families we observe cross-culturally are usually larger and quite varied. We have already noted that polygyny is common in preindustrial societies. Thus many families in societies with polygyny are larger than the nuclear family. In addition, most societies have extended families, with two or more families related by blood. A family that has polygynous marriages and that is an extended family can be very large indeed. Consider that if a household contained a polygynously married man with two co-wives, each of whom had two married sons (living there, patrilocally), there would be seven adults in addition to unmarried children.

So most societies in the ethnographic record had families containing more than two married adults. Single-parent families were rare. The reasons that families have decreased in size with industrialization, and the reasons that the frequency of single-parent families has increased in recent years all over the industrialized world, will be discussed later in this chapter. But first let us turn to the factors that may produce extended family households. There are two main varieties of extended family. *Stem* families contain couples from two generations, a pair of parents and a married child with spouse. *Joint* families have at least two from the same generation, for example, a pair of brothers and their spouses, and possibly the parents.

Comparison of societies around the world indicates a curvilinear relationship between family form and societal complexity. Families are more likely to be extended at the intermediate levels of complexity than in either simple or complex societies. Hunter-gatherers often have independent nuclear families. Extended families are more common in agricultural settings but decline again in the most complex (urban-industrial) societies.[9] There clearly is some relationship between agriculture and family extension but its nature is not well understood.

One suggestion is that families are simpler (and kinship generally less important) in urban-industrial-commercial contexts for the same reasons that neolocality is common in such societies. Public institutions assume many family and kin group functions while the economy encourages nuclear family independence. At the other extreme, the simplicity of hunter-gatherer families may reflect the fact that food is limited, which encourages mobility. The assumption here is that the families in a hunter-gatherer band have to split up frequently in order to find enough food; hence families are less likely to be extended. Agriculturalists are more likely to have extended families, presumably because agriculture produces a more stable food supply. According to this line of reasoning, cultivation enables and encourages sedentary life, and the ownership of land for cultivation makes extended families more likely.[10] But there are problems with these speculations.

Although it used to be assumed that hunter-gatherers usually lived from hand-to-mouth, we now realize that foraging (hunting, gathering, fishing) can be quite productive, even in environments that are marginal for agriculture.[11] Foraging usually supports multifamily groups (bands), in human as well as other primate societies. If a hunter-gatherer band can include more than one family, why couldn't there be extended families? Thus, if hunter-gatherers have extended families less often than cultivators, it is not because the economy cannot support extended families. There must be other reasons. Perhaps hunter-gatherers are less likely to have extended families simply because they have less reason to delay family division. After all, why should related couples endure unpleasant long-term associations if aggregations of independent nuclear families could manage? More than that, given marginal environments and simple technologies, migration and ability to aggregate and disperse as conditions warrant might confer a selective advantage on independent family mobility. Extended families might provide less flexibility and therefore be less adaptive under such circumstances.[12]

What is it about agriculture, then, that might discourage family division? Meyer F. Nimkoff and Russell Middleton point to the fact that cultivation requires more labor than hunting-gathering, engenders firmer notions of private property, and discourages land fragmentation.[13] Let us consider their ideas about private property and land fragmentation. They argue that when land becomes privately owned, which is more likely among agriculturalists than among hunter-gatherers, it is advantageous to keep the land undivided over time; hence extended family households should emerge.

Nimkoff and Middleton assume that the division of land into small parcels would be less productive than unpartitioned land. While it is possible that partition of land into small parcels may under certain circumstances be disadvantageous, we question whether those circumstances are common among agriculturalists in general.[14] It seems to us that there is possibly a problem only when there are acute land shortages, with nowhere for

excess family members to go. But this is not generally true for shifting horticulturalists who make up the majority of agriculturalists in Nimkoff and
Middleton's sample. (If they didn't have somewhere to go, they wouldn't be
shifting agriculturalists.)

And even when there are land shortages, we are not persuaded that
partition of land is necessarily disadvantageous. A certain amount of land
feeds the same number of people whether the land is partitioned or not.
Perhaps Nimkoff and Middleton were thinking of the inefficiency of independent family households, each needing to have its own traction (animal,
machine) and plow. This might be inefficient, but why must related families live together in the same extended family household in order to share a
plow and/or animals to pull it? There are also other ways to maintain or
even increase income after family partition. People may work harder, apply
fertilizer and irrigation more effectively, plant improved varieties or more
profitable crops, or engage in sideline enterprises.

Further, farm size is not the only determinant of labor need. Choice of
crops, watering conditions, and the requirements of other family enterprises and investments are also important. Even then there may be ways, apart
from family extension, to meet labor needs. Workers may be hired, and in
much of the world families exchange labor during critical periods of the
year. So it is not clear that labor needs by themselves make extended families more likely among cultivators than foragers.

It is true, of course, that cultivators generally have a greater demographic potential for large families. Among hunter-gatherers, women usually carry their infants as they work, nursing on demand, a practice that may
delay the resumption of ovulation and hence conception. Cultivators more
commonly leave infants home in the care of others, often a mother-in-law
in the same extended family. Nursing is therefore less frequent, birth spacing shorter, and fertility higher among cultivators. But we can hardly conclude that cultivators have extended families simply because they have
more children. More offspring could just as well translate into more conflict, earlier family division, and therefore a higher likelihood of independent (nonextended) families.

Apart from these theoretical difficulties, there are also empirical problems with the hypothesis that agriculture favors extended families. If we
look at the actual relationship between agriculture and type of household,
the association is statistically significant (unlikely to be due to chance), but
agriculture only weakly predicts extended family households. There are a lot
of societies not explained by the agriculture hypothesis. While 60 percent
of agricultural societies have extended families, 40 percent do not. And
while 56 percent of hunter-gatherers do not have extended families, 44 percent do.[15]

There is a more effective way to predict which societies *at any level of
complexity* are likely to have extended families. The three of us (Pasternak,

Ember, and Ember) conducted cross-cultural research that supports the idea that family extension is likely *in any society* when, in the absence of hired or slave labor, the activities of women or men regularly require them to be in two places at once. We call these *incompatible activity requirements*.[16] Recall that the Embers pointed to an incompatibility between a human mother's feeding requirements and her need to care for babies as probably the main reason that humans have marriage. In the case of marriage, a male and a female could share or divide the food-getting and baby-tending tasks. However, we are now referring to incompatible activities that one gender needs to perform at the same time.

So, for example, if women do most of the agricultural work because men are otherwise occupied in war or long-distance trade *and* women also need to tend their children, a family needs to contain two adult women (at least)—one to work in the fields and the other to mind the kids. If men have to clear their land at the same time that they are engaged in long-distance trade, then the family needs to contain at least two adult men. Incompatibility of activity requirements predicts extended family households much more strongly than agriculture. Indeed, in our cross-cultural study, we were also able to predict which nonagricultural cases would have extended families, and which agricultural cases would likely have nonextended families.

But we must ask why societies could not solve these incompatibility problems in other ways? Why couldn't a woman or man from another household cooperate in providing the needed help?[17] While this is certainly a logical solution, cooperation between neighbors would likely entail a kind of alternating arrangement. "I work in your fields today while you babysit; tomorrow we alternate." Or "I work in both fields, you babysit both sets of kids." But the problem with such alternation is that it is unreliable in crunch times, particularly when there are brief, critical times for planting, replanting or harvesting. If the previously cooperating people have competing demands, they are likely to favor their own fields, or their own children. But if the other person belongs to the same household, the demands on the cooperating persons are not so likely to be competing because the cooperators often share the proceeds of their activities.

And if the extended family is a three-generational family, there is likely to be an older woman without child care responsibilities who can help out. The older woman might not be as able to do a great deal of outside work anyway, but could be a very effective caretaker. If she takes on the caretaking responsibility full-time, she may free up the younger woman and her energy for work in the fields or in marketing. In short, an extended family probably provides the most reliable as well as efficient solution to the problem of incompatible activity requirements.[18]

The idea of incompatible requirements also helps explain why agricultural societies are somewhat more likely than hunter-gatherers to have extended family households. First, agricultural societies usually have more work, so both women and men are likely to be faced with incompatible activity requirements.[19] Second, agricultural women tend to have shorter birth spacing and more children, so child care needs are greater.[20] In industrialized societies, these incompatibilities can be overcome. Help can be hired and there are fewer children, either because birth rates are lower or because children so often spend much of their time in school. Nonetheless, help requires money, so it is not surprising that it is more often the poor than the rich in industrialized societies who must rely on family for the cooperation they need.

VARIATION WITHIN SOCIETIES

Joint families are usually more difficult to keep together than stem, polygamous, or nuclear families, even in societies that prize them. Why then do we find them more often in certain localities, and why do some families in a particular community resist division longer than others? Why are joint families more common at one time than another? To deal with such issues we must give *activity incompatibility* greater precision, exploring in specific contexts the conditions that discourage family division. Let us begin with the observation of many that there is some connection between class (politically or economically defined) and family extension.[21] Why should the wealthy and powerful in class-stratified societies more often have joint families, and yet why do we sometimes find joint families among the poor and powerless as well? The ethnography of China may provide some direction.

CHINESE CLUES

Among Western stereotypic notions about the Chinese is one that attributes to them a predilection for large, joint families. However, although highly valued, joint families comprise only a small proportion of families at any given time in China. Many people spend some part of their lives in them, but joint families tend to be short-lived and therefore statistically infrequent.[22] There is abundant evidence of class linkage; the wealthy achieved the ideal more often and maintained it longer than the poor. Some observers have suggested this was because they had more land and needed more labor. Others note that the wealthy were also better educated and more indoctrinated in Confucian virtues, like filial piety. Perhaps wealthy sons more often obeyed their parents, and younger brothers more commonly deferred to older siblings. Such filial piety might discourage family division.

The problem is that not all wealthy families were joint, while even some poor ones were. And abundant land would not necessarily require more family members if workers could be hired or land rented out. How then account for the endurance of joint families among the wealthy, and for their occurrence among some less well-off families as well? Studies of specific communities indicate that technological and/or economic incompatibilities may discourage family division especially among the wealthy, but sometimes also among those with relatively little.

The Chinese themselves (women as well as men) commonly attribute family division to arguments among women. As noted earlier, property traditionally passes in the male line, with adult sons enjoying equal rights to the family estate. Women do not share these rights and have access to productive property only through husbands and sons, a situation that pits mother-in-law against daughter-in-law, and sisters-in-law against each other. That competition poses a threat to harmony, especially in joint families.

When she marries, a woman pursues the loyalty of her husband. Since she will likely outlive him, her security in old age ultimately also depends upon her sons. In that regard she has competition from her daughters-in-law. That is why, in custom and symbol, the parent-child bond takes precedence over the conjugal one and why, in traditional contexts, marriage so often joins people from different communities. Initial familiarity between bride and groom more readily challenges the parent-child bond. It is also why overt, public expression of spousal affection is in poor taste.

While a mother-in-law has reason to keep her sons together, her daughters-in-law are motivated to press for family division. Each woman must look to the interests of her own children and conjugal unit. A few hypothetical situations will show why this is so. Consider the case of Mr. Hwang, head of a joint family, who decides to send a child of his eldest son to college. He is the smartest, most capable grandson, the one most likely to reward the larger family through advanced education. However, a younger son's wife resents the decision. Why should efforts of her conjugal unit subsidize family members who will eventually be independent? Concerned, she becomes what the Chinese sometimes call a "pillow ghost." In bed at night she presses her husband to demand family division.

Or consider an even more common situation in which one daughter-in-law has a child while another does not. The childless one may agitate for division on the grounds that her labor and that of her husband are being consumed by an unproductive nephew, a child who may well depart before matching their contribution. Her attitude will likely change, of course, once she has a child and her nephew is old enough to work a plow. Then her sister-in-law is likely to become the pillow ghost. Given the potential for conflict which patrilocal residence and equal patrilineal inheritance provide, it is hardly surprising that joint families rarely endure for long.

Still, we do find an unexpected number of them in some localities. Why there, and in those particular families, are centrifugal tendencies repressed? Recall Chungshe, the Taiwanese village described in connection with marriage, where rainfall dependence discouraged family division *even in poor families* by putting a premium on adult male labor. Farmers could prepare their fields only when it rained and the ground was wet. It rained on all fields at the same time, so everybody needed to work in the fields then; hence the possibility of cooperation was limited. Only men plowed, so every family wanted more than one man. In Chungshe then, there was good reason to resist the entreaties of pillow ghosts, and joint families were unusually common.

The durability of joint families had little to do with power, education, shared values, or wealth in Chungshe. Farmers were relatively poor and Confucian virtues were no more accepted than in other Taiwanese villages. Indeed, while there were many joint families, many villagers married matrilocally—a less than filial choice on the part of the in-marrying son-in-law. The situation changed once local authorities constructed a reservoir and network of canals to store and deliver water throughout the plain. Rotational irrigation meant that water was available over a longer period. Families no longer had to act at the same time, and in fact, could not do so. Once cooperation was possible, the frequencies of joint families and matrilocal marriages both dropped precipitously.

In Chungshe, then, technology affected marital residence and form of extended family by creating an unusual need for men. Data from another Chinese village shows how technology may discourage family division by putting a premium on the labor of women.[23] When some rice-growing families in Lungtu (Taiwan) began cultivating and processing tobacco, a cash crop, most of the work was assigned to women. The men continued to concentrate on rice. Women picked tobacco leaves as they ripened, carried them to family drying houses, regulated fires there day and night, and sorted the leaves when they had dried. Their skills were so crucial and specialized that tobacco growers married only tobacco growers.

While farmers growing rice had few joint families, those that additionally cultivated tobacco almost invariably had joint families because, for them, family division created special problems. Which son would inherit the very profitable drying house, and how would his brothers be compensated? More important, any family division would mean a diversion of female labor from tobacco to separate kitchens, pigs, and child care.

These examples illustrate our more general finding, mentioned earlier in connection with marriage, that activity or task incompatibility encourages family extension. In Chungshe there was more work than one man could do at certain crucial times, hiring labor was difficult and expensive, and exchanging labor even more so. In Lungtu the different tasks of women were at issue. But there are still other circumstances, especially relevant to the wealthy, that have a similar effect and that help us understand why, in traditional Chinese contexts and perhaps elsewhere, the wealthy more often have joint families than the poor.

The connection between stratification and family extension may depend less on the land a family owns or cultivates than on other correlates of wealth which, like tobacco or rainfall dependence, recommend keeping several women and/or men in the same family. One may own vast areas without cultivating any, just as one can farm without owning land (as a tenant). In the Chinese context, at least, wealthy families may delay division longer to facilitate and protect multienterprise family investments. To the extent that any family invests labor and capital in different enterprises, puts its eggs in many baskets, it stands to improve its security, ability to withstand economic fluctuations, and long term wealth. Consider the following illustration:

Mr. Lin manages a substantial family estate and heads a joint family consisting of four married sons and their respective wives and children. He lives with one son on the family farm, another lives in and runs the family wine house (and brothel) in town, the third lives elsewhere and manages the family brick factory, and the fourth son runs the family trucking firm. The family is thus invested in a number of enterprises, each of which operates on its own schedule. As they see it, the joint family is the minimal corporate kin group. The brothers live in different households, which short-circuits some of the conflict that might otherwise emerge. There are powerful economic reasons for avoiding family division. With the family intact, its manager can shift labor and capital from enterprise to enterprise, an advantage that would be lost if the brothers were to divide. Men and women are channeled to various family undertakings as needed. When the crop is brought in, sons and grandsons help. Assuming a good yield, the wine-house-brothel is busy and family members help there. During winter slack the brick factory needs workers, and at other times labor is needed for trucking.

By holding his family together, Mr. Lin meets these needs without hiring. He can shift capital as well and avoid borrowing at high rates of interest. The family wine-house-brothel, very profitable in good years, can be a serious burden when harvests are poor and farmers less free with their money. A family that can move labor and capital from one enterprise to another is better able to weather the fluctuations.

It would not be easy to divide this corporation in any event, for how does one assess the value of a brothel compared to a brick factory or farm? They have different values, potentials, requirements, and risks. In this case, then, it is not wealth per se that makes the difference as much as the way in which people invest it. In commercial-agricultural societies, where it is possible to avoid keeping eggs in a single basket, families may better conserve or increase wealth by remaining together and shifting resources around than by splitting up and depending on outsiders (whom they would have to pay). Joint families should be particularly favored where credit is scarce or where resources have to be conserved and kept fluid.[24]

FAMILY AND HOUSEHOLD

Our discussion of Mr. Lin's family highlights the pitfalls of confusing families and households, especially in complex societies.[25] In the Chinese context it is best to think of family as the minimal corporate kin group. Mr. Lin's family in that sense consisted of several residential units, or households. If we confuse the two here or elsewhere, we may underestimate the incidence of extended families. An East Indian store owner in Hoboken, New Jersey, might well constitute one segment of a larger family corporation centered in Bombay, India—one egg in a family basket. Similarly, the illegal Chinese boat person in New York, whose voyage was financed from family resources in China, may represent a family investment.

If we fail to recognize connections between households, it is easy to underestimate family complexity and mystify family dynamics. The risk is especially great in complex societies. We must take care not to confuse frequent neolocal residence with a propensity for nuclear families. And the distinction between family and household is easily overlooked. In a study of East Indians in Uganda, H. S. Morris observed that a cash economy is not conducive to joint family operation because

> wealth acquired by one member through his own efforts, which in traditional conditions is seldom an important category of property, can become of overriding significance. A man who has made a fortune by his own skill and who has invested it in property other than farming land may be reluctant to allow other members of the family to interfere in its management.[26]

But why should this be, if management of a multienterprise family investment can be so advantageous? In fact, Morris's description suggests he may have underestimated the persistence of *nonresidential* joint families. He claims Indians do not attain extended (and especially joint) families in Uganda. Yet,

> of the ninety households investigated, the heads of forty-four claimed to own property in India jointly with agnatic [patrilineal] relations. To this extent the concept of a joint family as a property-owning corporation had some relevance, even in Uganda, where the form of the family was in fact almost always individual. Most informants, moreover, regretted this practical disappearance of the joint family in East Africa, and attributed the loss to housing conditions, lack of proper religious training in the young, and European ideas which undermine control by the head of the household over sons and daughters-in-law.[27]

It would be interesting to know whether households in Uganda send or receive anything from relatives in India (i.e., from other members of a property-owning family corporation). Indians, like the Chinese, may subsidize far-flung ventures to increase resources and capabilities. If household heads in Uganda cannot make a go of it, can they exert a claim on some family estate in India? Still, we might wonder why Indians in Uganda rarely constitute joint families. Inadequate housing may require residential separation, but it would not prevent the formation and perpetuation of nonresidential joint families.

As for the impact of new ideas on marriage, under what conditions are people more or less likely to adopt such ideas? When, for example, would a rebellious wife be likely to prevail upon her husband to leave his father's home? Perhaps when there are no overriding economic arguments against it. Morris tells us that Ugandan property and inheritance laws provided no obstacles, and his description of family economics indicates that division was a simple matter. Furthermore, reliance on non-kin was a virtual necessity in Uganda:

> The migration and settlement of Indians in East Africa was by individuals and not by large blocks of patrilineal relatives; consequently a man in Uganda who wishes to rely on his lineage will be in difficulties. At the same time, in a trading community, men are in urgent need of support from friends and relatives. Capital and employment are often hard to come by and no one can afford to ignore any route that will lead him to successful help from a more powerful or rich man. No one can afford to ignore collateral or affinal links.[28]

In short, cooperation united Indians *as Indians* in Uganda, and this may be one reason why neither descent groups nor extended families emerged. While Indians did not produce many joint families in Uganda, the ethnographic record does not indicate that extended families are completely absent in urban-industrial or commercial societies everywhere.[29] Married students living apart from parents do not necessarily constitute separate families. That a husband lives near his factory does not mean his wife and children in the countryside are a separate family. A Chinese in southeast Asia who has not seen his brother in years, has not sent or received money from him, may not have renounced his claim upon their common property. So long as the family estate has not been partitioned, Chinese brothers consider themselves members of the same family, notwithstanding the national or international borders separating them. The family estate provides a kind of insurance they would not otherwise enjoy.

Some would have us believe that extended families (and larger kin groups) persist in complex societies only so long as the requirements of an industrial economy have not become fully operative, or only if other agencies have not developed to provide economic and social security in a tight, competitive labor market with high unemployment.[30] But perhaps some complex societies do not provide these functions because families and larger kin groups already do so. We should take nothing for granted and, in each instance, should determine the starting point for change—the sorts of kinship groups that existed when commercialization and/or industrialization began. While industry and commerce may encourage neolocality and nuclear families, it is clear that some societies, including many in western Europe, had nuclear family systems even before. Indeed, some suggest that industrialization and commercialization do not isolate individuals or conjugal units unless they are already isolated.

We have seen how the joint family may enable the wealthy to maintain or increase their wealth in complex societies. For precisely the same reasons, the poor may also benefit from some form of family or household expansion. The anthropologist Harumi Befu tells us that large families were adaptive in the face of poverty and near starvation in Nakagiri, Japan, for example. There, a need to economize and conserve resources made the difference.[31] And in Peru's urban slums, we find enlarged households with similar functions. They consist of one or more young families plus unrelated wage earners, sharing costs of rent, water, and fuel, and occasionally child care so mothers and young children can earn extra income.[32]

These examples support Myron L. Cohen's proposal, based on Chinese materials, that the "interdependent nature of the various economic activities undertaken by different family members" provides a key to perpetuation of the joint family. It is a form likely to endure longer where, in the event of family division, "the limited possibilities remained to each unit would not bring total returns as great as those derived from the total investments of the family as now constituted," or where "division would also mean a reduction in total income from present enterprises."[33] In short, extended families (especially joint families) may endure longer where defense of accumulated wealth (at one end of the socio-economic spectrum) or maintenance of minimal living standards (at the other) benefit from delaying family division. That may be especially likely in commercial-agricultural settings where productive resources are privately owned but constantly or periodically limited in supply.

Extended families are also common in pastoral societies where advantages flow from cooperation.[34] There, too, variation in the form and composition of families may reflect economic and environmental differences. In adapting to dissimilar habitats, the Jie and Turkana of East Africa, originally with the same culture, developed somewhat different family organizations.[35] Living under more favorable conditions, the Jie have permanent settlements and supplement transhumant pastoralism with horticulture. The typical *homestead* contains descendants of a single grandfather, with their wives, sons, sons' wives and children, and unmarried sisters and daughters. Homesteads, in turn, consist of *houses*, groups of full brothers, which are the main cattle owning units. While neither homesteads nor houses are free of strife, counter pressures delay partition in both. Few houses can accumulate bride wealth on their own; people usually seek the help of close (patrilineal) kinsmen. Houses also cooperate in tending livestock and for other purposes.

In contrast, the Turkana live in mobile, changing groups. Unpredictable vegetation encourages independence. They have joint families like the Jie, but theirs are not coresidential and are more prone to fission. Environmental conditions require herding animals of different sorts in different locations. As a result, the family normally consists of at least two separated homesteads. The situation clearly recommends impermanent kin and cross-kin alliances, and there are fewer incentives than among the Jie for enduring social units at any level.[36]

FEMALE-FOCUSED FAMILIES

Thus far, we have been describing families predicated on some form of marriage. Without explicitly saying so, we have assumed that families consisted of married couples and their offspring, abandoning our initial, simpler definition of family. As we have repeatedly observed, however, female-focused families (and households) are not uncommon in commercial-industrial societies, and sometimes also in simpler societies under their influence. Some years ago, the anthropologist Nancie González proposed that families with absent husband-fathers (consanguineal families) may constitute a modern alternative in societies with recurrent migratory labor and low wages.[37] The husband may work and live elsewhere, as is common in some Caribbean countries, or be absent because of military obligations, as among the Nayar of India. And then there are *matrifocal* families, which are quite different. González reserved that term for families or households, "in which the woman is dominant and plays the leading role psychologically."[38] Not all consanguineal families are also matrifocal in this sense. Families can be matrifocal, as among the Mescalero Apache, even when husband-fathers are present.[39] The Nayar have consanguineal households which are not matrifocal because authority is vested in the woman's brother. Researchers have not yet determined with precision the conditions under which families or households are likely to be female-dominated or matrifocal.

Let us leave the distinction between matrifocal and consanguineal families aside, then, and turn to a related issue.[40] As we noted earlier in this chapter, although single-parent families are relatively uncommon in most societies, their number has dramatically increased in Western countries recently, and in most cases (about 90 percent) they are female-headed. Many American families depart from the two-parent model and approach the minimal definition with which we began this chapter. A great many children now grow up in families without one biological parent. Families are also increasingly impermanent.

According to the most recent census, nearly 10 million children live with a stepparent, or with siblings less than full brothers and sisters. And there are sharp differences between groups in this regard. The census indicated that 56 percent of white, and 26 percent of black children, live with both parents. For Hispanics the figure is 37.8 percent. Fully 24 percent of all American children live in one-parent families, almost always with their mothers. Nineteen percent of white children live in single-parent families, compared to 31 percent for Hispanics and 49 percent for black children.[41]

What accounts for this trend? In some cases, single-parent families result from out-of-wedlock birth, death of a spouse, or simply from a single person's decision to adopt a child. More often they are the product of divorce or separation. In fact, some suggest that ease of divorce may be the most important source of single-parent families. During the late 1960s and early 1970s, changes in law did make divorce easier in many countries, and the percentage of one-parent families rose. But why did so many countries relax constraints on divorce at the same time? Did more accessible divorce produce new attitudes about marriage and family, or were more relaxed divorce laws reflective of changed values?

It would probably be a mistake to attribute the increase in single-parent families solely to changes in divorce. For one thing, more frequent divorce would produce more one-parent households only if people did not quickly remarry, as was the case in the United States during the mid-1960s, when remarriage rates declined, particularly among younger, better educated women. The percentage of single-parent households may have risen then for that reason. But in many other countries, one-parent households increased after divorce rates became stable during the 1980s, so ease of divorce cannot account for the recent general increase in single-parent families.

Although some people prefer a single life, many more would probably marry if they could. Cross-culturally, opportunities to marry vary. In some countries (and among some ethnic groups within countries) there are fewer males than females, and sometimes a high proportion of them have poor economic prospects. There are many more women than men in the former Soviet Union, for example, because more males died from war, alcoholism, and accidents.

The sex ratio is not unbalanced in the United States, but neighborhoods, particularly poor ones, sometimes have high young male mortality and high unemployment rates, especially for males. One study estimated that for every one hundred African-American women between the ages of twenty-one and twenty-eight, there are fewer than eighty available African-American men.[42] If we consider only *employed* men (full or part-time), then the number of men per one hundred women drops below fifty. Among non-Latino white Americans, there are more available men and a higher proportion are employed (ninety for every one hundred women). So there may be merit to the suggestion that the percentage of single-parent families (again, usually female-headed) will be high when a spouse (particularly an employed one) is hard to find.

Another suggestion is that one-parent families have become more common because our "welfare state" has made it easier for women to manage without husbands. In Sweden, unmarried and divorced mothers do enjoy many state-provided benefits, including allowances for maternity and education. While there are few comparable supports in Iceland, however, that country has the highest rate of out-of-wedlock births in Scandinavia. Nor does the welfare argument work very well in the United States. The "Aid to Families with Dependent Children" program mainly serves single mothers. If the theory about the effect of welfare were correct, increases in aid should increase the percentage of mother-headed households. What we actually find is that, while the percentage of families receiving aid (and the value of aid) *decreased* during the 1970s, the percentage of mother-headed households *increased*. And during the 1980s, when access to welfare became more restricted, the percentage of mother-headed households increased still further.

Some propose that the increasing involvement of women in work outside the home has encouraged single-parent families. Improvements in access to higher-paying jobs presumably also enabled more women to choose a single life-style. While these developments may explain the choices of some women, research indicates that employed women are generally *more* rather than less likely to marry. Still, there does seem to be some sort of relationship between commercial economies and the incidence of single-parent families.

Is there something about subsistence economies that promotes marriage or about commercial ones that discourages it? Recall from our earlier discussions that while marriage is not everywhere based on romantic love, it usually entails considerable interdependence, economic and otherwise. Such interdependence is particularly evident and necessary in societies with little commerce. In market economies, goods and services can be bought and sold, and governments often assume functions handled by the family and kin group in simpler societies. So the one-parent family is likely to remain a choice or even be a necessity for some people in our society.

OTHER IMPLICATIONS OF FAMILY VARIATION

The matter of variation in family form is not of interest simply for its own sake. We are not just interested in why families differ between and within localities, but also in the implications of these differences. We have already seen how life in a joint family may affect the nature of relations between women and their daughters-in-law, and between husband and wife. There is still much to learn about how family form impacts family relationships. In a patrilineal, patrilocal society (like China) a woman's well-being may well depend on the size and composition of the family into which she marries, on whether or not she knows her groom, and on her age relative to his. At what phase of family development does she enter, how many brothers does her husband have, and how many sisters-in-law must she deal with? Does family composition have any effect on the age at which women and men marry, or on the number of children they bear?

And for children, too, family form may be crucial. With how many cousins (and of what sex) are they in competition? How many caretakers are available, and what sorts of discipline can they apply? Many studies indicate that family form has implications for the way children are socialized, which in turn influences the kind of adults they become. In a study of Chinese families, for example, Nancy Johnston Olsen found that mothers in extended families are more likely to stress aggression control, to emphasize conformity, and to use punishment rather than shame-oriented discipline, than are mothers in nuclear families. They were also more likely to emphasize traditional values.[43] In nuclear families, mothers scored higher on independence training, insisted more on obedience, and were more inclined to use shame as a disciplinary technique than were mothers in extended families. The cross-cultural results are similar. Aggression is more likely to be punished in extended as compared with nonextended families.[44]

As Olsen points out, the socialization differences she found in Taiwan are like those associated with social class in the United States and many other countries. Mothers in Taiwanese extended families resemble American working-class and rural mothers in their use of punishment, in the value they place on conformity and tradition, and in the lack of emphasis they put on independence training. When she controlled on class differences (occupationally defined), and compared rural and urban Taiwanese families, she also found that class made a difference in much the same direction. Interestingly, however, the differences in socialization associated with family form persisted *even within classes*, indicating that family form was important independently of class, and apart from whether families were rural or urban.

Indeed, the differences in socialization as linked to variation in family form were significant even when dissimilarities in maternal education were considered. While Olsen attempts to sort out what it is about differences in family composition that produces the observed variation in child socialization, we cannot pursue that here. Enough has been said, however, to indicate the importance of following out the implications of being raised in, or living in, families of different size, form, and composition. In this regard our research is still in its infancy.

NOTES

1. From interview with Judith Bruce, an author of the Population Council study "Families in Focus," as quoted in *The New York Times International*, May 30, 1995.
2. William J. Goode, *The Family* (Englewood Cliffs, NJ: Prentice-Hall, 1964), p. 3.
3. George Peter Murdock, *Social Structure* (New York: Macmillan, 1949), p. 1.
4. Murdock himself noted (*Social Structure*, p. 8) that "sexual unions without economic cooperation are common, and there are relationships between men and women involving a division of labor without sexual gratification, e.g., between brother and sister, master and maid-servant, or employer and secretary."
5. Ibid., p. 8.
6. For classic formulations of this view, see M. J. Levy and Lloyd A. Fallers, "The Family: Some Comparative Considerations," *American Anthropologist* 61 (1959): 647–651; and Talcott Parsons, "The American Family: Its Relations to Personality and to the Social Structure," in *Family, Socialization, and Interaction Process*, eds. T. Parsons and R. F. Bales (New York: Free Press, 1955), pp. 3–33.
7. Levy and Fallers, "The Family," p. 650.
8. In a review and critique of efforts to define family and household, Sylvia Yanagisako, in "Family and Household: The Analysis of Domestic Groups," *Annual Review of Anthropology* 8 (1979): 199–200, wrote: "What is wrong is to decide a priori that the diverse array of social units we call families fulfill the same set of functions or that their primary function is always the same. If we are to cast aside this premise and instead seek out the functions of the family in each society, we must at the same time abandon our search for the irreducible core of the family and its universal definition. Our usage of the terms "family" and "household" will then reflect an awareness that they are, like "marriage" and "kinship," merely "odd-job" words, which are useful in descriptive statements but unproductive as tools for analysis and comparison. The dilemmas we encounter in cross-cultural comparisons of the family and household stem not from the conviction that we can construct a precise, reduced definition for what are inherently complex, multifunctional institutions imbued with a diverse array of cultural principles and meanings. Indeed, the only thing that has thus far proved to be unvarying in our search for the universal family is our willingness to reduce this diversity to the flatness of a genealogical grid."
9. For studies documenting the curvilinear relationship between family form and societal complexity, see Rae Lesser Blumberg and Robert F.

Winch, "Societal Complexity and Familial Complexity: Evidence for the Curvilinear Hypothesis," *American Journal of Sociology* 77 (1972): 898–920; and Meyer F. Nimkoff and Russell Middleton, "Types of Family and Types of Economy," *American Journal of Sociology* 66 (1960): 215–225.

10. Nimkoff and Middleton, "Types of Family and Types of Economy."

11. See Nimkoff and Middleton, "Types of Family and Types of Economy," p. 218, for one example of the notion that hunter-gatherers have limited food. For the opposite view that hunting and gathering may provide a satisfactory and stable food supply, see Richard B. Lee, "Kung Bushmen Subsistence: An Input-Output Analysis," in *Environmental and Cultural Behavior*, ed. Andrew P. Vayda (New York: Doubleday Natural History Press, 1969), pp. 47–79; James Woodburn, "An Introduction to Hadza Ecology," in *Man the Hunter*, eds. R. B. Lee and I. DeVore (Chicago: Aldine-Atherton, 1968), pp. 49–55, and "Stability and Flexibility in Hadza Residential Groupings," in *Man the Hunter*, eds. Lee and DeVore, pp. 185–199. We should also keep in mind that hunter-gatherers have not always inhabited marginal areas. Contrary to older beliefs, moreover, the greater potential of agriculture does not necessarily result in more leisure or better fed and healthier producers. In many instances, the rewards of agriculture are siphoned by landlords and tax-collectors who press for ever greater productivity.

12. See Woodburn, "Stability and Flexibility in Hadza Residential Groupings."

13. Nimkoff and Middleton, "Types of Family and Types of Economy," p. 220.

14. Burton Pasternak, Carol R. Ember, and Melvin Ember, "On the Conditions Favoring Extended Family Households," in Melvin Ember and Carol R. Ember, *Marriage, Family, and Kinship: Comparative Studies of Social Organization* (New Haven: HRAF Press, 1983 [originally published 1976]), pp. 129–130.

15. Ibid., pp. 130–131.

16. Ibid., pp. 133–149.

17. Ibid., pp. 135–138.

18. Ibid.

19. Marshall D. Sahlins, *Stone Age Economics* (Chicago: Aldine, 1972).

20. Ibid.

21. Nimkoff and Middleton, "Types of Family and Types of Economy"; see also Blumberg and Winch, "Societal Complexity and Familial Complexity"; and Remi Clinget and Joyce Sween, "Urbanization, Plural Marriage, and Family Size in Two African Cities," *American Ethnologist* 1 (1974): 221–242.

22. For more detailed discussions of complex families in China, see Arthur

P. Wolf and Chieh-shan Huang, *Marriage and Adoption in China, 1845–1945* (Stanford: Stanford University Press, 1980); Arthur P. Wolf, "Chinese Family Size: A Myth Revitalized," in *The Chinese Family and Its Ritual Behavior,* eds. Hsieh Jih-chang and Chuang Ying-chang (Taipei, Taiwan: Institute of Ethnology, Academia Sinica, 1992 [originally published 1985]), pp. 30–49; Myron L. Cohen, *House United, House Divided: The Chinese Family in Taiwan* (New York: Columbia University Press, 1976), and "Family Management and Family Division in Contemporary Rural China," *The China Quarterly* 130 (1992): 357–377; and Burton Pasternak, *Guests in the Dragon: Social Demography of a Chinese District, 1895–1946* (New York: Columbia University Press, 1983).

23. Cohen, *House United, House Divided.*

24. In the People's Republic of China, with productive property transferred to the collective and private enterprise discouraged, there was no reason for families to become more complex than stem. In that sense, collectivization undermined traditional sources of family complexity. Since recent economic reforms in China, economic diversification again encourages more complex families and there are already signs of a resurgence of the joint family. See Cohen, "Family Management and Family Division in Contemporary Rural China"; Elisabeth Croll, "New Peasant Family Forms in Rural China," *Journal of Peasant Studies* 14 (1987): 469–499, and "Some Implications of the Rural Economic Reforms for the Chinese Peasant Household," in *The Reemergence of the Chinese Peasantry,* ed. A. Saith (London: Croom Helm, 1987), pp. 105–137.

25. The point has been made by others. See, for example, Donald R. Bender, "A Refinement of the Concept of Household: Families, Co-Residence, and Domestic Functions," *American Anthropologist* 69 (1967): 493–504, and "De Facto and De Jure Households in Ondo," *American Anthropologist* 73 (1971): 223–241; and Yanagisako, "Family and Household."

26. H. S. Morris, "The Indian Family in Uganda," *American Anthropologist* 61 (1959): 779–789.

27. Ibid., p. 783.

28. Ibid., p. 788.

29. See, for example, Myron L. Cohen, "Variations in Complexity among Chinese Family Groups: The Impact of Modernization," *Transactions of the New York Academy of Sciences* 29 (1967): 638–644, "A Case Study of Chinese Family Economy and Development," *Journal of Asian and African Studies* 3 (1968): 161–180, "Developmental Process in the Chinese Domestic Group," in *Family and Kinship in Chinese Society,* ed. Maurice Freedman (Stanford: Stanford University Press,

1970), pp. 21–36, *House United, House Divided*, and "Family Management and Family Division in Contemporary Rural China"; Clinget and Sween, "Urbanization, Plural Marriage, and Family Size in Two African Cities"; Croll, "New Peasant Family Forms in Rural China," and "Some Implications of the Rural Economic Reforms for the Chinese Peasant Household"; Sidney M. Greenfield, "Industrialization and the Family in Sociological Theory," *American Journal of Sociology* 67 (1961–1962): 312–322; Erwin Johnson, "The Stem Family and Its Extension in Present Day Japan," *American Anthropologist* 66 (1964): 839–851; Burton Pasternak, *Kinship and Community in Two Chinese Villages* (Stanford: Stanford University Press, 1972), and *Introduction to Kinship and Social Organization* (Englewood Cliffs, NJ: Prentice-Hall, 1976); Bernard C. Rosen and Manoel T. Berlinck, "Modernization and Family Structure in the Region of São Paulo, Brazil," *America Latina* 11 (1968): 96; and Arnold Strickon, "Class and Kinship in Argentina," *Ethnology* 1 (1962): 500–515.

30. For an example of the former position, see William J. Goode, *World Revolution and Family Patterns* (London: The Free Press of Glencoe, 1963). See Melvin Ember, "The Emergence of Neolocal Residence," *Transactions of the New York Academy of Sciences* 30 (1967): 291–302, for an example of the second position.

31. Harumi Befu, "Origins of Large Households and Duolocal Residence in Central Japan," *American Anthropologist* 70 (1968): 309–319. Befu also pointed to fluctuations in yields and in the availability of critical productive resources as contributing to large families and households. Agriculturalists may be more susceptible than hunter-gatherers or fishing people to such fluctuations, which would contribute to the higher frequency of extended families among them.

32. E. A. Hammel, "The Family Cycle in a Coastal Peruvian Slum and Village," *American Anthropologist* 63 (1961): 989–1005.

33. Cohen, "Variations in Complexity among Chinese Family Groups."

34. See Blumberg and Winch, "Societal Complexity and Familial Complexity," pp. 914–915.

35. P. H. Gulliver, "The Jie of Uganda," in *Man in Adaptation: The Cultural Present*, 2nd ed., ed. Yehudi A. Cohen (Chicago: Aldine, 1968), pp. 323–345, and "The Turkana," in *Man in Adaptation*, ed. Cohen, pp. 346–361.

36. Gulliver, "The Turkana," pp. 351, 358.

37. Nancy L. Solien de Gonzalez, "The Consanguineal Household and Matrifocality," *American Anthropologist* 67 (1965): 1547; see also Peter Kunstadter, "A Survey of the Consanguine or Matrifocal Family," *American Anthropologist* 65 (1963): 56–66; Keith Otterbein,

"Caribbean Family Organization: A Comparative Analysis," *American Anthropologist* 67 (1965): 66–79, and "The Developmental Cycle of the Andros Household: A Diachronic Analysis," *American Anthropologist* 72 (1970): 1412–1419.

38. Solien de Gonzalez, "The Consanguineal Household and Matrifocality," p. 1544; see also Raymond T. Smith, *The Negro Family in British Guiana* (London: Routledge and Kegan Paul, 1956).

39. Ruth Boyer, "The Matrifocal Family among the Mescalero: Additional Data," *American Anthropologist* 66 (1964): 593–602.

40. The discussion in this section is based largely on Carol R. Ember and Melvin Ember, *Anthropology*, 8th ed. (Upper Saddle River, NJ: Prentice Hall, 1996), pp. 378–389.

41. As reported in the *New York Times*, August 30, 1994.

42. Daniel T. Lichter, Diane Kay McLaughlin, George Kephart, and David J. Landry, "Race and the Retreat from Marriage: A Shortage of Marriageable Men?" *American Sociological Review* 57 (1992): 781–799.

43. Nancy Johnston Olsen, "The Effect of Household Composition on the Child Rearing Practices of Taiwanese Families" (Ph.D. diss., Cornell University, University Microfilms Publications no. 71–22. Ann Arbor: University Microfilms, 1983).

44. John W. M. Whiting, "Cultural and Sociological Influences on Development," in *Growth and Development of the Child in His Setting* (Maryland Child Growth and Development Institute, 1959), pp. 5–9.

12

DESCENT GROUPS: KINSHIP BEYOND THE FAMILY

In all societies known to anthropology, people apply the concept of kinship to relatives beyond the family. Everybody has relatives in addition to parents, siblings, and children. Of particular importance to anthropology are the groups of kin we call *descent groups*, which we encounter in many societies. The members of a descent group consider themselves to be related because they say they have a common ancestor. But there is more to a descent group than common ancestry. After all, if common ancestry were the only element involved, all humans would constitute a kind of descent group because we are a single species and, therefore, we are all descended from the same ancestral parents. However, anthropologists would not like to call the entire human species a descent group because all humans do not do things together or own property together. We like to restrict the term *descent group* to groups of kin that behave or function collectively, as groups.

If there are descent groups in your society, the one(s) you belong to provide the structure of many aspects of social life. It (or they) may determine what productive property you have access to, what alliances you must be loyal to, which people you work with and depend on every day, and perhaps even what supernatural beings you worship. (Often, the members of a descent group worship common ancestors.) Indeed, kinship connections may have an important bearing on matters of life and death. If you are able-bodied and live in a prestate society, you could be called on to go to war in behalf of your kin group, or the community it is part of. Thus, in addition to everything else it does for you, your life may depend on knowing which group of people will defend or attack for you.

The biological meaning of *descent* is clear, but the term as used in anthropology also has a social or cultural meaning if it refers to a way of tracing kinship connections to justify a person's social status or access to property.[1] Although the two meanings usually coincide, that is not inevitable—people may adopt or disown children, for example. In this chapter we are concerned with descent as culturally defined; in this sense, few North Americans belong to descent groups. Indeed, it is unlikely that many of us could even name third cousins on either our mother's or father's side. So why do most societies known to anthropology (68 percent, 585 of 857, in one sample) have descent groups?[2] And why do the vast majority of those trace descent through men rather than through women (or both genders)? Let us look now at the sorts of groups that exist, and consider why they might develop and differ.

RECKONING DESCENT

Comparing societies reveals that people reckon descent in a limited number of ways. Most societies (61 percent in the ethnographic record) trace descent exclusively through people of the same sex (*unilineally*): If children belong to their mother's descent group from birth, descent is matrilineal (see Figure 12-1); if to their father's group, descent is patrilineal (see Figure 12-2). In a few

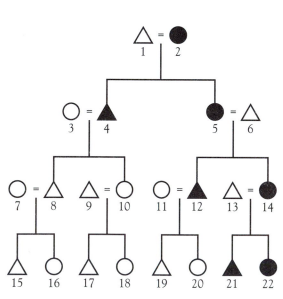

FIGURE 12-1
MATRILINEAL DESCENT

Individuals 4 and 5, who are the children of 1 and 2, affiliate with their mother's kin group, represented by the color black. In the next generation the children of 5 and 6 also belong to the black kin group, since they take their descent from their mother, who is a member of that group. However, the children of 3 and 4 do not belong to this matrilineal group, since they take their descent from their mother, who is a member of a different group; their father, although a member of the black matrilineal group, can't pass his affiliation on to them under the rule of matrilineal descent. In the fourth generation only 21 and 22 belong to the black matrilineal group, since their mother is the only female member of the preceding generation who belongs. Thus, individuals 2, 4, 5, 12, 14, 21, and 22 belong to the same matrilineal group.

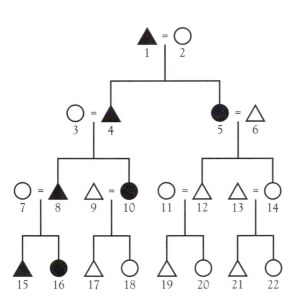

FIGURE 12-2
PATRILINEAL DESCENT

Individuals 4 and 5, who are the children of 1 and 2, affiliate with their father's patrilineal kin group, represented by the color black. In the next generation the children of 3 and 4 also belong to the black kin group, since they take their descent from their father, who is a member of that group. However, the children of 5 and 6 do not belong to this patrilineal group, since they take their descent from their father, who is a member of a different group. In other words, although the mother of 12 and 14 belongs to the black patrilineal group, she can't pass on her descent affiliation to her children, and since her husband (6) does not belong to her patrilineage, her children (12 and 14) belong to their father's group. In the fourth generation only 15 and 16 belong to the black patrilineal group, since their father is the only male member of the preceding generation who belongs to the black patrilineal group. In this diagram, then, 1, 4, 5, 8, 10, 15, and 16 are affiliated by patrilineal descent; all the other individuals belong to other patrilineal groups.

cases (3 percent), there are both matrilineal and patrilineal descent groups. In such *double descent* societies, individuals belong to the mother's group for certain purposes, to the father's for others. Among the Yakö of Eastern Nigeria, for example, political and landholding groups are patrilineal while movable property (e.g., livestock) is owned by matrilineal groups.[3]

In 4 percent of societies, people reckon descent sometimes through one and sometimes the other gender (i.e., *ambilineally*—see Figure 12-3). This is quite different from double unilineal descent, where every individual belongs to both a matrilineal and patrilineal descent group. In ambilineal societies, an individual belongs to a descent group because either his or her father or mother does, and other members also trace their descent from the common ancestor through males or females.

A descent group, unilineal or ambilineal, should not be confused with a *kindred*, which is a set of relatives (on the mother's *and* father's sides) who are

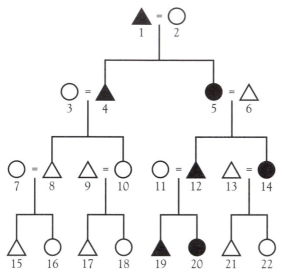

FIGURE 12-3
AMBILINEAL DESCENT

A hypothetical ambilineal group of kin is indicated by the color black. Members 4 and 5 belong to this group because of a male link, their father (1); members 12 and 14 belong because of a female link, their mother (5); and members 19 and 20 belong because of a male link, their father (12). This is a hypothetical example because any combination of lineal links is possible in an ambilineal descent group.

related *to you* (see Figure 12-4). The members of your kindred do not share a common ancestor; they are just related in various ways to you. (Societies lacking descent groups, that may have kindreds, are called *bilateral* societies.)

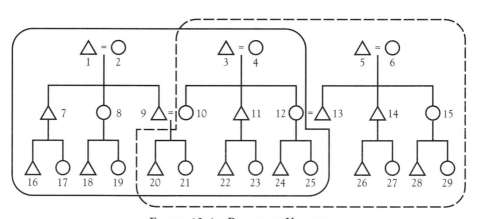

FIGURE 12-4   BILATERAL KINSHIP

In a bilateral system the kindred is ego-centered; hence, it varies with different points of reference (except for brothers and sisters). In any bilateral society, the kindred minimally includes parents, grandparents, aunts, uncles, and first cousins. So the close kindred of the brother and sister 20 and 21 (enclosed by the solid line) includes their parents (9 and 10), their aunts and uncles (7, 8, 11, and 12), their grandparents (1, 2, 3, and 4), and their first cousins (16–19 and 22–25). But the kindred of the brother and sister 24 and 25 (shown by the dashed line) includes only some of the same people (3, 4, 10–12, and 20–23); in addition, the kindred of 24 and 25 includes people not in the kindred of 20 and 21 (5, 6, 13–15, and 26–29).

While descent groups are rare among us (except for some very wealthy families whose family corporations are ambilineal descent groups), Americans do have kindreds. They are loosely defined circles of relatives, essentially the kin we invite to weddings and funerals. In fact, because their membership is indefinite, it is not always easy to decide whom we should and should not invite to these events. Kindreds are focused on the self rather than on an ancestor, so only siblings may have exactly the same kindred. They are usually nameless groups, ephemeral in the sense that they do not endure beyond the lives of their human focus (e.g., "Mary's relatives"). Your children will not invite all the members of your kindred to their weddings. In sharp contrast, descent groups generally persist through time; deaths may remove members but births add them. In a word, descent groups are perpetuating; kindreds are not.

Why do some societies have descent groups while others do not, and what determines whether people will trace descent through women or men? Why is it that many more societies reckon descent through men than through women (46 percent compared to only 14 percent of unilineal societies)? Consider first the societal preference for patrilineality. We have already learned that patrilocality aggregates men related through males, that matrilocality keeps women related through females together, and that avunculocal residence localizes men related through females. Thus, if people are patrilocal and if they have descent groups, then they will likely trace descent through the males. For the same reason, matrilocal peoples trace descent through women (if they have descent groups). Since avunculocality localizes men related through women (mothers), they too are likely to be matrilineal. But again, the nature of postmarital residence influences how people trace descent only if they organize descent groups. Under what circumstances are they likely to do that?

WHY DO DESCENT GROUPS DEVELOP?

While a majority of societies with unilineal descent (97 percent) also have a unilocal pattern of postmarital residence (matrilocal, patrilocal, or avunculocal), only 72 percent of unilocal societies have unilineal descent groups.[4] Clearly something in addition to a unilocal rule of residence is required for people to organize unilineal descent groups. Just because related males or related females may live together (because of patrilocal or matrilocal residence, respectively) does not mean that those people will actually view themselves as a descent group and function as such. So what else in addition to unilocality may give rise to unilineal descent groups?

One speculation is that a strong notion of private property together with a unilocal rule of residence favors the development of unilineal descent groups.[5] The idea here is that when people recognize private as opposed to common property, they must devise some way to define property rights clearly (or otherwise they would be fighting all the time over who has rights to what); and, according to this speculation, unilineal descent groups provide an unambiguous way to do that. There is no ambiguity about your rights because there is no ambiguity about which descent group you belong to. If there are patrilineal groups, for example, you belong to your father's group. The problem with this theory (about private property predicting unilineal descent groups) is that it does not fit the empirical realities of the ethnographic record. Only a small proportion of the world's known societies have private property, but most of them have unilineal descent groups. So how could something rare account for something common?

Still, the discreteness of unilineal descent groups (their nonoverlapping memberships) does suggest that the absence of ambiguity over who belongs to which group may be a key to why unilineal descent groups develop. Consider the possibility that private property rights developed in human history only when access to productive resources became problematic—that is, only when necessary things became scarce (because more people were now seeking them) and there was the possibility of conflict over access to those things. If this scenario is correct, private property and unilineal descent might both constitute responses, but alternative ones, to competition and potential conflict. Societies might develop either to minimize competition.

This argument assumes that people tend to adopt customs that preclude competition and violence. It would be nice if that were so, and it may be that people generally do want to minimize the possibility of violence, but the ubiquity of warfare in the ethnographic record belies such utopian assumptions. The fact of the matter is that people in most societies had fairly frequent warfare (within the society and/or with people in neighboring societies) when they were first described.[6] Might we not expect, then, that unilineal descent groups would occur most often *in nonstate societies* with warfare?

Where fighting is likely, natural selection may favor clearly defined groups of people who can be relied upon in time of danger. We need to limit our question to nonstate societies since states, by definition, claim a monopoly on force and use it (with military forces) to provide for defense. In societies like our own, political agencies of the state are supposed to provide internal security as well. Thus, people in complex societies call upon the state for defense and security. Where political development is not so elaborate, however, unilineal descent may constitute a favored response to the challenge of competing groups. This is strongly suggested by the finding that 91 percent of societies with unilocal residence and warfare have unilineal descent groups.[7]

ALTERNATIVE RESPONSES TO THE THREAT OF VIOLENCE:
CROSS-KIN ASSOCIATIONS AND AMBILINEAL DESCENT GROUPS?

Unilineal descent groups are the most common but not the only conceivable response to the threat of violence in nonstate societies. Some societies organize groups on the basis of gender and culturally defined age range, for example. Among the Jie pastoralists discussed earlier in connection with family, males belong to ordered generations, the most important of which are the senior or initiated generation and the junior or uninitiated one.[8] Every twenty-five years, special rituals establish a new generation of Jie. Individuals initiated during the same year belong to the same age-group, and three consecutive age-groups constitute an age-set within a given generation.

Societies with age-groups and age-sets often use them as fighting units in war, and they may also have ritual functions. They may even be the basis of political organization in general, as among the Karimojong of Uganda, where members of the active senior generation perform administrative, judicial, and religious functions while members of the junior generation are warriors and policemen. Noninitiates and members of the retired generation are essentially without function.[9] Among the Nyakyusa of southeastern Africa, members of a particular age-set even lived apart in age-villages.[10] The Cheyenne, Native Americans of the plains, organized warrior societies. Some five military associations were open to males of any age who could demonstrate fitness for war. These constituted the tribe's military and police force. Each society had its own costumes, dances, and songs. Their leaders were the important war chiefs of the tribe.[11]

Why did the Cheyenne and other societies, such as the Jie and Karimojong, develop age organizations or classes? Cross-cultural research indicates that age-sets and warrior societies are likely in societies that have warfare and local groups that change in size and composition throughout the year, or where a substantial proportion of men at any given moment are living away from settlements (as in a seminomadic pastoral society).[12] The age classes, which are cross-kin associations, make it possible to solicit support from a larger number of people than would be possible if one had to rely exclusively upon family members or on unilineal kin who were nearby at a given moment.

The evidence also indicates that age-class systems provide a means of integration that is *additional* rather than alternative to unilineal descent groups. That is, age-class systems are not found in the absence of unilineal descent groups. The implication of this finding is that, in meeting the challenge of violent competition, people are likely to expand upon the familiar notion of unilineal kinship first, and to add cross-kin associations only where kinship is not enough because kinsmen are often dispersed.

Although ambilineal descent groups would also provide unambiguous manpower for offense or defense, they are not, in fact, a common solution. This is probably because ambilineal descent is associated with bilocal residence, which in turn is predicted mostly by recent, dramatic depopulation (usually associated with Western conquest and disease). Ambilineal descent may thus be a relatively recent human invention, and, therefore, ambilineal descent groups are not a likely alternative to unilineal descent groups as a response to threat of violence in nonstate societies.[13]

SOCIETAL COMPLEXITY AND THE EVOLUTION
OF UNILINEAL DESCENT SYSTEMS

In the latter part of the nineteenth century and into the twentieth, it was believed that matrilineal descent systems evolved earlier than patrilineal ones, and that patrilineality emerged only when societies became more complex.[14] This belief became unfashionable early in the twentieth century when anthropologists began to reject all evolutionary thinking. The notion that matrilineality always came first was finally and firmly rejected when George Peter Murdock demonstrated that all modes of reckoning kinship (matrilineal, patrilineal, bilateral) occur in societies on all levels of cultural or social complexity.[15]

However, unilineal descent systems (matrilineal or patrilineal) are not completely unrelated to societal complexity. They are more commonly found in societies of midrange complexity (nonindustrial agriculture, no complex state); unilineal descent systems appear less often in simple hunting-gathering societies and tend to weaken and vanish in complex urban-industrial societies.[16] Unilineal descent is by no means absent among hunter-gatherers or in complex societies. In a large sample of societies, unilineal descent occurs in 54 percent of those that have no political integration beyond the local community or that are state-societies with populations exceeding one hundred thousand people; but in middle-range categories the proportions range from fifty-nine to eighty-five.[17] Thus, there is a somewhat curvilinear relationship between cultural complexity and unilineal descent systems: They are less likely at the lower and upper ends of the scale of cultural complexity, and more likely in the middle of the range.

But why should middle range societies be more likely to have unilineal descent systems? One theory is that the conditions of life in technologically simpler societies do not favor large aggregations of kin. When people make their living by hunting and gathering in marginal or difficult environments, local groups tend to be small, highly mobile, and flexible in composition. At the other extreme, descent groups lose viability in complex state-organized, commercial-industrial societies because non-kin agencies or the state assume many kin functions (e.g., defense, education, welfare, adjudication). In complex societies, it is individuals (not families or larger kin groups) who take advantage of economic or occupational opportunities; when someone moves to a new job, parents and siblings are not likely to go along (and cousins and aunts and uncles even less likely). Moreover, where populations are heterogeneous and the state provides for defense, people are more likely to identify with others in terms of socioeconomic position and territory, rather than in terms of kinship.[18]

Frederick Engels went so far as to claim an "irreconcilable opposition" between descent groups and the state, a view that has had many supporters.[19] We find it clearly expressed in the following passage from the work of anthropologist Yehudi A. Cohen:

> Part of the course of a state's vertical entrenchment is the arrogation by its leaders of the exclusive right to wage war, enact and administer laws, control productivity and redistribute wealth, lay claim to rights of eminent domain and administer tenure, exact tribute, and the like. These are among the rights that are also claimed by the controlling personnel of corporate kin groups and communities. Since such authority and other political activities can be carried out autonomously in only one of the two boundary systems, one of them must be subverted if the society is to remain stable.[20]

It is not simply that the state usurps functions of family or larger kin groups, but also that such societies are socially, politically, and economically heterogeneous. Many scholars assume that class differences invariably compete with, and take precedence over, bonds of kinship. As one writer put it,

> the process of differentiation within the clan, while for a long time taking place within this flexible unit, finally reaches the point where the interests of those of equal standing, in *all* the clans of the tribe, come into such sharp conflicts with the interests of the other strata that their struggles, the struggle of by now fully-fledged social classes, overshadows the old principles of clanship and finally leads to the break-up of clan, first as the dominating form of social organization and then to its final disappearance.[21]

Many scholars also believe that there is an incompatibility between commerce, another attribute of complex societies, and descent groups; markets presumably put overwhelming strains on the bonds of kinship because production is diverted from family and community to the market.[22] Thus, according to Marshall D. Sahlins,

> lineages, or like systems of extensive and corporate solidary relations, are incompatible with the external drain on household staples and the corresponding posture of self-interest required *vis-a-vis* other households. Large local descent groups are absent or inconsequential.

Instead, the solidary relations are of the small family itself, with various and changing interpersonal kin ties the only nexus of connection between households.[23]

Although cross-cultural evidence does provide support for the belief that descent groups are less common in very simple or very complex societies than in middle range societies, we need to note some reservations. First, as already mentioned, while unilineal descent systems are less common in the very simple and the very complex societies, they nonetheless occur in about half of them. Second, recent hunter-gatherers have often lived in areas of the world that cannot support many people (usually because agriculture is not possible), but this has not always been the situation for foragers. Humans were all hunter-gatherers until ten thousand years ago (and in many places until quite recently), even in places where there are now urban populations dependent on intensive agriculture. So the lower likelihood of unilineal descent systems among recent hunter-gatherers does not necessarily mean that hunter-gatherers in the more distant past lacked unilineal descent systems. Indeed, we would guess they often had such systems. We cannot go by the hunter-gatherers of the last two hundred years, who mostly live in (or had retreated to) places that were marginal for agriculture.

Given the difficult environments in which they have recently lived, it is hardly surprising that the hunter-gatherers known to anthropology often responded to resource scarcity and variability by shifting band membership. As we discussed in the preceding chapter, bilocality occurs in some recent hunter-gatherer societies probably because of resource fluctuation and small community size.[24] (As we have seen too, bilocality appears more often, indeed mostly, to be a response to dramatic depopulation, which in turn is a common consequence of recent contact with Western colonizers.) Bilocality is likely to transform unilineality into ambilineality, or to encourage bilateral reckoning (if descent groups disappear). The implication then is that unilineal descent groups were probably much more common among hunter-gatherers in the more distant past.

MATRILINEAL VERSUS PATRILINEAL DESCENT

If we compare the structure of matrilineal groups (Figure 12-1) with patrilineal (Figure 12-2), they look like mirror images. However, the two systems differ in a fundamental way. That difference has to do with who exercises authority. In patrilineal systems, people trace descent through males, who also exercise political authority. Another way of saying this is that, in patrilineal systems, lines of descent and authority converge. In a matrilineal system, however, even though descent is traced through females, they rarely exercise authority in their kin groups—males usually do. Thus, lines of authority and descent do not converge.[25] We do not fully understand why this should be so, but it could have something to do with the fact that polit-

ical decisions in matrilineal systems, too, often involve warfare, an enterprise in which women are rarely involved. In any case, because males do
exercise authority in matrilineal kin groups, an individual's mother's brother becomes an important authority figure. Father does not belong to one's
matrilineal kin group and has no say in kin group matters.

The divergence between authority and descent in matrilineal systems
has another effect on social structure. Most matrilineal societies practice
matrilocal residence. Daughters stay at home after marriage and their husbands come to live with them; sons leave home to join their wives. While
sons marry out, however, they eventually exercise authority in their own
kin groups. The situation clearly presents a problem. The solution in most
matrilineal societies is that, when grooms join their brides, they usually do
not move far. Indeed, as we have already noted, they often marry women
living in the same village. In short, matrilineal societies tend not to be
locally exogamous—that is, people often marry within their communities,
in contrast to the situation in patrilineal societies, which are often locally
exogamous.[26] Thus, the patrilocal Luo are locally exogamous; the matrilocal
Iroquois are locally agamous (neither exogamous nor endogamous).

As an example of how authority works in matrilineal systems, consider
the people of Truk, a group of small islands in the Pacific.[27] The Trukese have
property-owning matrilineages. The female lineage members and their husbands occupy a cluster of houses on matrilineage land. It is a female's eldest
brother, rather than her husband, who administers lineage property, allocat-
ing it for cultivation and assigning work. It is he who represents the descent
group in its dealings with the district chief and outsiders, and it is this brother whom people consult on matters affecting the descent group. The senior
female member of the descent group also enjoys a measure of authority, but
only insofar as the activities of women are concerned. She supervises their
cooperative work (they usually work separately from the men).

Within the nuclear family, father and mother are primarily responsible for raising and disciplining children. Once they attain puberty, however, paternal authority ends. Mother continues to provide discipline, however, and now the maternal uncle to some extent replaces father in matters of
discipline. This is possible because, on Truk, men rarely move far from their
birthplace. As Ward H. Goodenough pointed out, while matrilocal residence takes men from their families, "most of them marry women whose
lineage houses are within a few minutes' walk of their own."[28]

Descent Group Structures

We have long known that most of the world's peoples form groups on the
basis of common descent, but we have only slowly come to appreciate that,
apart from whether descent is traced through women or men, the *kinds* of

descent groups that develop may vary within as well as between societies. There are impressive differences in the size, geographic distribution, and structure of descent groups as well, and we realize now that the kinds of descent groups people construct reflect the economic and political attributes of the societies in which they live. It to these differences and their causes that we now turn.

DISTRIBUTION IN SPACE

If warfare is a catalyst for the formation of descent groups in societies with unilocal residence, the particular kinds of warfare that occur influence the kinds of descent groups people organize. Consider, for example, the spatial distribution of descent group members. The core members (e.g., men in patrilineal societies) may typically live contiguously, not interspersed with members of other descent groups, as among the Tiv and Luo in Africa. But in other cases the core members do not live contiguously; rather a particular descent group (or segment thereof) lives interspersed with other descent groups, as among the matrilineal Iroquois and Creek of native North America. Why are the core members of descent groups contiguous in some societies, but separated in others?

There is reason to believe that this aspect of variation may have something to do with the nature of the society's warfare—more specifically with whether fighting is *internal* (between territorial units of the *same* society) or *external* (between territorial units of *different* societies—populations speaking different languages). Why should this be the case? As we have already discussed in the chapter on marital residence, if fighting occurs between communities of the same society, the most pressing priority may be to have a way to mobilize a loyal fighting force as quickly as possible. Where fighting is at least sometimes internal and attacks can come from close by (providing little time to mobilize), males of a unilineal descent group may have to reside close to one another because the more of them there are close by, the better they can defend themselves.

We have already learned that if warfare is at least sometimes internal, unilineal groups are usually patrilineal because marital residence is usually patrilocal. Recall, too, that if internal war is newly emergent in a previously matrilocal and matrilineal society, residence might be avunculocal. In both cases, a core of unilineally related males lives contiguously. But in societies with purely external warfare, where attacks are more likely to come from greater distances, residential contiguity may be less necessary. In this case, all community males, unilineally related or not, would have reason to join in common defense (or offense) against the enemy. Some dispersal of kinsmen could even confer an advantage under these circumstances; having relatives in many areas might provide a bond of solidarity throughout the society that could be mobilized for the external warfare. As a matter of fact, cross-cultural research does indicate that societies with internal war are more likely to favor some degree of descent group contiguity than societies with purely external warfare.[29]

LINEAGES AND CLANS

Consider another aspect of structural variation. In some cases, people pay considerable attention to the precise connections among descent group members; in other societies the matter is of little interest. Where people take the trouble to *demonstrate* connections (trace their descent by way of known persons back to a common ancestor), we refer to their descent groups as *lineages*. If they are content simply to *stipulate* common descent (agreeing that they are members of the same descent group without specifying precise connections), we speak of *clans*. Societies may not have only demonstrated or only stipulated groups; there may be both kinds of descent group (and the clans may include sets of lineages).

And there also may be sets of supposedly related clans, or *phratries*. When the whole society is divided into two stipulated descent groups, which may or may not contain smaller descent groups, we say that there are *moieties*. Claude Lévi-Strauss and others thought that moiety systems reflected a dualism in the human mind. But if that were true, wouldn't all societies have moieties? As it turns out, societies with moieties may just be very small; moiety systems are almost always found in societies with less than nine thousand people (including children) in the entire population.[30]

Why should some societies find it useful to trace precise connections while others do not? One suggestion is that people who can recall connections are more likely to be attentive to them, and people near each other are in a better position to recall them.[31] If so, we would expect societies with internal warfare (and therefore more descent group contiguity) to have lineages more often than societies with purely external warfare. And cross-cultural research suggests that they do.[32]

Of course, there can be considerable distance between relatives who live contiguously, so we have to take physical distance into consideration as well. If we use population density as an indirect measure of physical distance (ethnographies rarely provide a more precise indicator), we do find cross-cultural support for the notion that proximity and lineages go together. In societies with unilineal descent groups and internal warfare, those with lineages are likely to have higher population density than those without lineages.[33] It may also be more difficult to remember genealogical connections in low density societies because they are usually highly mobile and people may not remain for long near the same relatives.

While societies with unilineal descent, internal warfare, contiguity, and high population densities are especially likely to have descent groups based on demonstrated descent (lineages), is this just because of ease in remembering kinship connections? Do people take the trouble to remember and pay attention to the precise links that connect them just because they can, or do they realize that potentiality for some good reason(s)? Internal warfare may be especially important in this regard.

We may speculate that people with high population density, other things (particularly political) being equal, may be particularly inclined to fight among themselves, and perhaps to do so more frequently than other people. Thus, the recurrence of internal warfare provides a more direct reason for remembering and tracing connections—to know precisely whom to call upon in time of war. We will have an example shortly, when we consider the Tiv. But the ranking and stratification commonly found in higher density populations, which often have internal warfare, can provide other reasons for paying attention to the linkages of descent, as we shall see.

SEGMENTATION AND RANKING

Descent groups also differ in internal structure—in the extent to which they are subdivided into segments, and in the way they are segmented. What accounts for this variation? We will see that the descent groups we find in any society reflect the society's political and economic characteristics. To illustrate, consider the patrilineal groups in four very different societies—among the reindeer-herding Tungus of Siberia, the shifting-agricultural Tiv in Africa, among the root- and tree-cropping Tahitians of Polynesia, and finally, among the sedentary cereal-cropping Chinese in pre-Communist southeastern China.

Exogamous, egalitarian Tungus clans provide rights in territory and reindeer, protect members, and enforce various social rules. Reflecting the fundamentally egalitarian nature of Tungus society, distinctions are not made among clan members; all are equally descended from the common ancestor.[34] The Tiv are also egalitarian; there is even resistance to unusual displays of authority.[35] The Tiv have neither legislators nor enforcers, only men of relative influence. Members of the Tiv patrilineage share territory and ceremony and have mutual obligations when it comes to feuding and warfare.[36] Because it includes people in different localities, the lineage serves to integrate groups. But there is a difference between Tungus clans and Tiv lineages—the latter give considerable attention to genealogy. Their patrilineages are organized in terms of a principle that some refer to as *segmentary opposition*:

> It is a projection of the idea that my brother and I are antagonistic to each other only so long as there is no person more distantly related to us who is antagonistic to both of us. I join my brother against my half brothers. My half brothers join me and my full brothers against the group of our father's brother's son. They join us, again, against our father's father's brother's son's sons.[37]

In Figure 12-5, /a/ and /b/ represent discrete groups descended from a common ancestor (i.e., from /1/). When it comes to political support, and especially in feuding, segment /a/ stands against /b/ unless someone from /c/ makes trouble, in which case /a/ and /b/ unite as /1/ to fight /2/. Should an altercation involve a member of /h/ there would be conflict between /A/ and /B/. If someone from /m/ fights with a member of /a/, confrontation could involve /I/ and /II/, and attack by outsiders would unite the entire descent group.

The Tiv are attentive to genealogy and have symmetrically segmented lineages because they must be clear about obligations and allies when it comes to fighting. Marshall D. Sahlins has suggested that the segmentary system is especially effective in tribal societies because its ability to organize more and more inclusive segments allows a group to intrude into new territory and take land from others with smaller descent groups. Individual lineage segments could call on support from related lineages when faced with border troubles. And conflicts within the society (between segments), especially in border areas, were often turned outward, "releasing internal pressure in an explosive blast against other peoples."[38] The Luo of Kenya, whom we described in the chapter on marital residence, also had a segmentary lineage system. Such a system probably aided them in their migration into areas of western Kenya that were already occupied by other societies.

But some societies with patrilineages consist of segments that are not balanced against each other in the Tiv or Luo fashion. Rather, the descent groups are differentially ranked with respect to each other, and sometimes even internally (branches are differentially ranked). Such a system of ranking obtained among the Tahitians of the South Pacific and the Nootka of the North American northwest coast—chiefdoms with descent groups that were differentially ranked in prestige, privilege, and obligation. Primogeniture determined relative position—first sons enjoyed higher rank than subse-

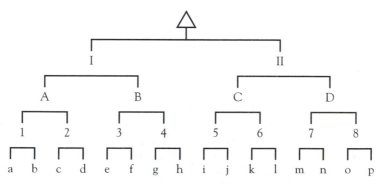

FIGURE 12-5   THE PRINCIPLE OF SEGMENTARY OPPOSITION

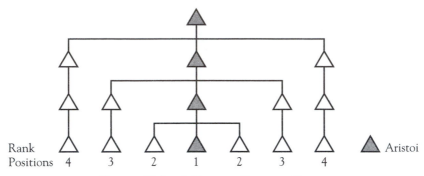

Rank
Positions   4   3   2   1   2   3   4   ▲ Aristoi

FIGURE 12-6   A CONICAL DESCENT GROUP

quent ones (Figure 12-6 provides a model), and groups descended from first sons ranked higher than groups descended from others. Structurally, their patrilineages displayed the inequalities of status and privilege that existed in the society as a whole. Genealogical nearness to the main line of descent (*aristoi*) was the major determinant of status and privilege.

In chiefdoms, rank translates into differences in prestige, influence, and consumption, but the dissimilarities are not as great as in fully *class-stratified* societies (like our own), in which there are differences of ownership such that some individuals, families, or other groups can deny access, or can demand payment for access, to the means of production. In chiefdoms, position in the kinship system confers prestige and privilege; in class-stratified societies, prestige derives not from kinship but from differences in wealth, and the inequality translates into power.

In chiefdoms, people donate to their chiefs, often in ritual contexts. The chiefs in turn redistribute what they obtain among their constituents. Generosity is the hallmark of the chief in such societies. But when differential access to strategic resources (class stratification) emerges and it becomes possible to accumulate wealth independently of kinship position (e.g., from trade or industry), the importance of genealogically determined rank declines. Those with special access to the means of production come to have more in common with each other than with less fortunate kin.

What, then, becomes of kinship obligations and descent groups when people can sell their products and labor in a supply-demand market and use what they earn to acquire new commodities like motorcycles, radios, and TV? People begin to cut back on kinship obligations, by diverting what they have traditionally provided to their kin or to the chief and selling it in the market instead. (The market need not be a physical place where buying and selling occur.) No longer does wealth derive from kinship position, but rather from effort in the market; and those who, by the rule of descent, should have the most prestige and privilege may actually have little, while those of low rank may have an abundance. A serious contradiction emerges when a genealogical nobody ends up a controller of strategic resources and a purveyor of political and economic influence.

Although stratification and state organization may indeed encourage the integration of society across and independent of kinship, as the curvilinear hypothesis suggests, this does not mean that there is an invariable incompatibility between descent groups per se and either stratification or state organization. Clearly, some kinds of descent groups accommodate both. The heterogeneous, stratified state, with its monopoly of force, must find a glue other than kinship to integrate local groups on a territorial basis. New structures and forms of organization develop while older ones change to meet new challenges. But differences in wealth and power do not necessarily signal the end of kinship in general, or of descent groups in particular. In some societies the structures of kinship have been modified and elaborated to accommodate commercial and political developments.

For example, lineages and clans survived quite well in China, one of the world's most highly stratified, centralized states, and the descent groups were particularly elaborated in the commercial southeast of the country.[39] If commercialization and political development always undermined descent groups, we would expect the poor in southeast China to have been more committed to the rituals and structures of descent than were the wealthy. But that is not what we find. On the contrary, interest in descent groups and their rituals was a sign of wealth and power in pre-Communist China, and is still so in many Chinese contexts. Far from balancing economic differences, ancestral rituals more often exacerbated them. Ancestral trusts, which underwrote rituals and provided a focus for clans, lineages, and their segments, were established not by the poor but by the wealthy—by those most given to market investment. The Chinese thus pose a challenge to conventional wisdom. Why did commerce and the differences in wealth it produced strengthen rather than weaken community integration, local commitment, leadership, and descent groups?

THE UNLIKELY CHINESE DESCENT GROUP

Why do descent groups survive, even flourish, in the complex state-society that is China?[40] The members of a traditional Chinese lineage are equally descended from their common ancestor. The Chinese share this understanding with the Tiv and Tungus. The difference between them and the Tungus and Tiv is that segmentation within the lineage is neither symmetrical nor simply a function of genealogy. In the Chinese case, segmentation reflects socio-economic position, differences in wealth and power, in society at large. Let us see how this all plays out.

The Chinese traditionally recognize two kinds of property—private property, which can be freely acquired, lent, rented, or sold, and which is ultimately to be divided equally among sons; and ancestral property which, once established, cannot be divided, alienated, or disposed of without the consent of the shareholders (i.e., the descendants of the common ancestor). A man of means could reserve a portion of his private property to establish an ancestral estate, the rents of which financed periodic sacrifices to his ghost after his death. A portion of the estate's profits could also be used by the elder leadership to underwrite the education of gifted descendants or provide relief for those in distress.

In the course of time, segments develop within the Chinese descent group. In contrast to those of the Tiv, however, they are not balanced, and unlike those of the Tahitians, Chinese lineage segments are not predictable in terms of genealogy. For a lineage segment to exist, an ancestral estate or trust must be established in the name of some focal ancestor. Often this is done posthumously by sons, grandsons, or later progeny. Establishment of such trusts depends on wealth which was unevenly distributed within the descent group. Accordingly, wealthy lines of descent within the group enjoyed access to more ancestral trusts than poorer ones.

In establishing these estates, moreover, it was important to ensure that profits would not be drained, diluted, or consumed by distant, often poorer kin. The more shareholders, the less benefit per share. Thus, it was usually preferable to select a nearer ancestor as the focus. If I establish a trust in my own name, I cut out my brother's progeny; if my brother and I together select our father as focus, we deny access to our cousins. This kind of selective denial of access is not unfamiliar in our own society, especially among the very wealthy. The Chinese descent group is much like a wealthy family trust here.

Consider the model presented in Figure 12-7. The progeny of ances-

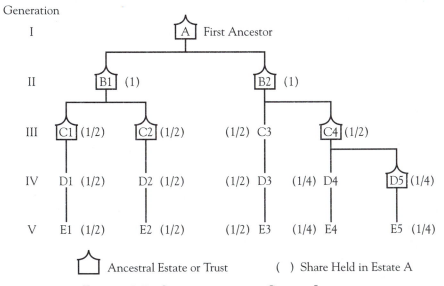

FIGURE 12-7   SEGMENTATION IN A CHINESE LINEAGE

tor /B2/ comprise a lineage segment within the larger descent group. They attend ancestral ceremonies and feasts memorializing /B2/ and also enjoy in common the profits of his ancestral trust. The descendants of /C4/ constitute a lineage segment in the same sense. But the progeny of /C3/, for whom no ancestral estate has been established, do *not* constitute a lineage segment because they are not incorporated; they did not establish an ancestral trust to unite his descendants. Now, the fact that /E5/ has access to more ancestral trusts than any other descendant of the first ancestor in his generation suggests that more of his ancestors had been especially wealthy, relatively well-educated, and probably also more influential than those of other descent group members. In theory, headship in the lineage or branch passed by age and generation—there was no main line of descent. But in reality, leadership and management of ancestral properties belonged to the wealthy and literate. Thus, the asymmetrical pattern of segmentation and the nature of leadership both reflected the unequal, stratified nature of Chinese society. We are not likely to find lineages of this sort in nonstate societies.

As the curvilinear hypothesis implies, when the Chinese state was strong, descent groups tended to be relatively weak; and when the state was weak, descent groups became stronger, sometimes even usurping state functions. But descent groups have been extraordinarily viable and tenacious over the long haul. The Chinese lineage seems to have been strengthened rather than weakened by social and political inequality. So long as real power remained in elite hands, and so long as genealogical authority was minimized, the descent group could hold its members together, fortifying them against their neighbors and softening the demands and exactions of the state. The wealthy and literate provided political and economic protection for all; the poor provided the muscle if push ever came to shove and, in turn, benefited by being able to rent lineage land and, in some cases, obtaining support in time of need.

Why, then, do we not find such descent groups more commonly in complex societies? While we have no definite answer at present, certain special characteristics of the Chinese state in late Imperial times (until the early years of the twentieth century) may have been conducive to maintenance of descent groups (and the rise of *warlords*) in many locations. China was an empire of enormous size, whose economy was based on a complex, extensive irrigation system which required centralized management to run, repair, and defend. To have relied exclusively on paid bureaucrats would have been costly. At some point, the administrative complexity needed to extract funds to run the state would have cost so much that funds reaching the center would have been reduced substantially. The center (the imperial court) resolved the problem by limiting the number of bureaucrats and delegating responsibility to localities. Descent groups (and their wealthy elites) were important in this regard. They often handled local matters like irrigation, maintenance of order, and sometimes even the collection of taxes due the state. One writer described the situation as follows:

> Since the effective leaders of the differentiated lineage were neither appointed by nor under the orders of the magistrate, and since if they were themselves scholars they could confront the magistrate on an equal footing, the will of the state could be restricted without a breach of administrative duty. Unless he was prepared to bring in the militia, the magistrate could only deal and treat with a recalcitrant lineage; he could not command it. By preventing a bureaucrat from serving in his own province the system attempted to avoid nepotism and corruption; but by allowing lineage leadership to take on a strong bureaucratic colouring without imposing any bureaucratic checks upon it, the state weakened its control of the lineage, however much it may have suffused its leadership with the correct ideology. With the gentry as a buffer, the differentiated lineage could oppose itself to the state and yet maintain its standing in official eyes.[41]

But the notion of common descent served other purposes in China, resulting in still other structures. In some instances the asymmetry of lineage segmentation may reflect, not some ongoing differentiation taking place within the descent group, but rather a process of *fusion*, an attempt to find commonalities that would join different lines of descent within the larger group. Consider the following example from southwestern Taiwan during the late eighteenth and early nineteenth centuries.

Hakka-speaking Chinese migrated to southwestern Taiwan some three hundred years ago. Finding the coastal plain occupied by Hokkien-speaking Chinese who had arrived earlier, the Hakka gravitated to the foothills further inland. The Hakka-Hokkien relationship was initially symbiotic, the Hakka opening lands rented from Hokkien landlords. The Hakka lived under hazardous conditions; aboriginal non-Chinese groups in the nearby mountains resented their presence and periodically descended to separate them from their heads. In time, an even greater threat menaced the Hakka. As their numbers and communities grew, they drew more water from rivers and streams to meet irrigation needs, a diversion keenly felt in Hokkien villages closer to the sea. The Hakka-Hokkien relationship turned hostile.

For defense, Hakka families lived together in nucleated villages. Within these villages common descent groups existed, but were not especially important apart from a ritual context. Hokkien lineages—larger, wealthier, politically more connected—were often able to defend their own interests more effectively. (Many of their communities consisted of a few descent groups, or even just one descent group.) In contrast, the more recent Hakka migrations had sometimes brought brothers and cousins, but there were simply not enough patrilineal kinsmen close by (among the Hakka) to depend upon when push came to shove. Within Hakka villages, therefore, people were inclined to deemphasize differences of descent and to elaborate on the commonalities of community instead.

Although descent groups had little importance *within* the Hakka communities, they became quite important *between* them. If a few families named Chen in one village discovered Chen from the same region of southeastern China in another, they might establish a small estate in the name of a common ancestor to create a bond of obligation between the families in different communities. The size of the estate was of less importance than the alliance it implied. If they subsequently discovered Chen in still more distant villages, ancestral estates in the name of more distant, perhaps even imaginary, common ancestors could be established, which would extend and widen the alliance. The result, over time, were lineages consisting of asymmetrically segmented units reflecting a process of *fusion* rather than fission within the descent group.

Many have believed that nonlocalized, or what Maurice Freedman called *higher-order*, lineages could not extend far, normally not beyond the local communities of a *vicinage*, or *standard marketing area*, because the state would not long tolerate such growth.[42] But the case of the Hakka in Taiwan does not contradict the supposedly inverse relationship between descent group systems and state-type political development. In southwestern Taiwan, when the Hakka competed with the Hokkien, there was no strong state, and there were lineages spanning vast areas and multiple standard marketing areas. Isn't this precisely the sort of situation in which we would expect to see the development of extensive lineages, judging by the cross-cultural evidence reviewed earlier? That is, we should expect strongly developed lineage organization in the presence of internal warfare *and* in the absence of a strong state able to prevent or monopolize fighting.

You can even have descent groups in cities, judging by China. In the cities, we are dealing not with lineages but with clans. When families move from the countryside to the city, there are often few close patrilineal kinsmen around with whom to cooperate. In this situation it is useful to extend kinship to families of the same surname with whom no direct linkage may be apparent. In this context, the interest is not in making distinctions but in forging useful alliances for economic or political purposes. To that end, families of the same surname contribute ancestral tablets and dues to a common clan association. It is hardly a coincidence, moreover, that the wealthy have a particular interest in urban clans. They have the most to gain from them. Perhaps clans generally develop in this way, by fusion of groups that want to do things together, and this may be true also for the noncommercial societies traditionally studied by anthropologists.[43]

In summary, while it is true that descent groups are less often found in very simple and very complex societies than in midrange (nonindustrial agricultural) societies, it is clear that there is more to discover. In particular, we still need to explore the conditions under which descent groups continue to play important roles in some societies but not in others. Kin groups have declined in importance in our own society and other Western societies; in places like China and Taiwan, kinship continues to be important. But is this because the central state apparatus in China is still not very strong? Or do descent groups persist (particularly in mainland China) because the countryside is still largely dependent on agriculture? In understanding how kinship and social structure vary in complex societies, we are still at the beginning.

NOTES

1. A. R. Radcliffe-Brown, *Structure and Function in Primitive Society* (New York: Free Press, 1952), pp. 32–49.

2. The authors made a count of types of descent from George Peter Murdock, "Ethnographic Atlas: A Summary," *Ethnology* 6 (1967): 109–236.

3. Daryll Forde, "Double Descent among the Yakö," in *African Systems of Kinship and Marriage*, eds. A. R. Radcliffe Brown and Daryll Forde (London: Oxford University Press, 1950), pp. 285–332.

4. See Table 2 in Carol R. Ember, Melvin Ember, and Burton Pasternak, "On the Development of Unilineal Descent," *Journal of Anthropological Research* 30 (1974): 69–74. Reprinted in Melvin Ember and Carol R. Ember, *Marriage, Family, and Kinship: Comparative Studies of Social Organization* (New Haven: HRAF Press, 1983).

5. See, for example, Robert H. Lowie, *Primitive Society* (New York: Harper, 1961 [originally published 1920]); and George Peter Murdock, *Social Structure* (New York: Macmillan, 1949).

6. See Carol R. Ember and Melvin Ember, "Violence in the Ethnographic Record: Results of Cross-Cultural Research on War and Aggression," in *Troubled Times: Osteological and Archaeological Evidence of Violence*, eds. David Frayer and Debra Martin (Langhorne, PA: Gordon and Breach, in press).

7. See Table 2 in Ember, Ember, and Pasternak, "On the Development of Unilineal Descent."

8. P. H. Gulliver, "The Jie of Uganda," in *Man in Adaptation: The Cultural Present*, 2nd ed., ed. Yehudi A. Cohen (Chicago: Aldine, 1968).

9. Neville Dyson-Hudson, *Karimojong Politics* (Oxford: Clarendon Press, 1966).

10. Monica Wilson, *Good Company: A Study of Nyakyusa Age-Villages* (Boston: Beacon Press, 1963).

11. E. Adamson Hoebel, *The Cheyennes: Indians of the Great Plains* (New York: Holt, Rinehart & Winston, 1960).

12. Madeline Lattman Ritter, "The Conditions Favoring Age-Set Organization," *Journal of Anthropological Research* 36 (1980): 87–104.

13. Ember, Ember, and Pasternak, "On the Development of Unilineal Descent."

14. Louis Henry Morgan, *Systems of Consanguinity and Affinity of the Human Family* (Washington, DC: Smithsonian Institution, 1870).

15. Murdock, *Social Structure*, p. 186.

16. On this issue, see David F. Aberle, "Matrilineal Descent in Cross-Cultural Perspective," in *Matrilineal Kinship*, eds. David M. Schneider and Kathleen Gough (Berkeley: University of California Press, 1961); Allan D. Coult and Robert W. Habenstein, *Cross Tabulations of Murdock's World Ethnographic Sample* (Columbia: University of Missouri Press, 1965); Burton Pasternak, *Introduction to Kinship and Social Organization* (Englewood Cliffs, NJ: Prentice-Hall, 1976); and Elman R. Service, *Primitive Social Organization* (New York: Random House, 1962).

17. See Table 8.2 in Pasternak, *Introduction to Kinship and Social Organization*, p. 113. The percentages presented there were calculated from data in Coult and Habenstein, *Cross Tabulations of Murdock's World Ethnographic Sample*. In societies with politically independent local groups not over 1,500 in average population, the percentage unilineal was 59; in those with peace groups transcending the local community, but where the basis of unity is not political, the percentage unilineal was 59; in minimal states—politically integrated with populations averaging between 1,500 and 10,000, it was 76 percent; and in small states—those politically integrated and averaging between 10,000 and 100,000, the percentage was 85.

18. Meyer Fortes, "The Structure of Unilineal Descent Groups," *American Anthropologist* 55 (1953): 17–41.

19. Frederick Engels, *The Origins of the Family, Private Property, and the State* (New York: International Publishers, 1942), p. 99.

20. Yehudi A. Cohen, "Ends and Means in Political Control: State Organization and the Punishment of Adultery, Incest, and Violation of Celibacy," *American Anthropologist* 71 (1969): 665–666.

21. Paul Kirchhoff, "The Principles of Clanship in Human Society," in *Readings in Anthropology*, vol. 2, 2nd ed., ed. Morton H. Fried (New York: Thomas Y. Crowell, 1968 [originally published 1955]), pp. 379–380; see also Paul Bohannan, *Social Anthropology* (New York: Holt, Rinehart & Winston, 1963), p. 136.

22. As we saw in the chapter on marital residence, neolocal residence becomes more likely with commercial exchange. This form of residence disperses related households, making it more difficult to keep track of connections.

23. Marshall D. Sahlins, *Stone Age Economics* (Chicago: Aldine, 1972), p. 225.

24. See Carol R. Ember, "Residential Variation among Hunters-Gatherers," *Behavior Science Research* 10 (1975): 199–227; see also Carol R. Ember and Melvin Ember, "The Conditions Favoring Multilocal Residence," in Ember and Ember, *Marriage, Family, and Kinship*, pp. 219–248.

25. See David M. Schneider, "The Distinctive Features of Matrilineal Descent Groups," in *Matrilineal Kinship*, eds. Schneider and Gough, pp. 1–35.

26. Melvin Ember and Carol R. Ember, "The Conditions Favoring Matrilocal versus Patrilocal Residence," *American Anthropologist* 73 (1971): 174. Reprinted with "Afterthoughts," in Ember and Ember, *Marriage, Family, and Kinship*.

27. David M. Schneider, "Truk,'" in *Matrilineal Kinship*, eds. Schneider and Gough, pp. 202–233.

28. Ward H. Goodenough, *Property, Kin, and Community on Truk* (New Haven: Yale University Press, 1951), p. 145.

29. Ember, Ember, and Pasternak, "On the Development of Unilineal Descent."

30. Ibid.

31. Mischa Titiev, "The Influence of Common Residence on the Unilateral Classification of Kindred," *American Anthropologist* 45 (1943): 511–530.

32. Ember, Ember, and Pasternak, "On the Development of Unilineal Descent."

33. Ibid.

34. Although we use somewhat different examples, and interpret them differently, much of the discussion to follow builds upon the work of Morton H. Fried, especially his classic article, "The Classification of Corporate Unilineal Descent Groups," *Journal of the Royal Anthropological Institute* 87 (1957): 1–29. The description of Tungus patriclans is from that work.

35. Paul Bohannan, "Extra-Processual Events in Tiv Political Institutions," *American Anthropologist* 60 (1958): 1–12.

36. Paul Bohannan, "The Migration and Expansion of the Tiv," *Africa* 24 (1954): 2–16.

37. Bohannan, *Social Anthropology*, p. 137.

38. Marshall D. Sahlins, "The Segmentary Lineage: An Organization of Predatory Expansion," *American Anthropologist* 63 (1961): 342.

39. See Maurice Friedman, *Lineage Organization in Southeastern China* (London: Athlone Press, 1958); see also Jack Potter, *Capitalism and the Chinese Peasant* (Berkeley: University of California Press, 1968).

40. Much of the discussion that follows builds upon the work of Maurice Friedman and Morton H. Fried. See Maurice Friedman, *Chinese Lineage and Society: Fukien and Kwangtung* (London: Athlone Press,

1966), and *Lineage Organization in Southeastern China*; see also Fried, "The Classification of Corporate Unilineal Descent Groups." For a general discussion of the relevance of their work for an understanding of Chinese descent groups, see Burton Pasternak, "The Disquieting Chinese Lineage and Its Anthropological Relevance," in *The Chinese Family and Its Ritual Behavior*, eds. Hsieh Jih-chang and Chuang Ying-chang (Nankang, Taiwan: Institute of Ethnology, Academia Sinica, 1985).

41. Friedman, *Lineage Organization in Southeastern China*, p. 138.

42. Friedman (in *Chinese Lineage and Society*) used the term *vicinage* for this local system of communities. G. William Skinner made essentially the same point but with respect to the villages comprising the *standard marketing* area. See G. William Skinner, "Marketing and Social Structure in Rural China," *Journal of Asian Studies* 24 (1964–1965): 3–43, 195–228, 363–399.

43. Cf. Ember, Ember, and Pasternak, "On the Development of Unilineal Descent."

13

REFLECTIONS

D oes what we have learned from this cross-cultural treatment of sex, gender, marriage, and kinship provide insights of relevance to ourselves and our future? What we have learned about societies around the world should at least make us sensitive to the constraints and probabilities that have shaped our choices in the past and will likely continue to do so in the future. We should pay special attention to themes that have appeared chapter after chapter. They point to factors that exert special force, shaping the way we organize ourselves and relate to each other. We have seen the degree to which warfare and the nature of work seem to predict a great deal of variation in social structure. And some elements of social structure appear to be influenced by societal complexity—bigger families and important kin groups beyond the family are most important at the midrange of complexity.

We review those findings briefly here, but understanding social structure is not our only purpose. We need to understand the implications of those structures for human relationships. It is that issue upon which we focus in this chapter. We reflect on how the gender focus of social groups and the culture of violence impact human relationships, then turn to the impact of increasing societal complexity, and conclude with speculations about the future.

THE GENDER FOCUS OF SOCIAL GROUPS

Among mammals, mothers nurse, so it is hardly surprising that they usually provide more infant care than do fathers. In most mammalian species biological fathers don't hang around once they have impregnated a female;

they play little role in bringing up the offspring they help conceive. For that reason alone, we might expect uterine groups (mothers and their children) to be the truly essential building blocks of social groups, at least until the young are grown. Indeed, mother-child units constitute the *only* social groups in some animal species. However, in some mammal and in most bird species, we find female-male bonding, in which case the father typically remains with the mother and offspring for some time, helping with care of the young directly or indirectly as a provider.

Humans are actually quite unusual among mammals. Most have either female-male bonding without larger groups, or belong to larger groups without female-male bonding. We are one of very few species that typically have female-male bonding, creating families that are in turn the constituents of larger social groups. In most traditional societies families belong to larger networks of kin. But societies differ in the nature of those larger groups, in the *sorts of kin* they contain and in the forms they take. That brings us to an important cultural invention that affects so many aspects of our lives and behavior. As we noted over and over in this book, whether larger kin groups focus on women or men has a profound influence on the nature of the family and family relations, on the roles women and men play, on their opportunities and constraints, and on their relative social positions.

What, then, determines whether society focuses on women or men when it organizes supra-familial kin groups? Recall that, because the familial incest taboo is universal, people cannot find mates within their own families. For that reason, and because the human condition involves relatively enduring female-male bonding, some children invariably leave their families when they marry and go to live with others. Societies typically do not leave the choice of which child will leave to whim or personal preference. Custom specifies who goes where, and which options are acceptable. Most often, one gender consistently remains at home while the other departs, and in the majority of traditional societies this translates into either patrilocal or matrilocal residence.

Cross-culturally, the nature of war (internal versus purely external) appears to largely predict whether couples will live with the husband's or the wife's parents. And in the presence of unilocal residence, war in nonstate societies appears to engender the formation of descent groups (almost always patrilineal if residence is patrilocal; usually matrilineal if residence is matrilocal). Residence not only shapes the composition of larger kin groups, but it also influences the composition of the household should extended families develop.

The core of patrilocal extended families is a group of men related through the male line, while central to a matrilocal extended family is a group of women related through the female line. So couples have traditionally lived in a social system oriented around males *or* around females by virtue of the rules of residence and descent, and the ethnographic record clearly indicates that male-oriented social structures have been far more common than female-oriented ones.

As we have seen, the nature of supra-familial kin groups has an importance that goes well beyond kinship relations themselves—beyond the matter of who is obliged to help whom in time of danger or need. The kind of descent group to which one belongs, whether female- or male-focused, influences sexuality—the degree to which it is restricted for each gender both before and after marriage. It affects the way we obtain marriage partners—the degree to which we consider and accommodate personal preferences, the criteria we employ in making matches, the nature of wedding and honeymoon customs, and perhaps most important, relations between husband and wife.

With respect to sexuality, we found that matrilocal, matrilineal societies impose the fewest restrictions on women as well as men, and tend to treat childhood and premarital sex rather casually as well. Perhaps this is because important economic resources accrue to children through the maternal line.

For people unfamiliar with genetic analysis, establishing maternity is certainly more straightforward than determining paternity, so there is less need for vigilance when it comes to a woman's sexuality. Mothers (and their brothers) usually know who the mother's children are. Where access to crucial resources comes through one's father, however, as in patrilocal, patrilineal societies, it is not so certain who fathered the children and, therefore, the continuity of the patrilineal descent group itself may be less certain. It is hardly surprising, then, that we find less tolerance of premarital license, particularly on the part of women, more concern about assurances of virginity at marriage, and more insistence that wives confine their sexual activity to the conjugal relationship in patrilineal societies.

In patrilocal, patrilineal societies, kin are likely to become involved in marriage arrangements. The extended family or descent group is likely to transfer goods to the bride's kin (bride-price or bride-wealth), apparently signaling the transfer of human reproductive potential from the bride's to the groom's group. Marriage celebrations tend to be elaborate, and special treatment that makes the new couple stand out (e.g., a honeymoon) is common. Not only do marriages take more time and effort to arrange, they are also more difficult to end in male-focused societies. It is particularly difficult for women to obtain divorce, while the men of such societies tend to base their claims to divorce either on wifely infidelity, or on the failure of wives to produce heirs. All these customs reflect a special concern for paternity in patrilocal, patrilineal contexts.[1]

There is evidence that males are especially assertive and dominant in patrilocal, patrilineal societies, and that matrilocality and matrilineality provide women a greater measure of equality in some areas of life. But in some respects males have the upper hand no matter what the social structure. In many matrilineal societies a woman's brother has authority over her. Indeed, males typically serve as political leaders in all societies, and are almost invariably the society's warriors. So even female-oriented social structures, or at least the ones that we know about so far, have their limits when it comes to the equality of women.

THE CULTURE OF VIOLENCE

Living in a society where war is part of life undoubtedly affects everyone in obvious, unambiguous ways. But fighting can also have more subtle yet no less profound effects on sexuality, gender roles, the status of women, marriage, and the character of marital relationships. To begin with, recall the association we found between high mortality of adult males in war and polygyny in nonstate societies.[2] Apart from having to share a husband's sexual favors with another woman, what else does polygyny mean for a woman? For one thing, it usually means less husband-wife intimacy. And we also know that polygynous societies are particularly likely to have long postpartum sex taboos (of a year or more), during which time the couple avoids sex. That custom alone encourages a certain aloofness.

Although it is relatively uncommon, matrilocal societies, too, can have polygyny. In that case it is almost always sororal; the husband lives with or near the parents of wives who are sisters. The spousal aloofness associated with polygyny is more characteristic of patrilocal societies, however, in part because polygyny is much more common in patrilocal societies. (Also, sisters who are co-wives usually live in the same house, so we would expect the husband to be more often around.)

But the coincidence of polygyny *and* patrilocality in societies engaged in internal warfare (i.e., fighting within the society) can greatly exaggerate husband-wife avoidance, especially where enemies live nearby. In these cases, men frequently go to war against the native villages of their wives. It is not difficult to appreciate that, in these circumstances, men might be inclined to maintain some distance, physical and psychological, from their wives (who literally come from the enemy camp). Similarly, we would expect that wives would also maintain some distance from their husbands.

One might also speculate that spousal aloofness may shape the attitudes young women and men develop toward each other, and their views about marriage. Recall John W. M. and Beatrice B. Whiting's proposal that sons with an absent father are likely to develop conflicts about their sexual identification. Believing initially, in the absence of their fathers, that mothers control important resources, boys first identify with their mothers. Subsequent realization that men really control the crucial resources, and have authority and power besides, produces psychic conflict. Boys and men may try to resolve the conflict by exaggerated displays of masculine behavior—by acting super tough and brave, by derogating women and avoiding association with them, by engaging in gratuitous violence.

An alternative scenario suggests that, when fathers are frequently absent, or away for long periods, boys may develop an exaggerated Oedipus complex. If boys develop especially strong early attachments to their mothers, and then have to dramatically repress them when father finally returns (e.g., after a long postpartum avoidance), then we might expect them later to manifest more spousal jealousy and violence than would otherwise be the case.

If custom creates strong attachments in boys for their mothers, which are thwarted and even disparaged later (because of the incest taboo), perhaps they generalize their repression and associated negative feelings to women other than their mothers. Wouldn't we then expect husbands to be very concerned about wifely fidelity, and about controlling women under these circumstances? And, indeed, we have found that the double standard with respect to extramarital relations is particularly strong in societies with long postpartum sex taboos.

Recall, too, the fear of sex with women characteristic of men in certain areas of highland New Guinea, where husbands hardly lived with wives (often women from nearby enemy villages). It is probably no accident, too, that wife-beating is more characteristic of societies with frequent fighting. Since such societies tend to encourage aggressiveness in boys, its manifestation later in life is hardly surprising.[3] Indeed, cross-cultural research suggests that wife-beating is part of a more general syndrome of violence which includes violent conflict-resolution within the community, physical punishment of criminals, and cruelty toward enemies.

The type of warfare people engage in, particularly whether they fight only with other societies (external warfare) or among themselves (internal warfare), also affects women's participation in the political arena. When fighting is internal and wives come from the enemy, as among the Mae Enga of highland New Guinea, wives are hardly good candidates for intimate relationships. In fact, contact with them requires caution—they are the enemy within and, therefore, potentially dangerous. For this reason women are usually excluded from any participation in war, from handling weapons, and from approaching meetings where war is discussed. In short, they are not trusted and perhaps for this reason alone are excluded from the political arena.

It is not clear that war has a uniformly negatively impact on the status of women, however. Martin K. Whyte found a slight improvement in women's status in some domains, perhaps because they filled roles that men vacated when they had to go off to war. But perhaps more important, fighting affects women through its influence on postmarital residence. Recall that people who fight only externally (only with people in other societies) are matrilocal, except in relatively rare cases where the division of labor is patridominant because men are *not* away fighting when subsistence work has to be done. Recall, too, that in matrilocal societies women fare better than in patrilocal ones.

If people sometimes fight among themselves (internal warfare), which is commonly the case, they are almost invariably patrilocal, presumably to keep sons at home to defend quickly against the nearby enemies. And it is from patrilocality that male-oriented social structures emerge, to the clear disadvantage of women. This suggests that the type of warfare may be more important than warfare itself. We may better understand the effects of warfare on women's status, then, if we can tease out the effects of different sorts of fighting.

Recall, too, that supra-familial social structures, that is, descent groups, are themselves adjustments to warfare in nonstate societies. We have found that, when political development is not elaborate and fighting is a problem, people are likely to rely on unilineal descent groups, unambiguous sets of related kin, for support. And since most societies in the ethnographic record are patrilocal, most of those with descent groups are also patrilineal.

If localizing men and moving women (patrilocality) constrains women, then patrilineality undoubtedly does so even more. In a patrilocal and patrilineal society, a woman has to contend not only with her husband's parents, brothers, and sisters-in-law, she must also respond to the concerns and interests of a larger set of men who share common descent.

SOCIETAL COMPLEXITY AND THE TRANSFORMATION OF KINSHIP

It is not just patrilocality, patrilineality, and violence that shape families, relations within them, and the nature of kinship beyond. Aspects of societal complexity, too, exert an influence. With the emergence of stratification, for example, parents are concerned about marrying children to the "right kind" of people, which encourages them to guard more closely against potentially compromising sexual liaisons before and after marriage. In some cases contact with the opposite sex is entirely eliminated before marriage, and where it is not it usually takes place under the watchful eyes of chaperones. The control that parents and kin groups exercise over marriage affects more than sexual behavior. For example, people are particularly likely to value obedience in children in stratified and politically complex societies, which makes it easier to control whom they marry as well as how and where they will live.[4]

The effects on kinship organization that technological and economic development bring about when societies become more complex are quite clear. As we have learned, extended families and important, functional unilineal kin groups are more characteristic of midrange agricultural societies than of either foraging or industrial-commercial societies, where we more often find independent nuclear families and bilateral kinship. In most of the very simple and very complex societies, there are no descent groups at all. Perhaps the most significant kinship change occurs in commercial-industrial contexts where, in most cases, we find a reduction in the size of effective kinship units.

As other agencies assume important functions formerly managed by families and larger kin groups (functions such as defense, education, and support when in need), as employment comes to depend on universalistic rather than familistic criteria (e.g., one's education and skill rather than one's family or kinship connections), and as making a living increasingly requires physical mobility of individuals rather than cooperation by groups of related families, the family becomes increasingly isolated from other kin. People more often marry neolocally and live in independent, nuclear families apart from other kin (often far apart). The obligations of kinship no longer have the force they once did, as people become more concerned with accumulating the means to acquire, for themselves, the consumer goods that become increasingly available. Money is nonperishable and hideable, so individuals can store it and decrease their dependence on others, kin included. Under such circumstances, extended families become the exception, and larger kin groups (descent groups) tend to atrophy or disappear altogether.

But there is a price we must pay. Who will tide us over when we lose a job? What becomes of us when we are old and can no longer work? What happens when one is sick? Who will care for children when their parents are at work, or away from home? How shall we manage such things if our incomes are not sufficient to hire strangers to stand in for kin? And who will attend to the interests of children, guarding them against abuse? In traditional societies the answers to such questions are straightforward—people rely on their families and kin.

For us and people like us, the matter is more complicated. In many developed countries, including our own, people call upon government to provide the safety net that kin provide in nonindustrial societies. Opinions vary widely as to how good the state is at doing this. While most people in our own society would agree that many support programs are not particularly effective or efficient, we are likely to disagree about what we should or can do about it.

Some would call on government to do a better job of getting people on their feet in adversity, arguing that it is far too late (and perhaps not even desirable) to recreate the sorts of kin structures and networks that have served more traditional societies. After all, would those structures not be out of place in our economy and, in any case, doesn't it seem that they could function only under conditions of more certain residential propinquity?

While a case could be made that the economy would no longer be hospitable to any large-scale reconstruction of extended families and larger kin groups, strict residential propinquity may not be all that necessary for suprafamilial kin structures to be effective. Consider the kin networks anthropologist Carol Stack found in the "Flats" of Chicago, a poor neighborhood. In one case, seven different households within a three mile area functioned as a single cooperating network. Most of the participants were related through women, or friends of those women. They often shared evening meals, cooperated in child care, and took in any network member that became homeless.[5]

In fact, some propose that the government should retreat as much as possible from the social services business, that we should invigorate and equip families to assume more of this work. They see families becoming smaller, and believe that isolation of the individual has gone too far in our society, that little sense of community remains. And the only "safety net" of consequence that remains kicks in too often when it is too late. But even if it were possible to revitalize families and larger kin groups, we would have to decide what sorts of families to encourage, and how best to do so. And even then there would probably be a price to pay.

Consider the plight of women. In some ways, they have benefited from the waning of kinship. As we have seen, family institutions and kin groups were for the most part structured around males in traditional societies. Patrilineality, patrilocality, conflict, and social stratification have all often translated into limited autonomy and opportunity for women—less access to productive property, more constraint over their sexuality, less to say politically, and little control over whom they marry or remarry. With the ebbing of kinship has come a more balanced focus, one that provides more options for women.

While there have been gains, however, there have also been losses. Women often find themselves on much shakier ground materially as the safety net provided by kinship shrinks. For women still bear the major burden of child care, whether or not they work outside the home. They can count on little help from within the household. In most cases, work outside only adds to their domestic burden. If they choose not to be or stay married, they may have a harder time still; unmarried mothers are especially likely to find themselves below the poverty line.

So any gain in autonomy for women that may accrue from the ebbing of male-oriented family and kinship systems may be costly. Greater autonomy is a mixed blessing if insecurity or poverty accompanies it. Children may pay a greater price still. A recent Carnegie Corporation report on the status of children shows that a great many children in America are now at terrible risk. Many lack adequate health care and adequate nutrition, do poorly in school, and find themselves getting into trouble. Single parents under stress are especially likely to be hostile or indifferent to their children. This does *not* mean, of course, that mothers living in poverty generally do poorly by their children. Indeed, most do very well, managing against all odds. But the numbers of children at risk are increasing, and it is urgent that we do the research that will tell us why some mothers do well while others do not.

Any simplification of family which reduces it to a unit smaller than the nuclear family—to the most basic uterine group—unavoidably draws our attention to the issue of absent fathers. A large body of research points to the problems commonly experienced by boys who grow up without fathers or other male role models. Often those boys create super-tough, super-brave images for themselves. They may derogate women, and are more likely than other boys to exhibit violence. Such attitudes and behaviors may be self-reproducing if boys end up passing them on to their children.

Is there some way we might reconcile the need of women for more equality and the need for broader networks of kin that might serve to back up faltering families? Judging from what we know about traditional matrilocal, matrilineal societies, women's lot was better than in male-focused contexts. Although it is unlikely we could ever recreate the formal patterns of matrilocality and matrilineality in modern societies, there is some indication that families may be inching toward more female-centered structures. In this country, for example, sociologists have frequently noted that married couples usually live closer to the wife's family, and visit them more often. We also know that single mothers often rely heavily on their own mothers, grandmothers, and sisters. But there are other possible routes to enlarging the networks upon which we can depend.

We still have much to learn about the effects of modernization and development, indigenous or imposed from the outside. Scholars in many disciplines are already at work on various related questions, but there is something extra to be gained from a systematically comparative perspective, as we have tried to convey in this book. Studies of contemporary and recent societies as described in the ethnographic record tell us how human societies have tried to adjust to their worlds. Whether or not they have been touched by global forces, all of them tell us what we may be capable of achieving. If we study them systematically, we can discover the causes and consequences of institutions we may take for granted but poorly understand.

Complex societies share with many simpler ones a preference for patrilocality, and sometimes for patrilineal descent as well. In some cases the institutions are gone, but residual customs and practices remain. For that reason, women often continue to pass their lives in male-focused social structures, or coping with the attitudes and assumptions they have left behind. Because women still join the families of their husbands in many developing and developed societies, they remain subject to, and dependent on, the good will of their husbands' relatives. And anticipating that daughters will eventually serve others, parents and kin groups still find no advantage in educating or otherwise investing in women.

When we look back at life in more traditional societies, we find reason to believe that, in many ways, women lost ground when societies became more complex; and when societies began to depend on intensive cultivation, women began to have more children and domestic work than in those dependent on foraging and nonintensive agriculture. The heavier burden of work in and around the house, together with customs designed to constrain and confine their sexuality, discourage women's participation in public affairs. Because women in such societies are more often separated, even isolated, there are few opportunities for them to display capabilities that might otherwise earn them respect outside the home. Further, the political hierarchies characteristic of complex societies are everywhere male-dominated, accentuating the importance of men in other areas as well.

On the other hand, the effects of industrialization and commercialization are complex; we are only at the beginning of sorting them out. All stratified societies are industrialized or commercialized, but they do not all display the same degree of sexual constraint or gender inequality. We, ourselves, have become less restrictive when it comes to premarital sex, and increasingly disposed to women having greater access to education, opportunity, and public participation—all signs of progress toward greater equality. Still, the greater control that women in our society exercise over their own sexuality, and their gradual and painful approach to equity in the workplace, are not paralleled in many societies that are also industrial and commercial. Indeed, where women had traditionally contributed *more* to the economy than men, industry and commerce have actually lowered the status of women.

Colonial intrusions into traditional societies, too, have had their impact, on family relations in general, and on the position of women in particular, sometimes exaggerating the consequences of male-focused social systems, and often creating new problems. To be fair, the effects have not always or uniformly been to the detriment of women. Consider the Coast Salish of western Washington State and British Columbia, who now have elected political councils. Although they played little role in traditional politics, women now constitute high proportions in the councils of some Salish communities. Comparing their electoral success in different Salish communities, Bruce G. Miller found that women more often won elections where they earned a higher proportion of household income as a result of having technical and service jobs. They did better politically in poorer communities where their wage contributions made the biggest difference, and in smaller ones where everyone knew them personally.[6]

Among the Abelam of Papua New Guinea, too, the introduction of Western-style courts benefited women who could now try to redress the grievances they had against men. Traditionally, only men participated in the resolution of disputes, and in that system women could not bring actions against men. Richard Scaglion and Rose Whittingham have observed that women in many parts of New Guinea are increasingly appealing to local courts for redress against sexual offenses (rape, incest, domestic violence, sexual jealousy). And they are achieving the same rate of success in court as men.[7] So in situations where men once almost exclusively dominated the political and judicial systems, new political institutions can sometimes work to women's benefit.

Still, it must be said that Western colonialism has generally been detrimental to women, in part because Westerners have been accustomed to dealing with men, and also because they found it convenient to take advantage of the relative docility of women in male-focused traditional societies. Women in such societies do not easily protest, form unions, or take to the streets. There are numerous examples of Europeans restructuring land ownership around men and teaching men modern farming techniques, where women were traditionally the principal farmers. In many colonial contexts men acquired a more direct access to cash, by selling their labor (particularly when work was at a distance) or through commerce (e.g., selling furs to Europeans). This advantage not only enhanced their importance within the family, but it also provided access to experience and knowledge about the outside world which justified and reinforced their political dominance.[8]

WHERE WILL IT ALL END?

Although we have concerned ourselves in this book with sexuality, gender, marriage, and kinship in the ethnographic record, what we have discovered does tell us some things about our own prospects. It is quite clear that during most of human history individuals have needed others, and it is likely we will continue to require the support of larger social groups. Whether they will be kin groups, friendship groups, or neighborhood groups, is difficult to say. But the fact that all human societies have had marriage and families of some kind suggests that those institutions are likely to form the basis of any larger social groupings.

But does it really make a difference if family and kinship become increasingly less important, even irrelevant, as societies everywhere transform, as they adjust to a global market economy? With this question we return to the issue raised at the outset, and to the very different perspectives provided by Lee Kwan Yew, Singapore's former Prime Minister, and by the group of women academics we quoted.

In Lee's view, you will recall, educating and allowing women economic and social independence are potential threats to the family, to what he and others believe to be the essential "building brick of society." For the academics cited, however, marriage, family, and the role of "wife" are intimately connected to the subordination of women. Are we, then, to guard the family and its extensions at all cost, because no other agency can perform their functions as well? Or would the costs be too high and the project unnecessary?

After all, is it not true that in some ways complex economies confer important advantages on women as well as men? Individuals have more freedom to move where opportunities present themselves. And, without kin around asking for food, money, and shelter, people can keep more for themselves. Indeed, the central importance of the individual has achieved a hallowed place in our own national politics and ideology. Not only is the individual said to be responsible for all that she or he achieves, but we often see the individual as solely responsible for failure as well. We are no longer inclined to hold the kin group and community responsible.

The contrast with thinking in many traditional, kinship-organized societies is stark. For not only do families and kin groups protect and provide for their members, but they also enjoy the fruits of their successes and assume responsibility for their failures. Some emphasis on the group over the individual persists even in many nation-states today. We see it clearly reflected in Lee Kwan Yew's observations about the "evils" of Western society, with its misguided focus on rights of the individual. Indeed, in places like Singapore, China, and Japan, the family (if not the larger kin group) continues to be important, and has passed fewer of its obligations to state agencies. In the People's Republic of China, the obligation of family members to support one another is written into constitutional law, and collective responsibility for the actions of family members remains a fact of life (much to the distress of many political outcasts).

In the end, we must leave it to the reader to decide whether a shift to smaller, less functional kin groups, and from collective to individual identification, is a positive or negative one. Whether we approve of it or not, however, it is occurring around the world. For that reason alone, we must be attentive to the consequences and study the evolution of social structures in all cultures known to us. Only by doing so will we obtain reliable insight into what is causing what, and only with that understanding can we hope to shape our own futures.

We have to decide, of course, what we want and what (or whom) we are willing to sacrifice to get it. It was not our intention to deal with these problems, nor did we set out to suggest optimal societal arrangements. Hopefully, however, we have delivered on the more modest promise with which we began—to lay out the various possibilities. We have described the variety of marriage forms and family and kinship structures that people have shown themselves capable of creating. We have discussed how issues of sex and gender are interleaved in these structures. And we have outlined what comparative research tells us about the possible or probable causes and implications of variation in social structure. Now we leave it to the reader to decide what is *better*, more *natural*, or *basic* in the domains of sex, gender, marriage, and kinship.

NOTES

1. In some patrilineal, patrilocal societies, however, descent groups assure their reproduction differently. Instead of restricting premarital sex, they allow it. We usually find this in age-graded societies (like the Masai), where men inhabit bachelor huts to which women make visits. Rather than dyadic pairing, premarital sex commonly involves a wider sharing of sexual favors, perhaps as a way of reinforcing age-grade solidarity. In these societies people usually think of paternity in sociological rather than biological terms; a man is considered the father of children mostly because his kin gave wealth to the bride's kin.

2. There are different interpretations of that relationship. Research by Melvin Ember suggests that the unequal sex ratio creates polygyny. Others (e.g., Napoleon Chagnon, Barbara C. Ayres, Bobbi Low) suggest that men compete for wives and the more successful are more likely to survive and acquire more wives. See Napoleon A. Chagnon, "Life Histories, Blood Revenge, and Warfare in a Tribal Population," *Science* 26 (February 1988): 985–992; Barbara C. Ayres, "Marriage Systems as Reproductive Strategies: Cross-Cultural Evidence for Sexual Selection in Man" (paper delivered at the annual meeting of the Society for Cross-Cultural Research, February 1976); Bobbi S. Low, "Plural Marriages," in *Encyclopedia of Cultural Anthropology*, vol. 3, eds. David Levinson and Melvin Ember (New York: Henry Holt, 1996), pp. 948–951.

3. Carol R. Ember and Melvin Ember, "War, Socialization, and Interpersonal Violence: A Cross-Cultural Study," *Journal of Conflict Resolution* 38 (1994): 620–646.

4. See Table 3 in Herbert Barry III, Irvin L. Child, and Margaret K. Bacon, "Relation of Child Training to Subsistence Economy," *American Anthropologist* 61 (1959): 51–63.

5. Carol Stack, "Domestic Networks: 'Those You Count On'," in *Gender in Cross-Cultural Perspective*, eds. Caroline B. Brettell and Carolyn F. Sargent (Englewood Cliffs, NJ: Prentice Hall, 1993), pp. 301–310.

6. Bruce G. Miller, "Women and Politics: Comparative Evidence from the Northwest Coast," *Ethnology* 31 (1992): 367–382.

7. Richard Scaglion and Rose Whittingham, "Female Plaintiffs and Sex-Related Disputes in Rural Papua New Guinea," in *Domestic Violence in Papua New Guinea*, monograph no. 3, ed. S. Toft (Port Moresby, Papua New Guinea: Law Reform Commission, 1985).

8. For reviews of the literature on this point, see Naomi Quinn, "Anthropological Studies on Women's Status," *Annual Review of Anthropology* 6 (1977): 85; and Mona Etienne and Eleanor Leacock, eds., *Women and Colonialization: Anthropological Perspectives* (New York: Praeger, 1980), pp. 19–20.

References

'Abd Allah, Mahmud M. "Siwan Customs." *Harvard African Studies* 1 (1917): 7, 20.

Aberle, David F. "Matrilineal Descent in Cross-Cultural Perspective." In *Matrilineal Kinship*, eds. David M. Schneider and Kathleen Gough. Berkeley: University of California Press, 1961.

Aberle, David F., Urie Bronfenbrenner, Eckhard H. Hess, Daniel R. Miller, David M. Schneider, and James N. Spuhler. "The Incest Taboo and the Mating Patterns of Animals." *American Anthropologist* 65 (1963): 253–265.

Abler, Thomas S. "Iroquois: The Tree of Peace and the War Kettle." In *Portraits of Culture: Ethnographic Originals*, eds. Melvin Ember, Carol R. Ember, and David Levinson. Englewood Cliffs, NJ: Prentice Hall/Simon & Schuster Custom Publishing, 1994.

Ackerman, Charles. "Affiliations: Structural Determinants of Differential Divorce Rates." *American Journal of Sociology* 69 (1963): 13–20.

Adams, David B. "Why Are There So Few Women Warriors?" *Behavior Science Research* 18 (1983): 196–212.

Adriani N., and Albert C. Kruyt. *De Bare's Sprekende Toradjas van Vidden-Celebes (de Oost Toradjas), Tweede Deel* [*The Bare-Speaking Toradja of Central Celebes (the East Toradja), vol. 2*]. Tweede, geheel omgewerkt druk, Koninklijke Nederlandse Akademie Van Wetenschappen, Verhandelingen, Afdeling Letterkunde, Nieuwe Reeks, vol. 55. Amsterdam: N. V. Noord-Hollandsche Uitgevers Maatschappij, 1951.

Aghajanian, Akbar. "Some Notes on Divorce in Iran." *Journal of Marriage and the Family* 48 (1986): 749–755.

Albers, Patricia C. "From Illusion to Illumination: Anthropological Studies of American Indian Women." In *Gender and Anthropology: Critical Reviews for Research and Teaching*, ed. Sandra Morgen. Washington, DC: American Anthropological Association, 1989.

Alexander, Richard D., and Katherine M. Noonan. "Concealment of Ovulation, Parental Care, and Human Social Evolution." In *Evolutionary Biology and Human Social Behavior: An Anthropological Perspective*, eds. Napoleon Chagnon and William Irons. North Scituate, MA: Duxbury Press, 1979.

Altschuler, Milton. "Cayapa Personality and Sexual Motivation." In *Human Sexual Behavior*, eds. Donald S. Marshall and Robert C. Suggs. Englewood Cliffs, NJ: Prentice Hall, 1971.

Ames, David W. "Plural Marriage among the Wolof in the Gambia: With a Consideration of Problems of Marital Adjustment and Patterned Ways of Resolving Tensions." Unpublished Ph.D. diss. Evanston, IL: Northwestern University, 1953.

Amoo, J. W. A. "The Effect of Western Influence on Akan Marriage." *Africa* 16 (1946): 228–237.

Ayres, Barbara C. "Bride Theft and Raiding for Wives in Cross-Cultural Perspective." *Anthropological Quarterly* 47 (1974): 238–252.

Ayres, Barbara C. "Intra-Societal Variation in the Incidence of Polygyny." Paper presented at the annual meeting of the Society for Cross-Cultural Research, Washington, DC, 1983.

Ayres, Barbara C. "Marriage Systems as Reproductive Strategies: Cross-Cultural Evidence for Sexual Selection in Man." Paper presented at the annual meeting of the Society for Cross-Cultural Research, February 1976.

Barnett, William Kester. "An Ethnographic Description of Sanlei Ts'un, Taiwan, with Emphasis on Women's Roles; Overcoming Research Problems Caused by the Presence of a Great Tradition." Ph.D. diss., Michigan State University, 1970, University Microfilms Dissertation no. 71–2026. Ann Arbor: University Microfilms, 1971.

Barry, Herbert III, Irvin L. Child, and Margaret K. Bacon. "Relation of Child Training to Subsistence Economy." *American Anthropologist* 61 (1959): 51–63.

Barth, Fredrik. "Father's Brother's Daughter Marriage in Kurdistan." *Southwestern Journal of Anthropology* 10 (1954): 164–171.

Bates, Ülkü Ü., Florence L. Denmark, Virginia Held, Dorothy O. Helly, Susan H. Lees, Sarah B. Pomeroy, E. Dorsey Smith, and Sue Rosenberg Zalk. *Women's Realities, Women's Choices: An Introduction to Women's Studies*. New York: Oxford University Press, 1983.

Bateson, Patrick. "Optimal Outbreeding." In *Mate Choice*, ed. Patrick Bateson. Cambridge, England: Cambridge University Press, 1983.

Bateson, Patrick. "Rules for Changing the Rules." In *Evolution from Molecules to Men*, ed. D. S. Bendall. Cambridge, England: Cambridge University Press, 1983.

Becker, Gary S., Elisabeth M. Landes, and Robert T. Michael. "An Economic Analysis of Marital Instability." *Journal of Political Economy* 85 (1977): 1141–1187.

Befu, Harumi. "Origins of Large Households and Duolocal Residence in Central Japan." *American Anthropologist* 70 (1968): 309–319.

Begler, Elsie B. "Sex, Status, and Authority in Egalitarian Society." *American Anthropologist* 80 (1978): 571–588.

Bell, Graham. *The Masterpiece of Nature: the Evolution and Genetics of Sexuality*. Berkeley: University of California Press, 1982.

Bender, Donald R. "De Facto and De Jure Households in Ondo." *American Anthropologist* 73 (1971): 223–241.

Bender, Donald R. "A Refinement of the Concept of Household: Families, Co-Residence, and Domestic Functions." *American Anthropologist* 69 (1967): 493–504.

Berreman, G. "Himalayan Polyandry and the Domestic Cycle." *American Ethnologist* 2 (1975): 127–139.

Berry, John W. *Human Ecology and Cognitive Style*. New York: John Wiley, 1976.

Betzig, Laura L. "Causes of Conjugal Dissolution: A Cross-Cultural Study." *Current Anthropology* 30, no. 5 (December 1989): 654–676.

Betzig, Laura L. *Despotism and Differential Reproduction: A Darwinian View of History*. New York: Aldine Publishing Company, 1986.

Betzig, Laura L. "Roman Polygyny." *Ethology and Sociobiology* 13 (1992): 309–349.

Bevc, Irene, and Irwin Silverman. "Early Proximity and Intimacy between Siblings and Incestuous Behavior: A Test of the Westermarck Theory." *Ethology and Sociobiology* 14 (1993): 171–181.

Bischof, N. "The Biological Foundations of the Incest Taboo." *Social Science Information* 11, no. 6 (1972): 7–36.

Bischof, N. "Comparative Ethology of Incest Avoidance." In *Biosocial Anthropology*, ed. Robin Fox. New York: Malaby Press, 1975.

Björkqvist, Kaj. "Sex Differences in Physical, Verbal, and Indirect Aggression: A Review of Recent Research." *Sex Roles* 30 (1994): 177–188.

Blumberg, Rae Lesser, and Robert F. Winch. "Societal Complexity and Familial Complexity: Evidence for the Curvilinear Hypothesis." *American Journal of Sociology* 77 (1972): 898–920.

Blurton-Jones, N. G., and M. Konner. "Sex Differences in Behavior of London and Bushman Children." In *Comparative Ecology and Behaviour of Primates*, eds. R. P. Michael and J. H. Crook. London: Academic Press, 1973.

Bock, R. D., H. Wainer, A. Petersen, D. Thissen, J. Murray, and A. Roche. "A Parameterization for Individual Human Growth Curves." *Human Biology* 45 (1973): 63–80.

Bogoras, Waldemar (Bogaraz-Tan, Vladimir Germanovich). *The Chukchee: Material Culture [Part 1], Religion [Part 2], Social Organization [Part 3].* New York: G. E. Stechert and Co., Memoirs of the American Museum of Natural History, 11, 1904 (Part 1), 1907 (Part 2), 1909 (Part 3).

Bohannan, Paul. "Extra-Processual Events in Tiv Political Institutions." *American Anthropologist* 60 (1958): 1–12.

Bohannan, Paul. "The Migration and Expansion of the Tiv." *Africa* 24 (1954): 2–16.

Bohannan, Paul. *Social Anthropology.* New York: Holt, Rinehart & Winston, 1963.

Bolton, Ralph. "Sex, Science, and Social Responsibility: Cross-Cultural Research on Same-Sex Eroticism and Sexual Intolerance." *Cross-Cultural Research* 28 (1994): 134–190.

Booth, Alan, and John N. Edwards. "Age at Marriage and Marital Instability." *Journal of Marriage and the Family* 47 (1985): 67–75.

Boserup, Ester. *Woman's Role in Economic Development.* New York: St. Martin's Press, 1970.

Boyer, Ruth. "The Matrifocal Family among the Mescalero: Additional Data." *American Anthropologist* 66 (1964): 593–602.

Bradley, Candice. "Keeping the Soil in Good Heart: Weeding, Women, and Ecofeminism." In *Ecofeminism: Multidisciplinary Perspectives*, ed. Karen Warren. Bloomington: Indiana University Press, 1995.

Brandt, Vincent S. R. *A Korean Village between Farm and Sea.* Cambridge, MA: Harvard University Press, 1971.

Broude, Gwen J. "Cross-Cultural Patterning of Some Sexual Attitudes and Practices." *Behavior Science Research* 11 (1976): 227–262.

Broude, Gwen J. "Extramarital Sex Norms in Cross-Cultural Perspective." *Behavior Science Research* 15 (1980): 181–218.

Broude, Gwen J. "Male-Female Relationships in Cross-Cultural Perspective: A Study of Sex and Intimacy." *Behavior Science Research* 18 (1983): 154–181.

Broude, Gwen J. "The Relationship of Marital Intimacy and Aloofness to Social Environment: A Hologeistic Study." *Behavior Science Research* 21 (1987): 50–69.

Broude, Gwen J. "Variations in Sexual Attitudes, Norms, and Practices." In *Cross-Cultural Research for Social Science*, eds. Carol R. Ember and Melvin Ember. Upper Saddle River, NJ: Prentice Hall/Simon & Schuster Custom Publishing, 1996.

Broude, Gwen J., and Sarah J. Greene. "Cross-Cultural Codes on Husband-Wife Relationships." *Ethnology* 22 (1983): 263–280.

Broude, Gwen J., and Sarah J. Greene. "Cross-Cultural Codes on Twenty Sexual Attitudes and Practices." *Ethnology* 15 (1976): 409–430.

Brown, Judith K. "Economic Organization and the Position of Women among the Iroquois." *Ethnohistory* 17 (1970): 1073–1078.

Brown, Judith K. "A Note on the Division of Labor by Sex." *American Anthropologist* 72 (1970): 837–853.

Bruce, Judith, et al. "Families in Focus." Population Council Study. Quoted in *The New York Times International*, May 30, 1995.

Burbank, Victoria K. "Female Aggression in Cross-Cultural Perspective." *Behavior Science Research* 21 (1987): 70–100.

Burch, Jr., Ernest S. "North Alaskan Eskimos: A Changing Way of Life." In *Portraits of Culture: Ethnographic Originals*, eds. Melvin Ember, Carol R. Ember, and David Levinson. Englewood Cliffs, NJ: Prentice Hall/Simon & Schuster Custom Publishing, 1994.

Burling, Robbins. *Rengsanggri: Family and Kinship in a Garo Village*. Philadelphia: University of Pennsylvania Press, 1963.

Burton, Roger V. "Folk Theory and the Incest Taboo." *Ethos* 1 (1973): 504–516.

Busby, Annette. "Kurds: A Culture Straddling National Borders." In *Portraits of Culture: Ethnographic Originals*, eds. Melvin Ember, Carol R. Ember, and David Levinson. Englewood Cliffs, NJ: Prentice Hall/Simon & Schuster Custom Publishing, 1994.

Busch, Ruth C., and James Gundlach. "Excess Access and Incest: A New Look at the Demographic Explanation of the Incest Taboo." *American Anthropologist* 79 (1977): 912–914.

Busia, K. A. *The Position of the Chief in the Modern Political System of Ashanti: A Study of the Influence of Contemporary Social Changes on Ashanti Political Institutions*. London: The Oxford University Press for the International African Institute, 1951.

Callender, Charles, and Lee M. Kochems. "The North American Berdache." *Current Anthropology* 24 (1983): 443–470.

Carneiro, Robert L. "Preface." In *The Evolution of Society: Selections from Herbert Spencer's Principles of Sociology*, ed. Robert L. Carneiro. Chicago: University of Chicago Press, 1967.

Chagnon, Napoleon A. "Life Histories, Blood Revenge, and Warfare in a Tribal Population." *Science*, February 26, 1988, pp. 985–992.

Chagnon, Napoleon A. *Yanomamö*. New York: Harcourt Brace College Publishers, 1992.

Chagnon, Napoleon A. "Yanomamö Warfare, Social Organization, and Marriage Alliances." Ph.D. diss. submitted to the University of Michigan, University Microfilms Publications no. 67–8226. Ann Arbor: University Microfilms, 1967.

Chance, Norman A. *The Eskimo of North Alaska*. New York: Holt, Rinehart & Winston, 1966.

Cherlin, Andrew J. "The Effects of Children on Marital Dissolution." *Demography* 14 (1977): 265–272.

Cherlin, Andrew J. *Marriage, Divorce, Remarriage*. Cambridge, MA: Harvard University Press, 1981.

Cherlin, Andrew J. "Work Life and Marital Dissolution." In *Divorce and Separation*, eds. G. Levinger and O. C. Moles. New York: Basic Books, 1979.

Chu, T'ung-Tsu. *Law and Society in Traditional China*. Paris: Mouton & Co., 1961.

Cipriani, Lidio. "Hygiene and Medical Practices among the Onge (Little Andaman)." *Anthropos* 56 (1961): 481–500.

Clinget, Remi, and Joyce Sween. "Urbanization, Plural Marriage, and Family Size in Two African Cities." *American Ethnologist* 1 (1974): 221–242.

Cohen, Myron L. "A Case Study of Chinese Economy and Development." *Journal of Asian and African Studies* 3 (1968): 161–180.

Cohen, Myron L. "Developmental Process in the Chinese Domestic Group." In *Family and Kinship in Chinese Society*, ed. Maurice Freedman. Stanford: Stanford University Press, 1970.

Cohen, Myron L. "Family Management and Family Division in Contemporary Rural China." *The China Quarterly* 130 (1992): 357–377.

Cohen, Myron L. *House United, House Divided: The Chinese Family in Taiwan*. New York: Columbia University Press, 1976.

Cohen, Myron L. "Variations in Complexity among Chinese Family Groups: The Impact of Modernization." *Transactions of the New York Academy of Sciences* 29 (1967): 638–644.

Cohen, Ronald. *The Kanuri of Bornu*. New York: Holt, Rinehart & Winston, 1967.

Cohen, Yehudi A. "Ends and Means in Political Control: State Organization and the Punishment of Adultery, Incest, and Violation of Celibacy." *American Anthropologist* 71 (1969): 658–687.

Condominas, George. "The Primitive Life of Vietnam's Mountain People." In *Man's Many Ways*, ed. R. A. Gould. New York: Harper & Row, 1973.

Coppinger, Robert M., and Paul C. Rosenblatt. "Romantic Love and Subsistence Dependence of Spouses." *Southwestern Journal of Anthropology* 24 (1968): 310–319.

Coult, Allen D., and Robert W. Habenstein. *Cross Tabulations of Murdock's World Ethnographic Sample*. Columbia: University of Missouri Press, 1965.

Crapo, Richley H. "Factors in the Cross-Cultural Patterning of Male Homosexuality: A Reappraisal of the Literature." *Cross-Cultural Research* 29 (1995): 178–202.

Creed, Gerald W. "Sexual Subordination: Institutionalized Homosexuality and Social Control in Melanesia." *Ethnology* 23 (1984): 157–176.

Croll, Elisabeth. "New Peasant Family Forms in Rural China." *Journal of Peasant Studies* 14 (1987): 469–499.

Croll, Elisabeth. "New Peasant Household." In *The Reemergence of the Chinese Peasantry*, ed. A. Saith. London: Croom Helm, 1987.

Croll, Elisabeth. "Some Implications of the Rural Economic Reforms for the Chinese Peasant Household." In *The Reemergence of the Chinese Peasantry*, ed. A. Saith. London: Croom Helm, 1987.

Crook, J. H. "Sexual Selection, Dimorphism, and Social Organization in the Primates." In *Sexual Selection and the Descent of Man, 1871–1971*, ed. B. Campbell. Chicago: Aldine, 1972.

Culshaw, W. J. *Tribal Heritage: A Study of the Santals*. London: Lutterworth Press, 1949.

Daly, Martin, and Margo Wilson. *Homicide*. New York: Aldine de Gruyter, 1988.

Daly, Martin, and Margo Wilson. *Sex, Evolution, and Behavior*, 2nd ed. Boston: Willard Grant Press, 1983.

Daly, Martin, Margo Wilson, and Suzanne J. Weghorst. "Male Sexual Jealousy." *Ethology and Sociobiology* 3 (1982): 11–27.

Davenport, William. "Sexual Patterns and Their Regulation in a Society of the Southwest Pacific." In *Sex and Behavior*, ed. Frank A. Beach. New York: John Wiley, 1965.

Davies, N. B. *Dunnock Behaviour and Social Evolution*. Oxford, England: Oxford University Press, 1992.

Davis, K. "Jealousy and Sexual Property." *Social Forces* 14 (1936): 395–405.

Davis, Susan Schaefer. "Morocco: Adolescents in a Small Town." In *Portraits of Culture: Ethnographic Originals*, eds. Melvin Ember, Carol R. Ember, and David Levinson. Englewood Cliffs, NJ: Prentice Hall/Simon & Schuster Custom Publishing, 1994.

Demarest, W. J. "Incest Avoidance among Human and Nonhuman Primates." In *Primate Biosocial Development: Biological, Social, and Ecological Determinants*, eds. Suzanne Chevalier-Skolnicoff and Frank E. Poirier. New York: Garland Publishing, 1977.

Diamond, Norma Joyce. "Collectivization, Kinship, and the Status of Women in Rural China." In *Toward an Anthropology of Women*, ed. Rayna R. Reiter. New York: Monthly Review Press, 1975.

Diamond, Norma Joyce. *K'un Shen: A Taiwan Village*. New York: Holt, Rinehart & Winston, 1969.

Divale, William T. "Migration, External Warfare, and Matrilocal Residence." *Behavior Science Research* 9 (1974): 75–133.

Divale, William T., and Marvin Harris. "Population, Warfare, and the Male Supremacist Complex." *American Anthropologist* 78 (1976): 521–538.

Draper, Patricia. "!Kung Women: Contrasts in Sexual Egalitarianism in Foraging and Sedentary Contexts." In *Toward an Anthropology of Women*, ed. Rayna R. Reiter. New York: Monthly Review Press, 1975.

Draper, Patricia, and Henry Harpending. "Father Absence and Reproductive Strategy: An Evolutionary Perspective." *Journal of Anthropological Research* 38 (1982): 255–273.

Dunning, R. W. *Social and Economic Change among the Northern Ojibwa*. Toronto: University of Toronto Press, 1959.

Durham, William H. *Coevolution: Genes, Culture, and Human Diversity*. Stanford: Stanford University Press, 1991.

Dyson-Hudson, Neville. *Karimojong Politics*. Oxford: Clarendon Press, 1966.

East, Rupert. *Akiga's Story: The Tiv Tribe as Seen by One of Its Members*. London: The International Institute of African Languages and Cultures, Oxford University Press, 1939.

Ellis, Lee. "Evidence of Neuroandrogenic Etiology of Sex Roles from a Combined Analysis of Human, Nonhuman Primate, and Nonprimate Mammalian Studies." *Personality and Individual Differences* 7 (1986): 525–527.

Ember, Carol R. "A Cross-Cultural Perspective on Sex Differences." In *Handbook of Cross-Cultural Human Development*, eds. Ruth H. Munroe, Robert L. Munroe, and Beatrice B. Whiting. New York: Garland Press, 1981.

Ember, Carol R. "An Evaluation of Alternative Theories of Matrilocal versus Patrilocal Residence." *Behavior Science Research* 9 (1974): 135–149.

Ember, Carol R. "Feminine Task-Assignment and the Social Behavior of Boys." *Ethos* 1 (1973): 424–439.

Ember, Carol R. "Men's Fear of Sex with Women: A Cross-Cultural Study." *Sex Roles* 4 (1978): 657–678.

Ember, Carol R. "The Relative Decline in Women's Contribution to Agriculture with Intensification." *American Anthropologist* 85 (1983): 288–289.

Ember, Carol R. "Residential Variation among Hunter-Gatherers." *Behavior Science Research* 10 (1975): 199–227. Reprinted in Melvin Ember and Carol R. Ember, *Marriage, Family, and Kinship: Comparative Studies of Social Organization*. New Haven: HRAF Press, 1983.

Ember, Carol R., and Melvin Ember. *Anthropology*, 8th ed. Upper Saddle River, NJ: Prentice-Hall, 1996.

Ember, Carol R., and Melvin Ember. "The Conditions Favoring Multilocal Residence." *Southwestern Journal of Anthropology* 28 (1972): 382–400. Reprinted in Melvin Ember and Carol R. Ember, *Marriage, Family, and Kinship: Comparative Studies of Social Organization*. New Haven: HRAF Press, 1983.

Ember, Carol R., and Melvin Ember. "The Evolution of Human Female Sexuality: A Cross-Species Perspective." *Journal of Anthropological Research* 40 (1984): 202–210.

Ember, Carol R., and Melvin Ember. "Resource Unpredictability, Mistrust, and War: A Cross-Cultural Study." *Journal of Conflict Resolution* 36 (1992): 251–252.

Ember, Carol R., and Melvin Ember. "Violence in the Ethnographic Record: Results of Cross-Cultural Research on War and Aggression." In *Troubled Times: Osteological and Archaeological Evidence of Violence*, eds. David Frayer and Debra Martin. Langhorne, PA: Gordon and Breach, in press.

Ember, Carol R., and Melvin Ember. "War, Socialization, and Interpersonal Violence: A Cross-Cultural Study." *Journal of Conflict Resolution* 38 (1994): 620–646.

Ember, Carol R., Melvin Ember, and Burton Pasternak. "On the Development of Unilineal Descent." *Journal of Anthropological Research* 30 (1974): 69–74. Reprinted in Melvin Ember and Carol R. Ember, *Marriage, Family, and Kinship: Comparative Studies of Social Organization*. New Haven: HRAF Press, 1983.

Ember, Melvin. "Alternative Predictors of Polygyny." *Behavior Science Research* 19 (1985): 1–23.

Ember, Melvin. "The Conditions That May Favor Avunculocal Residence." *Behavior Science Research* 9 (1974): 203–209. Reprinted with "Afterthoughts," in Melvin Ember and Carol R. Ember, *Marriage, Family, and Kinship: Comparative Studies of Social Organization*. New Haven: HRAF Press, 1983.

Ember, Melvin. "The Emergence of Neolocal Residence." *Transactions of the New York Academy of Sciences* 30 (1967): 291–302. Reprinted with "Afterthoughts," in Melvin Ember and Carol R. Ember, *Marriage, Family, and Kinship: Comparative Studies of Social Organization*. New Haven: HRAF Press, 1983.

Ember, Melvin. "On the Origin and Extension of the Incest Taboo." *Behavior Science Research* 10 (1975): 249–281. Reprinted in Melvin Ember and Carol R. Ember, *Marriage, Family, and Kinship: Comparative Studies of Social Organization*. New Haven: HRAF Press, 1983.

Ember, Melvin. "Taxonomy in Comparative Studies." In *A Handbook of Method in Cultural Anthropology*, eds. Raoul Naroll and Ronald Cohen. New York: Columbia University Press, 1973.

Ember, Melvin. "Warfare, Sex Ratio, and Polygyny." *Ethnology* 13 (1974): 197–206. Reprinted in Melvin Ember and Carol R. Ember, *Marriage, Family, and Kinship: Comparative Studies of Social Organization*. New Haven: HRAF Press, 1983.

Ember, Melvin, and Carol R. Ember. "The Conditions Favoring Matrilocal versus Patrilocal Residence." *American Anthropologist* 73 (1971): 571–594. Reprinted with "Afterthoughts," in Melvin Ember and Carol R. Ember, *Marriage, Family, and Kinship: Comparative Studies of Social Organization*. New Haven: HRAF Press, 1983.

Ember, Melvin, and Carol R. Ember. "Male-Female Bonding: A Cross-Species Study of Mammals and Birds." *Behavior Science Research* 14 (1979): 37–56. Reprinted with "Afterthoughts," in Melvin Ember and Carol R. Ember, *Marriage, Family, and Kinship: Comparative Studies of Social Organization*. New Haven: HRAF Press, 1983.

Engels, Frederick. *The Origins of the Family, Private Property, and the State*. New York: International Publishers, 1942.

Erchak, Gerald M. "Family Violence." In *Research Frontiers in Anthropology*, eds. Carol R. Ember and Melvin Ember. Englewood Cliffs, NJ: Prentice Hall/Simon & Schuster Custom Publishers, 1995.

Erchak, Gerald M., and Richard Rosenfeld. "Societal Isolation, Violent Norms, and Gender Relations: A Reexamination and Extension of Levinson's Model of Wife Beating." *Cross-Cultural Research* 28 (1994): 111–133.

Etienne, Mona, and Eleanor Leacock, eds. *Women and Colonialization: Anthropological Perspectives*. New York: Praeger, 1980.

Etkin, William. "Social Behavior and the Evolution of Man's Mental Faculties." *American Naturalist* 88 (1954): 129–142.

Evans-Pritchard, Edward Evan. *Witchcraft, Oracles, and Magic among the Azande.* Oxford: Clarendon Press, 1937.

Fallers, Lloyd A. "Some Determinants of Marriage Stability in Bugosa." *Africa* 27 (1957): 106–121.

Finkelhor, D. *Sexually Victimized Children.* New York: Free Press, 1979.

Firth, Raymond. *We, the Tikopia: A Sociological Study of Kinship in Primitive Polynesia.* London: George Allen and Unwin, 1936.

Fjellman, Stephen M. "Hey, You Can't Do That: A Response to Divale and Harris's 'Population, Warfare, and the Male Supremacist Complex.'" *Behavior Science Research* 14 (1979): 189–200.

Flinn, Mark V. "Uterine versus Agnatic Kinship Variability and Associated Cousin Marriage Preferences: An Evolutionary Biological Analysis." In *Natural Selection and Human Social Behavior*, eds. Richard Alexander and Donald Tinkle. New York: Chiron, 1981.

Ford, Clellan S., and Frank A. Beach. *Patterns of Sexual Behavior.* New York: Harper, 1951.

Forde, Daryll. "Double Descent among the Yakö." In *African Systems of Kinship and Marriage*, eds. A. R. Radcliffe-Brown and Daryll Forde. New York: Oxford University Press, 1958 (originally published 1950).

Fortes, Meyer. "The Structure of Unilineal Descent Groups." *American Anthropologist* 55 (1953): 17–41.

Frayer, David W., and Milford H. Wolpoff. "Sexual Dimorphism." *Annual Review of Anthropology* 14 (1985): 431–432.

Frayser, Suzanne G. *Varieties of Sexual Experience: An Anthropological Perspective on Human Sexuality.* New Haven: HRAF Press, 1985.

Freud, Sigmund. *Totem and Taboo.* New York: New Republic, 1931.

Fried, K., and A. M. Davies. "Some Effects on the Offspring of Uncle-Niece Marriage in the Moroccan Jewish Community in Jerusalem." *American Journal of Human Genetics* 26 (1974): 65–72.

Fried, Morton H. "The Classification of Corporate Unilineal Descent Groups." *Journal of the Royal Anthropological Institute* 87 (1957): 1–29.

Friedman, Maurice. *Chinese Lineage and Society: Fukien and Kwangtung.* London: Athlone Press, 1966.

Friedman, Maurice. *Lineage Organization in Southeastern China.* London: Athlone Press, 1958.

Friedman, Maurice. "Ritual Aspects of Chinese Kinship and Marriage." In *Family and Kinship in Chinese Society*, ed. M. Freedman. Stanford: Stanford University Press, 1970.

Fuller, Christopher J. *The Nayars Today.* Cambridge, England: Cambridge University Press, 1976.

Gaulin, Steven J. C., and Alice Schlegel. "Paternal Confidence and Parental Investment: A Cross-Cultural Test of a Sociobiological Hypothesis." *Ethology and Sociobiology* 1 (1980): 301–309.

Gaulin, Steven J. C., and James S. Boster. "Dowry as Female Competition." *American Anthropologist* 92 (1990): 994–1005.

Gelles, Richard J., and Murray A. Straus. *Intimate Violence.* New York: Simon and Schuster, 1988.

Gilligan, Carol. *In a Different Voice: Psychological Theory and Women's Development.* Cambridge, MA: Harvard University Press, 1982.

Gladwin, Thomas, and Seymour B. Sarason. *Truk: Man in Paradise.* New York: Wenner-Gren Foundation for Anthropological Research, Viking Fund Publications in Anthropology, no. 20, 1953.

Glen, Norval, and Michael Supancic. "Sociological and Demographic Correlates of Divorce and Separation in the United States: An Update and Reconsideration." *Journal of Marriage and the Family* 46 (1984): 563–576.

Gluckman, Max. "Kinship and Marriage among the Lozi of Northern Rhodesia and the Zulu of Natal." In *African Systems of Kinship and Marriage*, eds. A. R. Radcliffe-Brown and D. Forde. Oxford: Oxford University Press, 1950.

Gluckman, Max. "The Lozi of Barotseland in North-Western Rhodesia." In *Seven Tribes of British Central Africa*, eds. Elizabeth Colson and Max Gluckman. Manchester: Manchester University Press, 1959.

Goethals, George W. "Factors Affecting Permissive and Nonpermissive Rules Regarding Premarital Sex." In *Sociology of Sex: A Book of Readings*, ed. James M. Henslin. New York: Appleton-Century-Crofts, 1971.

Goldman, Irving. *The Cubeo: Indians of the Northwest Amazon*. Urbana: University of Illinois Press, Illinois Studies in Anthropology, no. 2, 1963.

Goldstein, Melvyn C. "Culture, Population, Ecology, and Development: A View from Northwest Nepal." Paris: Proceedings of C.N.R.S. International Conference on the Ecology of the Himalayas: The Life Sciences, 1977.

Goldstein, Melvyn C. "Fraternal Polyandry and Fertility in a High Himalayan Valley in Northwest Nepal." *Human Ecology* 4 (1976): 325–337.

Goldstein, Melvyn C. "Pahari and Tibetan Polyandry Revisited." *Ethnology* 17 (1978): 325–337.

Goldstein, Melvyn C. "Population, Social Structure, and Strategic Behavior: An Essay on Polyandry, Fertility, and Change in Limi Panchayat." *Contributions to Nepalese Studies* 4 (1977): 47–52.

Goodall, Jane. *The Chimpanzees of Gombe: Patterns of Behavior*. Cambridge, MA: Harvard University Press, 1986.

Goode, William J. *The Family*. Englewood Cliffs, NJ: Prentice Hall, 1964.

Goode, William J. "Family Disorganization." In *Contemporary Social Problems*, 3rd ed., eds. Robert K. Merton and Robert Nisbet. New York: Harcourt Brace Jovanovich, 1971.

Goode, William J. "The Theoretical Importance of Romantic Love." *American Sociological Review* 24 (1959): 38–47.

Goode, William J. *World Revolution and Family Patterns*. New York: Free Press, 1963.

Goodenough, Ward H. *Property, Kin, and Community on Truk*. New Haven: Yale University Press, Yale University Publications in Anthropology, no. 46, 1951.

Goodman, Madeleine J., P. Bion Griffin, Agnes A. Estioko-Griffin, and John S. Grove. "The Compatibility of Hunting and Mothering among the Agta Hunter-Gatherers of the Philippines." *Sex Roles* 12 (1985): 1199–1209.

Goody, Jack. "Bridewealth and Dowry in Africa and Eurasia." In *Bridewealth and Dowry*, eds. Jack Goody and S. J. Tambiah. Cambridge, England: Cambridge University Press, 1973.

Goody, Jack. *Production and Reproduction*. Cambridge, England: Cambridge University Press, 1976.

Gough, Kathleen E. "The Nayars and the Definition of Marriage." In *Marriage, Family and Residence*, eds. P. Bohannan and J. Middleton. New York: Doubleday Natural History Press, 1968 (originally published 1959).

Gould, James L., and Carol Grant Gould. *Sexual Selection*. New York: Scientific American Library, 1989.

Graham, Susan Brandt. "Biology and Human Social Behavior: A Response to van den Berghe and Barash." *American Anthropologist* 81 (1979): 357–360.

Granqvist, Hilma. "Marriage Conditions in a Palestinian Village." *Helsingfors, Commenationes Humanarum, Societas Scientiarium Fennica* 3 (1931).

Gray, J. Patrick. *Primate Sociobiology*. New Haven: HRAF Press, 1985.

Gray, J. Patrick, and Rob Brubaker. "Aloof Marriage, Subsistence, and the Socialization of Boys: A Multivariate Analysis." *World Cultures* 7 (1993): 7–23.

Gray, J. Patrick, and Linda D. Wolfe. "Height and Sexual Dimorphism of Stature among Human Societies." *American Journal of Physical Anthropology* 53 (1980): 441–456.

Greenfield, Sidney M. "Industrialization and the Family in Sociological Theory." *American Journal of Sociology* 67 (1961–1962): 312–322.

Gulliver, P. H. "The Jie of Uganda." In *Man in Adaptation: The Cultural Present*, 2nd ed., ed. Y. A. Cohen. Chicago: Aldine, 1968.

Gulliver, P. H. "The Turkana." In *Man in Adaptation: The Cultural Present*, 2nd ed., ed. Y. A. Cohen. Chicago: Aldine, 1968.

Gurdon, Philip R. T. *The Khasis*. London: David Nutt, 1907.

Guttentag, Marcia, and Paul F. Secord. *Too Many Women? The Sex Ratio Question*. Beverly Hills, CA: Sage, 1983.

Hall, Judith A. *Nonverbal Sex Differences: Communication Accuracy and Expressive Style*. Baltimore: John Hopkins University Press, 1984.

Hammel, E. A. "The Family Cycle in a Coastal Peruvian Slum and Village." *American Anthropologist* 63 (1961): 989–1005.

Handwerker, W. Penn, and Paul V. Crosbie. "Sex and Dominance." *American Anthropologist* 84 (1982): 97–104.

Hanks, Jane Richardson. *Maternity and Its Rituals in Bang Chan*. Ithaca: Cornell University, Department of Asian Studies, Southeast Asia Program, Data Paper no. 51, 1964.

Hanson, Allan F. "The Rapan Theory of Conception." *American Anthropologist* 72 (1970): 1444–1447.

Hareven, Tamara K. "Modernization and Family History: Perspectives on Social Change." *Signs* 2 (1976): 190–206.

Harner, Michael J. *The Jívaro: People of the Sacred Waterfalls*. Garden City, NY: Anchor Books, 1973.

Harrel, Steven, and Sara A. Dickey. "Dowry Systems in Complex Societies." *Ethnology* 24 (1985): 105–120.

Harris, Marvin. *Culture, Man, and Nature*. New York: Thomas Y. Crowell, 1971.

Hartung, John. "Matrilineal Inheritance: New Theory and Analysis." *The Behavioral and Brain Sciences* 8 (1985): 661–688.

Havelock, Ellis. *Sexual Selection in Man*. Philadelphia: F.A. Davis, 1906.

Heath, Dwight B. "Sexual Division of Labor and Cross-Cultural Research." *Social Forces* 37 (1958): 77–79.

Heer, David M., and Amyra Grossbard-Shectman. "The Impact of the Female Marriage Squeeze and the Contraceptive Revolution on Sex Roles and the Women's Liberation Movement in the United States, 1960–1975." *Journal of Marriage and the Family* 43 (1981): 49–65.

Heise, David R. "Cultural Patterning of Sexual Socialization." *American Sociological Review* 32 (1967): 726–739.

Hendrix, Lewellyn. "Varieties of Marital Relationships." In *Cross-Cultural Research for Social Science*, eds. Carol R. Ember and Melvin Ember. Upper Saddle River, NJ: Prentice Hall/Simon & Schuster Custom Publishing, 1996.

Hendrix, Lewellyn, and Willie Pearson, Jr. "Spousal Interdependence, Female Power, and Divorce: A Cross-Cultural Examination." *Journal of Comparative Family Studies* 26 (1995): 217–232.

Hirschfeld, Lawrence, James Howe, and Bruce Levin. "Warfare, Infanticide, and Statistical Inference: A Comment on Divale and Harris." *American Anthropologist* 80 (1978): 110–115.

Hoebel, E. Adamson. *The Cheyennes: Indians of the Great Plains.* New York: Holt, Rinehart & Winston, 1960.

Hoebel, E. Adamson. *Man in the Primitive World.* New York: McGraw Hill, 1949.

Hollis, A. C. "A Note on the Masai System of Relationship." *Journal of the Royal Anthropological Institute of Great Britain and Ireland* 40 (1910): 473–482.

Holmes, W. G., and P. W. Sherman. "Kin Recognition in Animals." *American Scientist* 71 (1983): 46–55.

Homans, G., and D. M. Schneider. *Marriage, Authority, and Final Causes.* New York: Free Press, 1955.

Hopkins, Keith. "Brother-Sister Marriage in Roman Egypt." *Comparative Studies in Society and History* 22 (1980): 303–354.

Hrdy, Sarah Blaffer, and Patricia L. Whitten. "Patterning of Sexual Activity." In *Primate Societies*, eds. Barbara B. Smuts, Dorothy L. Cheney, Robert M. Seyfarth, Richard W. Wrangham, and Thomas T. Struhsaker. Chicago: University of Chicago Press, 1987.

Huber, Joan, and Glenna Spitze. "Considering Divorce: An Expansion of Becker's Theory of Marital Instability." *American Journal of Sociology* 86 (1980): 75–89.

Hunt, Morton. *Sexual Behavior in the 1970s.* Chicago: Playboy Press, 1974.

Hupka, Ralph B., and James M. Ryan. "The Cultural Contribution to Jealousy: Cross-Cultural Aggression in Sexual Jealousy Situations." *Behavior Science Research* 24 (1990): 51–71.

Hyde, Janet Shibley. "Gender Differences in Aggression." In *The Psychology of Gender: Advances through Meta-Analysis*, eds. Janet Shibley Hyde and Marcia C. Linn. Baltimore: The John Hopkins University Press, 1986.

Jacobs, Sue Ellen, and Christine Roberts. "Sex, Sexuality, Gender, and Gender Variance." In *Gender and Anthropology: Critical Reviews for Research and Teaching*, ed. Sandra Morgen. Washington, DC: American Anthropological Association, 1989.

Jankowiak, William R., ed. *Romantic Passion: A Universal Experience?* New York: Columbia University Press, 1995.

Jankowiak, William R., and Edward F. Fischer. "A Cross-Cultural Perspective on Romantic Love." *Ethnology* 31 (1992): 149–155.

Jenness, Diamond. *The Life of Copper Eskimos.* Report of the Canadian Arctic Expedition, 1913–1918, 12, part A. Ottawa: F. A. Acland, 1992.

Johnson, Erwin. "The Stem Family and Its Extension in Present Day Japan." *American Anthropologist* 66 (1964): 839–851.

Kang, Gay E. "Exogamy and Peace Relations of Social Units: A Cross-Cultural Test." *Ethnology* 18 (1979): 85–99.

Kang, Gay E., Susan Horan, and Janet Reis. "Comments on Divale and Harris's 'Population, Warfare, and the Male Supremacist Complex.'" *Behavior Science Research* 14 (1979): 201–209.

Kanin, E. J. "An Examination of Sexual Aggression as a Response to Sexual Frustration." *Journal of Marriage and the Family* 29 (1967): 428–433.

Katz, A. M., and R. Hill. "Residence Propinquity and Marital Selection: A Review of Theory, Method, and Fact." *Marriage and Family Living* 20 (1958): 27–35.

Katz, Solomon. "Brewing an Ancient Beer." *Archaeology* (July/August 1991): 24–33.

Kaufman, Howard Keva. *Bangkhuad: A Community Study in Thailand.* Locust Valley, NY: Association for Asian Studies, Monographs 10, 1960.

Kelly, Raymond C. "Witchcraft and Sexual Relations: An Exploration in the Social and Semantic Implications of the Structure of Belief." Paper presented at the annual meeting of the American Anthropological Association, Mexico City, 1974.

Kenyatta, Jomo. *Facing Mount Kenya.* New York: Random House, 1979.

Kerckoff, Alan C. "The Structure of Conjugal Relationships in Industrial Societies." In *Cross-National Family Research*, eds. Marvin B. Sussman and Betty E. Cogswell. Leiden, The Netherlands: E. J. Brill, 1972.

Kirchhoff, Paul. "The Principles of Clanship in Human Society." In *Readings in Anthropology*, vol. 2, 2nd ed., ed. M. H. Fried. New York: Thomas Y. Crowell, 1968 (originally published 1955).

Kitahara, Michio. "Men's Heterosexual Fear Due to Reciprocal Inhibition." *Ethos* 9 (1981): 37–50.

Knez, Eugene I. "Sam Jong Dong: A South Korean Village." Ph.D. diss., Syracuse University, 1959, University Microfilms Publication no. 59–6308. Ann Arbor: University Microfilms, 1960.

Knox, Robert. *An Historical Relation of Ceylon, 1681*, cited in Nur Yalman, *Under the Bo Tree: Studies in Casto, Kinship, and Marriage in the Interior of Ceylon*. Berkeley: University of California Press, 1971.

Korbin, Jill E. "Introduction." In *Child Abuse and Neglect: Cross-Cultural Perspectives*, ed. Jill E. Korbin. Berkeley: University of California Press, 1981.

Kortmulder, K. "An Ethological Theory of the Incest Taboo and Exogamy." *Current Anthropology* 9 (1968): 437–449.

Kroeber, Alfred. *The Nature of Culture*. Chicago: University of Chicago Press, 1952.

Kunstadter, Peter. "A Survey of the Consanguine or Matrifocal Family." *American Anthropologist* 65 (1963): 56–66.

LaBarre, W. "The Aymara Indians of the Lake Titicaca Plateau, Bolivia." *Memoirs of the American Anthropological Association* 68 (1948): 1–250.

Lagae, C. R. *Les Azande ou Niam-Niam: L'organisation Zande, Croyances Religieuses et Magiques, Coutomes Familiales* [*The Azande or Niam-Niam: Zande Organization, Religious and Magical Beliefs, Family Customs*]. Bibliotheque-Congo, XVIII. Bruxelles: Vromant and Company, 1926.

Lancaster, Jane B. "Sex Roles in Primate Societies." In *Sex Differences: Social and Biological Perspectives*, ed. Michael S. Teitelbaum. Garden City, NY: Anchor Books, 1976.

Lancaster, Jane B., and Chet Lancaster. "Paternal Investment: The Hominid Adaptation." In *How Humans Adapt: A Biocultural Odyssey*, ed. D. Ortner. Washington, DC: Smithsonian Institution, 1983.

Land, Kenneth, and Marcus Felson. "A Dynamic Macro Social Indicator Model of Changes in Marriage, Family, and Population in the U.S.: 1947–1974." *Social Science Research* 6 (1977): 328–362.

Landes, Ruth. *The Ojibwa Woman*. New York: Columbia University Press, 1938.

Leach, Edmund R. "Aspects of Bridewealth and Marriage Stability among Kachin and Lakher." *Man* 57 (1957): 50–55.

Leach, Edmund R. "Concerning Trobriand Clans and the Kinship Category Tabu." In *The Developmental Cycle in Domestic Groups*, ed. Jack Goody. Cambridge, England: Cambridge University Press, 1971.

Leach, Edmund R. "The Structural Implications of Matrilateral Cross-Cousin Marriage." In *Rethinking Anthropology*, ed. Edmund R. Leach. London: The Athlone Press, 1961.

Leakey, L. S. B. "Some Notes on the Masai of Kenya Colony." *Journal of the Royal Anthropological Institute of Great Britain and Ireland* 60 (1930): 185–209.

Leavitt, Gregory C. "Inbreeding Fitness: A Reply to Uhlmann." *American Anthropologist* 94 (1992): 448–450.

Leavitt, Gregory C. "Sociobiological Explanations of Incest Avoidance: A Critical Review of Evidential Claims." *American Anthropologist* 92 (1990): 971–993.

Leavitt, Gregory C. "Sociobiology and Incest Avoidance: A Critical Look at a Critical Review Critique." *American Anthropologist* 94 (1992): 932–934.

Lee, Gary R. *Family Structure and Interaction: A Comparative Analysis*, 2nd ed. Minneapolis: University of Minnesota Press, 1982.

Lee, Gary R. "Marital Structure and Economic Systems." *Journal of Marriage and the Family* 41 (1979): 701–713.

Lee, Gary R., and Lorene Hemphill Stone. "Mate-Selection Systems and Criteria: Variation According to Family Structure." *Journal of Marriage and the Family* 42 (1980): 319–326.

Lee, Richard B. "Kung Bushmen Subsistence: An Input-Output Analysis." In *Environmental and Cultural Behavior*, ed. Andrew P. Vayda. New York: Doubleday Natural History Press, 1969.

Lévi-Strauss, Claude. *The Elementary Structures of Kinship*. Boston: Beacon Press, 1949.

Lévi-Strauss, Claude. *Structural Anthropology*. New York: Basic Books, 1963.

Levine, Nancy E. "Women's Work and Infant Feeding: A Case from Rural Nepal." *Ethnology* 27 (1988): 231–251.

Levins, R. *Evolution in Changing Environments: Some Theoretical Explorations*. Princeton, NJ: Princeton University Press, 1968.

Levinson, David. *Family Violence in Cross-Cultural Perspective*. Newbury Park, CA: Sage, 1989.

Levy, M. J., and L. A. Fallers. "The Family: Some Comparative Considerations." *American Anthropologist* 61 (1959): 647–651.

Lewin, Tamar. "Family Decay Global, Study Says: Troubled Households Are Not Just a U.S. Phenomenon." *New York Times International*, May 30, 1995.

Lewin, Tamar. "Sex in America: Faithfulness in Marriage Is Overwhelming." *New York Times National*, October 7, 1994, pp. A1, A18.

Lewis, Oscar. *Life in a Mexican Village: Tepoztlan Revisited*. Urbana: University of Illinois Press, 1951.

Lichter, Daniel T., Diane Kay McLaughlin, George Kephart, and David J. Landry. "Race and the Retreat from Marriage: A Shortage of Marriageable Men?" *American Sociological Review* 57 (1992): 781–799.

Lindenbaum, Shirley. "Sorcerers, Ghosts, and Polluting Women: An Analysis of Religious Belief and Population Control." *Ethnology* 11 (1972): 241–253.

Lindzey, Gardner. "Some Remarks Concerning Incest, the Incest Taboo, and Psychoanalytic Theory." *American Psychologist* 22 (1967): 1051–1059.

Linn, Marcia C., and A. Petersen. "A Meta-Analysis of Gender Differences in Spatial Ability: Implications for Mathematics and Science Achievement." In *The Psychology of Gender: Advances through Meta-Analysis*, eds. Janet Shibley Hyde and Marcia C. Linn. Baltimore: John Hopkins University Press, 1986.

Linton, Ralph. "The Natural History of the Family." In *Readings in Anthropology*, vol. 2., 2nd ed., ed. M. H. Fried. New York: Thomas Y. Crowell, 1968 (originally published 1947).

Linton, Ralph. *The Study of Man*. New York: Appleton-Century-Crofts, 1936.

Lovejoy, C. O. "The Origin of Man." *Science*, January 23, 1982, pp. 341–350.

Low, Bobbi S. "Marriage Systems and Pathogen Stress in Human Societies." *American Zoologist* 30 (1990): 325–339.

Low, Bobbi S. "Plural Marriages." In *Encyclopedia of Cultural Anthropology*, vol. 3, eds. David Levinson and Melvin Ember. New York: Henry Holt, 1996.

Lowie, Robert H. *Primitive Society*. New York: Harper, 1961 (originally published 1920).

Lowie, Robert H. *Social Organization*. New York: Rinehart & Company, 1956.

McCabe, J. "FBD Marriage: Further Support for the Westermarck Hypothesis of the Incest Taboo?" *American Anthropologist* 85 (1983): 50–69.

Maccoby, Eleanor E., and Carol N. Jacklin. *The Psychology of Sex Differences*. Stanford, CA: Stanford University Press, 1974.

McDowell, Nancy. "Mundugumor: Sex and Temperament Revisited." In *Portraits of Culture: Ethnographic Originals*, eds. Melvin Ember, Carol R. Ember, and David Levinson. Englewood Cliffs, NJ: Prentice Hall/Simon & Schuster Custom Publishing, 1994.

Macionis, John J. *Sociology*, 4th ed. Englewood Cliffs, NJ: Prentice Hall, 1993.

Mair, Lucy P. *An African People in the Twentieth Century*. London: George Routledge and Sons, 1934.

Malinowski, Bronislaw. *Argonauts of the Western Pacific: An Account of Native Enterprise and Adventure in the Archipelagoes of Melanesian New Guinea*. London: George Routledge and Sons, Ltd., 1922.

Malinowski, Bronislaw. *Coral Gardens and Their Magic*, vol. 1. New York: American Book Company, 1935.

Malinowski, Bronislaw. *A Scientific Theory of Culture*. New York: Oxford University Press, 1960 (originally published 1944).

Malinowski, Bronislaw. *The Sexual Life of Savages*. London: George Rutledge, 1929.

Malinowski, Bronislaw. *The Sexual Life of Savages in Northwestern Melanesia*, vol. I and II. New York: Horace Liveright, 1929.

Martin, M. Kay, and Barbara Voorhies. *Female of the Species*. New York: Columbia University Press, 1975.

Masters, William M. "Rowanduz: A Kurdish Administrative and Mercantile Center." Ph.D. diss., University of Michigan, 1953.

May, R. M. "When to Be Incestuous." *Nature* 279 (1979): 192–194.

Mead, Margaret. *Sex and Temperament in Three Primitive Societies*. New York: New American Library, 1950 (originally published 1935).

Meggitt, M. J. *Blood Is Their Argument: Warfare among the Mae Enga Tribesmen of the New Guinea Highlands*. Palo Alto, CA: Mayfield Publishing Company, 1977.

Meggitt, M. J. "Male-Female Relationships in the Highlands of Australian New Guinea." *American Anthropologist* 66, no. 4 (1964): 204–322.

Michael, Robert T., John H. Gagnon, Edward O. Laumann, and Gina Kolata. *Sex in America: A Definitive Survey*. Boston: Little, Brown and Co., 1994.

Middleton, Russell. "Brother-Sister and Father-Daughter Marriage in Ancient Egypt." *American Sociological Review* 27 (1962): 603–611.

Miller, Bruce G. "Women and Politics: Comparative Evidence from the Northwest Coast." *Ethnology* 31 (1992): 367–382.

Moore, Frank W., ed. *Readings in Cross-Cultural Methodology*. New Haven: HRAF Press, 1961.

Moore, Jim. "Sociobiology and Incest Avoidance: A Critical Look at a Critical Review." *American Anthropologist* 94 (1992): 929–934.

Moore, Jim and Rauf Ali. "Are Dispersal and Inbreeding Avoidance Related?" *Animal Behavior* 32 (1984): 94–112.

Morgan, Louis Henry. *Systems of Consanguinity and Affinity of the Human Family*. Washington DC: Smithsonian Institution, 1870.

Morgan, Phillip S., and Ronald R. Rindfuss. "Marital Disruption: Structural and Temporal Dimensions." *American Journal of Sociology* 90 (1985): 1055–1077.

Morris, Desmond. *The Naked Ape*. New York: McGraw-Hill, 1967.

Morris, H. S. "The Indian Family in Uganda." *American Anthropologist* 61 (1959): 779–789.

Mukherjea, Charulal. *The Santals*. Calcutta: A. Mukherjee and Co., 1962.

Mukhopadhyay, Carol C. and Patricia J. Higgins. "Anthropological Studies of Women's Status Revisited: 1977–1987." *Annual Review of Anthropology* 17 (1988): 473.

Muller, Jean-Claude. "On Preferential/Prescriptive Marriage and the Function of Kinship Systems: The Rukuba Case (Benue-Plateau Site, Nigeria)." *American Anthropologist* 75 (1973): 1563–1576.

Munroe, Robert et al. "Sex Differences in East African Dreams." *Journal of Social Psychology* 125 (1985): 405–406.

Munroe, Robert L., John W. M. Whiting, and David J. Hally. "Institutionalized Male Transvestism and Sex Distinctions." *American Anthropologist* 71 (1969): 87–91.

Munroe, Ruth H., Robert L. Munroe, and Anne Brasher. "Precursors of Spatial Ability: A Longitudinal Study among the Logoli of Kenya." *Journal of Social Psychology* 125 (1985): 23–33.

Munson, Martha L., and Larry L. Bumpass. "Determinants of Cumulative Fertility in Upper Volta, West Africa." *Working Paper* 73–76, mimeo. Madison: University of Wisconsin, 1973.

Murdock, George Peter. *Ethnographic Atlas*. Pittsburgh: University of Pittsburgh Press, 1967.

Murdock, George Peter. *Social Structure*. New York: The Free Press, 1965 (originally published 1949).

Murdock, George Peter. "World Ethnographic Sample." In *Readings in Cross-Cultural Methodology*, ed. Frank W. Moore. New Haven: HRAF Press, 1961 (originally published 1957).

Murdock, George Peter, and Catarina Provost. "Factors in the Division of Labor by Sex: A Cross-Cultural Analysis." *Ethnology* 12 (1973): 203–225.

Murdock, George Peter, and John W. M. Whiting. "Cultural Determination of Parental Attitudes: The Relationship between Social Structure, Particularly Family Structure, and Parental Behavior." In *Problems of Infancy and Childhood*, ed. Milton J. E. Senn. New York: Josiah Macy Jr. Foundation, 1951.

Murphy, Robert F., and Leonard Kasdan. "The Structure of Parallel Cousin Marriage." *American Anthropologist* 61 (1959): 17–29.

Nadler, Ronald D., and Charles H. Phoenix. "Male Sexual Behavior: Monkeys, Men, and Apes." In *Understanding Behavior: What Primate Studies Tell Us about Human Behavior*, eds. James D. Loy and Calvin B. Peters. New York: Oxford University Press, 1991.

Nag, Moni. *Factors Affecting Human Fertility in Nonindustrial Societies: A Cross-Cultural Study*. New Haven: Yale University Press, 1962.

Nag, Moni. "Marriage and Kinship in Relation to Human Fertility." In *Population and Social Organization*, ed. Moni Nag. The Hague: Mouton, 1975.

Needham, R. *Structure and Sentiment*. Chicago: University of Chicago Press, 1962.

Nerlove, Sara B. "Women's Workload and Infant Feeding Practices: A Relationship with Demographic Implications." *Ethnology* 13 (1974): 207–214.

Nimkoff, Meyer F., ed. *Comparative Family Systems*. Boston: Houghton Mifflin, 1965.

Nimkoff, Meyer F., and Russell Middleton. "Types of Family and Types of Economy." *American Journal of Sociology* 66 (1960): 215–225.

Oberg, Kalvero. "Crime and Punishment in Tlingit Society." *American Anthropologist* 36 (1934): 145–155.

Oboler, Regina Smith. "Nandi: From Cattle-Keepers to Cash-Crop Farmers." In *Portraits of Culture: Ethnographic Originals*, eds. Melvin Ember, Carol R. Ember, and David Levinson. Englewood Cliffs, NJ: Prentice Hall/Simon & Schuster Custom Publishing, 1994.

Ogburn, William F., and Meyer Nimkoff. *Technology and the Changing Family*. Boston: Houghton Mifflin, 1955.

Olsen, Nancy Johnston. "The Effect of Household Composition on the Child Rearing Practices of Taiwanese Families." Ph.D. diss., Cornell University, University Microfilms Publications no. 71–22. Ann Arbor: University Microfilms, 1983.

Opler, Morris Edward. *An Apache Life-Way: The Economic, Social, and Religious Institutions of the Chiricahua Indians*. Chicago: University of Chicago Press, 1941.

Otterbein, Keith. "Caribbean Family Organization: A Comparative Analysis." *American Anthropologist* 67 (1965): 66–79.

Otterbein, Keith. "The Developmental Cycle of the Andros Household: A Diachronic Analysis." *American Anthropologist* 72 (1970): 1412–1419.

Parker, Hilda, and Seymour Parker. "Father-Daughter Sexual Abuse: An Emerging Perspective." *American Journal of Orthopsychiatry* 56 (1986): 531–549.

Parker, Seymour. "Cultural Rules, Rituals, and Behavior Regulation." *American Anthropologist* 86 (1984): 584–600.

Parker, Seymour. "The Precultural Basis of the Incest Taboo: Toward a Biosocial Theory." *American Anthropologist* 78 (1976): 285–305.

Parker, Seymour. "The Waning of the Incest Taboo." *Legal Studies Forum* 11, no. 2 (1987): 205–221.

Parsons, Talcott. "The American Family: Its Relations to Personality and to the Social Structure." In *Family, Socialization, and Interaction Process*, eds. Talcott Parsons and R. F. Bales. New York: Free Press, 1955.

Pasternak, Burton. "The Disquieting Chinese Lineage and Its Anthropological Relevance." In *The Chinese Family and Its Ritual Behavior*, eds. Hsieh Jih-chang and Chuang Ying-chang. Nanking, Taiwan: Institute of Ethnology, Academia Sinica, 1985.

Pasternak, Burton. *Guests in the Dragon: Social Demography of a Chinese District, 1895–1946.* New York: Columbia University Press, 1983.

Pasternak, Burton. *Introduction to Kinship and Social Organization.* Englewood Cliffs, NJ: Prentice Hall, 1976.

Pasternak, Burton. *Kinship and Community in Two Chinese Villages.* Stanford: Stanford University Press, 1972.

Pasternak, Burton. "Seasons of Birth and Marriage in Two Chinese Localities." *Human Ecology* 6 (1978): 299–323.

Pasternak, Burton, Carol R. Ember, and Melvin Ember. "On the Conditions Favoring Extended Family Households." *Journal of Anthropological Research* 32 (1976): 109–123. Reprinted with "Afterthoughts," in Melvin Ember and Carol R. Ember, *Marriage, Family, and Kinship: Comparative Studies of Social Organization.* New Haven: HRAF Press, 1983.

Paulme, Denise. *Organisation Sociale Des Dogon (Soudan Francais)* [*Social Organization of the Dogon (French Sudan)*]. Paris: Editions Domat-Montchrestien, F. Loviton et Cie., 1940.

Pearson, Jr., Willie, and Lewellyn Hendrix. "Divorce and the Status of Women." *Journal of Marriage and the Family* 41 (1979): 375–385.

Potter, Jack. *Capitalism and the Chinese Peasant.* Berkeley: University of California Press, 1968.

Pusey, Anne E. "Inbreeding Avoidance in Chimpanzees." *Animal Behavior* 28 (1980): 543–582.

Quinn, Naomi. "Anthropological Studies on Women's Status." *Annual Review of Anthropology* 6 (1977): 181–225.

Radcliffe-Brown, A. R. *Structure and Function in Primitive Society.* New York: Free Press, 1952.

Rattray, R. S. *Ashanti Law and Constitution.* Oxford: The Clarendon Press, 1929.

Read, A. F., and P. H. Harvey. "Genetic Relatedness and the Evolution of Animal Mating Patterns." In *Human Mating Patterns*, eds. C. G. N. Mascie-Taylor and A. J. Boyce. Cambridge, England: Cambridge University Press, 1988.

Reichel-Dolmatoff, Gerardo. *Los Kogi: Una Tribu de la Sierra Nevada de Santa Marta, Columbia, Toma II* [*The Kogi: A Tribe of the Sierra Nevada de Santa Marta, Columbia, vol. II*]. Bogota: Editorial Iqueima (translated from the Spanish for the Human Relations Area Files by Sydney Muirden), 1951.

Richards, Audrey I. *Chisungu. A Girl's Initiation Ceremony among the Bemba of Northern Rhodesia.* London: Faber and Faber, 1956.

Ritter, Madeline Lattman. "The Conditions Favoring Age-Set Organization." *Journal of Anthropological Research* 36 (1980): 87–104.

Rivers, W. H. R. *The Todas.* Oosterhout, N.B., The Netherlands: Anthropological Publications, 1967 [originally published in 1906].

Robinson, Marguerite S. "Complementary Filiation and Marriage in the Trobriand Islands." In *Marriage in Tribal Societies*, ed. Meyer Fortes. Cambridge, England: Cambridge University Press, 1972.

Rohner, Ronald. "Sex Differences in Aggression: Phylogenetic and Enculturation Perspectives." *Ethos* 4 (1976): 58–72.

Rosen, Bernard C., and Manoel T. Berlinck. "Modernization and Family Structure in the Region of São Paulo, Brazil." *America Latina* 11 (1968): 96.

Rosenblatt, Paul C., and Paul C. Cozby. "Courtship Patterns Associated with Freedom of Choice of Spouse." *Journal of Marriage and the Family* 34 (1972): 689–695.

Rosenfeld, Henry. "An Analysis of Marriage Statistics for a Moslem and Christian Arab Village." *International Archives of Ethnography* 48 (1957): 32–62.

Ross, Heather L., and Isabel V. Sawhill. *Time of Transition: The Growth of Families Headed by Women.* Washington, DC: Urban Institute, 1975.

Ross, Marc Howard. "Female Political Participation: A Cross-Cultural Explanation." *American Anthropologists* 88 (1986): 843–858.

Rowell, Thelma E. *Social Behavior of Monkeys.* Harmondsworth, England: Penguin Books, 1972.

Rubin, J. Z., F. J. Provenzano, and R. G. Haskett. "The Eye of the Beholder: Parents' Views on the Sex of New Borns." *American Journal of Orthopsychiatry* 44 (1974): 512–519.

Russell, D. E. H. *Sexual Exploitation.* Beverly Hills: Sage Publications, 1984.

Sahlins, Marshall D. "Origin of Society." *Scientific American* (September 1960): 76–86.

Sahlins, Marshall D. "The Segmentary Lineage: An Organization of Predatory Expansion." *American Anthropologist* 63 (1961): 322–345.

Sahlins, Marshall D. *Stone Age Economics.* Chicago: Aldine, 1972.

Sanday, Peggy R. "Female Status in the Public Domain." In *Woman, Culture, and Society*, eds. Michelle Z. Rosaldo and Louise Lamphere. Stanford, CA: Stanford University Press, 1974.

Sanday, Peggy R. "Toward a Theory of the Status of Women." *American Anthropologist* 75 (1973): 1682–1700.

Savage-Rumbaugh, E. Sue. "Hominid Evolution: Looking to Modern Apes for Clues." In *Hominid Culture in Primate Perspective*, eds. Duane Quiatt and Junichiro Itani. Niwot, CO: University Press of Colorado, 1994.

Scaglion, Richard, and Rose Whittingham. "Female Plaintiffs and Sex-Related Disputes in Rural Papua New Guinea." In *Domestic Violence in Papua New Guinea*, monograph no. 3, ed. S. Toft. Port Moresby, Papua New Guinea: Law Reform Commission, 1985.

Scanzoni, John. "A Historical Perspective on Husband-Wife Bargaining Power and Marital Dissolution." In *Divorce and Separation*, eds. George Levinger and O. C. Moles. New York: Basic Books, 1979.

Scanzoni, John. "A Reinquiry into Marital Disorganization." *Journal of Marriage and the Family* 27 (1965): 483–491.

Scanzoni, John. *Sexual Bargaining: Power Politics in the American Marriage.* Englewood Cliffs, NJ: Prentice Hall, 1972.

Schlegel, Alice. *Male Dominance and Female Autonomy.* New Haven: HRAF Press, 1972.

Schlegel, Alice. "Status, Property, and the Value on Virginity." *American Ethnologist* 18 (1991): 719–734.

Schlegel, Alice. "The Status of Women." In *Cross-Cultural Research for Social Science*, eds. Carol R. Ember and Melvin Ember. Upper Saddle River, NJ: Prentice Hall/Simon & Schuster Custom Publishing, 1996.

Schlegel, Alice, and Herbert Barry III. *Adolescence: An Anthropological Inquiry.* New York: Free Press, 1991.

Schlegel, Alice, and Herbert Barry III. "The Cultural Consequences of Female Contribution to Subsistence." *American Anthropologist* 88 (1986): 142–150.

Schlegel, Alice, and Rohn Eloul. "Marriage Transactions: Labor, Property, Status." *American Anthropologist* 90 (1988): 291–309.

Schlesinger, Jr., Arthur M. *The Disuniting of America: Reflections on a Multicultural Society.* New York: W. W. Norton & Company, 1992.

Schneider, David M. "The Distinctive Features of Matrilineal Descent Groups." In *Matrilineal Kinship*, eds. David M. Schneider and Kathleen Gough. Berkeley: University of California Press, 1961.

Schneider, David M. "Truk." In *Matrilineal Kinship*, eds. David M. Schneider and Kathleen Gough. Berkeley: University of California Press, 1961.

Schneider, Jane. "Of Vigilance and Virgins: Honor, Shame, and Access to Resources in Mediterranean Societies." *Ethnology* 10 (1971): 1–24.

Schroeder, Theodore. "Incest in Mormonism." *American Journal of Urology and Sexology* 11 (1915): 415.

Seccombe, Karen, and Gary R. Lee. "Female Status, Wives' Autonomy, and Divorce: A Cross-Cultural Study." *Family Perspectives* 20 (1987): 241–249.

Segall, Marshall H., Carol R. Ember, and Melvin Ember. "Aggression, Crime, and Warfare." In *Handbook of Cross-Cultural Psychology, Volume 3, Social Behavior and Applications*, 2nd ed., eds. J. W. Berry, M. H. Segall, and C. Kagitcibasi. Boston: Allyn and Bacon, in press.

Seligman, Charles Gabriel, and Brenda Z. Seligman. *Pagan Tribes of the Nilotic Sudan.* London: George Routledge and Sons, Ltd., 1932.

Service, Elman R. *Primitive Social Organization.* New York: Random House, 1962.

Shapiro, Harry L. "The Family." In *Man, Culture, and Society*, ed. Harry L. Shapiro. New York: Oxford University Press, 1956.

Shepher, Joseph. *Incest: A Biosocial View.* New York: Academic Press, 1983.

Shepher, Joseph. "Mate Selection among Second Generation Kibbutz Adolescents and Adults: Incest Avoidance and Negative Imprinting." *Archives of Sexual Behavior* 1 (1971): 293–307.

Shimony, Annemarie Anrod. *Conservatism among the Iroquois at the Six Nations Reserve.* New Haven, CT: Yale University Publications in Anthropology, Yale University, 1961.

Silverman, Irwin, and Krista Philips. "Effects of Estrogen Changes during the Menstrual Cycle on Spatial Performance." *Ethology and Sociobiology* 14 (1993): 257–269.

Simons, Marlise. "African Women in France Battling Polygamy." *The New York Times International*, January 26, 1996, pp. A1, A6.

Skinner, William G. "Marketing and Social Structure in Rural China." *Journal of Asian Studies* 24 (1964–1965): 3–43, 195–228, 363–399.

Slater, Miriam. "Ecological Factors in the Origin of Incest." *American Anthropologist* 61 (1959): 1042–1059.

Small, Meredith F. *Female Choices.* Ithaca, NY: Cornell University Press, 1993.

Smith, Arthur. *Village Life in China.* Boston: Little, Brown and Company, 1970 (originally published 1899).

Smith, Carol A., ed. *Regional Analysis*. New York: Academic Press, 1976.

Smith, Raymond T. *The Negro Family in British Guiana*. London: Routledge and Kegan Paul, 1956.

Smuts, Barbara B. "Gender, Aggression, and Influence." In *Primate Societies*, eds. Barbara B. Smuts, Dorothy L. Cheney, Robert M. Seyfarth, Richard W. Wrangham, and Thomas T. Struhsaker. Chicago: University of Chicago Press, 1987.

Smuts, Barbara B. "Sexual Competition and Mate Choice." In *Primate Societies*, eds. Barbara B. Smuts, Dorothy L. Cheney, Robert M. Seyfarth, Richard W. Wrangham, and Thomas T. Struhsaker. Chicago: University of Chicago Press, 1987.

Solien de Gonzales, Nancy L. "The Consanguineal Household and Matrifocality." *American Anthropologist* 67 (1965): 1541–1549.

South, Scott J. "Economic Conditions and the Divorce Rate: A Time-Series Analysis of the Post-War United States." *Journal of Marriage and the Family* 47 (1985): 31–41.

South, Scott J., and Glenna Spritze. "Determinants of Divorce over the Marital Life Course." *American Sociological Review* 51 (1986): 583–590.

Spencer, Herbert. *Principles of Sociology*, vol. 1. London: Appleton, 1876. As referred to by Robert L. Carneiro in his preface to *The Evolution of Society: Selections from Herbert Spencer's Principles of Sociology*, ed. Robert L. Carneiro. Chicago: University of Chicago Press, 1967.

Spiro, Melford E. *Children of the Kibbutz*. Cambridge, MA: Harvard University Press, 1958.

Spiro, Melford E. *Gender and Culture: Kibbutz Women Revisited*. Durham: Duke University Press, 1979.

Spiro, Melford E. "Is the Family Universal? The Israeli Case." *American Anthropologist* 56 (1954): 839–846.

Spiro, Melford E. *Oedipus in the Trobriands*. Chicago: University of Chicago Press, 1982.

St. Erlich, Vera. *Family in Transition: A Study of 300 Yugoslav Villages*. Princeton, NJ: Princeton University Press, 1966.

Stack, Carol. "Domestic Networks: 'Those You Count On.'" In *Gender in Cross-Cultural Perspective*, eds. Caroline B. Brettell and Carolyn F. Sargent. Englewood Cliffs, NJ: Prentice Hall, 1993.

Stephens, William N. "A Cross-Cultural Study of Menstrual Taboos." *Genetic Psychology Monographs* 64 (1961): 385–416.

Stephens, William N. "A Cross-Cultural Study of Modesty." *Behavior Science Research* 7 (1972): 1–28.

Stephens, William N. *The Family in Cross-Cultural Perspective*. New York: Holt, Rinehart & Winston, 1963.

Stephens, William N. *The Oedipus Complex: Cross-Cultural Evidence*. Glencoe, IL: Free Press, 1962.

Stimpson, David, Larry Jensen, and Wayne Neff. "Cross-Cultural Gender Differences in Preference for a Caring Morality." *Journal of Social Psychology* 132 (1992): 317–322.

Stini, William A. "Evolutionary Implications of Changing Nutritional Patterns in Human Populations." *American Anthropologist* 73 (1971): 1019–1030.

Stogdill, Ralph M. *Handbook of Leadership: A Survey of Theory and Research*. New York: Macmillan, 1974.

Straus, Murray A. "Physical Violence in American Families: Incidence Rates, Causes, and Trends." In *Abused and Battered: Social and Legal Responses to Family Violence*, eds. Dean D. Knudsen and JoAnn L. Miller. New York: Aldine de Gruyter, 1991.

Strickon, Arnold. "Class and Kinship in Argentina." *Ethnology* 1 (1962): 500–515.

Talmon, Yonina. "Mate Selection in Collective Settlements." *American Sociological Review* 29 (1964): 491–508.

Textor, Robert B., comp. *A Cross-Cultural Summary*. New Haven: HRAF Press, 1967.

Tinbergen, Niko. *The Animal in Its World*, vol. 2. London: Allen and Unwin, 1973.

Titiev, Mischa. "The Influence of Common Residence on the Unilateral Classification of Kindred." *American Anthropologist* 45 (1943): 511–530.

Titiev, Mischa. *Old Oraibi: A Study of the Hopi Indians of Third Mesa*. Harvard University, Peabody Museum of American Archaeology and Ethnology, Papers 22, no. 1. New York: Kraus Reprint Co., 1971.

Topley, Majorie. "Ghost Marriages among the Singapore Chinese." *Man* 35 (1955): 29–30.

Topley, Majorie. "Ghost Marriages among the Singapore Chinese: A Further Note." *Man* 63 (1956): 71–72.

Trent, Katherine, and Scott J. South. "Structural Determinants of the Divorce Rate: A Cross-Societal Analysis." *Journal of Marriage and the Family* 51 (1989): 391–404.

Trivers, R. L. "Parental Investment and Sexual Selection." In *Sexual Selection and the Descent of Man 1871–1971*, ed. B. Campbell. Chicago: Aldine, 1972.

Tschopik, Jr., Harry. "The Aymara of Chucuito, Peru." *Anthropological Papers of the American Museum of Natural History* 44 (1951): 133–308.

Turke, Paul W. "Effects of Ovulatory Concealment and Synchrony on Protohominid Mating Systems and Parental Roles." *Ethology and Sociobiology* 5 (1984): 33–44.

Turnbull, Colin M. "The Mbuti Pygmies: An Ethnographic Survey." *Anthropological Papers of the American Museum of Natural History* 50 (1965): 139–282.

Turnbull, Colin M. *Wayward Servants: The Two Worlds of the African Pygmies*. Garden City, NY: The Natural History Press, 1965.

Tylor, E. B. "On a Method of Investigating the Development of Institutions: Applied to Laws of Marriage and Descent." *Journal of the Royal Anthropological Institute* 18 (1888): 245–269.

Uhlmann, Allon J. "A Critique of Leavitt's Review of Sociobiological Explanations of Incest Avoidance." *American Anthropologist* 94 (1992): 446–448.

Underhill, Ruth Murray. *Social Organization of the Papago Indians*. New York: Columbia University Press, 1939.

Unnithan, N. Prabha. "Nayars: Tradition and Change in Marriage and Family." In *Portraits of Culture: Ethnographic Originals*, eds. Melvin Ember, Carol R. Ember, and David Levinson. Englewood Cliffs, NJ: Prentice Hall/Simon & Schuster Custom Publishing, 1994.

Van den Berghe, P. L., and D. Barash. "Inclusive Fitness and Human Family Structure." *American Anthropologist* 79 (1977): 809–823.

Van den Berghe, P. L., and G. M. Mesher. "Royal Incest and Inclusive Fitness." *American Ethnologist* 7 (1980): 300–317.

Weiner, Annette B. *The Trobrianders of Papua New Guinea*. New York: Holt, Rinehart & Winston, 1988.

Werner, Dennis W. "Chiefs and Presidents: A Comparison of Leadership Traits in the United States and among the Mekranoti-Kayapo of Central Brazil." *Ethos* 10 (1982): 136–148.

Werner, Dennis W. "Child Care and Influence among the Mekranoti of Central Brazil." *Sex Roles* 10 (1984): 395–404.

Werner, Dennis W. "A Cross-Cultural Perspective on Theory and Research on Male Homosexuality." *Journal of Homosexuality* 4 (1979): 345–362.

Werner, Dennis W. "The Making of a Mekranoti Chief: The Psychological and Social Determinants of Leadership in a Native South American Society." Ph.D. diss., City University of New York, 1980.

Werner, Dennis W. "On the Societal Acceptance or Rejection of Male Homosexuality." M.A. thesis, Hunter College of the City University of New York, 1975.

Westermarck, Edward. *The History of Human Marriage.* London: Macmillan, 1922.

White, Douglas R. "On the Explanation of Polygyny: Additional Source Materials." *Current Anthropology* 31 (1990): 313.

White, Douglas R. "Rethinking Polygyny: Co-Wives, Codes, and Cultural Systems." *Current Anthropology* 29 (1988): 529–558.

White, Douglas R., and Michael Burton. "Causes of Polygyny: Ecology, Economy, Kinship, and Warfare." *American Anthropologist* 90 (1988): 871–887.

White, Douglas R., Michael Burton, and Malcolm M. Dow. "Sexual Division of Labor in African Agriculture: A Network Autocorrelation Analysis." *American Anthropologist* 83 (1981): 824–849.

White, Douglas R., Michael L. Burton, and Lilyan A. Brudner. "Entailment Theory and Method: A Cross-Cultural Analysis of the Sexual Division of Labor." *Behavior Science Research* 12 (1977): 1–24.

White, Leslie A. *The Science of Culture.* New York: Grove Press, 1949.

Whiting, Beatrice B. "Sex Identity Conflict and Physical Violence: A Comparative Study." *American Anthropologist* 67 (1965): 123–140.

Whiting, Beatrice B., and Carolyn P. Edwards. *Children of Different Worlds: The Formation of Social Behavior.* Cambridge, MA: Harvard University Press, 1988.

Whiting, Beatrice B., and Carolyn P. Edwards. "A Cross-Cultural Analysis of Sex Differences in the Behavior of Children Aged Three through Eleven." *Journal of Social Psychology* 91 (1973): 171–188.

Whiting, Beatrice B., and John W. M. Whiting, in collaboration with Richard Longabaugh. *Children of Six Cultures: A Psycho-Cultural Analysis.* Cambridge, MA: Harvard University Press, 1975.

Whiting, John W. M. "Cultural and Sociological Influences on Development." In *Growth and Development of the Child in His Setting.* Maryland Child Growth and Development Institute, 1959.

Whiting, John W. M. "Effects of Climate on Certain Cultural Practices." In *Explorations in Cultural Anthropology: Essays in Honor of George Peter Murdock,* ed. Ward H. Goodenough. New York: McGraw Hill, 1964.

Whiting, John W. M. "The Effect of Polygyny on Sex Ratio at Birth." *American Anthropologist* 95 (1993): 435–442.

Whiting, John W. M., and Beatrice B. Whiting. "Aloofness and Intimacy of Husbands and Wives: A Cross-Cultural Study." *Ethos* 3 (1975): 183–207.

Whiting, John W. M., Victoria K. Burbank, and Mitchell S. Ratner. "The Duration of Maidenhood across Cultures." In *School Age Pregnancy and Parenthood: Biosocial Dimensions,* eds. Jane B. Lancaster and Beatrix A. Hamburg. New York: Aldine De Gruyter, 1986.

Whyte, Martin K. "Cross-Cultural Codes Dealing with the Relative Status of Women." *Ethnology* 17 (1978): 229–232.

Whyte, Martin K. *The Status of Women in Preindustrial Societies.* Princeton, NJ: Princeton University Press, 1978.

Williams, G. C. *Sex and Evolution.* Princeton, NJ: Princeton University Press, 1975.

Williams, Walter L. "Amazons of America: Female Gender Variance." In *Gender in Cross-Cultural Perspective,* eds. Caroline B. Brettell and Carolyn F. Sargent. Englewood Cliffs, NJ: Prentice Hall, 1993.

Willner, D. "Definition and Violation: Incest and the Incest Taboos." *Man* 9 (1983): 134–159.

Wilson, Monica. *Good Company: A Study of Nyakyusa Age-Villages.* Boston: Beacon Press, 1963.

Wolf, Arthur P. "Adopt a Daughter In-Law, Marry a Sister: A Chinese Solution to the Problem of the Incest Taboo." *American Anthropologist* 70 (1968): 864–874.

Wolf, Arthur P. "Childhood Association and Sexual Attraction: A Further Test of the Westermarck Hypothesis." *American Anthropologist* 72 (1970): 503–515.

Wolf, Arthur P. "Childhood Association, Sexual Attraction, and the Incest Taboo: A Chinese Case." *American Anthropologist* 68 (1966): 883–898.

Wolf, Arthur P. "Chinese Family Size: A Myth Revitalized." In *The Chinese Family and Its Ritual Behavior*, eds. Hsieh Jih-chang and Chuang Ying-chang. Taipei, Taiwan: Institute of Ethnology Academia Sinica, 1992 [originally published 1985].

Wolf, Arthur P. "The Women of Hai-shan: A Demographic Portrait." In *Women in Chinese Society*, eds. Margery Wolf and Roxane Witke. Stanford, CA: Stanford University Press, 1975.

Wolf, Arthur P., and Chieh-shan Huang. *Marriage and Adoption in China, 1845–1945*. Stanford, CA: Stanford University Press, 1980.

Wolf, Margery. *The House of Lim: A Study of a Chinese Farm Family*. New York: Appleton-Century-Crofts, 1968.

Wolf, Margery. *Women and the Family in Rural Taiwan*. Stanford: Stanford University Press, 1972.

Wolf, Margery. "Women and Suicide in China." In *Women in Chinese Society*, eds. Margery Wolf and Roxane Witke. Stanford, CA: Stanford University Press, 1975.

Wolfe, Linda D. "Human Evolution and the Sexual Behavior of Female Primates." In *Understanding Behavior: What Primate Studies Tell Us about Behavior*, eds. James D. Loy and Calvin B. Peters. New York: Oxford University Press, 1991.

Woodburn, James. "An Introduction to Hadza Ecology." In *Man the Hunter*, eds. R. B. Lee and I. DeVore. Chicago: Aldine-Atherton, 1968.

Woodburn, James. "Stability and Flexibility in Hadza Residential Groupings." In *Man the Hunter*, eds. R. B. Lee and I. DeVore. Chicago: Aldine-Atherton, 1968.

Worthman, Carol. "Developmental Dysynchrony as Normative Experience: Kikuyu Adolescents." Paper delivered at the Social Science Research Council meeting on School-Age Pregnancy and Parenthood, 1982.

Yalman, Nur. *Under the Bo Tree: Studies in Caste, Kinship, and Marriage in the Interior of Ceylon*. Berkeley: University of California Press, 1971.

Yanagisako, Sylvia. "Family and Household: The Analysis of Domestic Groups." *Annual Review of Anthropology* 8 (1979): 161–205.

Zuckerman, Solly. *The Social Life of Monkeys and Apes*. London: Routledge and Kegan Paul, 1932.

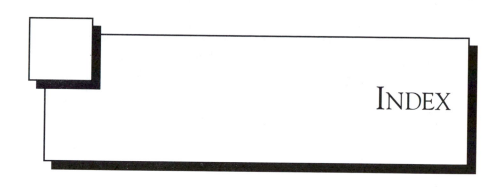

INDEX

Abelam (of Papua New Guinea), and human rights for women, 289–90
Africa:
  age-villages among Nyakyusa, 261
  attitude toward sexuality among Bemba, 33
  bride wealth in, 154
  division of labor among Tiv, 266, 268
  extramarital sex among Masai, 170
  gender differences among !Kung, 60
  and the incest taboo, 105, 129–30, 132, 137
  and jealousy among co-wives, 179, 180
  lineage among Tiv, 268–69, 271, 272
  marital residence among Tiv, 227
  sex during pregnancy among Kanuri, 167
  and sexual jealousy leading to homicide, 182
  See also specific countries
Africa, East:
  age-groups and age-sets among Jie, 261
  family extension among Jie, 245–46
  family form among Turkana, 245–46
Africa, West:
  attitude toward extramarital sex among Dogon, 169–70
  attitude toward masturbation among Ashanti, 20
  incest taboo among Ashanti, 128, 132
African-Americans, sex-ratio imbalance in U.S., 247
Age-groups and age-sets, 261
Aggression:
  gender differences in, 59–61, 62, 181–82, 284
  influence of family form on, 249
  and jealousy, 179, 180, 181–82
  sexual-agonistic linkage, 115
Agricultural societies:

  and dowry, 155
  and extended family, 235, 236–37, 238–39, 242
  and family size, 237, 239
Agta (of the Philippines), division of labor among, 50
Akan (of Africa's Gold and Ivory Coasts), and the incest taboo, 105, 129
AIDS epidemic, effect on extramarital and pre-marital sex, 19
Apache, Eastern. *See* Eastern Apache
Arapesh (of New Guinea):
  gender differences among, 59
  jealousy of co-wives among, 181
  marriage among, 104–5
Argentina, and child-support payments in, 3
Ashanti (of West Africa):
  attitude toward masturbation among, 20
  and the incest taboo, 128, 132
Aymara (of Peru):
  attitude toward childhood sexuality among, 19
  courtship among, 152
Ayres, Barbara C., 150
Azande (of the Sudan):
  attitude toward extramarital sex among, 173–74
  attitude toward homosexuality among, 31
Azande (of Zaire), gender stratification among, 57

Bang Chan (of Thailand), and sex during pregnancy, 167
Bateson, Patrick, 117
Bedouins (Arab), and cousin marriage, 105, 120, 139